SHAKESPEARE AND THE CLASSICS

Shakespeare and the Classics demonstrates that the classics are of central importance in Shakespeare's plays and in the structure of his imagination. Written by an international team of Shakespeareans and classicists, this book investigates Shakespeare's classicism and shows how he used a variety of classical books to explore such crucial areas of human experience as love, politics, ethics, and history. The book focuses on Shakespeare's favourite classical authors, especially Ovid, Virgil, Seneca, Plautus and Terence, and, in translation only, Plutarch. Attention is also paid to the humanist background and to Shakespeare's knowledge of Greek literature and culture. The final section, from the perspective of reception, examines how Shakespeare's classicism was seen and used by later writers. This accessible book offers the most rounded and comprehensive treatment of Shakespeare's classicism currently available and will be a useful first port of call for students and others approaching the subject.

CHARLES MARTINDALE is Professor of Latin at the Department of Classics and Ancient History, University of Bristol. He is the author of *John Milton and the Transformation of Ancient Epic* (London and Sydney 1986), *Redeeming the Text: Latin Poetry and the Hermeneutics of Reception* (Cambridge 1993), *Shakespeare and the Uses of Antiquity* (with Michelle Martindale, London and New York 1990) and editor of *Ovid Renewed: Ovidian Influences on Literature and Art from the Middle Ages to the Twentieth Century* (Cambridge 1988) and *The Cambridge Companion to Virgil* (Cambridge 1997).

A. B. TAYLOR is Retired Dean of Faculty (Humanities), The Swansea Institute. He is the editor of *Shakespeare's Ovid: The Metamorphoses in the Plays and Poems* (Cambridge 2000) and has published in *Shakespeare Survey, Notes and Queries, Connotations, English Language Notes*, and *Review of English Studies*.

SHAKESPEARE AND THE CLASSICS

EDITED BY

CHARLES MARTINDALE AND A. B. TAYLOR

CAMBRIDGE
UNIVERSITY PRESS

PUBLISHED BY THE PRESS SYNDICATE OF THE UNIVERSITY OF CAMBRIDGE
The Pitt Building, Trumpington Street, Cambridge, United Kingdom

CAMBRIDGE UNIVERSITY PRESS
The Edinburgh Building, Cambridge, CB2 2RU, UK
40 West 20th Street, New York, NY 10011–4211, USA
477 Williamstown Road, Port Melbourne, VIC 3207, Australia
Ruiz de Alarcón 13, 28014 Madrid, Spain
Dock House, The Waterfront, Cape Town 8001, South Africa

http://www.cambridge.org

First published 2004
Reprinted 2005

Printed in the United Kingdom at the University Press, Cambridge

Typeface Adobe Garamond 11/12.5 pt.   *System* LATEX 2ε   [TB]

A catalogue record for this book is available from the British Library

Library of Congress Cataloguing in Publication data
Shakespeare and the classics / edited by Charles Martindale & A. B. Taylor.
p.   cm.
Includes bibliographical references (p. 294) and index.
ISBN 0 521 82345 5 (hardback)
1. Shakespeare, William, 1564–1616 – Knowledge – Literature.   2. Shakespeare, William,
1564–1616 – Knowledge – Greece.   3. Shakespeare, William,
1564–1616 – Knowledge – Rome.   4. Classicism – England – History – 16th century.
5. Classical literature – Appreciation – England.   6. English literature – Classical influences.
I. Martindale, Charles.   II. Taylor, A. B. (Albert Booth)
PR3037.S56   2004   822.3′3 – dc22   2004040405

ISBN 0 521 82345 5 hardback

to
Jeannette, Mark, Chris, and Sue Taylor
to
Gabriel and Benjamin Martindale

Contents

Notes on contributors

GORDON BRADEN is Linden Kent Memorial Professor of English at the University of Virginia. He is author of *The Classics and English Renaissance Poetry: Three Case Studies* (New Haven 1978), *Renaissance Tragedy and the Senecan Tradition* (New Haven 1985), *Petrarchan Love and the Continental Renaissance* (New Haven 2000), and, with William Kerrigan, *The Idea of the Renaissance* (Baltimore 1989).

SARAH ANNES BROWN is a Fellow of Lucy Cavendish College, Cambridge. She has written *The Metamorphosis of Ovid: Chaucer to Ted Hughes* (London 1999) and *Devoted Sisters: Representations of the Sister Relationship in Nineteenth-Century British and American Literature* (Burlington, VT 2003), and is co-editor (with Charles Martindale) of Rowe's translation of Lucan's *Pharsalia* (London 1997). She has published several articles on influence and allusion and is currently working on the creative reception of *The Tempest*.

COLIN BURROW is Reader in Renaissance and Comparative Literature at the University of Cambridge and a Fellow of Gonville and Caius College. He is the author of *Epic Romance: Homer to Milton* (Oxford 1993), *Edmund Spenser* (Plymouth 1996), and is the editor of Shakespeare's *Complete Sonnets and Poems* (Oxford 2002).

STUART GILLESPIE is Reader in English Literature at Glasgow University. He is the editor of the journal *Translation and Literature*, author of *Shakespeare's Books: A Dictionary of Shakespeare Sources* (London 2001), and joint general editor of the forthcoming *Oxford History of Literary Translation in English*.

DAVID HOPKINS is Professor of English Literature at the University of Bristol. He is the author of *John Dryden* (Cambridge 1986), *John Dryden* (*Writers and their Work*) (Plymouth 2003); with Charles Martindale, editor of *Horace Made New* (Cambridge 1993), and with Paul Hammond, editor of *Dryden's Poems* (forthcoming). He has a particular interest in English / Classical literary relations, and is currently co-editing volume 3 (1660–1790) of the forthcoming *Oxford History of Literary Translation in English*.

HEATHER JAMES is Associate Professor of English and Comparative Literature at the University of Southern California. Her publications include *Shakespeare's Troy: Drama, Politics, and the Translation of Empire* (Cambridge 1997), and numerous essays on Shakespeare as well as George Sandys, John Milton, Baldassare Castiglione, and Marguerite de Navarre. Her current work focuses on Ovid's influence on poetic form and political thought in the Renaissance. She is co-editor of the *Norton Anthology of World Literature*.

RAPHAEL LYNE is a Lecturer in the Cambridge University Faculty of English, and a Fellow of New Hall. He is the author of *Ovid's Changing Worlds: English Metamorphoses* (Oxford 1998). He has a particular interest in classical traditions and has published articles on Shakespeare, Marlowe, Donne, Drayton and Golding.

CHARLES MARTINDALE, Professor of Latin at the University of Bristol, has a special interest in the reception of the classics in English poetry. He is author of *Redeeming the Text: Latin Poetry and the Hermeneutics of Reception* (Cambridge 1993); with Michelle Martindale, of *Shakespeare and the Uses of Antiquity* (London and New York 1990); and editor of *Ovid Renewed* (Cambridge 1988) and *The Cambridge Companion to Virgil* (Cambridge 1997). He is currently writing a book on Latin poetry and the Kantian tradition in aesthetics.

A. D. NUTTALL FBA is Professor of English, New College, Oxford; his works include *A New Mimesis* (London 1983), *Why Does Tragedy Give Pleasure?* (Oxford 1996), and *The Alternative Trinity: Gnostic Heresy in Marlowe, Milton, and Blake* (Oxford 1998). He is interested in relations between philosophy and literature and in links between classical and English literature.

YVES PEYRÉ is Professor of English at Université Paul Valéry (Montpellier) and general editor of *Cahiers Elisabéthains*. He is author of *La voix des mythes dans la tragédie élisabéthaine* (Paris 1996), and a contributor to *Shakespeare in the Twentieth Century*, ed. J. Levenson, J. Bate, and Dieter Mehl (Delaware 1999), and *Shakespeare's Ovid: The Metamorphoses in the Plays and Poems*, ed. A. B. Taylor (Cambridge 2000).

WOLFGANG RIEHLE is Professor of English at the Karl-Franzens-Universität Graz and a member of the Austrian Academy of Sciences. His books include *The Middle English Mystics* (transl. B. Standring) (London and Boston 1981), *Shakespeare, Plautus, and the Humanist Tradition* (Woodbridge 1990), and in German, a biography of Geoffrey Chaucer (Reinbek 1994), a study of Shakespeare's dramatic art in his trilogy *King Henry VI* (Heidelberg 1997), and a biography of Daniel Defoe (Reinbek 2002).

JOHN ROE is Senior Lecturer in English and Related Literature, University of York. He is editor of *Shakespeare: The Poems* (Cambridge 1992), and author of *Shakespeare and Machiavelli* (Woodbridge, Suffolk 2002).

ERICA SHEEN is Lecturer in English Literature and Film at the University of Sheffield. She has published on Shakespeare, David Lynch, and Hollywood cinema.

MICHAEL SILK is Professor of Greek Language and Literature at King's College London; his works include *Interaction in Poetic Imagery* (Cambridge 1974), *Nietzsche on Tragedy* (with J. P. Stern, Cambridge 1981, rev. edn 1983), *Homer: The Iliad* (Cambridge 1987, 2nd edn 2003), *Tragedy and the Tragic: Greek Theatre and Beyond* (ed., Oxford 1996, rev. edn 1998), *Aristophanes and the Definition of Comedy* (Oxford 2000, rev. edn 2002).

A. B. TAYLOR, formerly Dean of Humanities at The Swansea Institute, edited *Shakespeare's Ovid: The Metamorphoses in the Plays and Poems* (Cambridge 2000), and is currently working on *The Wound of Love in a World of Shadows: A Study of 'A Midsummer Night's Dream'*.

VANDA ZAJKO is Lecturer in Classics at the University of Bristol. She has wide-ranging interests in the reception of classical literature, and contributed a chapter to *The Cambridge Companion to Homer* (2004).

Abbreviations

ELH	English Literary History
ELR	English Literary Renaissance
HLQ	Huntington Library Quarterly
JEGP	Journal of English and Germanic Philology
MLN	Modern Language Notes
MLQ	Modern Language Quarterly
MLR	Modern Language Review
N&Q	Notes and Queries
n.s.	new series
OED	Oxford English Dictionary
PMLA	Publications of the Modern Language Association of America
PQ	Philological Quarterly
RES	Review of English Studies
RQ	Renaissance Quarterly
ShQ	Shakespeare Quarterly
ShS	Shakespeare Survey
ShSt	Shakespeare Studies
SEL	Studies in English Literature
SP	Studies in Philology
TLS	Times Literary Supplement

Introduction

In his own terms, Ben Jonson was right to remark on his friend's 'small Latine & lesse Greek', for to his eyes a grammar-school education, which may have been incomplete, had clearly left Shakespeare an ill-equipped classicist. If Shakespeare considered it necessary, he could read Latin texts: writing *The Rape of Lucrece* for the Earl of Southampton, he apparently studied the relevant section of Ovid's *Fasti* and also consulted the Latin notes by Paul Marsus in the standard edition; and for *The Comedy of Errors*, for a highly literate audience at the Inns of Court, he seems to have made extensive direct use of Plautus' *Menaechmi*, still untranslated at the time. But it is no coincidence that he could have studied both these works in school. In terms of the authors he used, Shakespeare seldom moved beyond the grammar-school ambit, and even within that ambit, perhaps partly because reading Latin texts clearly involved some effort, he habitually had recourse to available translations. For example, for his favourite Latin work, Ovid's *Metamorphoses*, parts of which he demonstrably knew well in the original, he also constantly used Arthur Golding's translation, as well as occasionally dipping into other partial versions such as that provided by Abraham Fraunce in *Amintas Dale*. There is no evidence that his 'lesse Greek' (whatever quite that may mean) enabled any approach to texts in that language; the only Greek author he used heavily, Plutarch, paradoxically for his Roman plays, was accessed via an English translation of a French translation of the Greek text.

Yet ill-equipped as Shakespeare might have seemed to Jonson, if his interests were taken by Roman history or mythology or classical tragedy, he read omnivorously and blended what he had absorbed into his work with awesome power and subtlety. Hybrid though his sources were, if one wants to see, transmuted into English, Ovid's depiction of the swift and silent movement of time, or the magic of the myths of the *Metamorphoses*, or Seneca's defiant, tragic individuality, or Plutarch's study of the array of contradictory tensions within men's characters, not only caught but made into something miraculously new, it is to Shakespeare that one must turn. Along with particular features, the general ambience of the Graeco-Roman heritage which inspired the humanists of the Renaissance has been effortlessly absorbed and was explored in Shakespeare's work as never before.

Knowledge of the ancients which the humanists called the *studia humanitatis* informs his work throughout. In *Hamlet* it shapes the values of the 'sweet prince' who is taken from a philosophical and cultured dream of study of all that man might be, to be embroiled in a shuddering confrontation with the sordid reality of what is ugly in human nature. In *The Tempest*, that other embodiment of the humanist dream, the magus Prospero, controlling life on his own private island, finally has to put away his magic to renew his embrace of imperfect humanity, some of which is unrepentant and unshaken in its commitment to evil.

In the view of many scholars the classics were no more useful to Shakespeare than any other literature. This book is predicated on the obverse principle: that the classics are of central importance in Shakespeare's works and in the structure of his imagination. This was the result of the prestige of antiquity, the influence of Renaissance humanism and the character of the educational curriculum (not to mention the quality of the classical texts in their rich medieval and Renaissance receptions). Most time at grammar school was spent reading and writing Latin; if Shakespeare was not a learned man, he had still read a very great deal of Latin by today's standards. Investigating Shakespeare's classicism is thus not simply a matter of locating 'sources' (something already well done by T. W. Baldwin and others) but of showing how he was enabled by a variety of classical books to explore such crucial areas of human experience as love, politics, ethics, and history.

Our volume, while not attempting to provide any kind of survey, is designed as an early port of call for anyone interested in Shakespeare and the classics, including students and their teachers. There is no single book which currently performs this job in an entirely satisfactory way. Although there have been some fine studies of individual aspects of Shakespeare's use of the classics (for example, Jonathan Bate's *Shakespeare and Ovid*), the only attempt to present a rather more comprehensive account in recent years has been *Shakespeare and the Uses of Antiquity* by Charles and Michelle Martindale (London and New York 1990). Before that one has to go back to J. A. K. Thomson's rather jejune *Shakespeare and the Classics* in the 1950s. In contrast to the Martindales who opted for a more topic-centred approach, this volume concentrates on individual classical authors and the ways the great poet and dramatist knew and made use of them. Some of these he first met in school, Ovid, Virgil, Plautus, possibly Seneca; others like Plutarch (who, along with Lucian, was an author much more admired and widely read in the Renaissance than later) he devoured later as material for the playhouse. Contributors were asked not merely to introduce their subjects but to engage the reader with sophisticated and novel treatments, while not taking previous knowledge for granted.

This volume uses the talents of classical and Shakespearean scholars (some established, some younger and emergent) from the UK, the USA, and Europe. Inevitably it lacks the individually focused vision that a single author could have brought to the task. But multi-authorship has compensating and great advantages. It enables the reader to experience a range of approaches, from New Historicism (Sheen), varieties of feminism (James, Zajko), the poetics of space (Lyne), reception theory (Brown) to more traditional humanistic approaches. No effort has been made to impose an artificial orthodoxy, and the differences of view should spur the reader to further reflection. Thus the book includes numerous exemplary readings of particular instances of intertextuality, reflecting this or that theoretical approach, in such a way that the reader should be encouraged to explore other instances with a different play, or ancient author, or theme.

We begin with an introductory chapter which provides an initial perspective on Shakespeare's classical knowledge, and in which Colin Burrow examines Shakespeare's humanistic culture and suggests that the dynamic in his work derives from a response to its problems and inconsistencies. There follows a series of studies of Shakespeare's use of favourite classical authors and genres. In a book of this kind any organisation will necessarily emphasise some aspects of the subject at the expense of others, and thus have disadvantages as well as advantages. Concentrating on authors has obvious convenience for both reader and contributor, but it must of course always be remembered that often Shakespeare drew on a range of classical writings in combination (Virgil and Ovid in particular are constantly entwined). The structure also embodies a particular ideological belief: an unFoucauldian commitment to the importance of individual authorship and the notion of 'genius' which often accompanies it.[1] Since Latin was of far more moment to Shakespeare than Greek, we start with Roman authors in their approximate order of importance for Shakespeare, Ovid incontestably first, then Virgil and the dramatists. Although after he left school Shakespeare may not have read many words of Greek, Greece and Greek literature have left their mark on his plays, through translations (into Latin and English), through imitations in the vernaculars, and through intermediaries like Erasmus. Comparatively little work has been done on Shakespeare's Greek, so the chapters on Plutarch, the romances, and Greek drama will help to fill out the picture of Shakespeare's classicism currently available.

Michael Silk's essay on Shakespeare and Greek tragedy (often compared, though Shakespeare had probably had no direct encounter even with Euripides, the best known of the dramatists at the time) leads smoothly to the two chapters which deal, by way of conclusion and in necessarily synecdochal fashion, with the reception of Shakespeare's classicism, and explore some important moments in this vital ongoing process. In this way we highlight the issue of Shakespeare's classicism within the wider perspective of reception. This is an integral part of the project as we have conceived it. We want readers to be aware of the limitations of the positivism which (despite frequent protestations to the contrary) still holds sway in source studies, since we believe that the processes of interpretation and reception are always implicated in each other in a form of continuing dialogue. For example, Shakespeare used Plutarch among other ancient writers in constructing his view of Rome; that view in turn nourished subsequent literature, criticism, and culture in a way that affected later responses to Shakespeare's Rome, including ours. Thus the relationship between Shakespeare and the classics, it could be said, has been created as much as simply discovered by later writers. Part of the book's function is to get away from the idea that the dramatist's classicism is primarily a matter of sources, references, allusions. Rather, as the final essay shows, there is a far deeper interrelationship between 'Shakespeare' and 'Antiquity' (where 'Shakespeare' means 'all the forces that created the plays and their reception'). Though this chapter concludes the volume, it does not seek to impose closure: the relationship between Shakespeare and the classics has not yet run its course.

Documentation and full bibliographical details will be found in the notes to individual chapters. The bibliography is not a bibliography to the book, but a select bibliography to the subject of Shakespeare's classicism, organised for maximum utility to likely users. Although it offers a more rounded treatment of the subject than is available elsewhere, this book obviously cannot claim to be comprehensive; the bibliography gives material on authors known to Shakespeare but not treated here (including Apuleius, Cicero, Horace, Livy). The editors would like to thank: Jo Paul for compiling this bibliography; Sarah Stanton, their understanding editor at CUP; the three readers chosen by CUP to referee the original project for numerous invaluable suggestions; Stuart Gillespie who helped with the bibliography; Colin Burrow, Mark Llewellyn, and Liz Prettejohn; as well as the individual contributors.

Finally, we would also like to dedicate this book to the memory of Thomas M. Greene (17 May 1926 – 23 June 2003), distinguished author of *The Light in Troy: Imitation and Discovery in Renaissance Poetry*. Thomas Greene was originally to have been a contributor but his untimely final illness supervened.

C. A. M., A. B. T.
September 2003

NOTE

1. See Jonathan Bate, *The Genius of Shakespeare* (London and Basingstoke 1997).

PART I

AN INITIAL PERSPECTIVE

CHAPTER I

Shakespeare and humanistic culture

Colin Burrow

No one knows exactly how and when Shakespeare read 'the classics', or even what he might have thought they were. Indeed it may be slightly misleading to talk about 'the classics' in relation to Shakespeare at all. The word is not recorded before the eighteenth century in the sense 'A writer, or a literary work, of the first rank and of acknowledged excellence; esp. (as originally used) in Greek or Latin' (*OED* B.1), and Shakespeare does not use any form of the word 'classic' or 'classical' at any point in his career. It's highly unlikely that he had a rigid or restricted sense of a fixed canon of texts which he regarded as the ultimate literary authorities. There was for him much weaker an imaginary boundary than there is now between the Augustan 'classics' – Virgil, Horace, and Ovid – and a larger sphere of reading which encompassed, probably in a hodge-podge of languages and surrounded by a variety of levels of commentary, Plutarch, Greek prose romance, a sprinkling of Lucan, the distiches of Cato, a dash of Homer, and perhaps some of Philostratus' *Imagines*, some of Aphthonius' dialogues, a little Livy, some Cicero, a bit of Quintilian, all of which would be tumbled together with quotations from classical authors which were used to illustrate grammatical points in Lily's Grammar or in Erasmus' educational works. Shakespeare read, remembered, misremembered and hybridised the works which we call 'the classics'.[1]

He did this in ways which are distinctive to him, but which also reflect recognisably Tudor humanist methods of reading. These were in all probability drummed into him at school from about the age of seven, and several more or less successful attempts have been made to peer into the satchel of the young Shakespeare as, like the young Lucius in *Titus Andronicus* 4.1, he set off to school with a copy of Ovid tucked under his arm. T. W. Baldwin, in his massive survey of grammar-school curricula *William Shakespere's Small Latine and Lesse Greeke*, argued that Shakespeare read more Latin at school than most classics undergraduates do at university today, and that 'William Shakespere was trained in the heroic age of grammar school rhetoric in England, and he shows knowledge of the complete system, in its most heroic proportions.'[2] Baldwin's view of Shakespeare as by modern standards a learned author took a while to take root, but is now effectively an orthodoxy.[3] The line from Ben Jonson's elegy on Shakespeare which gave Baldwin his title ('And, though thou hadst small Latin and less Greek') was read as a direct criticism of Shakespeare's ignorance of the classics by later seventeenth-century readers, and was often taken to support a view that Shakespeare studied nature rather than books by most critics before the twentieth century. Commentators since Baldwin, however, have tended to gloss Jonson's remark as a counterfactual speculation rather than a direct attack on Shakespeare's ignorance: "'Even if you had little scholarship" – which was not the case – "I would not seek to honour you by comparing you with classical poets"'.[4] This may well be to overstate Jonson's generosity of spirit, just as Baldwin may have overstated Shakespeare's learning. But in the late 1970s Emrys Jones and Joel Altman argued not just that Shakespeare read a lot of Latin and perhaps some Greek, but that central aspects of his habits of thought derived from the Latinate rhetorical training which he received at school.[5] Pupils in the higher forms of Elizabethan grammar schools would have learnt to argue, in Latin, on either side of the question, and to compose orations in the persona of historical characters. Both Jones and (less explicitly) Altman argued that without this training Shakespeare could not have staged debates on either side of a question between Cassius and Brutus, or between Brutus and his conscience. The long-term result of this work has been a high measure of consensus that there was effectively a straightforwardly supportive relationship between Shakespeare's works and his classical education at school.

More recent studies of humanistic forms of education, however, have tended to argue that it was not as spiritually liberating or as effective as it set out to be. For Anthony Grafton and Lisa Jardine the predominantly rhetorical and 'literary' educational system deriving from Erasmus, which filtered throughout England as grammar school after grammar school emu-lated the Erasmian statutes and ideals of St Paul's School, was far less suited to the practical needs of its pupils than the forms of logical instruction which it replaced.[6] They emphasise the practical failings of the system: even pupils such as the young Edward VI, who is frequently presented as the greatest product of Erasmian forms of education, had an imperfect grasp on the finer points of Latin grammar. The emphasis in the human-ist classroom on rote learning, on the authority of a master, and on the authority of Latin texts, they suggest, helped to fashion docile servants of absolutist regimes. This is certainly debatable: there is strong evidence to suggest that there was in fact a delicate balance between magisterial authority and freedom in the Tudor classroom.[7] Erasmus encouraged his students to argue whether democracy was preferable to monarchy, and to compose orations condemning the tyranny of Julius Caesar.[8] Pupils who had learned to conduct such debates might not be expected to be simple slaves to monarchs.

This chapter will suggest that Shakespeare's grammar-school education did not feed simply and beneficially into his poems and plays. But it will not argue that we should adopt the iconoclasm of Grafton and Jardine, and assume that Shakespeare's grasp on Latin literature was slight. Rather there were a number of failings, both practical and theoretical, in how Shakespeare was trained to read the classics in his early years, and, oddly enough, those failings were part of what made his later responses to his reading so powerful. Emrys Jones is correct to say that 'Without humanism . . . there could have been no Elizabethan literature: without Erasmus, no Shakespeare';[9] but this chapter will suggest that the quirks of and failings within humanist methods of responding to the classics mattered for Shakespeare as much as, or perhaps more than, their successes.

First things first. What did Shakespeare read at the King's Free Grammar School at Stratford? The statutes and records of this tiny school, refounded by the humanist prodigy Edward VI in 1553 and crammed into an upstairs room in the Guildhall in Stratford, do not survive.[10] As a result we do not have certain proof that Shakespeare attended it at all. If he did attend it, he would have done so from about 1571.[11] Our knowledge of what he may have read at school depends entirely on inference from what we know about other schools, and often the surviving evidence about these consists of statements of principles and ideals (curricula and timetables) rather than detailed descriptions of what actually happened in practice. Stratford's single master, who was reasonably paid at £20 per annum and was usually a graduate, probably aspired to follow something similar to the educational regime laid out in the statutes and curricula of St Paul's School in London. St Paul's had been founded by Dean Colet in 1509,[12] and for its foundation Colet had solicited from Erasmus the *De Ratione Studii* ('Concerning the Method of Study'), which was supplemented by what was to become one of the most influential books in the sixteenth century: the *De Duplici Copia Verborum atque Rerum* ('Concerning the Double Abundance of Words and Matter'). The *De Copia*, a handbook describing how to achieve a rich and eloquent style, went through 150 editions before 1572.[13] Colet's statutes were designed to produce pupils skilled in Latin and

Greek, who would go on to thrive in the formal disputations required of students at the universities, and eventually perhaps to act as secretaries to noblemen or even as counsellors to monarchs. Colet insisted that the study of literature was the best way to achieve these outcomes: 'I would they were taught always in good literature bothe Laten and Greeke, and good autors such as have the verraye *Romayne* eloquence joined with wisdom, specially Christen autors that wrote their wisdome with clean and chaste Laten.'[14] Colet's emphasis on moral content led him to present a curriculum which was not, to modern eyes, very 'classical', including as it did

Institutum Christiani Hominis, which that Learned Erasmus made at my requeste, and the boke called *Copia* of the same Erasmus. And then other authors Christian, as *Lactantius*, *Prudentius*, and *Proba*, and *Sedulius*, and *Juvencus*, and *Baptista Mantuanus*, and suche other as shall be thought convenient and most to purpose unto the true Laten speech . . . I saye that fylthiness and all suche abusion whiche the later blynde worlde brought in, whiche more rather may be called *Blotterature* then *Litterature*, I utterly abannyshe and exclude out of this Scole, and charge the Maisters that they teche alwaye that is beste.[15]

St Paul's School, along with Westminster and Eton, certainly provided the model for the statutes of many Tudor grammar schools, but this does not mean that all schools were like them in practice.[16] Even William Lily, the first High Master of St Paul's and the author of a Latin grammar which was to be prescribed by statute as the only one to be used in schools, noted that 'The varietie of teaching is diuers yet, and alwaies wil be.'[17] Richard Brinsley's *Ludus Literarius*, printed in 1612, a century after Colet's statutes, is probably our best guide to Shakespeare's school, since it was explicitly designed to assist provincial schoolmasters rather than teachers at elite urban institutions such as St Paul's or Westminster. Brinsley, schoolmaster at Ashby-de-la-Zouch, fifty miles from Stratford and a similar distance from London, begins by emphasising the exhaustion and demoralisation of the provincial schoolmaster: 'I wax vtterly wearie of my place, and my life is a continual burden vnto me.'[18] It is likely that keeping order and keeping going was the highest priority for masters in the poorer schools.[19] Brinsley has a clearer conception than Colet of the ancient texts which might be most worthy of imitation by modern pupils: 'And therefore I would haue the cheifest labor to make these purest Authors our owne, as Tully for prose, so Ouid and Virgil for verse, so to speake and write in Latine for the phrase, as they did.'[20] It is very likely that Shakespeare would have read at least some of 'Cato, Corderius dialogues, Aesop's fables, Tullies [Cicero's] epistles gathered by Sturmius, Tullies Offices, de Amicitia, Senectute, Paradoxes, Ovid's *Tristia* and *Metamorphoses*, Virgil. Also *Terentius Christianus*.'[21]

This reading would in all probability have been carefully graded for difficulty: students at Canterbury grammar school (which was larger and better endowed than Stratford's school) would cut their teeth on Cato's *Distiches* and would move on to Terence and the neo-Latin *Eclogues* of Mantuan (the poetic nick-name of Baptista Spagnuoli) in the third form. It is just possible that Shakespeare studied English translations along with the Latin originals, although the evidence here is thin. Charles Hoole in 1659 was to urge his pupils to 'procure some pretty delightful English Poems, by perusal whereof they may become acquainted with the Harmony of English Poesie. *Mr. Hardwicks* late Translation of *Mantuan*, Mr *Sandys* of *Ovid*, Mr. *Ogleby's* of *Virgil*, will abundantly supply them with Heroick Verses.'[22] As Hoole's choice of translations indicates, this practice seems to have become fashionable only in the later seventeenth century, as the value of translations to the growth of the national tongue came to be more generally recognised. Brinsley embarked on an ambitious programme of translating some of the key texts used in Tudor classrooms, such as Cicero's *De Officiis*, but his cribs did not begin to appear until the early years of the seventeenth century. Shakespeare may conceivably have had access to Phaer's *Aeneid* or Golding's Ovid in the classroom, but there is little evidence that teachers at this date were making use of translations.[23] These early years would have been chiefly spent in exercising the memory: pupils would learn the whole of Lily's Latin grammar by heart, and were in most grammar schools supposed to speak Latin at all times. Here too though Tudor educational ideals and actual practice were almost certainly at odds. Brinsley is clear that Elizabethan schoolboys were not angelic swots: 'if we could bring them to speake Latine continually, from that time that they beginne to parse in Latine: but this I haue had too much experience of, that without great seuerity they will not be brought vnto: but they will speake English, and one will wink at another, if they are out of the Masters hearing'.[24]

The older boys would not simply read Ovid, Virgil, or Cicero. They would in theory write them too. In a method known since Roger Ascham's *The Schoolmaster* (printed in 1570) as 'double translation', students would be presented with a passage of Latin which they would be required to translate into English prose. The original would then be removed, and the poor students would be set the task of replicating the original as closely as they could. Learning to produce lines that scanned in the quantitative metre of Latin was as hard then as it is now: even the mild-mannered Brinsley has to confess that versification was the most painful part of grammar-school work: 'my schollars haue had more feare in this, then in all the former, and myselfe also driuen to more seuerity'.[25] Presumably those with excellent memories stood a better chance of succeeding in replicating the style and the content of the original: 'By which daily contentation you shall find, that those who take a delight in Poetry and haue sharpness & dexterity accordingly, will in a short time attaine to that ripeness, as that they who know not the places which they imitate, shall hardly discerne in many verses, whether the verse bee Virgils verse, or the schollars.'[26]

The practice of double translation might seem on the face of it to endorse Grafton and Jardine's claim that humanistic education was aimed to instil in its victims a sense that classical culture was a given which had to be mastered and emulated mechanically. Students with good memories must certainly have found 'double translation' much easier than those who had painstakingly to reinvent their Latin originals from the ground up. But actually the removal of the source text and the requirement to reconstruct it must have been intimidating and liberating in equal measure: who now gets to *write* Virgil, and who now is rewarded for inspired misrememberings of the classics? Humanist education may well have fostered a cult of memorial reconstruction of classical texts rather more than its professed aim of encouraging their creative imitation. But that practical failure was absolutely central to Shakespeare's treatment of his reading. There are several moments in his works when bad memories of a classical education create both broad comedy and exquisitely subtle attempts to retrieve, and to dramatise the dissemination of, classical works. Schoolmasters in Shakespeare's plays are dogged by the difficulty of recalling Latin texts to mind. The pedantic provincial master Holofernes in *Love's Labour's Lost* (4.2.93–4) misquotes the opening lines of Mantuan's first Eclogue, that staple of the early years of Latin reading. This may simply be a compositorial slip, or a joke at the expense of the failing memories of provincial schoolmasters; but whether intentional or not, it is a moment when a failure accurately to recall a past text serves to characterise a particular person in the drama. The fallible processes of recalling and construing Latin also generate the great moment in *The Merry Wives of Windsor* when a schoolboy called William (and that name hints at autobiography) is tested on his grasp of Lily's grammar by Sir Hugh Evans. The scene represents not just a battle to remember, but also very deliberately embeds the Latin tongue in a variety of vernacular influences. Evans, like Thomas Jenkins, master at Stratford school from 1575, is Welsh, and the lesson is overheard by two women, William's mother and Mistress Quickly, neither of whom know Latin:

EVANS What is your genitive case plural, William?
WILLIAM Genitive case?
EVANS Ay.
WILLIAM *Genitivo*: '*horum, harum, horum*'.
MISTRESS QUICKLY Vengeance of Jenny's Case! Fie on her! Never name her,
     child, if she be a whore. (4.1.52–7)

Remembering and mishearing here run together in the treatment of the
classical tongue, which is rapidly translated by the bawdy phonic imagination of Mistress Quickly into a sexual scandal. This scene makes Latin a
marvellously rebellious language, which breeds whores from its 'horums'
and bawdy puns from its cases (the word could mean 'vagina'). Mistress
Quickly, a woman, and consequently excluded from grammar school, is not
simply embodying female ignorance or feminine loquacity: she is rather
representing onstage the kinds of linguistic revenge which any Latinless
members of the audience might reap on the learned tongue presented to
their ears.[27] They hear it as a schoolboy might, as English and as rude.

     This leads on to a crucial point: to argue whether Shakespeare's educa-
tion was liberatingly dialectical or whether it was crushingly grounded in
the authority of the classics is not very fruitful. Shakespeare's works exploit
the slippage between the august ideals of humanist education and its practical shortcomings, between its ambitions and its unintended consequences.
Misremembering and mishearing the classical tongues can be as much a
response to 'the classics' as careful imitations and artful echoes. In this connection it is remarkable how often jolts to the memory precede extended
allusions to Virgil in Shakespeare's works: even the moment when Lucrece
seeks out the picture of the sack of Troy to use as a vehicle for her woe
is preceded by '*At last she calls to mind* where hangs a piece / Of skilful
painting, made for Priam's Troy' (1,366–7; my emphasis), and the picture
when it is described seems very, very old, as though the memory of Troy is
fading from recall. The Player's speech on Hecuba and the sack of Troy in
Hamlet is at some level an *imitatio* of Virgil, but is presented as a virtuoso
act of memory ('if it live in your memory', 2.2.449–50) of a piece of English
paraphrase which clearly belongs to the lexical world of decades before the
play in which it is set. The concern with memory can leak out, as it were,
from the classical texts to the plays in which they are set. *Hamlet* is, after all,
a play as much or more about remembering as it is a play about revenge.[28]
Even *The Tempest*, in which allusions to the *Aeneid* tend to be glancing
and fragmentary, is primarily concerned with recalling and re-enacting
past usurpations: Ariel's quasi-Virgilian appearance as a harpy is designed

to jog the fading memories of the courtly characters that they are 'men of
sin' (3.3.53). Ben Jonson, who attended the metropolitan hothouse of Westminster School under the great scholar and antiquarian William Camden,
never presents the recall of a classical text as a task to tax the memory:
Virgil *reads* from the *Aeneid* in *Poetaster* (5.2.56–97), rather than labouring
to recall his poem. The different attitudes of these two authors towards
classical learning are clearly connected with their differing and politically
inflected conceptions of authority.[29] But they also went to very different kinds of school. In Stratford 'the classics' may well have partly meant
labouring to recall – not in a sense of appreciating the gulfs of time that lay
between the modern scholar and the past, but in the humdrum sense of
trying to remember what those old poets wrote. This is not to revive the old
claim that Shakespeare knew little Latin. Rather it is to argue that the thick,
distorting medium of memory can turn a classical text into something new,
and indeed can make the classical text seem so antiquated as to be entirely
secondary to the newly constructed memory of it.

Shakespeare exploited the theoretical shortcomings of the form of education he received just as creatively as he made use of its practical deficiencies.
The first and most radical of these shortcomings concerns the ends of the
highly literary and almost exclusively literary training. What was it for? If
this question is asked at a merely instrumental level a number of problems
immediately arise. It was to equip students with the *copia*, or fullness of
language and knowledge, which would enable them to delight an audience,
to persuade, to praise, or to obtain work as lawyers, secretaries to noblemen, or perhaps even counsellors to the monarch. But fullness of language
has as its nightmarish double an ability to paraphrase, circumlocute, and
ornament in a manner which serves no instrumental purpose at all. Erasmus confronted this danger at the very start of his *De Copia*: 'We find that
a good many mortal men who make great efforts to achieve this godlike
power of speech fall instead into mere glibness, which is both silly and
offensive. They pile up a meaningless heap of words and expressions without any discrimination.'[30] There are indeed moments when Erasmus seems
to encourage his students to produce 'a meaningless heap of words': he lists
no fewer than 148 alternative methods of saying 'Dear Faustus, thank you
for your letter', which expand from *Tuae literae me magnopere delectarunt*
('your letter greatly delighted me') into the outer reaches of hyperbole. A
student who had diligently grasped this art would be equipped to draw
on a rich store of synonyms in whatever rhetorical circumstances he found
himself, and might also enjoy parodying such circumlocution by creating
pedantic abusers of the art of *copia* such as Holofernes. If one adds to

this skill the art of even-handedly arguing either side of the question it is clear that the ideal humanist schoolboy was not going to be someone who simply gets things done. Hamlet's 'To be or not to be' soliloquy is in its deliberative structure precisely the kind of *quaestio* (open-ended argument on either side of the question) which all grammar-school boys were trained to produce, and Hamlet, a good humanist scholar, elsewhere can weave pieces of Quintilian into his soliloquies.[31] But 'To be or not to be' is of course notoriously *not* followed by Hamlet's sweeping to his revenge. This is scarcely surprising: *Hamlet*'s author was trained in the arts of copious expression and of deliberation on either side of a question. Repeatedly he transfers those skills to characters within his plays and poems in ways that wryly recognise both the fascination of those methods and their potential for sicklying o'er the name of action with a pale cast of words.

By the late sixteenth century it was clear that the output of the grammar schools exceeded the number of vacancies for eloquent young men. In 1581 Richard Mulcaster, the first headmaster of the Merchant Taylors' School in London and a devoted follower of Ascham in his educational principles, voiced a fear that the spread of Erasmian education in grammar schools was resulting in the oversupply of young men with the wrong kinds of skills to suit the commonwealth and its needs. As a result 'there must be a *restraint*, and that all may not passe on to learning, which throng thitherwards, bycause of the inconueniences, which may ensue, by want of preferment for such a multitude, and by defeating other trades of their necessarie trauellours'.[32] According to Mulcaster, the unemployed victims of this educational overproduction were a threat to social equilibrium. In London in the 1580s and '90s a significant number of those produced by the Tudor educational machine ended up not as rebels or ne'er-do-wells, but as poets and playwrights. They were people who are not Prince Hamlet and who were never meant to be, but who shared Hamlet's lack of a clear role in life, who could turn out a *quaestio* to order, and who could remember, some time back, learning about Hecuba and the sack of Troy. For these men the contradictions and excesses in what they had been taught become a vital literary resource: they could turn the very goddess of love, Venus herself, into someone who could argue with endless copiousness that it is better to marry than to remain single, and could make her rhetorical failure to persuade the resistant Adonis a reflection, perhaps, of the lack of fit between their own rhetorical sophistication and any practical purchase on the world. They could ornament and embellish Ovid, as Shakespeare does in *Venus and Adonis*, weaving him in to a mass of textual authorities culled from a wide range of classical and post-classical reading, encrusting him

so thoroughly with adages and *exempla*, chronographies and *sententiae*,
that his original outlines were entirely obscured. They would be able to
hybridise, as Shakespeare does in the description of the painting of the
sack of Troy in *Lucrece*, a Virgilian scene with passages from the *Imagines*
of Philostratus,[33] and to embellish both of these sources with memories of
how Erasmus characterised particular heroes at the siege of Troy.[34]

This argument could be pressed further: that the way in which
Shakespeare learned to read and imitate the classics had the effect of ultimately making the classics almost invisible in his work. Humanist education
encouraged the pragmatic use of earlier literature. Erasmus advocated the
compilation of commonplace books, which were notebooks with headings,
usually in alphabetical order, designed to enable the storing and retrieval of
passages of classical literature to suit particular occasions.[35] The headings
might be rhetorical (under the heading 'chronographies' for example a student might record rhetorically elaborate descriptions of particular times of
day, such as *Aeneid* 4.522–7, to which he would look back when composing
a passage of his own, as Shakespeare may have done when composing the
great set piece chronographies in *Venus and Adonis*, 1–6, 853–8). Other topics might include 'Old Age', or 'Time', or 'Sleep'. Perhaps not surprisingly
many students found it much easier to compile lists of headings than to
undertake the organised programme of reading required to store the headings with examples.[36] Nonetheless this method was both a way of reading
and a means of converting that reading into writing. As such it provided a
counterbalance to the method of double translation: where double translation encouraged a mastery of, and perhaps a servility to, the style and
lexis of one particular author, commonplacing fostered a quite different set
of implied attitudes: a phrase from *any* author might be set down under a
particular heading next to a phrase from any other author, and often such
phrases might be entirely divorced from any indication of authorship when
they were set down in commonplace books. This did not exactly mean
that literature, classical or otherwise, acquired an individual and specific
meaning for each reader; but it did mean that any given piece of textual
matter could have a particular use for and applicability to any particular
person who happened to have a particular rhetorical need for it. As Bacon
remarked 'one man's notes will little profit another, because one man's
conceit doth so much differ from another's'.[37] This form of reading and
recalling creates a precondition for a type of drama which generates effects
of intersubjectivity by presenting a variety of characters onstage who have
different experiences and needs, and whose response to what they read
is determined by those particular needs. And this vitally influences how

Shakespeare represents the classics. So for Hamlet the grief of the player for the fate of Hecuba is rebuke to himself for having felt too little; for Polonius, who seems to read entirely for *sententiae* and plunderable ornaments, it is 'too long', though a good source of fine epithets ('"mobbled queen" is good', 2.2.506). Habits of commonplacing do not turn 'the classics' into unassailable objects of cultural authority; they rather make them objects of contention, and sometimes of deliberate appropriation.

For a dramatist versed in this form of learning, phrases from the classics could be embedded within a scene in which different characters perceive different things in, and want different things from, those ancient texts. In early Shakespearean drama these effects are particularly sharply defined, perhaps to a fault. So when in *Titus Andronicus* the schoolboy Lucius brings onstage a copy of Ovid's *Metamorphoses* the book is for him just a school text-book. He is chased by his aunt Lavinia, whose hunger for this particular book results from her need to communicate the fact that she has been raped and had her tongue and hands cut off by Chiron and Demetrius. For Lavinia, Ovid has a particular pragmatic purpose: he can reveal what she has suffered, and can, in a limited way, speak for her. Her rapists had attempted to overgo Ovid's Tereus by both cutting out her tongue and chopping off her hands, like grotesque parodies of Elizabethan schoolboys who had been taught to imitate, learn from, and overgo Ovid.[38] The physical presence of the *Metamorphoses* onstage, however, enables Lavinia to communicate, fitting as it does her circumstances and her needs. She 'quotes' [i.e. points at] the leaves with her stumps, and with the classical text before her she writes in Latin '*Stuprum* – Chiron – Demetrius' (*Titus Andronicus* 4.1.77).

Although the classical text is present on stage, it is no one thing: rather it is at the centre of an interpersonal drama. It is one of the many suggestive weaknesses of *Titus* that it is not explained why Lavinia needs to have the *Metamorphoses* itself before her before she can write down the names of her assailants. But the theatrical awkwardness testifies to the power of classical texts for Shakespeare: rather than being objects of unqualified veneration, they can be used within the lives of their readers to enable them to communicate. Classical books speak for present occasions. Even late in Shakespeare's career a classical book onstage can bring together disjoined perspectives in a way that sends shivers down the spine: the book which Imogen (presumably) innocently reads in bed in *Cymbeline* 2.2 is not named until Iachimo spies on her while she sleeps. Only then is it revealed to be 'The tale of Tereus' (2.2.45). The presence of the classical book onstage menacingly registers the difference of perspective between the two characters – for Imogen it is presumably just what she happened to be reading before she slept, while for Iachimo it suggests a literal template for the kind of metaphorical violation of Imogen which he intends.

It is often said that classical allusions in later Shakespearean drama are less explicit than they are in the Shakespeare of the 1590s. It is certainly the case that the Ovidian tale of Pyramus and Thisbe in *Midsummer Night's Dream* or the explicit allusions to the fall of Troy in *Hamlet* and *Lucrece* have no direct equivalent in Shakespeare's works after 1600, but Shakespeare did not lose interest in the classics as his career advanced.[39] It is partly that his later career draws extensively on 'classical' works which we do not think of as being classical (notably Plutarchan history and Greek prose romance), but it is also the case that his *methods* of reading came to dominate, and in some cases even to erase, the content of what he read. In his works from *c.*1600 (with the exception of the example from *Cymbeline*) onstage classical books tend not to be identified by name, and can as a result sometimes appear to be created by characters in order to convey particular concerns to their addressees. This tendency to rewrite the classics from within the framework of a Shakespearean scene can be found in *Hamlet*. The 'words, words, words' by the 'satirical slave' which Hamlet is reading when he is disturbed by Polonius (2.2.195–203) have often been said since Warburton in 1747 to be Juvenal's satires (10.190–5):[40]

the satirical slave says here that old men have grey beards, that their faces are wrinkled, their eyes purging thick amber or plum-tree gum, and that they have a plentiful lack of wit, together with most weak hams.

> sed quam continuis et quantis longa senectus
> plena malis! deformem et taetrum ante omnia vultum
> dissimilemque sui, deformem pro cute pellem
> pendentisque genas et talis aspice rugas
> quales, umbriferos ubi pandit Thabraca saltus,
> in vetula scalpit iam mater simia bucca.

(but how great and continual are the miseries of old age! Look at the foul and ugly face, unlike its former self; see the unsightly hide that serves for a skin and the sagging cheeks and the wrinkles like those which a mother ape carves on her aged cheeks where Thabraca spreads its shady groves)

The differences between Hamlet's impersonal 'says here that' and Juvenal's direct appeal to 'look' are so great as to suggest that the resemblance between the two passages is the result of (at best) a distant memory of a classical text, which has been remade by being partially forgotten (it is a great shame that Hamlet forgets Juvenal's wrinkled mother ape). Hamlet's words do not exactly have a source; rather the book which contains them is rewritten – perhaps even invented – to suit his immediate occasion. At this moment Hamlet's desire obliquely to sting Polonius by strategically directing commonplaces against him effectively makes a Juvenalian satire appear in his hand. It is as though classical literature is being *made* by dramatic contingencies.

This is not an isolated example. Ulysses in *Troilus and Cressida* (3.3.90–4) is reading a book by 'a strange fellow' about the impossibility of enjoying fame if your deeds are not observed:

> A strange fellow here
> Writes me that man, how dearly ever parted,
> How much in having, or without or in,
> Cannot make boast to have that which he hath,
> Nor feels not what he owes, but by reflection.

Achilles responds with 'Nor doth the eye itself, / That most pure spirit of sense, behold itself, / Not going from itself'. Largely as a result of Achilles' response to Ulysses, some have thought the book might be Plato's *First Alcibiades* 133A ('Then an eye viewing another eye, and looking at the most perfect part of it, the thing wherewith it sees, will thus see itself?'). Others have argued for Cicero's *Tusculan Disputations* ('The soule is not able in this bodye to see him selfe. No more is the eye whyche although he seeth all other thinges, yet (that whiche is one of the leaste) can not discerne his owne shape').[41] Both classical passages have resemblances to the conversation between the two heroes, but neither is in any simple sense a 'source' for the dialogue. Effectively the dialogue becomes the source for them, since the book is invented in order to serve Ulysses' need to quote a source which will rebuke Achilles. The oddest feature of the exchange is that it is Achilles, who is not holding the book, who picks up and develops the commonplace of classical and Renaissance ethics that the eye cannot see itself, rather than Ulysses, who has the book in his hand. As a result the book seems to be being read, even perhaps written, between the two characters, rather than by Cicero or Plato. The onstage book is the product of a process of mirroring and distorting of whatever might be its 'source' through the skewed perspectives of these two characters.[42] For this reason *what* Shakespeare read (even if we could reconstruct it) matters less than *how* he read it – indeed the 'how' can often supplant the 'what'. He does not directly mirror sources, or seek transpicuously to adapt classical writing to the concerns of his present. He read for situations and interpersonal dramas, and could write imaginary classical-seeming sources for his works which would fit into those scenes: Achilles and Ulysses know a body of *sententiae* (memorable maxims) and *loci communes* (commonplaces) so well that they need not quote from or imitate any particular source, and Shakespeare uses the (probably imaginary) book as an object of debate against which the characters calibrate their own points of view. He certainly does not treat it as a 'classical' text to which he alludes in order to give his audience a single authoritative commentary on the events onstage.

That is why the subject of 'Shakespeare and the Classics' needs to generate another book. Since the significance of classical texts is determined by what they mean to whom at particular moments in the drama, the subject of Shakespeare's classical learning cannot be approached simply by the tabulation of sources. Nor can one simply characterise Shakespeare's relationship to his classical reading by a single epithet ('eristic' or 'dialectical' or what you will), since that relationship is invariably tangled up with complex relationships between speaking characters and different points of view. Classical books can turn into ghostly volumes which are constructed by the methods by which and the aims for which they were studied, and they can also be quite different things for different characters onstage. This celebrated passage from the end of *The Merchant of Venice* illustrates the point:

LORENZO   in such a night
  Troilus, methinks, mounted the Trojan walls,
  And sighed his soul toward the Grecian tents
  Where Cressid lay that night.
JESSICA   In such a night
  Did Thisbe fearfully o'ertrip the dew
  And saw the lion's shadow ere himself,
  And ran dismayed away.
LORENZO   In such a night
  Stood Dido with a willow in her hand
  Upon the wild sea banks, and waft her love
  To come again to Carthage.
JESSICA   In such a night
  Medea gatherèd the enchanted herbs
  That did renew old Æson.
LORENZO   In such a night
  Did Jessica steal from the wealthy Jew,
  And with an unthrift love did run from Venice
  As far as Belmont.
JESSICA   In such a night
  Did young Lorenzo swear he loved her well,
  Stealing her soul with many vows of faith,
  And ne'er a true one.

LORENZO In such a night
Did pretty Jessica, like a little shrew
Slander her love, and he forgave it her.
(*Merchant of Venice* 5.1.3–22)

Jonathan Bate has argued that a Renaissance audience would have been well aware that all of the classical love-affairs alluded to by the lovers here end unhappily, and proposes an ironic reading of the passage as a result.[43] Charles Martindale has objected to this view: 'the timbre of the allusions remains on my reading firmly unironic, overwhelmingly sweet and romantic', and has insisted that Shakespeare here is Francis Meres' 'honey-tongued Ovid' reborn.[44] Significantly neither of these critics reproduces the speech-headings of the dialogue when they quote it, and as a result they reduce the relationship between Shakespeare and his classical sources to a relatively simple three-way interaction between Shakespeare, his (mostly Ovidian) sources, and his audience. The scene seems rather to explore at least a four-way relationship between new and nervous lovers and a variety of *exempla* from Ovid, Virgil, and elsewhere (through whom they are attempting to shape what they feel for and fear about each other), between Shakespeare and his characters, between Shakespeare's audience and Ovid, and between his characters and his audience. This gives the allusions an extraordinary volatility of tone, hedged in with love and fear and playfulness. Lorenzo begins by comparing himself to the love-lorn Troilus, and may want both to romanticise himself and to hint that Jessica might, like Cressida, not merit her lover's languishing. She replies with a tale about a fearfully loyal woman, Thisbe. Lorenzo takes the hint, and turns to an abandoned classical type of female loyalty, but again teasingly, and perhaps to Jessica's ears cruelly, does not recognise that a breezily beautified *exemplum* of Dido, the archetypical abandoned classical woman, is likely to sound harsh in the ear of a woman who has given up her religion and her family to be with him. That is why she responds with an allusion to the disastrous tale of Medea, who rejuvenates Jason's father, but then is abandoned by Jason, and why she then, part playfully, turns Lorenzo into a modern *exemplum* of infidelity. To call the allusions 'ironic' is to flatten the delicate interpersonal play which is worked through them, and the way that they suggest the simultaneously nervous and playfully exploratory voices of early love. To call them 'sweet' is doubtless to describe them as some members of an audience in the 1590s would have done, but the epithet does not acknowledge that a shared repertoire of classical learning here is what is doing the talking between lovers. The two are competing in classical learning, joying in sharing a language and playing with its resources, while neither of them seems fully in control of the effects of their allusions on either their onstage audience of one or on the larger audience offstage. The audience witnessing the scene is likely to become aware that to different people and to different sexes the same classical *exempla* can mean different things. Shakespeare is not here instructing his listeners to remember Ovid, nor is he (as both Bate and Martindale imply) as author alluding to or imitating Ovid in a way that is calculated to make his readers draw particular inferences from the allusions: rather he is mobilising a language of humanism, in which classical allusions can become part of the texture of conversation, and in which particular texts can be evoked and interpreted differently by different people with different pragmatic and social needs from those texts. A large part of the creativity of Shakespeare lies in his willingness to overlayer one shard of 'the classics' with another (as Dido here may borrow a willow wand from the abandoned Ariadne in *Heroides* 10.40–2), to misremember, and to reinvent what he has read. And a significant part of his artistry comes from his awareness that classical allusions, as much as any other use of a shared language, can bring people together at the same time as drawing the finest lines between them by their unpredictable reverberations. A large part of his willingness to do these things derived from the ways in which he learned to use his reading at school. But he learned as much from the failings of his masters, and from the unintended consequences of the way they taught, as from their successes.

NOTES

1. Useful studies include Stuart Gillespie, *Shakespeare's Books: A Dictionary of Shakespeare's Sources*, Athlone Shakespeare Dictionary Series, ed. Sandra Clark (London and New Brunswick, NJ 2001) and Robert S. Miola, *Shakespeare's Reading*, Oxford Shakespeare Topics (Oxford 2000).
2. T. W. Baldwin, *William Shakespere's Small Latine and Lesse Greeke*, 2 vols. (Urbana, IL 1944), vol. II, p. 378.
3. J. A. K. Thomson, *Shakespeare and the Classics* (London 1952), is the exception: he claims of *Lucrece*, for example, that 'Of classical *learning* there is no trace' (p. 42).
4. Brian Vickers, ed., *English Renaissance Literary Criticism* (Oxford 1999), p. 539. Richard Brome, *Five New Plays* (London 1659), sig A4*v* clearly regarded it as an insult: Jonson 'threw in [Shakespeare's] face . . . "small Latin and less Greek"'. Dryden saw the poem as 'an insolent, sparing, and invidious panegyric' (John Dryden, *Essays*, ed. W. P. Ker, 2 vols. (Oxford 1900), vol. II, p. 18).

5. Emrys Jones, *The Origins of Shakespeare* (Oxford 1977) and Joel B. Altman, *The Tudor Play of Mind: Rhetorical Inquiry and the Development of Elizabethan Drama* (Berkeley and London 1978).

6. Anthony Grafton and Lisa Jardine, *From Humanism to the Humanities* (London 1986).

7. Rebecca W. Bushnell, *A Culture of Teaching: Early Modern Humanism in Theory and Practice* (Ithaca, NY 1996), p. 18 notes in Tudor schoolmasters 'an admiration of variety and range in reading struggling against a will to control'. Cf. Margaret Tudeau-Clayton, *Jonson, Shakespeare, and Early Modern Virgil* (Cambridge 1998), ch. 2.

8. Desiderius Erasmus, *Collected Works of Erasmus 24, Literary and Educational Writings 2, De Copia / De Ratione Studii*, ed. Craig R. Thompson (Toronto, Buffalo, and London 1978), pp. 637, 680.

9. Jones, *The Origins of Shakespeare*, p. 13.

10. For a history, see Levi Fox, *Early History of King Edward VI School, Stratford-Upon-Avon* (Oxford 1984).

11. Baldwin, *Small Latine*, vol. 1, p. 468. Thomas Jenkins, a graduate of St John's College, Oxford, was to become his schoolmaster.

12. M. L. Clarke, *Classical Education in England* (Cambridge 1959), p. 180 notes that the foundation was not complete until 1512, and Colet's statutes date from 1518.

13. H. D. Rix, 'The Editions of Erasmus' *De Copia*', *Studies in Philology* 43 (1946), 595–618, 601.

14. Nicholas Carlisle, *A Concise Description of the Endowed Grammar Schools*, 2 vols. (London 1818), vol. ii, p. 76.

15. Ibid., pp. 76–7.

16. Baldwin, *Small Latine*, vol. 1, p. 163 emphasises that curricula are broadly similar in Eton, Peterborough, and Saffron Walden: 'the same fundamental routine evidently continues in these schools and the others throughout the sixteenth century and beyond'. This seems implausibly optimistic: Brinsley's testimony strongly suggests that however much provincial schools emulated the regulatory structures of St Paul's, they nonetheless did not in practice achieve the same level of tuition.

17. William Lily, *A Short Introduction of Grammar Generallie to Be Used* (Geneva 1557), sig. a2r.

18. John Brinsley, *Ludus Literarius: Or, the Grammar Schoole; Shewing How to Proceede from the First Entrance into Learning, to the Highest Perfection Required in the Grammar Schooles* (London 1612), p. 3. Baldwin's claim (vol. ii, p. 355) that Brinsley was thinking of schools 'meaner and ruder than that at Stratford' is unsubstantiated; cf. the more modest account of Stratford Grammar in Fox, *Early History of King Edward VI School, Stratford-Upon-Avon*.

19. This was something of a humanist topos: Melancthon's oration *De Miseriis Paedogogorum* (*c*.1526) emphasises how exhausting it is to correct errors, and how thankless and poorly paid a task it is. See Philip Melancthon, *Opera*

Quae Supersunt Omnia, ed. Carol Gottleib Bretschneider, 24 vols., *Corpus Reformatorum* (Halis Saxonum 1843), vol. XI, pp. 121–30.

20. Brinsley, *Ludus Literarius*, p. 195.

21. Ibid., p. 121.

22. Charles Hoole, *A New Discovery of the Old Art of Teaching Schoole* (London 1659), p. 158.

23. Shakespeare did, however, evidently make use of Golding later in life, as many articles by A. B. Taylor have shown.

24. Brinsley, *Ludus Literarius*, p. 219.

25. Ibid., p. 191.

26. Ibid., p. 194.

27. Cf. the argument in Patricia Parker, *Literary Fat Ladies: Rhetoric, Gender, Property* (London 1987), pp. 27–34.

28. John Kerrigan, 'Hieronimo, Hamlet, and Remembrance', *Essays in Criticism* 31 (1981), 105–26, repr. in John Kerrigan, *Revenge Tragedy: Aeschylus to Armageddon* (Oxford 1996).

29. As Tudeau-Clayton, *Jonson, Shakespeare, and Early Modern Virgil* argues.

30. Erasmus, *De Copia*, p. 295.

31. Jones, *The Origins of Shakespeare*, p. 22.

32. Richard Mulcaster, *Positions* (London 1581), p. 141.

33. William Shakespeare, *The Complete Poems and Sonnets*, ed. Colin Burrow (Oxford 2002), p. 318.

34. Erasmus, *De Copia*, pp. 584–5: 'Ulysses must be cunning, lying, deceitful, able to endure anything; Agamemnon rather lacking in force but eager for power'.

35. See ibid., pp. 635–8. On commonplace books, see Peter Beal, 'Notions in Garrison: The Seventeenth-Century Commonplace Book', in *New Ways of Looking at Old Texts*, ed. W. Speed Hill, *Medieval and Renaissance Texts and Studies* 107 (Binghamton, NY 1993), pp. 131–47, and Anne Moss, *Printed Commonplace-Books and the Structuring of Renaissance Thought* (Oxford 1996).

36. Cambridge University Library MS Dd.IV.5, dating from the late 1580s or early 1590s, has a large number of entries for some topics ('Amor' and 'Amicitia'), but none for many others (including 'Studium' and 'Stultitia'). A later hand has filled many of the blank pages with notes on sermons.

37. Sir Francis Bacon, *Works*, ed. James Spedding, Robert Lesley Ellis, and Douglas Denon Heath, 14 vols. (London 1857–74), vol. IX, pp. 25–6.

38. See Jonathan Bate, *Shakespeare and Ovid* (Oxford 1993), ch. 3.

39. Some argument against this view is in Bate, *Shakespeare and Ovid*, ch. 5.

40. William Shakespeare, *Hamlet*, ed. Horace Howard Furness, 2 vols., *A New Variorum Edition of Shakespeare*, vol. III (London and Philadelphia 1877), vol. I, p. 151.

41. Marcus Tullius Cicero, *The Fyve Questions Which Marke Tullye Cicero, Disputed in His Manor of Tusculanum*, trans. J. Dolman (London 1561), sig. E6v, translating 1.67.

42. See William Shakespeare, *Troilus and Cressida*, ed. Harold N. Hillebrand, *A New Variorum Edition of Shakespeare* (Philadelphia and London 1953), pp. 411–15 for a summary of various hypotheses.
43. Bate, *Shakespeare and Ovid*, pp. 154–7.
44. Charles Martindale, 'Shakespeare's Ovid, Ovid's Shakespeare: A Methodological Postscript', in *Shakespeare's Ovid*, ed. A. B. Taylor (Cambridge 2000), pp. 198–215, 203.

PART II

'SMALL LATINE'

OVID

CHAPTER 2

Petruchio is 'Kated': The Taming of the Shrew *and Ovid*

Vanda Zajko

How does the assertion that *The Taming of the Shrew* contains allusions to Ovid add to its interest or enliven our engagement with it? This question should be held in mind continuously when thinking about how to characterise Shakespeare's sources for his play. We are aware by now that to describe any play as Ovidian is to open up and not close down interpretative possibilities,[1] and the relationship between Shakespeare and Ovid has been too thoroughly explored for there to be much to be gained from reference spotting.[2] If we work within the particular area of literary criticism that is concerned to construct a classical tradition, more is required of us than to identify possible intertextualities in order to establish contexts for the interpretation of particular words. Part of our project must surely be to continue to think about the kind of Ovid Shakespeare himself creates and to allow that creation to impact on our readings both of Shakespeare and of Ovid.

When it comes to *The Taming of the Shrew*, one of the challenges for the critic is how to write about a play that dramatises the process of control and subjugation of a woman without seeming to collude in it. The unease that is triggered by Kate's final speech is made evident by the strategies adopted by both critics and performers to explain it: these include references to irony or to humour or, most prevalently, to history.[3] The speech is impossible to ignore because of its emphatic position in the final scene, but the questions it raises about dominance and submission are uncomfortable for those who like to believe that love resides in mutuality and not in coercion. The problem of negotiating the sexual politics of the play is one that preoccupies present-day critics for whom sexual relationships are key markers of identity, and the power struggle between Kate and Petruchio fascinates those attentive to contemporary power struggles between men and women. But this particular relationship is just one of those that Shakespeare chooses to explore. Within the play he also shows us the courtship of Lucentio and Bianca and the wooing of the rich widow by the cynical Hortensio.[4]

If our attention is drawn to and held by the relationship between Kate and Petruchio, it is partly because of this juxtaposition with other less demanding relationships which fail to capture the imagination in such a compelling way. Kate's transformation, however we define it, challenges us to think about the potential for change created by the interaction between two individuals, whereas the role playing of Bianca and her suitor leads only to stasis. Ovid provides models for both kinds of liaison, and, if the *Metamorphoses* is the text that underpins the relationship between Petruchio and Kate, the elegiac texts perform a similar role for the play's other couples. Shakespeare's use of Ovid inflects, then, both the connection between the different layers of plot within the play and the larger more controversial issues.

It became a commonplace to claim that Shakespeare was fascinated by the individual's capacity for change and Ovidian myths of transformation have been described as 'the metamorphic matter of Shakespearean romantic comedy'.[5] The dramatic potential of such myths is clear and it is possible to locate some kind of transformation at the heart of every plot. But if we do this we run the risk of talking about both something and nothing. As John Velz puts it: 'The risk of an analysis of "metamorphosis" in Shakespeare is that one may be tempted to discuss changes that are not really matters of morphosis. Since all traditional drama is about change through action (cf. the etymon of drama), the net catches everything in the action, making metamorphosis mean too much and (ergo) too little.'[6]

In the case of *The Taming of the Shrew* we can identify a whole range of Shakespearean transformations from the subterfuge surrounding Sly and the theatrical performances of the players, through the disguises of Tranio, Hortensio, and Lucentio, to the wordplay and manipulative rhetoric of Petruchio.[7] Why, then, should we identify Kate's transformation in particular with the transformations of the *Metamorphoses*? The question most relevant to this chapter is not simply what *is* the basis for such an identification but what *could* be the basis? The process of interpreting the change in Kate as a comment on, response to, or elaboration of Ovid's epic (by which I mean a poem in hexameters)[8] involves deciding what kind of reader of Ovid we imagine Shakespeare to have been.

Contemporary critics tend to stress the potential for reading Ovid meta-poetically.[9] The diversity of viewpoint involved in representing metamor-phosis (the juxtaposition of before and after that involves for the reader the responsibility of deciding where the before ends and the after begins) is regarded as a distinctive feature of Ovid's text, and metamorphosis is evaluated primarily as a literary trope.[10] So Andrew Feldherr writes:

The changing implications of metamorphosis among the many kinds of literary discourse in which it occurs make it a narrative element that invites contrasting readings and opens out interpretative possibilities. Ovid himself participates in this process by introducing multiple points of view on transformation itself as well as raising questions about the generic status of his work. Thus metamorphosis continually compels readers to refigure their relationship to the text, their understanding of the narratives it contains, and ultimately how it functions as a literary representation.[11]

Feldherr goes on to forge a connection between the literary-critical debates contemporaneous with Ovid and his immediate predecessors and those of the present day. He grounds his own interpretation of the poem, with its emphasis on multi-determinacy, in the 'historical' Ovid whom he creates from his reading of a selection of ancient poems. On this reading the *Metamorphoses* becomes a text preoccupied with its own literariness, and its sinuous capacity for intertextual interpretation becomes part of its grand design.

But while he emphasises the narrative techniques of the poem and the implications of its theme for evaluation of its genre, Feldherr downplays other ways of thinking about metamorphosis, for example cosmological or psychological allegory, that have been popular in the intervening historical periods. The essays collected in *The Cambridge Companion to Ovid* demonstrate that for the majority of today's leading Ovidians the dominant mode of criticism is a kind of formalism which seals off the poem and restricts its significance to narratological matters. It is the argument of this chapter that Shakespeare's reading of Ovid is not like this: his fascination with the Roman poet is provoked by the capacity of metamorphosis to explore the continuities and development of human personality, and the Ovid we meet as a result of our engagement with Shakespeare's plays is a poet whose interest in the manifold possibilities for expression of love and desire is central to his vision. Shakespeare's encounter with Ovid leads him to ponder these possibilities, and in *The Taming of the Shrew* he responds to and elaborates upon Ovidian models of love, drawing out their implications for the lives of men and women. If we give our reading this focus, the play becomes part of the literary tradition of writing about love that continues to provide us with resources for thinking about our own desires.[12]

Germaine Greer has argued that Shakespeare 'projected the ideal of the monogamous heterosexual couple so luminously in his matings that they irradiate our notions of compatibility and co-operation between spouses to this day'.[13] It is true that Shakespearean comedy is replete with examples of sparring couples whose destiny beyond the play arouses curiosity about what a happy ending might entail. But Greer's formulation suggests a complacency that is hard to justify, and the model of the heterosexual couple that the plays construct is less homogeneous than she would have us believe. What is clear is that Shakespeare has an interest in lasting relationships and the grounds for their very possibility, given what is commonly the transient nature of desire. This interest is what lies at the heart of the assorted couplings in *The Taming of the Shrew*, and it gives emphasis to the contrasting responses of the women to the challenge thrown out by their men in the final scene. The question the scene poses is which, if any, of the three relationships has the capacity to endure. The answer depends upon the position we adopt regarding Kate's transformation.

Let us turn now to those moments within the play that are most evidently Ovidian. Is it the case that there are generic differences between the allusions that correspond to the different kinds of relationship with which they are associated? Ovid is more often linked with sexual desire and the processes and pitfalls of seduction than with the institution of marriage, since the latter is identified closely with the Augustan regime to which he is assumed to be hostile. However it is acknowledged that the scope of the *Metamorphoses* allows for more exploration of the role and entailments of marriage than the didactic and elegiac poems.[14] Although there are interpretations of Roman elegy which regard it as having captured an authentic expression of love, in recent years commentators have tended to stress the genre's preoccupation with role play, manipulation and rhetoric. This has particularly been the case with the Ovidian texts, and especially the explicitly didactic *Ars Amatoria*. Duncan Kennedy outlines the position as follows:

> In treating love as a *system* which can be taught and learned, Ovid's *Ars amatoria* similarly views it as a discursive artefact. The phrase *tu mihi sola places* ('you are the only one for me') functions as an expression of the lover's exclusive devotion to the beloved (e.g. Propertius 2.7.19). In prefixing to it the words *'elige cui dicas'* ('choose to whom you may say', *Ars* 1.42), the *magister amoris* makes of it a script to be performed. Within this way of viewing things, to be in love is to think one's self 'in love' and 'act' accordingly.[15]

The 'Ovidian' perspective that Kennedy sets up complicates any notion of sincerity or authenticity regarding the expression of love. It is interesting, then, that it is the *Ars* that Lucentio is reading when accosted by Bianca at 4.2.6 ff.:

> LUC. Now, Mistress, profit you in what you read?
> BIAN. What, master, read you? First resolve me that.

LUC. I read that I profess, The Art to Love.
BIAN. And may you prove, sir, master of your art.
LUC. While you, sweet dear, prove mistress of my heart.

We are reminded that when Lucentio arrived in Padua he was keen to pursue his studies in philosophy but that he quickly accepted Tranio's advice not to neglect the study of Ovid (1.1.33). He has taken to heart the exhortation to 'study what you most affect' (1.1.40) and, disguised as a teacher, ostentatiously reads a text which will teach him how to be an effective lover. It has long been recognised that the courting of Bianca follows literary convention.[16] Lucentio's reaction to his first glimpse of Bianca conversing with her father and sister is immediately recognisable as participating in a tradition of 'love at first sight' (1.1.148 ff.) with its symptomology of burning, pining, and wasting away. Tranio's enquiry 'I pray, sir, tell me, is it possible / That love should of a sudden take such hold?' (1.1.146–7) can be read retrospectively as being rather arch, and indeed, as the scene progresses, it becomes clear that Lucentio's entreaties to Tranio for help position the servant as an Ovidian *magister amoris*: he is the one who recognises what is going on and urges that a practical solution be found to the problem of unfulfilled desire. Lucentio expresses his yearning for Bianca in terms which emphasise her sexual power, and yet, within the discourse of elegy, 'the common self-portrait of the lover as "slave" and his beloved as his *domina*, his mistress, can be considered, from the point of view of its rhetoric, as supporting the lover's position in his manipulation of the balance of erotic power'.[17] So how are we to evaluate the representation of Lucentio here? Does it depend on how we choose to interpret the Ovidian allusion?

In a very different reading from mine, Jonathan Bate argues that the Bianca/Lucentio relationship offers *The Taming of the Shrew*'s most positive model of courtship and marriage.[18] This is particularly interesting because Bate agrees that Ovid's amorous poetry and not the *Metamorphoses* constitutes the key set of intertexts for understanding the relationship. He bases his idea that reciprocity is at the heart of Lucentio and Bianca's liaison on an interpretation of 1.1.167–70, where Lucentio compares his own reaction on seeing Bianca to that of Jupiter when he first saw Europa:

> O yes. I saw sweet beauty in her face,
> Such as the daughter of Agenor had,
> That made great Jove to humble him to her hand,
> When with his knees he kiss'd the Cretan strand.

Bate suggests that in these lines Lucentio 'empties Jupiter's disguised wooing of Europa of its deceit and interprets it in terms of male humility'. He argues that Jupiter's metamorphosis entails a change of status and the adoption of a humbler role (animal rather than god) that is paralleled by Lucentio's own disguise as a servant.[19] But whereas Jupiter's transformation remains manipulative, Lucentio's transformation is 'wholly creative' because 'the love turns out to be mutual'. Bianca is said to share in 'the wonder of love's metamorphosis', and the Bianca/Lucentio plot overall proposes a model in which 'the chain of being is disrupted . . . in the name of a shared love'.[20] In this case, Bate implies, the ends justify the means, and the fact that the disguised wooing results in seduction rather than rape is enough to justify a positive rather than a negative judgement about the strategic choice of the lover. Lucentio may deceive Bianca as to who he really is, but in spite of his self-concealment she recognises him as the one she desires. She recognises, we might say, the script of the lover's discourse that he acts out so efficiently, and she plays her own part to equally good effect.

Bate interprets the reference to Jupiter as a reference to the story of Europa in the *Metamorphoses*, and claims that it is boldly reworked to produce a different kind of tale.[21] But in the context of the amatory poetry that we observe Lucentio read, the disguise and manipulation of the god do not seem out of place and Lucentio's identification with him is comprehensible without elaborate reworking. The process of seduction is accomplished by the reading of 'all books of love',[22] and there are explicit references to the *Heroides* and the *Ars Amatoria*. It may be significant, then, that there is another allusion to Europa in the Ovidian corpus, at *Amores* 1.3.23–4. Here she is invoked as someone who has inspired great poetry in the hope that her example will convince the addressee that she too should submit to being the subject of a poem (and to the desire of the lover). As Kennedy has demonstrated, the association of the beloved with Europa in this context, alongside Io and Leda, leads to the correlation of the lover with Jupiter that draws attention to his potential promiscuity, rather than to the fidelity which ostensibly he declares.[23] If we select this poem as an intertext for the passage from *The Taming of the Shrew*, the self-identification of Lucentio with the adulterous god is not as reassuring an image as Bate would have us believe; rather the particularity of the feelings he and Bianca have for each other is called into question.

The two references to the *Heroides* open up interpretative possibilities that are equally subversive of Bate's position. The first at 1.2.242–5 is less clear-cut than the second and is probably an allusion to *Heroides* 17.103–4, the letter from Helen to Paris. In these lines Tranio compares Bianca with

Helen, the daughter of Leda, and Lucentio with Paris, whose courtship of a married woman began the Trojan war:

> Fair Leda's daughter had a thousand wooers,
> Then well one more may fair Bianca have.
> And so she shall. Lucentio shall make one,
> Though Paris came, in hope to speed alone.[24]

The force of these lines is hyperbolic. Bianca is conceived of as having one more suitor than the most beautiful woman from the mythological and literary past, whilst it is envisaged that Lucentio would be successful in his conquest even if he were competing with Paris who did, after all, have the personal backing of the goddess of love. The exaggerated merits of the two protagonists match the inflated accounts of the beloved's desirability given by the poet/lover throughout the *Ars Amatoria*. But the Ovidian intertextuality is more complex still, because, in the third book of the *Ars*, the female reader is encouraged to study the *Heroides* if she wants to secure her man.[25] It is as if Bianca has heeded this advice, because when we see her being 'taught' by Lucentio disguised as her tutor at 3.1.26–83, it is clear that she is as knowledgeable as he. The text the pair construe is the first of the epistles, the letter from Penelope to Odysseus, and for each line Lucentio 'translates' Bianca 'translates' one in turn.[26] Bate interprets this symmetry as a sign of mutuality, and infers that their marriage will be one between equals. But, again, it is possible to take a less optimistic view:[27] what the couple share is nothing more than familiarity with the literary conventions of love.[28] The lack of distinctiveness in their interaction casts doubts on their capacity to sustain their interest in each other in the longer term.

What then of the other sister and the other Ovidian text? If we turn first to the Induction scene, possible traces of the *Metamorphoses* are visible everywhere, and the images of disguise, hunting and pursuit they introduce set up clear thematic links with the rest of the play.[29] The pictures the Lord and his servingmen offer to bring to delight Christopher Sly all depict episodes familiar from the epic and they provide a range of models for the pairings which follow. In addition to these apparently illustrative moments, the scene is shot through with a variety of transformations which we might or might not judge to be inspired by the subject matter, narrative style, or ideology of the *Metamorphoses*, depending on what we consider those to be. A single example will demonstrate how the evaluation of Shakespeare's Ovidianism in this scene relates to our evaluation of the transformation of Kate. At lines 58–61 the Third Servingman describes a picture of Daphne that he intends to fetch for Sly:

> Or Daphne roaming through a thorny wood,
> Scratching her legs that one shall swear she bleeds,
> And at that sight shall sad Apollo weep,
> So workmanly the blood and tears are drawn.

This picture calls to mind that of Daphne and Apollo in the first book of the *Metamorphoses*. In particular, it seems to gloss the following lines in Golding's translation which are articulated by Apollo himself:

> alas alas how woulde it grieve my heart,
> To see thee fall among the briers, and that the bloud should start
> Out of thy tender legges, I wretch the causer of thy smart.

It may seem perverse to take Apollo's sadness seriously given the part he has played in causing Daphne to suffer. And the lines can certainly be read as both threatening and persuasive given that it is only if she runs away that Daphne will be harmed. However, the ability she has to cause Apollo pain could be seen as articulating something important about the experience of desire. The play of power between the two that is rendered visible by the shifts of perspective in the way the story is told makes it hard to read it as a straightforward rape narrative. Daphne's initial metamorphosis can be regarded as an escape from violence that allows her to preserve something of herself untouched, or as an act of annihilation that completely destroys her identity. Then there is Apollo's appropriation of the laurel: is it a final gesture of humiliation and brutality, or a redemptive moment, signifying that the influence of Daphne is not at an end?[30] Feldherr outlines two possible ways of reading the story, and his analysis suggests that the choice of interpretation will hinge on the transformation.[31] The capaciousness of Ovid's metamorphic narrative is such that large-scale issues about the design and order of the world and the definition and scope of human personality are always involved when we make a judgement about how to evaluate the elements of change and continuity in any individual episode.

Shakespeare fully exploits the capaciousness of the poem. The Ovidian moments of the Induction scene can be read as programmatic for *The Taming of the Shrew*,[32] but this does not release us from the necessity of making interpretative decisions. William Carroll expresses a strong sense of the scene's potential:

Is it possible to say what kind of metamorphosis the Induction predicts for Kate? I think not. The Induction gives too many possibilities: transformations that are incomplete, transformations that are of clothes only, transformations that are both physical and emotional, transformations that are either erotic and desirable or frightening, transformations that are resisted and then accepted, mimetic transformations that are strictly the result of a suspension of disbelief, transformations that thin the blood and triumph over disease. Kate's change at the end partakes of all these possibilities.[33]

My argument that there is a potent connection between Shakespeare's treatment of Daphne and his subsequent depiction of Kate depends upon the idea that in this play Shakespeare utilises the *Metamorphoses* to explore the dynamic potential of relationship. In doing so he contributes to a tradition which figures Ovid, in this appropriation, as proto-psychoanalytic[34] and emphasises literature's role as a source for psychological theory. Literature has often been figured like this. As Shoshana Felman famously declared:

> Literature has claimed priority and authority over psychoanalysis as its influential historical source, as its ancestor or its predecessor in the discovery of the unconscious . . . The key concepts of psychoanalysis are references to literature, using literary proper names – names of fictional characters (Oedipal complex, Narcissism) or of historical authors (masochism, sadism). Literature, in other words, is the language which psychoanalysis uses in order to speak of itself. . . Literature is therefore not simply outside psychoanalysis, since it motivates and inhabits the very names of its concepts, since it is the inherent reference by which psychoanalysis names its findings.[35]

Leonard Barkan has commented on the way that Shakespearean comedy particularly draws upon those Ovidian myths that illustrate the various ways an individual might desire,[36] and one such myth is referred to in the vital scene for Kate's transformation at 4.5.27 ff. where she agrees to call the sun the moon. Petruchio instructs her to address Vincentio as if he were a woman, and she does this in words reminiscent of Salmacis' address to Hermaphroditus at *Met.* 4.320–8.

> Young budding virgin, fair, and fresh, and sweet,
> Whither away, or where is thy abode?
> Happy the parents of so fair a child,
> Happier the man whom favourable stars
> Allots thee for his lovely bedfellow.

Bate describes the Ovidian context for the lines as 'the classic source of sexual role-reversal', and proposes that 'the fact that Shakespeare went to Salmacis for the image is enough to suggest that the idea of marriage as mutuality rather than subjugation was in his mind as he wrote the play'.[37] Roberts' historicising account claims that 'the hermaphrodite was a popular Elizabethan emblem for the miracle of marriage, which joined male and female'.[38] The mutuality of the relationship between the protagonists surely is what is being emphasised here, but the image is neither bland

nor comfortable. Salmacis actively pursues the young man just as Apollo
pursues Daphne, and she sets about seducing him in spite of his resistance.
She persists in the face of his struggles ('Strive, struggle, wrest and writhe
(she said) thou forward boy thy fill: / Doe what thou canst thou shalt
not scape'),[39] and it is she who prays that they might be transformed so
that she can hold onto him forever. Only at the end of the episode does
Hermaphroditus use his voice, and then it is to pray that any man bathing
in the nymph's pool subsequently will be as emasculated as he himself has
been.

The allusion to the Salmacis story is subtle rather than explicit, and yet
it makes a striking contribution to the intertextual nexus surrounding Kate
and Petruchio. There is a clear emphasis on the dominance of the female and
on her capacity to be the aggressor, so that there is no equality of desire in
the stalking or its outcome. The final image of their bodies joined together
'Like as if a man should in one barke beholde / Two twigges both growing
into one and still togither holde'[40] is hardly reassuring since it continues to
be stressed that it is she who is grasping him. It seems easier to interpret this
as an image of non-consensuality rather than as an emblem of successful
marriage as the commentators suggest. But here we return to the question
of Shakespeare's priorities in relation to Ovid. There are some readers for
whom the *Metamorphoses* consists of revelation or clarification, for whom
the central paradox of the poem is that it represents changes which preserve,
alterations which maintain identity.[41] Shakespeare however is not one of
these. For him the fascination of change resides not in the shape-shifting
of bodies but in its internal, psychological aspect, and in this aspect the
process is continuous and potentially without end.

If the patterns of flight and sexual aggression alluded to in the Ovidian
myths contribute to an understanding of what is going on between Petruchio and Kate, they do so by drawing attention to a dynamics of sexual
power in which neither male nor female is automatically in control. The
fight for supremacy between the equally matched protagonists in *The Taming of the Shrew* consists not in physical combat, but in a battle of wits
that threatens the very survival of the personalities involved. As Barkan
describes it, 'set in a context of the metamorphic images of love among
the minor characters, the relationship of Petruchio and Kate details the
struggle, through tests of will and perception, to hammer out individual
identity within the warring pair'.[42] The process involves Petruchio just as
much as Kate. Originally interested in marrying for money, when he meets
his bride to be he finds her intellect as enticing as her dowry. Throughout
the scene of their first engagement (2.1.183–273) the couple embark on a

round of fast-flying observations and insults, replete with sexual innuendo, that allows each to observe the wit, pugnaciousness, and tenacity of the other. Kate throws everything she has at Petruchio in the clear expectation that he will be repulsed. But by the end of the scene he has seen enough to recognise how well matched they are:

> Now, Kate, I am a husband for your turn,
> For by this light, whereby I see thy beauty,
> Thy beauty that doth make me like thee well,
> Thou must be married to no man but me.[43]

It is the appreciation of Kate's particular qualities that enables Petruchio to woo her effectively, manipulating his appearance, language and personality to provide her with a fitting mate. Petruchio is 'Kated'.[44] Kate, in her turn, comes to understand something of the singular nature of her suitor and responds to her new insights in a strikingly courageous way. Her final public statement and Petruchio's recognition of its value is evidence of a process of significant and mutual change.

The ambiguity that surrounds the ending of the Ovidian stories concerning what, if anything, survives the physical transformations is translated into uncertainty concerning the transformed Kate. The last two lines of the play articulate a sense of doubt as to whether the transformation is genuine:

HOR. Now go thy ways, thou hast tam'd a curst shrew.
LUC. Tis a wonder, by your leave, she will be tam'd so.

As Petruchio points out, Hortensio and Lucentio have just been very effectively humiliated by their wives ('We three are married, but you two are sped'),[45] and the prospect of any sympathy between Petruchio and Kate is likely to be threatening to them. But a sceptical reading is certainly available, particularly if we regard Kate as simply bending to her husband's will.[46] Kate's psychological change, like Daphne's physical one, could be seen as a strategic means of avoiding male domination, the pretence of obedience providing her with some psychic space in which to hide. Alternatively, if we choose to stress the rhetoricity of every articulation of love, the sparring of Kate and Petruchio becomes merely another kind of role-playing and the speech delivered by Kate just another move in the game. I have argued above, however, that it is partly the contrast with the conventional love-making of Lucentio and Bianca that gives the relationship its power. What is made visible in the portrayal of Petruchio and Kate is the peril involved in the process of genuine self-exposure to another. Our psychological shape can be altered as a result of such a process. Shakespeare might, just, be daring us to risk this kind of change.[47]

NOTES

1. See, for example, Charles Martindale, 'A Methodological Postscript', in A. B. Taylor, ed., *Shakespeare's Ovid* (Cambridge 2000), p. 210: 'Few will deny that there is a highly significant relationship between Ovid and Shakespeare. The disputes are about how the character of that relationship is to be described, or, as I would prefer to put it, (re)constructed and (re)negotiated. Any Ovidian writer can be represented as "like" Ovid, or as "unlike" Ovid – to the extreme point of being "anti-Ovid" – and likewise valued for being like, or unlike, or both in shifting combinations. Ovid moreover can always be seen as changing in his reception – "Ovid" then as well as Ovid.'

2. Important discussions of Ovid and Shakespeare include Leonard Barkan, *The Gods Made Flesh: Metamorphosis and the Pursuit of Paganism* (New Haven 1986), Jonathan Bate, *Shakespeare and Ovid* (Oxford 1993), William Carroll, *The Metamorphoses of Shakespearean Comedy* (Princeton 1985), Lynn Enterline, *The Rhetoric of the Body From Ovid to Shakespeare* (Cambridge 2000), A. B. Taylor, ed., *Shakespeare's Ovid* (Cambridge 2000), M. L. Stapleton, *Harmful Eloquence: Ovid's Amores from Antiquity to Shakespeare* (Ann Arbor 1996).

3. See, for example, Michael Billington on the Bogdanov production at Stratford in 1978, cited in Penny Gay, *As She Likes It: Shakespeare's Unruly Women* (London 1994), p. 108: '[T]his production is entirely about the taming of Petruchio . . . what we see in the final scene is the ultimate humiliation of Petruchio by a mature, witty and ironic Kate.' Or Janet Suzman describing her own performance of Kate in Judith Cook, *Women in Shakespeare* (London 1980), p. 29: 'In that scene about the moon and the sun we made a useful discovery; if you can laugh with somebody you can't fight them any more. What Petruchio is doing in that scene is teaching Kate a small lesson in humour.' The following comment in Gay, *As She Likes It*, p. 86 is typical of attempts to alleviate the potential brutality of the play by placing it firmly in its historical context: 'The story implied by its title is more thoroughly rooted in a medieval and Elizabethan way of thinking about women and their relation to the patriarchy than any other of Shakespeare's plays (excluding the histories).'

4. Bate, *Shakespeare and Ovid*, p. 121 suggests that if the original form of the play is correct, it would have presented four versions of courtship and/or marriage: Petruchio and Kate, Bianca and Lucentio, Hortensio and his widow, and Christopher Sly and his off-stage wife. For a full exposition of the arguments concerning the relationship of *The Shrew* published in the First Folio to the play *The Taming of A Shrew* printed in 1594 see the introduction to Brian Morris' 1981 Arden edition. For the purposes of this chapter I am working with the text of *The Shrew* as published in the Morris edition.

5. Barkan, *The Gods Made Flesh*, p. 274.

6. John Velz, 'Shakespeare's Ovid in the Twentieth Century: A Critical Survey', in Taylor, *Shakespeare's Ovid*, p. 190.

7. Petruchio's 'false' descriptions of Kate and the world around her have the potential to transform reality both for her and the audience. For example, at 2.1.236 ff. he woos her as if she were the woman she is not, emphasising her 'courteous', 'gentle', 'soft', and 'affable' nature. It is as if he can see her latent possibilities, possibilities which become potential realities for the audience as he describes them.

8. There is substantial discussion of the debate surrounding the use of this generic term in Stephen Hinds, *The Metamorphoses of Persephone: Ovid and the Self-Conscious Muse* (Cambridge 1987).

9. Whatever else he is writing about Ovid is assumed to be writing about writing poetry. So, for example, Alison Sharrock, 'Gender and Sexuality', in Phillip Hardie, ed., *The Cambridge Companion to Ovid* (Cambridge 2002), p. 99: 'Writing poetry, for Ovid, is not just *about* "sexuality"; it is itself an erotic experience, in which it is impossible to distinguish clearly between sex and poetry.'

10. It is a notable feature of contemporary Ovidianism that it seeks to make the availability of the text for diverse interpretation a particular feature of Ovid's writing rather than of Latin literature or of literature generally.

11. Andrew Feldherr, 'Metamorphosis in the *Metamorphoses*', in Hardie, *The Cambridge Companion*, p. 165.

12. See Duncan Kennedy, *The Arts of Love* (Cambridge 1993), pp. 64–5: 'From such a perspective, it is disconcerting to feel that the phrase "I love you" may have emerged from our mouths already equipped with inverted commas, that we may have been acting out a script that has been played out, with much the same plot and much the same words, by many before us, that what we say and feel in love may not be unique to each of us, but moulded and refined by many before us.'

13. Germaine Greer, *Shakespeare* (Oxford 1986), p. 124.

14. See Charles Martindale in the Introduction to Martindale, ed., *Ovid Renewed* (Cambridge 1988), p. 8: 'The romantic is not the only unfamiliar Ovid. Another is the poet of marriage . . . Perhaps not since Homer had a major poet written with more sympathetic interest about married love; one thinks for example of Ceyx and Alcyone, Cephalus and Procris, and Baucis and Philemon, or Ovid's relationship with his third wife as conveyed in the exile poetry.' Sharrock in Hardie, *The Cambridge Companion*, p. 105 selects the same examples to illustrate Ovid's interest in marriage as part of a discussion of the poet's attitude towards the Augustan adultery laws.

15. Kennedy, *The Arts of Love*, p. 65. He goes on to argue that the Propertian and Ovidian positions are often represented as opposites but that from a recuperative 'Ovidian' perspective the 'authentic' Propertian position can be read as 'a dramatic mimesis of the lover's discourse'. This is hugely relevant to my argument later.

16. See, for example, Alexander Leggatt, *Shakespeare's Comedy of Love* (London 1987), pp. 46 ff.

17. Kennedy, *The Arts of Love*, p. 73. See, for example, 1.1.219–20: LUC. 'And let me be a slave, t'achieve that maid / Whose sudden sight hath thrall'd my wounded eye.'
18. Bate, *Shakespeare and Ovid*, pp. 120 ff.
19. Paula Berggren in '"From a God to a Bull": Shakespeare's Slumming Jove', *Classical and Modern Literature* 5 (1985), 280 agrees that the image of Jupiter here is one of humiliation: 'As the play proper gets under way, Europa is alluded to, not as Jove's victim but as his superior. . . In the ensuing action, Lucentio, who speaks these lines, will humble himself to win Bianca's hand, becoming "Cambio," the spirit of change, and giving up his own identity to his servant. This early reference to Jove as bull suggests that for Shakespeare, the god so disguised signifies social abasement rather than sexual prowess.' However in *The Merry Wives of Windsor* Shakespeare went on to explore the issue further and he avoided this easy polarity. When Falstaff appears in horns at the end of the play (5.5.3–13) he sees himself as the adulterous Jupiter: 'Remember, Jove, thou wast a bull for thy Europa; love set on thy horns. O powerful love, that in some respects makes a beast a man; in some other, a man a beast.' In the words of Barkan, *The Gods Made Flesh*, p. 282 Falstaff perceives 'both the glory and the degradation of amorous metamorphosis'.
20. The lines which form the basis for these conclusions are 5.1.112–17:

    BIAN. Cambio is chang'd into Lucentio.
    LUC. Love wrought these miracles. Bianca's love
    Made me exchange my state with Tranio,
    While he did bear my countenance in the town,
    And happily I have arriv'd at the last
    Unto the wished haven of my bliss.

21. The story of Europa appears at *Met.* 2.836 ff. and as one of the stories woven by Arachne at 6.103–7. Commentators point out that Shakespeare seems not to have followed the story exactly, since in Ovid, Jupiter appears to Europa on the beach at Tyre and then carries her off to Crete. The story is generally identified as Ovidian because the subject was made so popular by artistic representations which draw on details of the Ovid. It is relevant to my argument here that there is nothing which unequivocally links the passage of the play with either passage in the *Metamorphoses*.
22. *Taming of the Shrew* 1.2.145.
23. Kennedy, *The Arts of Love*, p. 68: 'The lover presents himself as in the power of his addressee, who has, he says, made him her prey (cf. *praedata . . . est*, 1) and to whom he is prepared to be a slave through the long years (cf. *deserviat*, 5), and as one who knows how to love with absolute fidelity (*pura . . . fide*, 6). The lover requests of her that she make herself available as a subject for his poetry, promising that poems will result that are worthy of their source of inspiration (19–20). However, the lover's invocation of three mythological heroines (Io, Leda, and Europa, 21–4) to illustrate the fame that poetry can

confer serves to identify him with the single figure who seduced all three, the archetypal adulterer Jupiter, thus casting doubt on the "sincerity" of his earlier protestations.'

24. The Ovidian lines are as follows: *tunc ego te vellem celeri venisse carina, / cum mea virginitas mille petita procis; / si te vidissem, primus de mille fuisses* ('I wish that you had come in your swift ship at the time when my virgin hand was sought by a thousand suitors. If I had seen you, of the thousand you would have been the first').

25. *Ars Amatoria* 3.345–6.

26. Bate, *Shakespeare and Ovid*, pp. 126–7 acknowledges that 'there may be a contextual irony in that the letter in question is written by Penelope while she is surrounded by wooers whom she'd rather be without'. But it is possible to develop a much more sinister reading than this.

27. Particularly if we consider that what they are reading are elegiac couplets which proverbially in Ovid are never equal: one of the two would have to take the hexameter and the other the pentameter.

28. There is a substantial debate concerning whether or not the *Heroides* should be read as attempting to express something genuine about the experience of love and about whether the heroines' accounts of their experiences differ substantially enough from each other to render them authentic in this regard. Kennedy explores the various positions in 'Epistolarity: the Heroides', in Hardie, *The Cambridge Companion*, pp. 217–32. The point about recuperation mentioned under n. 15 above is relevant here.

29. This thematic cohesion based on the *Metamorphoses* is a strong argument for the inclusion of the scene in the original play. See n. 3 above. For Adonis and Cytherea see *Met.* 10.520–739, for Io see *Met.* 1.588–600, and for Daphne and Apollo see *Met.* 1.452–567.

30. The lines in which Daphne/the tree seems to acquiesce in his action might allow for such an optimistic reading: 'The Lawrell to his just request did seem to condescende, / By bowing of hir newe made boughs and tender braunches downe, / And wagging of hir seemely toppe, as if it were hir crowne.' See Arthur Golding, *Shakespeare's Ovid* (London 1961), p. 34.

31. Feldherr in Hardie, *The Cambridge Companion*, pp. 173–4: 'The readings offered so far suggest that the event of metamorphosis in Ovid mobilizes two coherent interpretations of the poem, and that the choice between them depends on the point of view adopted on the transformation itself. First, to focus on the new shape, which is often a form familiar from the actual experience of the reader, in several senses normalizes metamorphosis, subordinating a manifestly unbelievable process to an undeniably real product . . . The alternative, to continue to recognize the human subjects of metamorphosis, dissolves the epic structure of the poem by making metamorphosis seem ultimately both inexplicable and very much the end of the story.'

32. Bate, *Shakespeare and Ovid*, p. 119 suggests that it is 'almost a program for Shakespeare's subsequent Ovidianism'.

33. Carroll, *The Metamorphoses*, p. 46.
34. So, for instance, Martindale, *Ovid Renewed*, p. 17: 'Ovid is perhaps best described as a psychologist rather than as a delineator of character and personality . . . Ovid's concern is with the behavioural patterns and psychological drives which constitute the ground of human nature.'
35. Shoshana Felman, 'To Open the Question', *Yale French Studies* 55/6 (1977), 9.
36. Barkan, *The Gods Made Flesh*, p. 273: 'Salmacis and Hermaphroditus, the two lovers who are fused into one being, are balanced by the inevitable Ovidian parallel of Narcissus, one being who becomes two lovers and must torture himself with the paradoxes of individuality. The power of these myths owes something to Aristophanes' myth in Plato's *Symposium*, which traces human origins to twin eggs that have been split apart and are yearning to be reunited in love.'
37. Bate, *Shakespeare and Ovid*, pp. 123–4.
38. Jeanne Roberts, 'Horses and Hermaphrodites: Metamorphoses in *The Taming of the Shrew*', *ShQ* (1983), 168.
39. Golding, *Shakespeare's Ovid*, 4.459–60.
40. Ibid., 464–5.
41. See e.g. Joseph B. Solodow, *The World of Ovid's Metamorphoses* (Chapel Hill 1988), p. 174.
42. Barkan, *The Gods Made Flesh*, p. 281.
43. *Taming of the Shrew* 1.265–8.
44. Ibid., 3.2.243.
45. Ibid., 5.2.186.
46. E.g. Bate, *Shakespeare and Ovid*, pp. 120–1: 'But what about *The Taming of the Shrew*? Can it any way be construed as a happy comedy of fulfilled love? Petruchio never hits Kate, but surely real violence is done in this play – to the woman's mind. Is this not a drama in which women are subjugated, as Jupiter subjugates Io? As the only release for Daphne was to become a tree, is not the only release for Kate to become a branch of Petruchio, bent to his will?'
47. I would like to thank the following for help with this chapter: Duncan Kennedy, Marie Hanley, Genevieve Liveley, Charles Martindale, A. B. Taylor.

CHAPTER 3

Ovid's myths and the unsmooth course of love in A Midsummer Night's Dream

A. B. Taylor

THESEUS AND HIPPOLYTA AND THE PLAY'S OPENING

The moonlight and rich poetry at the opening of *A Midsummer Night's Dream* tend to overshadow the fact that Shakespeare's marriage play also ironically opens in the wake of a full-scale war between the sexes in which women, the legendary Amazons, have been beaten by the men of the Athenian army. But the savagery of war having given way to the 'gentle concord' of love, the newly discovered harmony is epitomised in the coming union of the leaders of the opposing sides. And as he and his bride-to-be await their wedding day, resolving to wed her 'in another key', Theseus remarks on the strangeness of their coming together:

> Hippolyta, I woo'd thee with my sword,
> And won thy love doing thee injuries
>
> (1.1.16–17)[1]

These lines would have met with the approval of an Elizabethan audience imbued with patriarchal values: rebellious and disruptive womanhood, in the person of a warrior queen who had tried to overthrow one of the oldest civilisations, has been forced to submit to the 'natural' order and is in the process of being returned to the civilised fold through marriage. And, unusual as are the circumstances that occasion them, these lines contain a pattern found in some outstanding Elizabethan writing on courtship: of peace and harmony achieved in a relationship only after conflict in which there is violence and aggression on the man's part (the evocative image of the sword) and pain and suffering on the woman's (the equally evocative image of the wounding). One thinks of Spenser's brilliant, symbolic depiction of a woman's distress in Amoret's sufferings in 'The House of Busyrane', or Shakespeare's vivid portrayal of male aggression and violence in the farcical, at times brutal, wooing of Kate by Petruchio, another suitor who – whatever degree of irony one reads into the play – could claim to have 'won' a woman's love doing her 'injuries'.

49

When Theseus is subsequently called upon to suppress another rebellious female, Hermia, by her enraged father, and does so by recourse to law, he might seem a patriarchal ruler in his pomp. But for all his authority and eloquence, he is uneasy. He has ruled in favour of Egeus but his sympathy is clearly with the young lovers. Her father wants Hermia to marry Demetrius or he wants her dead – 'her death, according to our law / Immediately' (44–5). It is Theseus who introduces a third alternative, that the girl take up 'the livery of a nun', tries in vain to talk Egeus round, and buys time by postponing her having to announce her decision until his own wedding day. But praiseworthy though his motives are, Theseus' unease is increased by the noticeable reaction of a silent but important observer of this scene, his bride-to-be – 'Come, my Hippolyta; what cheer, my love?' (122). Hippolyta's reaction is perhaps because he could have been more deci-sive in helping the young lovers; moreover, in the little he did do, he has clumsily if unintentionally cast a dark, possibly bloody shadow over their wedding day.

This disharmony provides a small illustration of the different values he and Hippolyta place upon love. Although Theseus' references to it are, as one might expect, rich and eloquent – consider his reference to his own wedding day, the 'sealing-day betwixt my love and me / For everlasting bond of fellowship' (84–5), essentially his attitude is earthy, practical, and typically masculine. In their opening conversation, for example, it is his own needs as a man that are uppermost in his mind; his concern is for '*my* desires' (1.1.4; *my italics*) and what impedes their fulfilment which he refers to as the collection of a young man's 'revenue'. Hippolyta, by con-trast, sees love as romantic and exalted; for her, it is concerned with higher things. She is the first in the play to associate love with dreams in the very beautiful 'Four nights will quickly dream away the time' (7), and her view of their marriage is far removed from the collection of material things like 'revenues'. To her, it represents the beginning of something mysterious and exalted, conjuring thoughts of the 'silver bow' of the new moon in the heavens giving light to a darkened world (9). This disharmony is a reminder that Theseus and Hippolyta are at the beginning of a relationship in which there must be adjustment and compromise. For his part, Theseus, the conqueror of women, needs to discover the 'woman' in himself, while by implication, Hippolyta, paradoxically, given her Amazon background, needs to be more 'manly'. Before they achieve the kind of marital union, exemplified later in the play by the hermaphrodite, Theseus and Hippolyta both need to shift into and explore the 'sexual margins', a movement bril-liantly analysed by Catherine Belsey in a seminal article on the Comedies.

It involves the 'fragmentation of sexual identity in favour of . . . fluidity . . . plurality':

> The point is not to create some third, unified, androgynous identity which elim-
> inates all distinctions . . . It is rather to define through the internalization of dif-
> ference a plurality of places, of possible beings, for each person in the margins of
> sexual difference, those margins which a metaphysical sexual polarity obliterates.[2]

The shift into the 'sexual margins' is not a pronounced feature of this early but accomplished work, but it is implicit in the central, overarching relationship; and it is indicative that the opening movement closes with Theseus, its dominant male,[3] turning anxious eyes towards Hippolyta whose silence is eloquent.

The play's opening is remarkably free of any direct influence of its prime subtext, the *Metamorphoses*, which, in what is arguably Shakespeare's most Ovidian play, is elsewhere pervasive. At the outset, Shakespeare has asserted his humanistic faith in man; where chaos is resolved in classical texts by divine intervention, here the resolution of the savage sexual chaos comes with the mysterious and sudden appearance of no more than human love. It is as if, as his play begins, Shakespeare wants to set out his own stall before involving his favourite classical poet. But setting his play in a constantly changing, shifting world dominated by the 'inconstant' moon, Shakespeare repeatedly turns to Ovid's poem of changing shapes where 'nothing standes at stay'. And as he depicts the distinctly unsmooth course of love in this dramatic world, myths from Ovid's poem – Pyramus and Thisbe, Ino and Athamas, Salmacis and Hermaphroditus – make a major but not always obvious or recognised contribution.

THE YOUNG LOVERS

Both the difficulties involved in love and the use of Ovidian myth are to the fore with Hermia and Lysander, the other lovers in the play's opening movement. Both are quite remarkably young. Hermia is no more than a young girl trembling on the edge of womanhood, looking back nostalgically to the lost 'paradise' of her childhood. And Lysander's idea of striking out for independence is to run away from difficulties in Athens to a surrogate mother-figure. Their immaturity and inability to cope are evident when within a short time, like children in fairytales, they get lost in an enchanted wood. Their naivete also manifests itself in other ways: their pretty duet on the way love is oppressed in this world is led by Lysander and based not on experience but on books ('aught that I could ever read',

1.1.133); and they blurt out their secret plans to run away to the first person
who comes along, Helena, who as they both know dotes on Demetrius,
their enemy. Such rashness is particularly typical of Lysander who tends to
speak before he thinks – witness his tactless, offensive, and unhelpful gibe
inviting Demetrius to wed Hermia's father delivered within earshot of both
Egeus and Theseus. He also gets so carried away by his own thoughts he
is incapable of listening even to Hermia. After they conclude that love is
one of the 'quick bright things' rapidly devoured by 'the jaws of darkness'
(1.1.148–9), Hermia counsels 'let us teach our trial patience' (152). Lysander
immediately responds approvingly, 'A good persuasion' – then promptly
suggests running away. To this, Hermia, who has the wiser but not older
head, nervously agrees, referring to the doomed Dido and 'the false Trojan'
and 'all the vows that ever men have broke' (174–5). Yet naive though they
may be, these young lovers are also prepared to give up everything for each
other and defy the world to be together; inspired by their passion, they do
indeed strike out for themselves in their naive way, and their journey into
the wood outside Athens represents, as we shall see, their first fumbling
steps towards adulthood. And it is their deep love for each other, together
with their extreme youth and their tragic view of love, that explains why
they are identified with Pyramus and Thisbe, passionate Ovidian lovers
who were themselves little more than children. For an Elizabethan moralist
like Arthur Golding, Ovid's Babylonian myth was 'a piteous tale' showing
a 'headdie and frenticke' young love doomed to end in 'wo and payn';
and ominously Lysander's proposal that he and Hermia run away, echoes
Golding:

> *Steal forth thy father's house* tomorrow night
> And in the wood, a league *without the town*
> (Where I did meet thee once with Helena
> To do observance to a morn of May),
> There will I stay for thee.   (4.164–8)[4]

Unlike Pyramus and Thisbe whose flight takes them to a place of death
('Ninus' tomb'), however, Lysander and Hermia's destination proves in the
event to be a Shakespearean green world. To construct such a world, the
dramatist used a diversity of material but he widened the immediate back-
cloth of Ovid's myth by borrowing from another story featuring Babylon.[5]
The location of the '*wood*' '*a league without the town*' points to the use of
Huon of Bordeaux as does the addition of an enchanted forest inhabited by
fairies under their king Oberon. Those who enter the wood in *Huon* are terrified by 'tempestes with thonder and lyghtenynges, so that it shal seme to

you that all the worlde sholde pereshe' in 'a grete runnynge river, blacke and depe'. Although external factors play their part, the 'grete . . . river, blacke and depe' that almost overwhelms Shakespeare's young lovers, Hermia and Lysander, who are joined by Helena and Demetrius, primarily comes from within themselves. Hermia and Lysander quickly become aware that love, in addition to external oppression, suffers from internal dangers, when on their first night in the wood Lysander, with characteristic thoughtlessness, attempts to 'lie with' the girl and is firmly but politely repulsed. His words at this point, 'One heart, one bed, two bosoms, and one troth' (2.2.47), are steeped in irony; they recall Ovid's wordplay at the tragic moment when Thisbe kills herself, resolving on 'a double death' (*gemini . . . cruoris*, 4.161) – *tu quae ramis arbor miserabile corpus / nunc tegis unius, mox es tectura duorum* (157–8; 'you, o tree, who cover the poor body of one, are soon about to cover the bodies of two').[6] Pre-marital intercourse in Elizabethan England could represent the 'double death' of public humiliation for a couple indulging in it; it could also spell ruin for any children the woman bore after wedlock by incurring declarations of illegitimacy and disinheritance.[7] It is, too, piquant dramatic irony that within moments Puck, mistaking the identity of the sleeping Lysander, should upbraid him as a 'churl' and 'kill-courtesy' (2.2.76–7); this recalls Golding's lines on Pyramus and Thisbe at the wall,[8] for Lysander's selfish attitude has also become a barrier to love.

And Lysander's failure to control his libido leads to the poignant moment when Hermia awakens from sleep in the forest in fear calling out to the lover who has already deserted her:

> Help me, Lysander, help me! Do thy best
> To pluck this *crawling* serpent from *my breast*!
> Ay me, for pity! What a dream was here!
> Lysander, look how I do quake for fear.
> Methought a serpent ate my heart away,
> And you sat smiling at his cruel prey.
>
> (2.2.144–9; *my italics*)

The serpent can be explained in Freudian terms as the mental anguish of a virginal girl at the prospect of a man entering her body. But the hitherto unrecognised mythic source of Hermia's dream also points to deeper implications. In book 4 of the *Metamorphoses,* when Juno descends to the underworld to enlist the aid of the Furies in punishing Ino, it is Tisiphone who ascends to confront the unfortunate victim who is found with her husband Athamas. At the sight of the fury 'splaying forth hir filthie armes beknit with Snakes about', the terrified couple would have fled but 'there stoode the Fiend, and stopt their passage out' (4.605), and then Tisiphone,

> from amyd hir haire two snakes with venymed hand she drew
> Of which she one at Athamas and one at Ino threw.
> The snakes *did craule about their breasts, inspiring in their heart*
> *Most grievous motion of the minde:* the bodie had no smart
> Of any wound: *it was the minde that felt the cruell stings.*
> (4.611–15; *my emphases*)[9]

The power and drama of Golding's translation of this episode impressed Shakespeare: he used it in Othello's 'Arise black vengeance from thy hollow cell';[10] and here he takes from it the nightmarish image of snakes 'crawling'[11] over a person's 'breast' doing no actual physical harm but leaving them in intense mental anguish. Lysander 'smiling' as Hermia is destroyed also reflects the *madness* of his counterpart in the source, where Athamas, bereft of his wits, devastates the life of Ino, the woman he loves, by murdering their child. Similarly, when he tried to lie with Hermia, Lysander descends into a madness that, as noted above, threatened to ruin her life and also the lives of her future children. But most important of all is the reason Juno takes action against Ino: she is furious because here is a mortal woman who 'knew nothing of grief' (*expers . . . doloris erat*, 4.418–19). The snake that crawls about Ino's breast thus signals her entry to a world of woe, and by implication, the 'crawling' serpent on Hermia signals her own entry into the realm of grief and suffering. The innocent child who left her father's house is making the transition to the flawed adult world of experience. The medieval tradition of seeing Biblical truths in Ovidian myth was also still in evidence in Elizabethan literature;[12] and given Hermia's earlier reference to the innocence of her childhood as a lost 'paradise' (1.1.205), and the fact that her entry into a world of woe is signalled by a 'serpent'[13] (in the source it was a 'snake'), it is also probable that Hermia's dream also conjures at the deepest level shades of the story of Eve and the Fall.

Certainly, after her dream, as Marjorie Garber has shown, the girl emerges into a fallen world,[14] and her dream signals the start of a totally confused and progressive nightmare for all four young lovers. At its heart is the flower 'Love-in-idleness'. The name is puzzling if one thinks of 'idleness' in the modern sense as 'inactivity'; but in the sixteenth century the word also meant 'delirium', 'being out of one's senses' (*OED*). And the 'delirium' by which the young people are afflicted is to be of crucial importance to what happens to them in the forest. In it, as the men woo sword in hand by each attempting to kill his rival, causing the women, for different reasons, to suffer intensely, we are witnessing a variation on the pattern established by Theseus and Hippolyta. Torn by the 'briers' of love, stumbling their way to exhaustion, all four come to know that love involves hardship that takes the initial form of violence and aggression on the man's part and suffering and distress on the woman's. All these young people normally express their feelings about love in conventional Petrarchan language, but when reduced to the nakedness of basic human need as they are in the forest, they also give vent to animal snarls when someone threatens to encroach upon their erotic territory. And this new starker attitude to, and more basic, earthy knowledge of love comes through experience – *of a kind*. The magic of the play, the Shakespearean dramatic legerdemain, is that this experience is endured only at a psychic level. In a more intense and uncomfortable way than another Shakespearean lover in another forest, Orlando, these young people experience love's toils and difficulties without actually having to experience them. Their sufferings are illusory; like the 'grete . . . river, blacke and depe' in *Huon,* they have no reality; like Ino and Athamas, it is only in their minds they felt 'the cruell stings'. They will carry knowledge of what they have experienced back into their lives, but only as something hazy, dreamlike, seen 'with parted eye, / When everything seems double' (4.1.186–7). But it is because they have suffered some of the basic truth and adversity that real, as opposed to naive young love involves that they emerge from the forest worthy of marriage and of resuming their place in society.

As has been widely recognised, the description of the flower that is the catalyst for their behaviour, 'before, milk-white; now, purple with love's wound' (2.1.166), recalls from Ovid's myth the death of Pyramus and the mulberry's change of colour which follows the boy's suicide. It has been recognised that Ovid cleverly interweaves a strand of sexual imagery into his narrative with the purpose of conjuring shades of the physical union and sexual fulfilment his beautiful young lovers long for but never achieve. And the language he uses to describe this moment makes it a spectacular but grotesque addition to this feature. To Carole Newlands, for instance, Pyramus' death 'suggests a gigantic orgasm':

He plunges his sword into his groin (*ilia,* 119); his blood 'ejaculates' on high (*ejaculatur,* 124) with the accompanying violence of the sexual act (*ictibus . . . rumpit,* 'bursts . . . with its blows', 124); the blood produces a new colour in the fruit that are described as 'offspring' (*fetus,* 125). Moreover, *vitiato* ('corrupted', 122) is a word commonly used as a metaphor for the act of defloration.[15]

And Shakespeare, a most gifted and responsive reader of Ovid, was aware of the sexual implications of the myth's language; he saw, for instance, the link between Thisbe's thin veil (*tenues amictus*, 104),[16] torn and stained with blood, and the girl's virginity. In the burlesque of the myth at the end of *A Midsummer Night's Dream,* it is immediately after finding her veil 'stain'd with blood' (271–2), that the dramatist has his 'Pyramus' conclude that Thisbe has been 'deflower'd' (281). At one level, Bottom as 'Pyramus' has simply, and not for the first time, mixed up the words of Peter Quince's script but, at a deeper level, Shakespeare is associating the girl's veil with the hymen. And after the grotesque ejaculation when she arrives at the scene of Pyramus' death, the girl finds her lover's limbs writhing not in erotic ecstasy but in death (*tremebunda videt pulsare cruentum / membra solum*, 133–4; 'she sees his limbs beating the bloodstained ground uncontrollably'). At this, carefully positioning the boy's sword beneath her breast so that it will pierce her heart, she falls forward on the weapon still warm with his blood (*incubuit ferro, quod adhuc a caede tepebat*, 163). Given the age-old associations of the sword with the penis and of blood with semen,[17] Thisbe's literally dying as Pyramus' sword enters her body becomes a sad, rather moving parody of the love-making they so desired. As such, when one considers Ovid's awareness of Virgil, it is doubtless inspired by the example of Dido who also fell on her lover's sword in a death scene invested with similar sexual ambivalence:

Aeneas' sword, the surrogate penis, piercing her body and destroying her life, is a frightful inversion of the role of the husband's penis – penetration in order to give his wife a child, that is, to transmit new life.[18]

Allowing for the one moment of dubious taste in the grotesque ejaculation, the way Ovid fuses the language of sexual fulfilment with his young lovers' sad story is a powerful reminder of how technically accomplished this great Roman poet was. And, in the aetiological scheme of the poem, the dark fruit of the mulberry tree remains as an emblem of a young love tragically wasted outside society.

The 'sword', the shedding of blood, and 'love's wound' take one to the very heart of Shakespeare's marriage play which centres upon and is built around the more natural 'wound' of love that brings not death but life. It is inflicted when a man takes symbolic and physical possession of a woman on the wedding night and sheds her blood in the act of defloration. And it is in the play from the first – as Louis Montrose reminds us, 'the sexual act in which man draws blood from the woman is already implicit at the beginning of the play in Theseus' vaunt: "Hippolyta I woo'd thee with my sword, / And won thy love doing thee injuries"'.[19] It is parodied as the play moves toward its end in the burlesque in the business of Thisbe's veil, as we have seen. And the play reaches its crowning moment on the wedding night when the three bridegrooms inflict 'love's wound' upon their brides. Pointedly engaging and reversing Ovid's clever parody of the central erotic motif of the 'wound of love' in his myth, Shakespeare restores it to its natural place in human life, and to its proper place in marriage; and in the process he is doing what he does elsewhere – rewriting Ovid.[20] The result is that where Ovid's dark fruit symbolises a tragic young love set outside society, the dramatist's dark flower, in what for him is an unique venture into aetiology, symbolises, in its eventual effect, a happy and fruitful young love within a social setting (and elsewhere in the play a love restored).

Having embraced Pyramus and Thisbe in spirit in *Romeo and Juliet*, Shakespeare, feeling the need to conform to the standards of his patriarchal society as he writes its sister play celebrating marriage among the nobility, subtly but consistently subverts it. The process is not overt or harsh and involves intricate and considerable artistry, but it reaches a gloriously overt and hilarious climax with the burlesque. As I have shown elsewhere, on matters of style, the burlesque takes a scatter-gun to a host of targets, including Ovid and Shakespeare himself.[21] But as the principal event in the celebrations of the wedding party, this wonderfully comic and hugely enjoyable bowdlerisation of Ovid, even though the myth survives only in outline, still shows the dangers of young love outside society. Of course, it gleefully and cleverly debunks much of the play's romantic language as well as mockingly parodying events that had gone before but, as the recent film showed in its treatment of Thisbe's lament, it is not totally drained of tragic feeling; and it must have had a salutory effect on at least two young members of its onstage audience who had found themselves in the wild countryside outside Athens after the girl, like Thisbe, had also 'stolen' out of her father's house.

THE MARRIED LOVERS

The play's one study of married love with Oberon claiming rights as Titania's 'lord' (2.1.63), which she denies him by forswearing 'his bed and company' (62), is set in the fairy world. Traditionally fairies tended to be local and had only a peripheral effect on human life; they could occasionally put a curse on the livestock of some farmer who had offended them or be held responsible for 'changelings' but generally they lived apart from humans, keeping themselves to themselves.[22] Shakespeare transformed a fairly thin literary

tradition in this country by blending elements of folklore with classical
literature in an unprecedented way, in the process giving the fairy world
new powerful dimensions and relevance. As has long been recognised, he
invests Titania, Oberon, and Puck with shades of Ovid's Juno, Jove, and
Mercury,[23] as well as rifling the lesser levels of the Ovidian pantheon in
ways that have not always been fully recognised. Nor is the debt only to
Ovid; as I have shown elsewhere, he also endows both his theme of love
and his fairy world with universal proportions by taking both the central
idea and several features of Titania's speech on the widespread effects of
her and Oberon's quarrel from one of the very greatest works on love,
the *Symposium*, although doubtless *via* some intermediary source.[24] Plato,
however, was exceptional; Ovid is staple, if occasionally unexpected. As he
both enters and leaves the play, Oberon, for example, fills the role of the
goddess Juno as a deity of marriage and childbirth.

Leonard Barkan has written brilliantly on the play and focused a splendid
analysis of Titania and Bottom on the Actaeon myth as a violation of the
boundary between the animal/human and immortal worlds.[25] Indeed, he
has done so to such effect that attention has been diverted away from an
Ovidian myth that also makes a substantial contribution. Beyond the name
she shares with Diana, basically Titania has little in common with Ovid's
austere, chaste, and cruel goddess of chastity. Diana demands her followers
live life as literally a 'cold fruitless' 'maiden pilgrimage'; when Callisto is
raped by Jove and can no longer conceal her pregnant state, the goddess
is remorseless, expelling the nymph from her company (*suo . . . coetu*,
2.465). But when a 'vot'ress' of her 'order', the mother of the changeling
boy, becomes pregnant, Titania makes the woman her bosom companion,
and

> in the spiced Indian air by night
> Full often hath she gossiped by my side
> (2.1.124–5)

With her warm, sensual nature, the figure in the *Metamorphoses* with
whom Titania has a certain affinity is one also introduced to Elizabethan
readers by Golding as a 'fayry' 'haunting' the countryside, the nymph
Salmacis.[26] Both have a taste for indolence, Titania spending time in her
'flowery bed', Salmacis being in the habit of 'nicely' laying herself on her
own bed of 'soft sweete hearbes or soft greene leaves' (Golding 4.382–3,
380). Both have a penchant for floral decoration, Salmacis plucking 'gayes'
'to make a Posie', Titania adorning both the changeling child and the

transformed Bottom's head with flowers (4.1.3). And, more important, both uninhibitedly embrace the generative life-cycle: besides Titania's devotion to the changeling boy and his mother, this is apparent even in an incidental reference like that to trading ships whose 'sails conceive / And grow big-bellied with the wanton wind'; and it is very evident in Salmacis' initial approach to Hermaphroditus with its reference to the babe feeding at the nurse's breast, the joys of parenting, and those of the marriage bed. What separates the two is that, apart from the dubious 'forgeries of jealousy', Titania's behaviour is restrained and responsible, but the predatory Salmacis is prepared to use violence and force to get her sexual pleasure. However, when Titania is drugged by Oberon with 'Love-in-idlenes' and her sensual nature is distorted and uncontrolled, she becomes Salmacis-like. So when she, too, is inflamed by a passing stranger who ventures into her domain, she angrily refuses to allow him to leave. Titania's anger when Bottom initially wants to leave – 'Out of this wood do not desire to go. / Thou shalt remain here, whether thou wilt or no' (3.1.143–4) – is paralleled by Salmacis' in the pool when Hermaphroditus tries to escape her clutches – 'Strive, struggle, wrest and writhe (she said) thou froward boy thy fill: / Doe what thou canst thou shalt not scape' (4.459–60). Bottom may be an unlikely Hermaphroditus to Titania's Salmacis, but, in her drugged state, she sees him as 'beautiful', and although she promises to 'purge' him of 'mortal grossness' (3.1.153), her plans for him are far from neoplatonic.

Titania's being prepared to use force, however, proves temporary; unlike Salmacis, who is one of the female counterparts of a succession of male rapists headed by Jove in the *Metamorphoses*, in the fairy queen's case, after her initial outburst, her customary gentle and generous nature reasserts itself in her treatment of Bottom. In the crucial scene in her bower, which hardly supports the modern theatrical and filmic tradition inspired by Jan Kott[27] that sexual intercourse takes place, as she woos him, stroking his head, kissing his 'fair large ears', providing 'music', Bottom, innocent as ever and as always in a world of his own, is preoccupied by thoughts not of sex but of food ('a peck of provender', 'a bottle of hay' 4.1.31–3). And when Titania closes in and winds him in her arms, her words reflect how far force is from her mind:

> So doth the woodbine the sweet honeysuckle
> Gently entwist; the female ivy so
> Enrings the barky fingers of the elm.
> O how I love thee! How I dote on thee!
>
> (4.1.41–4)

It seems one could not be farther from Salmacis, the violent female 'rapist'; first embracing his body, then taking his hand, Titania is all softness. But the second image involving the elm supporting a weaker plant would recall the marriage theme of Shakespeare's play but for one jarring detail; the plant the elm supports in the marriage image is not 'the female ivy' but the vine.[28] The ivy as a parasitic plant which drains strength from the elm, is out of place. And as Titania strives in her own way to seduce her own 'beautiful' passing stranger, she is again Salmacis-like, for the ivy is taken from the nymph's rapacious struggle with the boy in the pool. It features in the great triple simile; beginning with the eagle, its talons entangled by the snake, it passes on to *ut . . . solent hederae longos intexere truncos* (4.365; 'as *ivy* is wont to embrace great trees'), and ends with the octopus destroying its victim beneath the waves. Hermaphroditus, the Ovidian boy who had wished to remain apart and untouched by life and its debilitating cares, is caught up, *via* the nymph's embrace, in the vortex of destructive appetite to be seen in sky, on land, and in the sea. As in the case of his fellow virginal recluse, Narcissus, it is the irruption of passion into his life that will destroy Hermaphroditus. Although to the Elizabethans, when pictured together with Hermaphroditus, Salmacis could be seen *in bono* as a figure for an ideal marriage, when referred to on her own she tended to be read *in malo* as lust, the 'voluptuous lyfe' which 'breedes sin' (Golding, *Epistle* 115–16). What we have then in Titania's lines where the 'ivy' has replaced the vine with the elm is an image of a marriage blighted by female lust, the vice to which, in the eyes of a patriarchal society, wives were most prone.[29]

But it is not lust of which Oberon is curing his wife: he is exploiting her sensual nature to cure her of the most fundamental fault of all in marriage, the fault from which all others spring, a wife's disobedience of her husband. And after Oberon has punished her and released her from her delirium by the use of 'Dian's bud', Titania resumes her proper marital role, and obeys her husband without question as, in an imperative mood, he issues her with a series of commands – 'Silence a while', 'music call', 'take hands with me' (4.1.79, 80, 84). Thereafter in public she speaks only after her husband, who is addressed as her 'lord' (98), has spoken. She is now adding her lesser to his greater strength: the vine has been reunited with the elm. The consequence is that we have the strange spectacle of two fairies, who were reputed as wild and menacing creatures not known for their sexual fidelity, emerging as a model Elizabethan patriarchal marriage.

THESEUS AND HIPPOLYTA AT THE CLOSE

When Theseus and Hippolyta re-enter proceedings after the others emerge from the forest, the Duke's attitude has changed. Confronted once again by Egeus' request for vengeance on Lysander, he chooses to temper strict adherence to the law with wisdom and compassion; he not only brushes objections aside but arranges for all four young lovers to be married. He does not explain his reasons, but it is significant that, prior to the discovery of the lovers, harmony had been the subject of his and Hippolyta's conversation; and one result of his revised ruling will be to make their wedding day a truly harmonious and festive occasion. And it is no coincidence that having amended his previous unfortunate ruling, it is to his bride-to-be that he immediately turns with 'Come, Hippolyta' (4.1.185). More significantly, after their marriage, when to Hippolyta he is 'my Theseus', when he comments on the dreamlike experience of the young people in the forest, expounding on the dangers of 'strong imagination' (5.1.2–22) and extolling the virtues of 'cool reason' in a magisterial speech, he suffers her to have the last word. In his speech, he had made the case that lovers are carried away by imagination by referring to a lover being deluded and seeing 'Helen's beauty in a brow of Egypt' (10). In her response, Hippolyta focuses on the incongruity of his dismissal of love apropos the young lovers in the forest, by emphasising that in their case it was not just one lover carried away by individual fantasy but all four experiencing the same fantasy – '*all* their minds transfigured so together' (24; *my italics*). And when she concludes that the lovers' shared experience 'grows to something of great constancy' (26), she is unchallenged by Theseus even though she is contradicting him.[30] He is thus tacitly acknowledging the shortcoming in his value-system, and admitting that 'there are more things in heaven and earth' than even 'cool reason comprehends'. Neither the more practical, down-to-earth husband nor the more imaginative, romantic wife have absolute truth on their side; but as they continue each to exercise tolerance in their relationship and grow together, they will constitute formidable pooled strength and wisdom. That his earlier difficulties have led to Theseus listening to his 'other half', also prompts a tempting question. In a play indebted to the *Symposium* and using Salmacis and Hermaphroditus, a myth long acknowledged to have its source in the legendary third sex, is Shakespeare also thinking of the 'man-woman' whose reunion healed what Plato called 'the human sore'?[31] It is intriguing that the four-legged, four-armed third sex was born of the celestial body that dominates the play, the moon.[32]

Catherine Belsey has highlighted the value-shift that allowed 'dynastic' (patriarchal) and 'affective' (based on love and shared responsibility) views on marriage to co-exist in the sixteenth century.[33] Of the marriages in the play, those of the young lovers and that of Oberon and Titania conform rather more stringently than is comfortable to the stereotypical patriarchal model. There is about Oberon's treatment of his queen a disturbing brutality and fierceness of will; and it is notable that, after their marriage, both the young brides observe the silence patriarchal society saw as virtue in wives. But the central, pivotal relationship evolves to a point where a man is disposed to learn from a woman, and here is the green shoot that will lead to Orlando and Orsino, and the beginning of the fertile exploration of the sexual margins that will enrich the comedies and lead to a much more complex Shakespearean dialogue on marriage.

POSTSCRIPT

Distinguished by an incredible control, normally Shakespeare's use of Ovidian myth is also marked by an extraordinary richness. As I have shown in some detail in *Shakespeare's Ovid*, in the space of only two lines a range of different sources can be invoked to colour an Ovidian reference, each chosen to make a precise contribution.[34] In this play, however, one particular source tends to predominate, Arthur Golding's translation of the *Metamorphoses*. It is unusual not only to find the translator looming so large but also to find one particular facet of his work echoing strongly in the background, the prefatory moralisation of Ovid, which was coloured by his intense and rather narrow Calvinism. And the reason it does so returns us to the fact that the dramatist is in a conformist mood as he writes his marriage play for the nobility.[35]

NOTES

1. Reference is to *A Midsummer Night's Dream*, ed. H. F. Brooks (London 1979).
2. See Catherine Belsey, 'Disrupting Sexual Difference: Meaning and Gender in the Comedies', in *Alternative Shakespeares*, ed. John Drakakis (London 1985), pp. 166–190, 189.
3. For discussion of the various *personae* of Theseus present in the play, see Peter Holland, 'Theseus' Shadows in *A Midsummer Night's Dream*', *ShS* 47 (1994), 139–52.
4. Moralising this story Golding writes in the *Epistle to Leicester*,

> The piteous tale of Pyramus and Thisbee doth conteine
> The headie force of frenticke love whose end is wo and payne.
>
> (109–10)

while his translation of their story tells how they plan,

> To steale out of their fathers house . . .
> . . . to meete without the towne
>
> (4.106–8)

(Reference is to *The xv Bookes of P. Ovidius Naso, Entytuled Metamorphosis 1567*, ed. W. H. D. Rouse (London 1904, repr. 1961)).

5. Gerames is telling Huon how to start his journey to Babylon, 'yf ye take the shorter way ye most passe throwout a wood a.xvi.leges of length . . . in that wood abydeth a kynge of the fayrey namyd Oberon'. (Reference to *Huon* is to 'Source Materials' reprinted in *A Midsummer Night's Dream*, ed. Brooks.)

6. Reference is to a standard sixteenth-century text of the *Metamorphoses* containing the notes of Regius, Micyllus, and Petrus Lavinius, *Metamorphoseon Publii Ovidii Nasonis* (Venice 1545).

7. See, for example, *Half Humankind: Contexts and Texts of the Controversy about Women in England*, ed. Katherine Usher Henderson and Barbara F. McManus (Urbana 1985), pp. 57–8.

8.
> . . . at least make roume to kisse.
> And yet thou shalt not finde us churles: we thinke our selves in det
> For the same piece of courtesie . . .   (4.94–6)

9. For a slightly fuller version of what follows, see my 'Golding and the Myth Underlying Hermia's Dream', *N&Q* 248 (2003), 31–2.

10. See my 'Shakespeare and Golding', *N&Q* n.s. 37 (1991), 492–9.

11. Golding's translation of Ovid's verb describing the snakes' movement, *pererrant* (497), as 'did craule' is distinctive but slightly inaccurate. According to the standard Latin–English dictionary of the day, Thomas Cooper's *Thesaurus*, the verb meant 'to wander over and over'; George Sandys more accurately conveys the snakes' movement with they 'up and down about their bosoms roule' (references are to Thomas Cooper, *Thesaurus Linguae Romanae & Britannicae* (London 1565), and George Sandys, *Ovid's Metamorphoses Englished* (Oxford 1632), ed. S. Orgel (New York 1976)).

12. The standard edition of the *Metamorphoses* in the sixteenth century, for instance, contained the commentary of Petrus Lavinius comparing events in book 1 to those in Genesis; and Golding's translation is prefaced by the conviction that Ovid 'the first foundation of his woorke from Moyses wryghting tooke' (*Epistle* 143).

13. 'Now the serpent was more subtil then anie beast of the field', Genesis 3.1 (reference is to *The Geneva Bible: A Facsimile of the 1560 Edition* (Madison, Milwaukee 1969)).

14. Marjorie Garber, *Dream in Shakespeare: From Metaphor to Metamorphosis* (New Haven 1974), p. 73.

15. Carole Newlands, 'The Simile of the Fractured Pipe in Ovid's *Metamorphoses*', *Ramus* 15 (1986), 143. (In some versions of the myth, the lovers abscond because Thisbe is pregnant.)

16. Sixteenth-century readers would know that *amictus*, which could be a cloak or a veil, was the latter from Raphael Regius' philological notes alongside the text in the standard edition of the *Metamorphoses* of the day, where *amictus* is rendered *velum* ('a veil'); accordingly, the garment Pyramus finds when he arrives, *vestem* (107), is also rendered a veil. There is further discussion of this point in my '"When Everything Seems Double": Peter Quince the Other Playwright in *A Midsummer Night's Dream*', *ShS* 56 (2003), 55–66. (I am indebted here to the generosity of Ceri Davies, Professor of Classics at Swansea.)

17. The sword as a symbolic representation of the penis has been traced back to Plautus in Roman literature (see R. F. Moorton Jr., 'Love as Death: The Pivoting Metaphor in Virgil's Story of Dido', *Classical World* 83 (1990), 162); blood and sexuality are discussed by Charles Segal in *Landscape in Ovid's Metamorphoses* (Wiesbaden 1969), p. 50. For the symbolic relationship between the sword and the penis, see W. Burkert, *Homo Necans*, English trans. Peter Bing (Berkeley 1983), p. 59 ff.

18. D. Gillis, *Eros and Death in the Aeneid* (Rome 1983), p. 49; cf. Moorton, 'Love as Death', p. 163: 'Dido impales herself on the sword of Aeneas (4.663–665) . . . this is a symbolic act of intercourse'.

19. Louis Montrose, 'Shaping Fantasies: Figurations of Gender and Power in Elizabethan Culture', *Representations* 1 (1983), 92.

20. For a recent discussion of an example of this, see my 'Shakespeare Rewriting Ovid: Olivia's Interview with Viola and the Narcissus Myth', *ShS* 50 (1997), 81–9.

21. See Taylor, 'When Everything Seems Double', and Kenneth Muir, 'Pyramus and Thisbe: A Study in Shakespeare's Method', *ShQ* 5 (1954), 141–53.

22. For details of the fairies' ways, see K. Briggs, *The Anatomy of Puck* (London 1959); M. W. Latham, *The Elizabethan Fairies: The Fairies of Folklore and the Fairies of Shakespeare* (New York 1930).

23. See W. F. Staton Jr., 'Ovidian Elements in *A Midsummer Night's Dream*', *HLQ* 26 (1962–3), 165–78; and Niall Rudd, 'Pyramus and Thisbe in Shakespeare and Ovid', in *Creative Imitation and Latin Literature*, ed. D. West and T. Woodman (Cambridge 1976), pp. 173–93.

24. See Taylor, 'Plato's *Symposium* and Titania's Speech on the Universal Effect of her and Oberon's Quarrel', scheduled to appear in *N&Q* (Sept. 2004).

25. Leonard Barkan, *The Gods Made Flesh: Metamorphosis and the Pursuit of Paganism* (New Haven 1986), pp. 252 ff.

26.   A Nymph did haunt this goodly Poole . . . .
                     Of all the Waterfayries she alonly was unknowne
                     To swift Diana . . .   (4.368–70)

27. See Jan Kott, *Shakespeare Our Contemporary*, trans. B. Taborski (London 1964), p. 17.

28. The figure, which is also Biblical, is related to marriage during the myth of Pomona and Vertumnus (see *Met.* 14.665–6). There are occasions in Elizabethan literature when the ivy replaces the vine without violating the

marriage image, but Adriana's address to Antipholus of Syracuse, who she thinks is her husband in *The Comedy of Errors*, makes clear this is not Shakespeare's view:

> Thou art an elm, my husband, I a vine
> If aught possess thee from me, it is dross,
> Usurping ivy, briar or idle moss,
> Who all for want of pruning, with intrusion,
> Infect thy sap, and live on thy confusion.
>
> (2.2.173–9)

29. See, for example, Henderson and McManus, eds., *Half Humankind: Contexts and Texts of the Controversy about Women in England*, pp. 8 and 30 ff.
30. What underlies this moment is the Elizabethan debate on 'affection' or 'imagination' which was associated with dreams and the unreal and could be very dangerous unless carefully controlled. (For an excellent discussion of this debate, see William C. Carroll, *The Great Feast of Language in Love's Labour's Lost* (Princeton, 1976), p. 99 ff.)
31. See *Symposium* D1, p. 136 (Loeb). For this passage as source for Ovid's myth, see Sandys, *Ovid's Metamorphoses Englished*, p. 160.
32. Of the three original sexes described by Aristophanes, the male was the offspring of the sun, the female of the earth, and 'that which partook of both sexes was born of the moon, for the moon also partakes of both' (see B3–5, p. 136).
33. See Belsey, 'Disrupting Sexual Difference: Meaning and Gender in the Comedies', *passim*; and *Shakespeare's Lost Eden* (Chicago 2000), *passim*.
34. See *Shakespeare's Ovid: The Metamorphoses in the Plays and Poems* ed. A. B. Taylor (Cambridge 2000), pp. 5–9.
35. I do not share the view, however, advanced by Barbara Freedman in her essay, 'Dis/Figuring Power: Censorship and Representation in *Midsummer Night's Dream*'. The predominant ethos of the play is undoubtedly patriarchal but as I have shown, this is questioned and undermined in its course by the central relationship; to see the play as Freedman does, as 'fawning collaboration with state ideology' (p. 180) is far too severe and simplifies its complex richness drastically. (Freedman's essay is in *A Midsummer Night's Dream: Critical Essays*, ed. Dorothea Kehler (London and New York 1998))

Drafts of this essay have been read by Gordon Braden, Andrew Gurr, Catherine Belsey, Heather James, A. D. Nuttall, and Charles Martindale. To all I am indebted for their patience and wisdom.

CHAPTER 4

Shakespeare's learned heroines in Ovid's schoolroom

Heather James

The dramatic action of *A Midsummer Night's Dream* begins when an angry father hauls his young daughter before the Duke of Athens to stage a trial of her modesty. In a scene Shakespeare will repeat and vary throughout his dramatic career, the young woman is pressed into public speech before the masculine authorities most likely to bind her tongue.[1] Hermia has refused to marry the man chosen by her father, Egeus, who consequently invokes 'the ancient privilege of Athens' (1.1.41), a death penalty granted to the fathers of disobedient daughters.[2] In a memorable piece of dialogue, Duke Theseus explains to Hermia the political theory behind Egeus' prerogative:

> To you your father should be as a god,
> One that composed your beauties, yea, and one
> To whom you are but as a form in wax,
> By him imprinted, and within his power
> To leave the figure or disfigure it.
>
> (1.1.47–51)

Constitutionally bound to uphold a law that he 'by no means . . . may extenuate' (1.1.120), Theseus counsels Hermia on her duty to her godlike father.[3]

He animates his lesson with an arresting rhetorical figure of a waxen form in an artist's shaping control. As a trope for the pressures that men exert over women, the image comes to Shakespeare's play in the first instance from the printing press and in the second from Ovid's tale of Pygmalion, where it describes the sensation felt by the sculptor-turned-lover when his ivory statue becomes flesh. 'The Ivory wexed soft', in Arthur Golding's translation, and

> yeelded underneathe his fingars, as wee see
> A peece of wax made soft ageinst the Sunne, or drawen too bee
> In divers shapes by chaufing it betweene ones handes
>
> (10.308–11)[4]

66

Just as the ivory maid warmed to Pygmalion's authorial touch, so should Hermia submit to her father's prodding and grow 'pliable by being plied'.[5]

Hermia, however, declines to be shaped and moved by her father's harsh demands or Theseus' sobering counsel. Implicitly rejecting the ideal of maidenhood as silent and static but infinitely malleable, Hermia speaks before the Duke with a boldness she does not claim to understand:

> I do entreat your grace to pardon me.
> I know not by what power I am made bold,
> Nor how it may concern my modesty
> In such a presence here to plead my thoughts
> *(Dream* 1.1.58–61)

On one level, this is mad blood stirring: Hermia's love for Lysander and adolescent resistance to arbitrary and tyrannical authority will impel her to venture with Lysander into the Athenian woods, where the risks she assumes are potentially fatal. Luckily for Hermia, Shakespeare relegates his comedy's death-laden plot to the play-within-the-play, the 'very tragical mirth' of Ovid's Pyramus and Thisbe (5.1.57) staged by the craftsmen for Theseus' wedding. At another level, however, the force that moves Hermia to speech remains mysterious in its source and suggestive in its effects.

The power that makes Hermia and other Shakespearean women bold has ties to Ovid which defy the common understanding of imitation as a strictly poetic exercise. There is a certain appeal to saying that Hermia finds her rhetorical boldness in the same creative wellspring that Theseus found his image of female compliance. There is also persuasive logic to the comparison of Hermia, in a comedy saturated with Ovidian allusion and transformation, to the passionate Ovidian heroines who violate propriety, custom, and law. Shakespeare's learned heroines, however, aspire to more than local identification with Ovid's ardent and articulate heroines. They want the bold speech of Ovid himself.

Ovid's poetic audacity famously earned him exile in his lifetime and immortality beyond it. Seneca the Elder regretted Ovid's 'licentious song' (*licentiam carminum*), while Quintilian felt Ovid was 'too much a lover of his own wit'.[6] But Ovid's wit (*ingenium*) was also the basis for his immortal reputation as a poet. Near the beginning of the *Metamorphoses*, Ovid associates his own poetic voice with boldness (*audacia*) in representing the political affairs of the heavens and earth, and at its end, he asserts that his poem will endure, as Golding puts it, even '*Joues* feerce wrath' (984):[7]

Yit shall the better part of mee assured bee to clyme
Aloft above the starry skye. And all the world shall never
Be able for too quench my name. For looke how farre so ever
The Romane Empyre by the ryght of conquest shall extend,
So farre shall all folke reade this woork.

(989–92)

Ovid's 'better part' was understood, in the Renaissance, precisely as his wit. As Raphael Regius wrote in his important edition, 'Nothing better than wit can pertain to a human being. For, as Cicero writes in his *Brutus*, the glory of humankind is wit' and the soul of wit is 'eloquence'.[8]

Shakespeare's learned heroines read, quote, and adapt Ovid's work and aim for his bold eloquence if not his fame. Unlike their male counterparts, they do not read Ovid to flirt with poetic and social conventions. To the contrary, they often struggle to avoid the Ovidian scenarios that come trippingly to their suitors' tongues: Ovid's repertoire of precepts, plots, and visual scenarios tends, after all, to frame women as pictures for a male viewer's delectation and, too often, as objects of his violence. What Shakespearean women really want from Ovid is far more audacious and ambitious than a moment's dalliance with the pleasures of the text: they want the expressive liberties Ovid takes with erotic, rhetorical, and social conventions. What Shakespeare in turn wants from his female characters, who reach for their Ovid to think through and resist arbitrary protocols or even laws, is a means to identify and articulate the essentially political character of bold speech in his own plays.[9]

LEARNING TO SPEAK IN THE COMEDIES

Among the first comic heroines to learn bold speech from Ovid's arts is Bianca of *The Taming of the Shrew*. Set to work in Ovid's amatory classroom, she proves a better student than her designing teacher, Lucentio, who has far to go if he is to become a desirable husband or, in fact, a husband at all. From his first glimpse of Bianca, Lucentio hopes to play the part of Ovid's philandering and rapacious Jove. He is dying, he declares to his man Tranio, to 'achieve . . . this young modest girl' (1.1.150). Just as Jove assumed the form of a bull to gain Europa (ll. 161–4), so will he 'be a slave t'achieve that maid' (l. 213). Bianca unsurprisingly wants more than life as an erotic figure in her lover's fancy, whether it is the silent ideal of 'Maid's mild behavior and sobriety' (l. 71) or the picturesque Europa, whose 'sweet beauty . . . made great Jove to humble him to her hand' (ll. 161–3). Bianca has no intention of becoming the equivalent of Daphne, Io, or Venus in the 'wanton pictures' (Induction 1.43) possessed by the lord of the Sly plot. She aims to traverse the considerable distance between the sweet but passive *puella* ('girl') of Roman New Comedy and the *docta puella* ('learned girl') of Ovidian elegy. Bianca uses Ovidian poems to put Lucentio, a self-proclaimed successor to the 'schoolmaster of love', through his paces.[10]

In her first lesson Bianca challenges the constructions placed by her Latin master upon an ostensibly tame text from Ovid: '*Hic ibat Simois, hic Sigeia tellus, / Hic steterat Priami regia celsa senis*' (3.1.28–9; 'Here flowed the Simois; here was the Sigeian land; here the high palace of old Priam had stood'). Taken from the first letter of the *Heroides,* where Penelope writes to the absent Ulysses, the lines evoke more than they sketch, which is simply the topography of Troy.[11] Ovid salts his *Ars Amatoria* with allusions to the Trojan War, noting in one place that Troy's fall gives assurance that any woman, even Penelope, may be conquered (1.1.477–8). When Lucentio reconstructs Ovid's couplet, the environs of Troy provide the setting for seduction:

'*Hic ibat*', as I told you before – '*Simois*', I am Lucentio – '*hic est*', son unto Vincentio of Pisa – '*Sigeia tellus*', disguised thus to get your love – '*hic steterat*', and that Lucentio that comes a-wooing – '*Priami*', is my man Tranio – '*regia*', bearing my port – '*celsa senis*', that we might beguile the old pantaloon. (3.1.31–6)

Shakespeare uses the pedagogical scene to present a hilarious juxtaposition of genres: King Priam of Troy has probably never endured a wilder free-fall than here, where Lucentio pushes him from the palace walls of epic tragedy into the lows of *commedia dell' arte*, where he rubs elbows with the pantaloon (thus mingling clowns and kings). Lucentio, however, is not obviously in control of the comic jarring he produces. He seems utterly unconcerned with the text from Ovid, whose Latin he arbitrarily breaks up to make space for an amatory plot based on Roman New Comedy and Italian *commedia*. He deftly identifies Bianca as the girl (*puella*) whose love he seeks as comedy's 'young man' (*adolescens*), and then reveals that his clever servant (*servus callidus*) Tranio is already in disguise and hard at work in his task of circumventing the traditional blocking figures of the genre. These are the old lover (*senex amator*) who rivals the young man and the father (*durus pater*) that Lucentio is bound to anger with his tricks. Hortensio, the older rival who tries to prise Bianca away from her Latin teacher (and interest in his gamut), is the old fool closest to hand. Yet Lucentio is also preparing his own father, Vincentio of Pisa, as well as Bianca's, to serve as additional dupes.

Lucentio is skilled in comic plotting but invention fails him when it comes to words: he has no gift in the art of double meaning most treasured by Ovid (*Ars Amatoria* 1.569–70, 601–2). Only one juxtaposition of English and Latin in his school lesson is artful. Knowing that the clever servant is allowed by the laws of comedy to be master for a day, Lucentio adroitly pairs '*Priami*' with 'my man Tranio'. The figure of Priam neatly anticipates both the high authority and mighty fall that the clever servant can expect from the play. By contrast with her master Bianca is an Ovidian pupil, 'apt to learn, and thankful for good turns' (2.1.163), as her father awkwardly puts it. She shows greater tact with the rules of courtship as well as the meters and phrasing of Latin poetry:

> Now let me see if I can construe it. '*Hic ibat Simois*', I know you not – '*hic est Sigeia tellus*', I trust you not – '*hic steterat Priami*', take heed he hear us not – '*regia*', presume not – '*celsa senis*', despair not. (3.1.40–3)

Bianca outdoes Lucentio by identifying the flaws in his plan while preserving, as he does not, the syntactical integrity of Ovid's Latin. The boy actor or modern actress playing Bianca may scan the metre, hopelessly broken up by Lucentio, so that Ovid's lines flow over the mock-translations almost as descant to burden.[12] Her emphasis in the second line then falls on the old man ('*Priami . . . senis*'), whose figure spans the vernacular risks ('take heed!') and lofty Latin prospects ('*regia celsa*') of Lucentio's presumptuous but interesting plot. Hortensio, who will inform her father of any amorous adventuring on her part, presents the immediate danger. Bianca's translation makes it clear that rich Baptista, who has opened his home to a Trojan horse of disguised men, is 'old Priam' on the eve of Troy's fall.

Swiftly rising to the top of Ovid's class, Bianca encourages Lucentio to live up to the promise of the erotic arts he professes. When her lover claims to practise what he teaches in '*The Art to Love*' (4.2.8), she rejoins, 'may you prove, sir, master of your art' (4.2.9). Ovid, it will be remembered, concludes the second book of the *Ars Amatoria* by instructing his male pupils on the method of achieving simultaneous orgasm. Bianca's hopes may be high indeed, if she also recalls Ovid's boast, in *Amores* 3.7, that he once came nine times in one night.[13] Her freedom with speech, in any case, compromises her modesty in the eyes of jealous characters within the play, such as Hortensio, as well as critics of the play.[14] The conservatism of *Taming of the Shrew* militates against the invention of a female Ovid, which a friendlier genre might celebrate in Bianca, who plays music, produces original translations of received materials, and exercises an agile and irreverent wit. Yet Bianca handles her cards well in the game of love, considering that Lucentio's first wish was to play Jove to her Europa and redeem his passion with the least personal cost ('*Redime te captum queas minimo*', 1.1.156). When the couple elopes and returns home to find not one but two angry fathers,

Lucentio exclaims, 'Bianca's love' has 'wrought these miracles' (5.1.105). He has a point: she has transformed his campaign of seduction into marriage and she does not, as Kate arguably does, surrender her speech to her husband.

The comic heroine most positively associated with eloquence is Portia of *The Merchant of Venice*. Her stirring speech on the quality of mercy serves the interests of the Christian authorities of Venice and, more subtly, offers creative resistance to the rule of silence imposed on her by the will of her dead father. Portia's courtroom experience is, among other things, a trial of her wit and speech. Her emancipation is assured only if she delivers Antonio from the Jew and takes her courtroom victory home to Belmont and the play's domestic plot. Her forensic victory guarantees the success of her marriage, already solemnised but as yet unnegotiated, to Bassanio. To become fully hers, Bassanio must be weaned from his swaggering ideas of mythical conquest (he speaks of Portia as the golden fleece at 1.1.170) and freed from his debt to Antonio, whose emotional and economic claims on Bassanio threaten the success of the play's heterosexual plot.[15]

In its denouement, the play recalls and mythologises Portia's forensic powers. Her triumph permeates Belmont in the form of music, which almost literally clears the play of the air of the contagion picked up in the courtroom scene along with the erotic tensions that make up the other half of this comedy. Music arrests the attention of Lorenzo and Jessica, caretakers of Belmont in Portia's absence, who have been singing a love-duet and reawakening the play's theme of erotic strife. The couple rehearse the dangers for women (and perhaps also for men) of venturing into trials of love and faith. After pausing on the legendary figures of Troilus and Cressida, Lorenzo and Jessica invoke a succession of ardent and star-crossed women from Ovid's poetry:

> JESSICA   In such a night
>   Did Thisbe fearfully o'ertrip the dew
>   And saw the lion's shadow ere himself,
>   And ran dismayed away.
> LORENZO   In such a night
>   Stood Dido with a willow in her hand
>   Upon the wild sea banks, and waft her love
>   To come again to Carthage.
> JESSICA   In such a night
>   Medea gather̀d the enchanted herbs
>   That did renew old Aeson.   (5.1.7–14)

If one hears the love-duet as a meditation on the fortunes of the romantic heroine who is returning home to Belmont, the series of Ovidian women adumbrates Portia's ethical journey from a stumbling and fearful lover (Thisbe trips on dew and flies from the shadow of a lion) to a woman prepared to assume erotic and linguistic risk. Whereas Antonio hazarded three thousand ducats for Bassanio, Portia vows 'six thousand . . . Double six thousand, and . . . treble that', before overwhelming the 'petty debt' representing Antonio's love by offering that sum 'twenty times over' (3.2.297–305). Her expressive powers, too, increase exponentially until their co-ordinates are mythological: Portia is like Ovid's Dido, striving to convey Aeneas back to Carthage through the charm of elegy, and Medea, plying her lyrical enchantments for the sake of Jason.[16]

The theme of power in speech passes through the sequence of Ovid's bold women and coalesces in the single figure of the same poet's Orpheus. When Jessica remarks that she is never merry when she hears sweet music, Lorenzo explains the power of music to suspend what is bloody, hard, and unregenerate in human nature:[17]

> Therefore the poet
> Did feign that Orpheus drew trees, stones, and floods,
> Since naught so stockish, hard, and full of rage
> But music for the time doth change his nature.
> (5.1.78–81)

Editors commonly refer the allusion to the *Metamorphoses*, which recounts how Orpheus brings the very trees and beasts into harmonious assembly (10.86–105, 143–4). He temporarily sways even the stones hurled by the enraged bacchantes, who at last drown out his eloquence and then kill and dismember the bard. Even in death, thanks to the river that carries his head downstream, Orpheus' tongue continues its song. Does Orpheus' entry into the repertoire of Ovid's female lovers serve as a correction of the large powers the play has surrendered to Portia at a cost to male authority? If so, the figure of the poet remains male and assertive women are recast as irrational maenads.

Shakespeare, however, melds the famous account of Orpheus with a resonant passage from the *Ars Amatoria*, where Orphic powers belong to women. Considering the question of whether music, a persuasive and not merely ornamental art, should rank among the skills of women, Ovid decides in the affirmative. After pausing on the 'monstrous' sirens, he fastens upon the creative figures of Arion and Orpheus:

nec plectrum dextra, citharam tenuisse sinistra
nesciat arbitrio femina docta meo.
saxa ferasque lyra movit Rhodopeïus Orpheus,
tartareosque lacus tergeminumque canem.
(*Ars Amatoria* 3.319–22)

(Nor in my opinion should a learned woman fail to know how to hold the quill in her right hand and the lyre in her left. With his lyre Orpheus of Rhodope moved rocks and wild things [i.e. beasts and barbarians] as well as the lakes of Tartarus and the three-headed dog [Cerberus].)[18]

That Shakespeare knew this passage is clear from *Titus Andronicus*, where Marcus gazes at his mutilated niece and unhappily recalls the persuasive arts that have been violently stripped from her. Had the 'monster seen those lily hands / Tremble like aspen-leaves upon a lute,' Marcus says, he 'would not then have touched them for his life' (2.4.44–6),

> Or had he heard the heavenly harmony
> Which that sweet tongue hath made,
> He would have dropped his knife and fell asleep,
> As Cerberus at the Thracian poet's feet.
> (*Titus Andronicus* 2.4.48–51)

Portia gains precisely where Lavinia loses: the idea of female invention can only enter into the revenge tragedy as a threat (in Tamora) or a loss (in Lavinia), but it may seal the comic triumph of *The Merchant of Venice*. Portia cannot bring the disparate interests of Venetian community into harmonious consent but she may bring into being a new dispensation for marriage as a union fundamental to civic society. To the extent that the play is able to envision a redistribution of social authority, it does so in its domestic plot, where Portia's bold eloquence makes her a peer of Ovid and Orpheus.

FORGETTING TO BE A WOMAN: THE BOYHOOD OF COMIC HEROINES

Under what conditions may comic heroines find the courage to be 'Ready in gibes, quick-answered, [and] saucy' (*Cymbeline* 3.4.158)? Portia chooses to separate eloquence from bawdiness (taken up by Gratiano). Other heroines, however, want the full range of Ovid's rhetorical, erotic, and social liberties, summed up in the following Ovidian keywords from Thomas Cooper's *Thesaurus Linguae Romanae & Britannicae*:[19]

Audacia. foolehardinesse: rashnes: presumption: courage: truste: confidence in ones selfe: auenturous boldnes: stomacke: hardines.

Ingenium. The nature, inclination, disposition, or propertie of a thyng: also wit.

Lasciuia. wantonnes: malaperte toying: ribaudous iestying or behauour.

Os. The mouth. The uisage or countenance: The proportion of all the bodie. Presence. Language. Audacitie, boldenesse, or hardinesse.

To gain full access to Ovid's wanton and bold wit, the comic heroine must 'forget to be a woman' (*Cymbeline* 3.4.154) and become a boy.

Rosalind of *As You Like It* and Viola of *Twelfth Night*, in fact, undergo something like an Ovidian change of shape. Accidents – exile and shipwreck, respectively – depress the fortunes and spirits of both women until they conclude they will fare better as boys.[20] Their spirits elevated at the prospect of being saucy boys, they enter Ovidian worlds, where they appear as either sex and appeal to both (like Ovid's Narcissus).[21] Their choices among Ovidian genres, however, differ in ways that profoundly influence their approaches to love and sexuality. Putting on 'doublet and hose' (2.4.5) and the name of Ganymede, Rosalind throws herself into the world of erotic games and theatre delineated in Ovid's early poems, the *Ars Amatoria* and *Amores*, in which love and poetry alike are games and toys.[22] As the eunuch Cesario, Viola is by contrast swept up in the world of shape-shifting and polymorphous desires summed up by the *Metamorphoses*.

The different epistemological claims that disguise makes upon each woman are especially evident in the response of each to the discovery that she is loved by another woman. Rosalind solves the fascinating problem of Phoebe's error within moments of discovering it: Silvius, although rejected by Phoebe, is to satisfy her desires in the end. For Rosalind's plan to succeed, Phoebe must choose aright once she discovers the true sex of her first choice, Ganymede. Love and marriage become a kind of game – oddly comparable to modern reality shows – in which Phoebe, lured by Ganymede as bait, narrows her amorous prospects to the two persons, Ganymede and Silvius, chosen by Rosalind. As director of her own comedy, Rosalind even arranges for the Roman god of marriage, Hymen, to sort the various lovers into properly heterosexual couples at the play's end. Having rigged the game of love, Rosalind is in the meantime free to toy with the amorous shepherdess for slightly mysterious reasons examined below.

When Viola realises, at the parallel moment in *Twelfth Night*, how strange a love triangle binds her, Orsino, and Olivia, she puzzles over the ambiguity of her bodily form and her responsibilities to the other two lovers. Both her body and duties seem profoundly shaped by the passions of the other two:

> How will this fadge? My master loves her dearly,
> And I, poor monster, fond as much on him,
> And she, mistaken, seems to dote on me.
> What will become of this? As I am man,
> My state is desperate for my master's love.
> As I am woman, now alas the day,
> What thriftless sighs shall poor Olivia breathe!
>
> (*Twelfth Night* 2.2.31–7)

The 'knot' (l. 39) of confused sexualities is too hard, she concludes, to disentangle: unlike Rosalind, Viola claims no mastery over erotic games. Instead, she feels controlled by narrative alternatives that will determine her partner in love and her very sex.

Viola's confusion is remarkable, as is her dismay over Olivia's welfare in love. Her feeling for Olivia's plight even dampens her sense of Orsino's interests. Although he is part of the love triangle that she is considering, the desperation that rivets Viola's attention in the last four lines pertains only to herself and Olivia. The bond forged between them is based on the 'unnatural' passion they share: love for Orsino makes a 'poor monster' of Viola/Cesario, while Olivia's love for the cross-dressed girl makes her equally pitiable. Their plight, as Viola meditates on it, recalls Ovid's story of Iphis, a girl raised as a boy and engaged to another girl, Ianthe. In that tale, Iphis views herself as a 'monster' (9.736) and her love as a hopeless and strange prodigy (9.727–8). The tale ends happily when the goddess Isis, responding to many ardent prayers – including Ianthe's – to bless the upcoming nuptials, effects a sexual metamorphosis in Iphis:

> Her face continued not so whyght.
> Her strength encreased, and her looke more sharper was too syght.
> Her heare grew shorter, and shee had a much more lively spryght,
> Than when shee was a wench. For thou O *Iphys* who ryght now
> A moother wert, art now a boay.   (Golding, 9.925–9)

Ovid plays lightly with Iphis' sexual ambiguity. One might expect at least one toying reference to genital change, but he inventories only secondary sexual characteristics and cultural markers of masculinity. In Golding's translation, Iphis 'Did take *Iänthee* too his wyfe, and so her love enjoy' (937), while Ovid leaves the reader to construe the gender of the possessive pronoun, *sua*: it may refer to Iphis' possession of either 'his' or 'her' Ianthe (*potiturque sua puer Iphis Ianthe*, 9.797).[23] Although Hymen is present at the marriage, the god does not 'bar confusion' (5.4.14) of sexual categories in the way that Rosalind's theatrical Hymen does.[24] At the end of *Twelfth Night*, Sebastian thoughtfully reflects on how close Olivia comes to being like Ianthe to an Iphis composed of Viola and her male twin: 'You would have been contracted to a maid, / Nor are you therein, by my life, deceived. / You are betrothed both to a maid and man' (5.1.259–61).

Ovid brings more than epistemological confusion to Viola: he also brings erotic and poetic inspiration. Olivia's 'proud' withdrawal from the world of men causes Viola to abandon her prepared speech on Orsino's behalf and conjure a fantasy, drawn from the passion of Ovid's Echo for Narcissus, of how she herself would woo Olivia. She would

> Write loyal cantons of contemned love,
> And sing them loud even in the dead of night;
> Halloo your name to the reverberate hills,
> And make the babbling gossip of the air
> Cry out 'Olivia!' O, you should not rest
> Between the elements of air and earth
> But you should pity me.
> (*Twelfth Night* 1.5.239–45)

As she is a woman, Viola is 'patience on a monument' (2.4.113): she imagines her metamorphosis into a monument (both a tribute and warning) to her story of impossible love, heroic silence, and self-sacrifice. But as she is a man, she imagines bringing nature itself under her power. To win Olivia's heart, she would conscript Echo, the 'babling' nymph whose earthly elements vanished, through 'restlesse carke and care', into 'ayre' (Golding, 3.443, 493, 495). The verbal and thematic elements of Echo's tale migrate from Viola's song to Olivia's passions, creating an extraordinary emblem of poetry's powers over the sympathetic imagination. With her persuasive and unabashedly 'loud' voice, Viola would transform her lady's self-love into sympathy of feeling.

Rosalind never doubts her ability to organise erotic experience, and her confidence separates her from the metamorphic world of Viola. She favours the games and playful precepts of Ovid's early love poems, which she uses to shower Orlando with 'good counsel' (3.2.330).[25] Adapting her inventory of symptoms of love-sickness from the *Ars Amatoria* (1.723–38), she first doubts that a robust man like Orlando is a lover at all. She tends only to the gravely ill: like 'doctor' Ovid in the *Remedia Amoris* (1.314), she will not 'cast away [her] physic but on those that are sick' (3.2.325–6). Her remedy, also like

Ovid's, is satire: the lover must harp on his lady's flaws, even he must make them up by transposing her adorable charms to disgusting faults (*Remedia* 1.315–30). Women mistakenly believe they are lovable, Rosalind continues, echoing the *Ars Amatoria* (1.613; *sibi quaeque videtur amanda*): 'That is one of the points in which women still give the lie to their consciences' (3.2.352–3).

Rosalind also advises Phoebe, on whom she unleashes the scabrous wit of the third book of the *Ars Amatoria*. Gone is the ebullience of the books of instruction to male pleasure-seekers. In its place is withering advice on how to maintain the female reader's apparently tenuous charms: tame that wild hair (3.133–6) and shave those hairy legs (3.193–6)! Choose clothes and assume physical postures that conceal unsightly blemishes from the sensitive eyes of your lovers. Above all, never reserve sexual favours, since your physical appeal will not last. To Phoebe, Rosalind volunteers discouraging advice about her prospects if she rejects Silvius:

> Know yourself; down on your knees
> And thank heaven, fasting, for a good man's love;
> For I must tell you friendly in your ear,
> Sell when you can. You are not for all markets.
> Cry the man mercy, love him, take his offer . . .
>
> (*As You Like It* 3.5.58–62)

It is not clear why Rosalind intrudes into the affairs of Silvius and Phoebe or why she reviles the shepherdess for rebuffing her suitor's clichés (e.g. her frowns wound and her eyes kill). Yet Rosalind notices affectation in Phoebe alone, and her insistence that Phoebe is vain must influence theatrical performance, since it is not obvious in her language (Olivia's vanity has a clearer textual basis). Momentarily startled by Phoebe's sudden attraction for her as Ganymede, Rosalind is soon delighted to 'sauce her with bitter words' (ll. 69–70). The bitter brew is Ovidian: 'I am falser than vows made in wine' (l. 74), she asserts, recalling Ovid's instructions, in the *Ars Amatoria*, to pretend to be tipsy when swearing love. The drunk cannot be held accountable for their vows.[26]

The reactions of Rosalind and Phoebe towards each other could not be more polarised if Cupid struck them with his leaden and golden arrows. Rosalind's distaste for the shepherdess is as instantaneous and irresistible as Phoebe's passion for the 'peevish boy' (3.5.111). Rosalind, I suggest, is repelled by the failed ambition that haunts Phoebe's speech: although the shepherdess has a share of eloquence, she cannot persuade Silvius to drop his amorous suit or compel the sympathies of Rosalind. Her speech has no hope of success, given the prevailing conventions of love and gender. This view gains support from Rosalind's manner of deriding Phoebe's love letter, which has, she facetiously asserts, 'a boisterous and a cruel style, / A style for challengers' (4.3.31–2). Phoebe aims to please, but according to Rosalind, she rails, chides, and writes 'Like Turk to Christian': 'Women's gentle brain, / Could not drop forth such giant rude invention' (ll. 33–4). As Rosalind knows, women cannot invent at all without risking the charge of colossal presumption. Should a woman exercise her wit, she casts doubts on her modesty along with her sources and very literacy: 'I say she never did invent this letter', Rosalind proclaims, 'This is a man's invention, and his hand' (ll. 28–9). In pursuing her man, Phoebe attempts to use the rhetorical, sexual, and social liberties that Rosalind has provisionally garnered for herself. Rosalind, who needs 'Gargantua's mouth' (3.2.205) to express her passion for Orlando, wants distance from the 'giant rude' presumption of the shepherdess and, above all, the pathetic inefficacy of her words.

For her part, Phoebe falls in love with the expressive liberties of the saucy but 'pretty youth' (l. 114), who looks so much like a woman. Her inventory of Rosalind/Ganymede's height, complexion, leg, lip ("Twas just the difference / Between the constant red and mingled damask', 3.5.123–4), and cheek is too well known to need full rehearsal. What may not be immediately remembered is that Phoebe's rapturous blazon begins with a meditation on the persuasive powers of speech:

> 'Tis but a peevish boy. Yet he talks well.
> But what care I for words? Yet words do well
> When he that speaks them pleases those that hear.
> (*As You Like It* 3.5.111–13)

Phoebe is manifestly thinking of the pleasure she herself would like to bring through her own inventive words. Her amorous blazon represents a yearning to possess a saucy voice and wounding tongue even more than the boy's body (which is 'but so-so', 3.5.120). Struck with a passion for a compelling voice and masterful verse of her own, Phoebe charmingly ends her speech with a decision to compose a letter.

Olivia also responds to the saucy tongue of a feminine boy, whose voluble wit represents a more effective means of securing the autonomy she has been seeking in melancholy withdrawal. She tells Cesario that she did not invite him into her home to hear his prepared speech on behalf of Orsino but to 'marvel' at the boy who was 'saucy at [her] gate' (1.5.174–5). Like Phoebe, she is 'sauced' with the boy's wit, and consequently comes to 'feel this youth's perfections / With an invisible and subtle stealth / To creep in at [her] eyes' (1.5.266–8). By the scene's end, she is remembering the 'peevish' boy (1.5.270) in a 'five-fold blazon' that begins with the tongue and proceeds to the face, limbs, actions, and spirit (1.5.262–3). Her associative chain leads from adoring parts of the boy's body to meditating on bodily and mental forms of human agency that she might possess through imitation.

Olivia's five-fold blazon also recalls, if only fortuitously, the expanding significance that Cooper attributes to the mouth (*os*). The 'tongue' leads to the 'uisage or countenance' and the 'proportion of all the bodie' before assuming abstract forms in 'Presence, Language, Audacitie, boldenesse, or hardinesse'. Such an extension of spirit or genius is for Ovid the machinery of immortality: as he asserts at the very end of the *Metamorphoses*, he will live forever so long as he is on the lips of his readers (*ore legar populi*, 15.878). At the ultimate moment of his most ambitious work, Ovid imagines transcending the world. Encounters with Ovidian poetry make Shakespeare's women, on the other hand, begin to dream of entering into it.

BOLD SPEECH, HONEST OVID, AND THE DEAD SHEPHERD

I am here with thee and thy goats as the most capricious poet honest Ovid was among the Goths. (Touchstone to Audrey, *As You Like It* 3.3.5–6)

Shakespeare's learned women, this chapter has argued, come into their own as romantic heroines at the moment they conceive and act on a passion for the expressive liberties and audacious wit of Ovid. Their imitative goals and practice differ markedly from those of classic humanists. Petrarch and Erasmus, for example, discuss imitation as a means to derive legitimacy and prestige from one's models; the immediate rewards are authorial self-definition and lustre.[27] Shakespeare, however, deviates from the recommended path to prestige. Instead of surrounding himself with distinguished models to assure his own pedigree, he hands imitative invention over to his resourceful heroines, who in turn pursue precisely the wrong commodities in their Ovidian ventures.[28] They properly experiment with form from metres to tropes, but do so to gain the qualities of Ovid's poetry that brought criticism and censure upon him: the bold speech and licence that Quintilian regarded as rhetorical abuse and Augustus Caesar judged to be a punishable moral offence. In this context, the imitative practices of Shakespeare's heroines suggest political thought as well as poetic skill.

As Ovid emphasises in his own identification with *audacia*, bold speech is a political prerogative that flourishes in republics but is a liability to subjects in imperial monarchies.[29] The price Ovid paid for his audacity was steep. From exile in Tomis on the Black Sea, surrounded by heavily armed (and hairy) Goths, Ovid wrote home to say that his very eloquence (*facundia*) had brought him harm. In his poetry of exile, translated by Thomas Churchyard as Ovid's 'bookes of Sorowes' (1580), the poet pleaded for the emperor to repeal his banishment.[30] That Ovid was never recalled came as a shock to his Renaissance admirers: for them, his exile counted against the emperor far more than his licentious subject. Julius Caesar Scaliger, for example, composed a poem in Ovid's voice that denounces the emperor as a tyrant and, with the power of the victim's curse, orders Augustus himself to go into exile.[31] Shakespeare's defence of Ovid is subtler but nonetheless insistent: Tranio cannot bear that Ovid be 'an outcast quite abjured' (*Shrew* 1.1.33), while Touchstone invokes 'the most capricious poet honest Ovid . . . among the Goths' (3.3.5–6). Because Tranio is urging Lucentio to study Ovid's amatory lessons alongside of Aristotle's ethical philosophy, his counsel sounds rather like a plea for schoolmasters to enlarge Ovid's place in the curriculum. Touchstone goes further when he juxtaposes the horny love poet's honesty and caprice (or insouciant wit), thus tacitly denying their opposition.[32] The very qualities of wit that repelled Elizabethan moralists as well as the Roman emperor charmed Ovid's Elizabethan translator and Shakespeare's clown: what strict authorities saw as licentious, they found 'pleasant'.[33]

Shakespeare's clowns worry over the ethics of Ovid's exile and his comic heroines evince passion for the daring wit that put the poet in jeopardy. What of Shakespeare himself?[34] According to Francis Meres, the 'sweet and witty soul of Ovid' found its way into the 'mellifluous and hony-tongued Shakespeare'.[35] Shakespeare might have agreed, early in his career, when he presented himself as the 'craftier Tereus' who, in *Titus Andronicus*, trims Lavinia of her tongue and hands, so she may neither speak nor weave her complaint (2.4.41–3). The evidence, however, suggests that philosophical differences with the other great Ovidian of Elizabethan England, Christopher Marlowe, persuaded Shakespeare to change his style and purpose in Ovidian imitation.

No one recalled the spirit of Ovid more boldly than Marlowe, who found in Ovid's myths and poetic 'toys' a powerful language to represent yearning for worldly satisfaction. His love of Ovid may relate, more closely than scholars have hitherto considered, to his poetic and political interest in Lucan, author of the republican *Civil War*, whose first book Marlowe translated. Marlowe also translated Ovid's *Amores* as his own *Elegies*, turned

Ovidian epyllia into a sensation with his *Hero and Leander*, and composed Ovidian rhapsodies for his Dido, Edward II, and Doctor Faustus, who would rather die than forsake the distinctive erotic promise that Ovid represents. The amorous invitation that began in Marlowe's slender lyric, 'The Passionate Shepherd', grew into a voracious demand in his narrative poem and tragedies. Marlowe's mighty line did not go unpunished: six years after his violent death, his Ovidian elegies were condemned and burned in the Bishop's Ban of 1599 (the probable year of *As You Like It*'s composition).

In a way that can only be deepened by remembrance of Ovid's history, the expression of bold desires and wit in Marlowe's plays seems often to be accompanied by the melancholy of exile or alienation from society. Marlowe generally finds homes for Ovidian expression in his tragic rebels against the tyranny of state, church, and custom: his Dido, Faustus, and Edward II consequently make a case both for and against the staging of expressive liberties. Shakespeare, I suggest, took Marlowe's tragic rebels and Marlowe himself as a challenge to daring in his own poetic line and stagecraft. His dramatic method of adapting Ovid and Marlowe was to reverse the magnetic polarity of Marlowe's mighty line and 'high astounding terms'.[36] Whereas Marlowe draws all audacity in his plays to a centre in his tragic protagonists and himself, Shakespeare irradiates the social worlds of his comic plays with contagious desires for boldness of speech. Shakespeare does not disclaim but disperses the radicalism Marlowe restricted to exceptional heroes and anti-heroes. Shakespeare's plays have their share of restless social energies, but they often come in unexpected and deceptively light vessels: comedies, clowns, and modest heroines of good family and education.

One humble character to remember Marlowe is Phoebe of *As You Like It*, who calls on him at the exact moment that she recovers her breath and presence of mind, addled by Ganymede: 'Dead shepherd,' she says, quoting from *Hero and Leander*, 'now I find thy saw of might: / "Who ever loved that loved not at first sight?"' (3.5.82–3). Through Phoebe, Shakespeare commemorates Marlowe as a poet on a par with Daphnis of Theocritus' first idyll and the dying Gallus of Virgil's tenth eclogue. Like 'capricious' Ovid among the Goths or goats (*caper* = goat), the shepherd Marlowe inspires and haunts Shakespeare's most pastoral play.[37] The brilliant but troubled careers of both poets – bold Ovid and even bolder Marlowe – gave Shakespeare every reason to distance himself from audacity in speech but equal reason to discover that paradoxical thing, a discreet means in which to pursue it.

NOTES

1. The image of being pressed into speech comes from *Richard II*, where Richard's queen experiences the gardeners' homily on kingship as torture. Heroines who sense the danger in being called to speak before male authorities include Desdemona, Cordelia, Marina, and Hermione. In the comedies, the scenario is no less demanding of poise, whether the heroine is Kate pleasing her tetchy husband or Isabella uttering her difficult petition for Angelo's life.

2. All references to Shakespeare are to the Norton Shakespeare, ed. Stephen Greenblatt (New York and London 1997).

3. Egeus' privilege appears to be based on a relic of Athenian constitutional history; Theseus recognises the 'sharp Athenian law' (1.1.162) but ultimately overbears Egeus' will (4.1.176). In one of the quieter plots of *Dream*, greater political authority passes to Theseus during the course of the play.

4. All references to Arthur Golding, *The. XV. Bookes of P. Ouidius Naso, entytuled Metamorphosis* are to the edition by W. H. D. Rouse (Carbondale, IL 1961).

5. Translations, unless otherwise specified, are my own; Ovid's phrase is *fit utilis usu* (10.286). A commonplace from antiquity, the notion that women have 'waxen minds' is used elsewhere by Shakespeare with no particular reference to Ovid's tale of Pygmalion.

6. Seneca the Elder, *Controversiae* 2.2.12. Quintilian's full remark runs, *Lascivus quidem in herois quoque Ovidius et nimium amator ingenii sui, laudandus tamen in partibus* (*Institutiones Oratoriae* 10.1.88).

7. At the moment that Ovid, in the *Metamorphoses,* introduces the topical politics of Rome into his description of the heavens, he signals his own boldness: *hic locus est, quem, si uerbis audacia detur, / haud timeam magni dixisse Palatia caeli* ('this is the place, which, if boldness were put into words, I would scarcely fear to call the Palatine of the great heavens', 1.175–6). I discuss this episode and Ovid's association of his poetic voice with open and bold speech in 'Ovid and the Question of Politics in Early Modern England', *ELH* 70 (2003), 343–73.

8. *Ingenio quo nihil melius contingere homini potest. Nam, ut Cicero in Bruto scribit, hominis decus est ingenium. Ingenii uero ipsius eloquentia.* Ovid, *Opera*, ed. Jacobus Micyllus (Basel 1543), p. 353.

9. Annabel Patterson, *Shakespeare and the Popular Voice* (Oxford 1989), provides a politically liberal reading of *Dream* and other Shakespearean plays. Patricia Parker, *Shakespeare from the Margins: Language, Culture, Context* (Chicago 1996), teases out the ideological implications of other rhetorical tactics in the play (pp. 83–115).

10. Ovid pervasively refers to and addresses the traditional *docta puella* of love elegy. For a study of Roman elegy that combines strong rhetorical readings with social history, see Sharon L. James, *Learned Girls and Male Persuasion* (Berkeley 2003).

11. Given the furious pace at which Shakespeare's Roman comedies dish out complex wordplay and stage business, contemporary and modern audiences alike must often feel that there was more to the joke they just heard than they quite

picked up on. One such joke concerns Lucentio's chosen epistle. The lines quoted in the play are also quotations in the letter, where Penelope imagines the war stories of returning husbands and envies each woman who 'hangs upon the lips of her husband as he tells the tale' (*Heroides* 1.30). In Ovid as in Virgil, the woman who listens raptly to a man's tragic war narrative is likely to be loved and left. Lucentio, in short, has chosen a text that aggrandises his role as an amorous conqueror and assumes a narrative outcome in which he remains free to wander erotically and geographically on his Grand Tour of Italy. See the discussion of the passage in *Ovid's Heroides: Select Epistles*, ed. Peter E. Knox (Cambridge 1995), p. 95.

12. Shakespeare uses the idea of such a musical division in *The Rape of Lucrece*, where Lucrece addresses Ovid's Philomela: 'For burden-wise I'll hum on Tarquin still / While thou on Tereus descants better skill' (1,133–4).

13. Critics who suspect Bianca of using her wit to undercut rather than encourage her lover will remember that Ovid reminisces about that happy occasion during a humiliating night of impotence. Bianca may hope to match Ovid's record or anticipate disappointment, rather in the way that Cressida appears to expect Troilus to let her down in bed: 'They say all lovers swear more performance than they are able, and yet reserve an ability that they never perform' (*Troilus and Cressida* 3.2.78–9).

14. This is the astute point of Lorna Hutson, *The Usurer's Daughter: Male Friendship and Fictions of Women in Sixteenth-Century England* (London 1994), pp. 214–18.

15. No one has written more persuasively about these concerns than Lars Engle, *Shakespearean Pragmatism* (Chicago 1993).

16. Jonathan Bate notes that the 'most sinister' of the figures in the Ovidian sequence is Medea, who is gathering 'the enchanted herbs / That did renew old Aeson' (5.1.13–14). He shrewdly notes the ironic relationship of Medea's renewal of Aeson to Portia's effort to coerce old Shylock into baptismal renewal and recalls the trick Medea plays on the daughters of Pelias, who dismember their father in the tragically mistaken belief that they are restoring his youth. See *Shakespeare and Ovid* (Oxford 1993), pp. 152–7.

17. Lorenzo's epithets for virtually intractable human nature recall Ovid's own aetiologies of human creation from stone (what is 'hard') and blood signifying a disposition to rebel against authority (what is 'full of rage').

18. Ovid is apparently thinking of Horace's allusions to Orpheus and Amphion as builders of civilisation in the *Ars Poetica* 391–401.

19. Thomas Cooper's *Thesaurus Linguae Romanae & Britannicae* (London 1565) defines Latin vocabulary with copious illustrations from Roman poetry and prose. The entry for *ingenium* provides examples of the word's ethical sense as well as of its rhetorical – and Ovidian – meaning of 'wit'. Cooper quotes Ovid's dismay at the political trouble into which his wit plunged him with Augustus: 'My witte and mynde was astonied with the miseries that I susteyned.' For the words *lascivia, lascivus,* and *lascivio,* Cooper offers more illustrations from Ovid than any other poet; Horace is a close second.

20. The devoted reader of Ovid will notice that exile and shipwreck, from the perspective of the *Tristia*, are virtually interchangeable accidents of fortune. Ovid
draws a strong comparison between his sentence of exile and the shipwreck he
fears on his passage to Tomis on the Black Sea. Rosalind and Viola experience
the disaster of Ovid's career at the beginning of their plays and feel liberated –
on the theory that there's nothing left to lose – to indulge in the bold liberties
of Ovidian expression.

21. In the *Metamorphoses*, Narcissus 'might seem either a boy or a young man' (*puer
iuvenisque*, 3.352) and is desired by both men and women. Even Malvolio is
inspired by the appearance of Cesario to describe him in erotic terms (1.5.139–
44).

22. Ovid repeatedly uses a theatrical metaphor for the erotic games he teaches his
male pupils in the *Ars Amatoria*: 'But most of all I would haue thee stir / At
the play time vnto the Theater' (1.69–70), he says, before detailing the Rape
of the Sabines in the Roman theatre. I quote from Thomas Heywood's *Art of
Love*, ed. M. L. Stapleton (Ann Arbor 2000).

23. Ovid almost settles matters by referring to Iphis as a *puer*, but in fact only *vir*
(man) would do the trick: the third meaning of *puer* listed in the *Oxford Latin
Dictionary* is 'a boy favourite' or 'catamite'. Although he is not shy about punning allusions to male genitals, as his reference to his *nervus* (vigour, sinews, and
penis) in the *Amores* (1.1.18) demonstrates, he bypasses an opportunity to give
Iphis' newfound vigour (9.790) a genital origin by choosing the word *vigor*.

24. Valerie Traub, 'The Homoerotics of Shakespearean Comedy', in *Desire and
Anxiety: Circulations of Sexuality in Shakespearean Drama* (London 1992), argues
that the corrective Rosalind's Hymen offers to the play's provisional sexualities
is less lasting than it seems. See also the influential discussions of *As You Like It*
in Jean Howard, *The Stage and Social Struggle in Early Modern England* (London
1994) and of *Twelfth Night* in Stephen Orgel, *Impersonations: the Performance
of Gender in Early Modern England* (Cambridge 1996). Omitting the tale of
Iphis from his discussion, Mario DiGangi argues that the plays use Ovidian
tales to represent a natural bias in both sexes towards the love of men in *The
Homoerotics of Early Modern Drama* (Cambridge 1997), ch. 2.

25. Jonathan Bate, in *Shakespeare and Ovid*, p. 159 notes her role as *praeceptor
amoris:* 'her sexual pragmatism [is] as down-to-earth and her wit as sharp as
they are in Ovid'.

26. This is only one game to be played with wine: see the detailed account in *Ars
Amatoria* 1.565–602.

27. See Thomas M. Greene, *The Light In Troy: Imitation and Discovery in Renaissance Poetry* (New Haven 1982) and Terence Cave, *The Cornucopian Text: Problems of Writing in the French Renaissance* (Oxford 1979).

28. Shakespeare is equally experimental but profoundly concerned with authorship
in his narrative poems and especially *The Rape of Lucrece*. See Wendy Wall,
The Imprint of Gender: Authorship and Publication in the English Renaissance
(Ithaca 1993), for an illuminating argument about Shakespeare's use of gender
difference to negotiate his own authorial identity. Lynn Enterline, *The Rhetoric*

of the Body (Cambridge 2000), extends the sources of Shakespeare's project to Ovid.

29. See my 'Ovid and the Question of Politics', especially the discussions of Jove's charade of soliciting senatorial advice and of the debate between Pallas and Arachne over the interpretation of Athens' civic origins.

30. See Stephen Hinds, 'Booking the Return Trip: Ovid and *Tristia* 1', *Proceedings of the Cambridge Philological Society* 31 (1985), 13–32. See also M. L. Stapleton, *Harmful Eloquence: Ovid's Amores from Antiquity to Shakespeare* (Ann Arbor 1996).

31. 'P. Ovidius Naso', *Scaligeri Heroes* (Lugduni: apud G. & M. Beringos, 1546), pp. 293–4.

32. Ovid's defence appears in *Tristia* 2.1.354, where he concedes that his Muse is playful (*iocosa*) but insists that his life is modest (*verecunda*). Modesty is not quite the same, however, as honesty. The word comes up in versions of the *Life of Ovid*. Petrus says, 'Ovid was preeminent in honest behavior (*moribus . . . honestis*) and had wondrous facility in reconciling the dispositions (*ingenia*) of men in his favor (which is worthy of the greatest admiration).' Petrus cites Ovid's honesty to impeach that of Augustus, whom he suspected of incestuous relations with Julia. The second reference alludes in more barbed form to the same legend: 'They say that he had seen Augustus lying with insufficient honesty with his daughter, which the poets wish to be communicated in this little verse of his: "why did I see something, why did I make eyes knowing?"', Ovid, *Opera Omnia*, ed. Jacobus Micyllus (Basel 1543–50).

33. Thomas Churchyard, *The Three first Bookes of Ouid de Tristibus* (London 1580), p. 15r. On the same page, he translates the *verecundia* of Ovid's life as 'shamefast'.

34. Shakespeare's removal of all evidence of self-interest from the political ideas in his plays suggests to some scholars that the quality of detachment called 'negative faith' by S. T. Coleridge means Shakespeare lacks political opinions or embraces orthodox ones. My argument is that Shakespeare demonstrates, through his Ovidian imitations and articulate heroines, a passionate faith in bold speech that is implicitly political.

35. Francis Meres, *Palladis Tamia: Wits Treasury* (New York 1973), pp. 281–2.

36. *Tamburlaine Part One* (prologue, l. 5), from *The Complete Plays of Christopher Marlowe*, ed. Irving Ribner (New York 1963).

37. It may be relevant that Ovid too commemorated Gallus, who was no longer dying of love but dead, a suicide in the aftermath of his political disgrace and formal rejection by Augustus. See *Amores* 1.15, *Tristia* 2.1, and *Ex Ponto* 4.16. Even if Gallus lost the world, Ovid argued, his elegies would endure the envy of detractors, the wrath of Jove (i.e. political censure), and time itself. Yet Gallus' poems did not in fact survive. Ovid's own early poems were themselves censored at the time of his banishment (and Ovid thinks with pain, in the *Tristia*, of the empty space on the shelves of the public libraries where his *Ars Amatoria* once sat). The legacy of Gallus survives chiefly in the poetry of his friends and in later commentaries that continue the work of mourning *mortuus Gallus*, the dead shepherd of erotic elegy and casualty of a prince's anger.

VIRGIL

CHAPTER 5

Shakespeare and Virgil

Charles Martindale

> J. W. Velz's claim that a full study of Virgil and Shakespeare is a key
> desideratum is . . . misplaced; we at least would rather be spared it.[1]

This interdiction, overly dogmatic and itself perhaps misplaced, sprang
from an irritation with the excesses and lack of rigour of much current
source-hunting. Leonard Digges' assertion 'look thorough / This whole
book, thou shalt find he doth not borrow / One phrase from Greeks, nor
Latins imitate',[2] even if we regard it as false or misleading, must at least
have seemed *plausible* to many of Shakespeare's early readers (Dr Johnson
later made a not dissimilar claim). Still, there can be no reasonable doubt
that Shakespeare read some Virgil in Latin at school, and that allusions and
references to Virgil are found throughout his work.[3] No one has undermined the demonstration by Root, made more than a century ago, that
Shakespeare's classical mythology derives primarily from Ovid and Virgil,
Ovid's influence being four times greater than Virgil's.[4] The main focus
of Shakespeare's interest in Virgil was in three episodes from the *Aeneid*,
the tragedy of Dido, the sack of Troy, and Aeneas' visit to the Underworld
(episodes that have been favourites throughout history, from St Augustine
in his *Confessions* onwards). Whether Shakespeare read the second half of
the poem, either in Latin or in the translation of Phaer and Twyne (1584),
cannot be proved, though it is likely enough. The mythological allusions
taken from Virgil do not, as a group, differ in style from those taken from
elsewhere. In the words of A. D. Nuttall, 'These passages, above all, are
of their time: mannered, ornamental, clever – manifestly poetry of the
English Renaissance. Shakespeare is seldom less Virgilian than when he is
citing him.'[5] In the main they exemplify that 'sweet, witty' style, in the well-
known characterisation of Francis Meres, that made Shakespeare seem like
the English Ovid.

I thus remain of the view that Shakespeare is not usefully to be described
as a Virgilian poet. By that I mean that his reading of Virgil did not result

in a profound modification of his sensibility and imagination in the way that his reading of other books did (Marlowe, for example, or Montaigne, or Plutarch). And Shakespeare did not substantially influence the way that Virgil's poems were subsequently read and thus our sense of the kind of poet that Virgil is. In other words Shakespeare's encounter with Virgil was not like Dante's with Virgil, or T. S. Eliot's with Dante, or indeed his own with Ovid. Nonetheless *Shakespeare and the Uses of Antiquity* significantly understates the importance of Virgil in the works, and this chapter thus functions as somewhat of a palinode. Furthermore, Virgil is one among those pervasive and diffused classical presences within Renaissance culture which, in the words of Leonard Barkan, 'are present everywhere in the formation of the plays via some deep acculturation'; in this connection Barkan acutely evokes 'Foucault's designation of "transdiscursive", by which he refers to Marx and Freud'.[6]

Let us start our enquiry with the most evocative of Shakespeare's ten mentions of the most celebrated Virgilian heroine.[7] Antony, falsely believing Cleopatra dead, and planning to follow her, imagines for them an Elysian reunion among other fabled lovers:

> Eros! – I come, my queen. – Eros! – Stay for me.
> Where souls do couch on flowers we'll hand in hand,
> And with our sprightly port make the ghosts gaze.
> Dido and her Aeneas shall want troops,
> And all the haunt be ours. Come, Eros, Eros!
>
> (4.15.50–4)

This marvellous and marvellously phrased picture is of course in conflict with the *Aeneid*. For, as every schoolboy knew, it was Sychaeus, her Phoenician husband, with whom Dido was reunited in the Underworld, while from Aeneas, like Homer's Ajax with Achilles, she turned in angry silence as he stammered out his justifications, a gesture used later by Arnold to characterise his 'Scholar Gipsy';

> Averse, as Dido did with gesture stern
> From her false friend's approach in Hades turn.
>
> (208–9)

This was the scene, with 'perhaps the most telling snub in all poetry', that Eliot, supporter of Virgil's imperial vision (which entailed the subordination of private happiness to the requirements of destiny), and who clearly identified with Aeneas' stance of painful embarrassment, described as 'not only one of the most poignant, but one of the most civilized passages in poetry'.[8] What then are we to make of this discrepancy between Virgil and

Shakespeare? In the eighteenth century William Warburton pedantically emended 'Aeneas' to 'Sychaeus', destroying all romance.[9] We might suppose that Shakespeare had simply forgotten the Virgilian scene, or chosen to ignore it. Or we might rather think the mythological mistake Antony's, not Shakespeare's, rather as Antony blunders over the conduct of his death in the high Roman manner, or, with ludicrous care, invites Cleopatra to trust only Proculeius. Or we could recall that the historical Antony died before the composition of the *Aeneid*, before Virgil made his version the canonical one. The play, it should be remembered, is much concerned with a contestation of authority, with who controls interpretation, as characters seek to establish their own version of events. So we may decide that Shakespeare, or Antony – or both? – is rewriting to his own vision 'Vergil's great fiction of erotic abnegation'.[10] Cleopatra, herself an 'immanent enactor of fictions',[11] subsequently outmanoeuvres Caesar's desire to shape her story, with her perfectly staged suicide. A young male actor performs Cleopatra performing her latest gender role – more like a Roman man than a Roman woman. The performance is flawless: Cleopatra becomes her role as Stoic suicide, and, in her version of performativity, her role becomes her. Caesar, ever the politician, sees the need for lofty acquiescence: 'She shall be buried by her Antony. / No grave upon the earth shall clip in it / A pair so famous' (5.2.352–4). The lovers' story is an aesthetic even more than an erotic triumph.[12] And Antony too has already, in our passage, more than proved himself as a poet of love: tender ('hand in hand'), graciously feminised ('Dido and her Aeneas'), creating, along with a sense of mutuality, a mood of wistfulness and wonder with his depiction of the ghosts; that his servant Eros bears the name of the Greek god of sexual desire adds a further resonance.

We should remember too that, whereas for most moderns Dido is primarily a Virgilian creation, Shakespeare inherited a rather more complex tradition. Scholars in antiquity and in the early modern period were well aware that the chronology meant that Dido and Aeneas could never have met. There was a rival story of an exemplary Dido, found for example in both Petrarch and Boccaccio, who died to preserve her chastity. The distinction between these two Didos lies behind the curious and rather listless exchanges between the courtiers in *The Tempest* 2.1. To Gonzalo's chaste 'widow Dido' Sebastian and Antonio jeeringly oppose the Virgilian 'widower Aeneas'. The matter was complicated by the at least partial identification of Queen Elizabeth ('Eliza') and Dido, whose alternative name was Elissa. For example, the so-called 'Sieve' portrait of *c.*1580–3, attributed to Cornelius Ketel, which associates the queen with the chaste Vestal Virgin

Tuccia, has scenes from the *Aeneid* in the background.[13] A medal celebrating victory over the Armada bore the Didonian legend *Dux Foemina Facti* ('a woman was leader of what was done', *Aen.* 1.364).[14]

Of more immediate significance, *Heroides* 7, a letter from Dido to Aeneas, was far more widely admired before the nineteenth century than it has been since. In it Ovid retains the basic shape of the Virgilian narrative but 'transvaluates' it from the perspective of elegiac love and in the light of the regular abandonment of women by men. In most of the plays in which Shakespeare evokes Virgil we find him combined with Ovid in imitative *contaminatio* (the scholars' word for the conflation of models), and in many cases it is Ovid who imaginatively triumphs and more obviously modifies Shakespeare's style. A Didonian instance occurs in a glamorously erotic exchange between lovers from *The Merchant of Venice* (5.1.9–12):

> In such a night
> Stood Dido with a willow in her hand
> Upon the wild sea banks, and waft her love
> To come again to Carthage.

Shakespeare here seems to be recalling details from the story of Ariadne, another of Ovid's heroines, as Englished by an earlier Ovidian, Chaucer (*Heroides* 10; *Legend of Good Women* 2,189 ff.). Chaucer indeed regularly sets Virgil and Ovid in collision as rival authorities; his version of Dido (*Legend* 924 ff.) starts with a strong nod to Virgil but soon is presenting Aeneas as a faithless lover, earning Chaucer the subsequent rebuke of Gavin Douglas as 'evir (God wait) all womanis frend' (verse prologue to his translation of *Aeneid* 4.449). Matthew Arnold famously cited the passage from *Merchant* as an example of the 'Celtic' (i.e. unclassical) element in English literature, describing it as 'drenched and intoxicated with the fairy-dew of . . . natural magic'.[15] In the grandest of all Virgilian operas, *Les Troyens*, Berlioz, whose literary gods were Shakespeare and Virgil, found an accommodation between the two writers and between the two sides of his own musical personality conventionally thought to be in conflict, the admirer of the neo-classical Gluck and the unfettered Romantic. He patterns an exchange, unimaginable in the *Aeneid*, in which Dido and Aeneas express their mutual love, on the nocturne in *Merchant*: the duet *Nuit d'ivresse* with its refrain *par une telle nuit*. (The 6/8 time means that for one critic Shakespeare in French recalls Virgil's hexameters.[16]) As we have seen, Shakespeare had Ovid as a precedent for rewriting Virgil in *Antony and Cleopatra*. Not dissimilarly Ovid reunited Orpheus and his twice-lost Eurydice in the Underworld, undoing the Virgilian tragic ending and wittily depriving the fateful backward glance of its potency (*Met.* 11.64–6): *hic modo coniunctis spatiantur passibus ambo, / nunc praecedentem sequitur, nunc praevius anteit / Eurydicenque suam iam tuto respicit Orpheus* ('here with conjoined steps both strode, now he follows her as she precedes, now walking ahead he goes in front, and at his Eurydice, now in safety, Orpheus *looks back*').[17]

We need, then, to be alert to the modes in which Shakespeare made his acquaintance with Virgil. Like other early modern writers, Shakespeare often encountered passages from classical poetry in recontextualised forms in florilegia, commonplace books, and the like.[18] The set-piece on Adonis' horse (*Venus and Adonis* 259–324) derives in part from Virgil's *Georgics* (3.75–94), but Shakespeare probably took the passage from Mirandula's popular compilation, *Illustrium Poetarum Flores*, or from another of the anthologisers. (Scholars too often assume that Shakespeare was like them (or their ideal images of themselves), and that therefore if he knew a passage of classical literature, he also knew its original context in the work as a whole.) More interesting is a famous line from *Henry V*. This play, with its heroic subject and narrative prologues, is perhaps the most epical in the corpus, so it would not be surprising if Shakespeare when writing it thought of the most admired epic poem. But in fact it is the *Georgics*, with its analogies between the state of the land and that of the commonwealth, nature and politics, that has left a stronger mark, in particular in two passages: the Archbishop of Canterbury's description of the bee community (1.2.187–204), and Burgundy's ruminations on the ruined state of the French countryside (5.2.23–67).[19] Shakespeare's bees recall Virgil's in *Georgics* 4 (for example 'to the tent royal of their emperor', 196, translates *circa regem atque ipsa ad praetoria,* 75), but the best and best-known line does not come from Virgil: 'The singing masons building roofs of gold' (198). Bees do not sing in Virgil; indeed Jasper Griffin made this point the basis of his interpretation of the whole of the fourth *Georgic*, according to which the bees – communal, laborious, Stakhanovite, *Roman* – contrast with Orpheus, the individual singer who loses all for love.[20] But Shakespeare, as Baldwin showed, used the commentary of Willichius, and got from there his insect songsters. For Willichius Virgil 'here depicted, allegorically, the form of the best state'; and he differentiated the various types of bees, including 'sirens, which are called thus from the song of the Sirens'.[21] Empson has a quite superb analysis of Shakespeare's line:

Bees are not forced by law or immediate hunger to act as *masons*; 'it all comes naturally to them'; as in the Golden Age they *sing* with plenty and the apparent freedom of their social structure. On the other hand bees only *sing* (indeed, can only sing) through the noise produced by their working; though happy they are not idle; and the human opposition between the pain of work and the waste of play has been resolved by the hive into a higher unity, as in Heaven. . . .

Roofs are what they are *building*; the culmination of successful work, the most airy and striking parts of it; also the Gothic tradition gave a particular exaltation to *roofs*, for instance those magnificent hammer-beam affairs which had angels with *bee*-like wings on the hammers, as if they were helping in the *singing* from a heavenly choir; and to have *masons*, building a stone *roof*, with mortar instead of nails, is at once particularly like the methods of *bees* and the most solid and wealthy form of construction. But *bees build* downwards from the *roof*, so that they are always still *building* the *roof*, in a sense; the phrase is thus particularly applicable to them, and the comparison with men makes this a reckless or impossible feat, arguing an ideal security. In the same way, both parties are given wealth and delicacy because the yellow of wax is no surface gilding, not even such as in the temple of Solomon (built without sound of hammer, in the best *bee* tradition, though it was) shone thickly coated upon ivory, but all throughout, as the very substance of their labours, in its own pale ethereal and delicious *gold*.[22]

Now of course Willichius could not show Shakespeare how to write like that, but Virgil perhaps could, with his shifting perspectives and occasional bee's-eye view (e.g. when he presents a small stream as a very ocean to the bees, 28–9, or sees their stings as looking like human weapons of war, 73–4). Shakespeare indeed had Virgil's bees so vividly in his mind that he recalled a striking line (*ingentis animos angusto in pectore versant*, 83) when he describes England itself, eager for valiant deeds against a foe superior in number, as 'Like little body with a mighty heart' (act 2, Prologue, chorus, 17).

Curiously enough, there is a case for saying that it is in *Titus Andronicus* that Shakespeare – if he is the author – had his most sustained dialogue with Virgil. The play is most usually described today as Ovidian[23] (more rarely as Senecan). But the statistics in Root (even if inexact) – 14 references to Ovid, 14 to Virgil – are suggestive of a broadly diffused Virgilian presence.[24] The young Shakespeare was not concerned, as he was in the later Plutarchan plays, to create the sense of a very specific moment in Roman history – T. J. B. Spencer's quip is well-known: 'the author seems anxious, not to get it all right, but to get it all in'.[25] But in a rather generalised way the play is best regarded as set in late antiquity (as in the narrative, preserved only in an eighteenth-century chap-book, that many scholars think was Shakespeare's source), hence the prominent role played by the Goths and a Moor.[26] The portrayal of Rome reduced to 'a wilderness of tigers' (3.1.54) thus operates as a kind of supplement to Virgil's picture of *imperium sine fine*, rather in the manner of Auden's poem 'Secondary Epic', which mocks Virgil for his inability to predict the true course of subsequent events:

No, Virgil, no:
Not even the first of the Romans can learn
His Roman history in the future tense,
Not even to serve your political turn;
Hindsight as foresight makes no sense.

(1–5)

To the humanists the *Aeneid* was a guide to right living, and *pius* Aeneas a prime exemplary hero. 'Only let Aeneas be worn in the tablet of your memory', averred Sidney in his *Defence of Poesie*,[27] while for Jonson Aeneas was 'the most exquisite pattern of piety, justice, prudence, and all other princely virtues' (*The Haddington Masque*, note on 214). As a result, in Jonson's words, 'the reading of Homer and Virgil is counselled by Quintilian as the best way of informing youth, and confirming man' (*Discoveries* 2240). Shakespeare always took a rather more complex view of the connections between actions, character, and ideology. The prime icon of Aeneas' *pietas* (his devotion to family, community, and the gods) was the tableau of his carrying his old father Anchises out of burning Troy. When in *Julius Caesar* (1.2.112–15) Cassius appropriates this *exemplum* for his relationship with Caesar (whom he will kill), claiming for himself the traditional virtue, it is difficult not to read with irony:[28]

> I, as Aeneas, our great ancestor,
> Did from the flames of Troy upon his shoulder
> The old Anchises bear, so from the waves of Tiber
> Did I the tired Caesar.

Similarly *Titus* can be read as interrogating humanist belief in the straightforwardly exemplary value of ancient literature, and expressing scepticism over the virtue of *pietas* so central to the Virgilian vision.[29] What indeed are we to make of the classics? The play inter alia examines the role of literature for dealing with violence and crisis, and constantly involves the self-conscious use of classical texts both by Shakespeare and by his characters. The murderer and rapist Chiron correctly identifies an ode of Horace (1.22, *Integer vitae, scelerisque purus / Non eget Mauri iaculis, nec arcu*, 'The man who is entire of life and pure of crime does not need the darts of the Moor nor the bow'): 'O, 'tis a verse in Horace, I know it well; / I read it in the grammar long ago' (4.2.22–3: this is an archly anachronistic reference to Lily's Latin grammar, standard in Tudor schools). What Chiron does not recognise is either the moral function of the text as promoted by the schoolmasters or its intended application by Titus to the current situation (*Mauri* is designed to refer to Aaron the Moor). Reading Latin literature has clearly not achieved any civilising or educative effect in his case.

And what anyway would be entailed by imitating Aeneas or other Roman heroes? Titus himself, surnamed Pius (1.1.23), 'the good Andronicus, / Patron of virtue' (1.1.64–5) has all the right Virgilian qualifications, including a daughter Lavinia who shares the name of Aeneas' Latin bride. His killing of his son Mutius for disobedience may have good Roman precedent in the virtuous filicides Brutus the Liberator and Titus Manlius Torquatus. But this act and the execution of Tamora's son to appease the dead of his own family ('Why suffer'st thou thy sons unburied yet, / To hover on the dreadful shore of Styx?', 1.1.87–8, another close Virgilian echo) put the notion of *pietas* under intense pressure. The logic of Tamora, evil as she may be, is inexorable:

> But must my sons be slaughtered in the streets
> For valiant doings in their country's cause?
> O, if to fight for king and commonweal
> Were piety in thine, it is in these.   (1.1.112–15)

The sacrifice of Alarbus ('cruel, irreligious piety', 1.1.130) sets in motion the disastrous events of the play, but Titus could have cited the precedent of Aeneas, who, on the pattern of Homer's Achilles (oddly in view of a general Roman distaste for human sacrifice), slew Latin captives at the funeral of Pallas, and who, at the poem's end, shows no mercy for the defeated Turnus helpless at his feet. Titus eventually kills his dishonoured daughter, appealing to the story of Virginia (threatened with rape by Appius and slain by her father to preserve her good name) as 'a pattern, precedent, and lively warrant' (5.3.43), an act that surprises even the vicious Saturninus. Rome in this play is more than usual a textual construct, endlessly involved in citation and precedent. The past, and the texts of the past, have become burdens 'till every view is a postcard signed by great names'(Walcott, *Omeros* 36.1).

The grand hunt in the second act of *Titus* is patterned on Dido's hunt in *Aeneid* 4, with its fatal denouement in the cave, as Tamora's speech makes clear (2.2.21–4):

> And after conflict such as was supposed
> The wandering prince and Dido once enjoyed
> When with a happy storm they were surprised
> And curtained with a counsel-keeping cave . . .

The humanist educator Thomas Elyot thought Dido's hunt provided rousing material for the young aristocrat: 'If the child have a delight in hunting, what pleasure shall he take of the fable of Aristaeus [in *Georgic* 4], semblably in the hunting of Dido and Aeneas which is described elegantly in his book of *Eneidos*' (*The Governor*, book 1, ch. 10). Shakespeare was alert to more sinister possibilities and made hunting a prime metaphor in *Titus*.[30] Shakespeare noticed a pattern in Virgil concerned with hunting that links it with war and sexual aggression. Aeneas' first act in the poem is the killing of some deer; Dido is later compared to a deer slain by an unwitting huntsman; she and Aeneas become lovers during the famous hunt and storm; Ascanius starts the war in Italy by unwittingly killing the pet stag of the Latin Silvia, Woodland Woman (*Aen.* 1.184–94; 4.68–73, 129–72; 7.483–510) – the persistence of the motif hints at the cost to others of Aeneas' mission. During the hunt in *Titus* Tamora, as we have seen, becomes a perverted Dido, while 'like a travesty of Aeneas, Aaron abandons love for the higher destiny of war'.[31] Shakespeare's version of the cave is the pit, site of murder and violation, with its suggestions of the female genitalia (2.3.198–201). The rapists, using the discourse of poachers, refer to Lavinia as a 'dainty doe' (2.2.26), and she herself, when ravished, becomes a version of the wounded Dido with 'unrecuring wound' (3.1.89–90). As Berry puts it, 'The ritual of the hunt, with its uniquely literal attempt to bring the bestial within the order of civilization, provided Shakespeare with a vivid set of images for a problem he pursued throughout his career: the tragic inability of ceremonial ideals to withstand the violent impulses within human nature.'[32]

After the rape Virgil is, to an extent, displaced by Ovid, in particular the Philomela story, for the revenge plot. But Virgil returns again at the close as some form of political order is restored. Lucius' Gothic followers are given a Virgilian bee simile ('We'll follow where thou lead'st, / Like stinging bees in hottest summer's day / Led by their master to the flowered fields', 5.1.13–15). Another simile ostentatiously reminds us of the story of Troy's sack and the treachery of Sinon, as told by Aeneas to Dido (5.3.79–86). But Lucius' final act in denying Tamora burial, a last rejection of pity (related like piety to the Latin *pietas*) gives no great assurance for a future different from the past. Pity is the play's last word, but only the birds of prey are to show it.

Just possibly Virgil may also have left his mark on the most famous (or notorious) speech in the play, Marcus' response to the mangled Lavinia (2.4.11–57):

> Speak, gentle niece, what stern ungentle hands
> Hath lopped and hewed and made thy body bare
> Of her two branches, those sweet ornaments
> Whose circling shadows kings have sought to sleep in,
> And might not gain so great a happiness
> As half thy love. Why dost not speak to me?
> Alas, a crimson river of warm blood,

Like to a bubbling fountain stirred with wind,
Dost rise and fall between thy rosed lips,
Coming and going with thy honey breath.
But sure some Tereus hath deflowered thee
And, lest thou shouldst detect him, cut thy tongue. . . .
Fair Philomel, why she but lost her tongue,
And in a tedious sampler sewed her mind.
But, lovely niece, that mean is cut from thee.
A craftier Tereus, cousin, hast thou met,
And he hath cut those pretty fingers off
That could have better sewed than Philomel.
O, had the monster seen those lily hands
Tremble like aspen leaves upon a lute
And make the silken strings delight to kiss them,
He would not then have touched them for his life. . . .

This set-piece is usually seen as Ovidian, which is fair enough in view of its conceits and its arabesques on the Philomela story. But what seems especially distinctive is the combination of an intense lyrical beauty with extreme violence. This over-ripeness of style is not really characteristic of Ovid, but it is sometimes found in the *Aeneid*. One example is the passage describing Lavinia's blush (*Aen.* 12.64–70), which Shakespeare may indeed have put into service for the moment when his Lavinia opens her mouth and the blood rises and falls between her rosed lips (22–5). Still more relevant, in its aestheticisation of blood and death, is the languorously eroticised picture of the dying Euryalus (9.433–7), lines that are opulent, somnolent, smooth, self-indulgent, self-consciously beautiful, redolent of a sort of *fin-de-siècle* 'decadence' (I use the word non-pejoratively):

> volvitur Euryalus leto, pulchrosque per artus
> it cruor inque umeros cervix conlapsa recumbit;
> purpureus veluti cum flos succisus aratro
> languescit moriens, lassove papavera collo
> demisere caput pluvia cum forte gravantur.

(Euryalus rolls over in death; over his fair limbs the blood flows and his neck collapses and slumps over his shoulders; as when a purple flower cut from below by the plough languishes as it dies, or poppies droop their heads with tired neck when once weighed down by rain.)

But if Shakespeare was inspired by Virgil to write in this way, it was not an experiment that he repeated.

Some scholars (Miola, Bono, James) have argued that Virgil continues to be a crucial shaping presence in the later Roman plays, so that 'a tacit

dialogue' is established with the *Aeneid*.[33] The evidence is less than irresistible. True, there are a few allusions certain or probable (including the
one from *Julius Caesar* I have already cited), but to me the truth is as obvious
as it is banal, that it was simply re-reading Plutarch which revolutionised
Shakespeare's vision of Roman history – Virgil had little to do with it. Even
where a direct Virgilian allusion seems at first glance a distinct possibility,
it may be illusory. For example, one might think that Cleopatra's sublime
chutzpah 'Husband, I come! / Now to that name my courage prove my title'
(5.2.282–3) reflects the argument between Dido and Aeneas about whether
they are married, an issue complicated by the weird cosmic wedding ceremony that accompanies their union in the cave (*Aen.* 4.165–72; cf. 316,
338–9). But all the material that Shakespeare needed is there in Plutarch:
Cleopatra 'called him her lord, her husband, and emperor, forgetting her
own misery and calamity' (*Life of Antony*, ch. 77, North).

   Much more complicated, and more interesting, is the case of *The Tempest*.
Scholars, following the lead of Donna Hamilton, increasingly present the
play as a sustained *imitatio* of the *Aeneid*.[34] And certainly there is a trail of
references to Virgil throughout (more than to any other single 'source').[35]
The problem is to know quite what to do with them, since they combine
a certain tenuousness with a curious persistence. For today's sophisticated
critics intertextuality is of course always A Good Thing. The problem here
is that Shakespeare fails to carry over into *The Tempest* the power of the
passages recalled. Virgil's fearful Harpies are reduced to a banal allegory of
greed and a matter of smoke and mirrors, 'a Halloween trick or treat'.[36]
The feeble jokes about 'widow Dido' (which appear partly to depend on
a mistake over the syllabic quantities of Dido's name) have palled with
many critics. If the relationship of Ferdinand and Miranda makes of them
a modern Aeneas and Dido, they seem a rather pallid equivalent (the meat
of the play surely isn't here). Hamilton herself is forced to admit as much:
'In his portrayal of Ferdinand, Shakespeare flattened Virgil, weakening
the tensions that dominate the parent work.'[37] That is, to say the least,
putting it mildly. Her view that, in effect, any combination of sameness
and difference constitutes imitation means that the creation of significant
relationships unlikely to register outside the study becomes fatally easy.[38]
In a general way one can see that there is in *The Tempest* a Virgilian sense
of time and fate ('the dark backward and abysm of time'). As Kermode has
well observed, the theatrical analogy with which the play constantly works
'stirs in one's mind the deep-seated parallel between the notion of destiny
and the role of the author who plans ahead and writes parts appropriate
to his cast'.[39] In that sense at least Prospero is like Shakespeare, or Virgil's

Jupiter, or indeed Virgil himself (another putative magus). But any good account of the matter must acknowledge the ghostly quality of all this, so well described by John Pitcher: 'The Virgilian presence in *The Tempest* is often of this spectral kind, a half-seen image of death, or damnation, or despair at the back of an episode, a line, or even a single word.'[40]

Today's orthodoxy sees *The Tempest* as a play above all about power and colonisation. This reading is a product of our post-colonial sensibilities, practices, and concerns (nothing wrong in that, of course, and it is a reading that has opened a rich hermeneutical vein). Unsurprisingly scholars seize happily on any Virgilian features, since the *Aeneid* is the great foundation poem of Western colonisation and empire. But to say that Shakespeare 'reworks the chiefly contested issues of national politics'[41] seems at best only a half-truth. Those who find rather themes of metamorphosis, art, illusion, and self-referentiality are more inclined to stress the elements from Ovid[42] (and to Ovid is owed one of the supreme moments of the play, Prospero's renunciation of his powers). For others we have a designed *contaminatio* in which Virgilian epic is played off against Ovidian romance (Prospero may start out as a Virgilian, using sequences from the *Aeneid* to control his enemies, but his is not the only voice). To my thinking it is difficult to shape either set of traces into a wholly clear pattern of meaning. Perhaps Shakespeare simply felt the need for a purely formal scaffolding which he took primarily from Virgil's *Aeneid*. Or the scattered and imperfect allusions to Virgil may be readable as part of the play's concern with the ethical interest of attenuated recalls of past actions and their re-enactment.[43] But the issue continues to perplex.

Shakespeare constantly returned to his favourite books, and his responses to many of them changed and deepened over time. *The Winter's Tale*, with its serio-comic texture and bold reworkings of Ovidian myths (Proserpina, Pygmalion) gives a different, and in some respects richer, sense of Ovid than earlier plays. *Macbeth* (for which Shakespeare seems to have prepared himself by reading a number of Seneca's plays, including *Medea* and *Hercules Furens*) is more profoundly Senecan and classical than *Titus* or *Richard III*.

Why did the same process not happen with Virgil? One could adduce a number of possible reasons. First, Shakespeare, though a perfectly competent reader of Latin, liked also to use translations, many of which were indeed engrossing works of literature in their own right, like Golding's Ovid or North's Plutarch. By contrast, apart from the energetic version of the *Aeneid* by Gavin Douglas in Middle Scots, and Surrey's rather stiff blank-verse rendering of *Aeneid* 2 and 4, there were no compelling translations of Virgil available (the Phaer and Twyne complete *Aeneid* in lumbering

fourteeners, standard in the period, is no more than serviceable). Secondly –
and closely linked to this first point – Virgil is an exceptionally difficult poet
to imitate. Perhaps not until Milton did anyone find a wholly satisfactory
English equivalent.[44] Ben Jonson had a classicising view of Virgil as a pure
and restrained writer.[45] It is true that Virgil does not employ the conceits and
verbal coruscations of Ovid, but his verse has extraordinary resonance and
musicality, as he draws endless verbal magic by the artful employment of
ordinary words in unexpected ways (what, according to Donatus' *Life of
Virgil*, an unpersuaded contemporary called *nova cacozelia*, a new form
of stylistic affectation). Jonson's translation, in *Poetaster*, of part of *Aeneid* 4
(a reworking, unwisely, of Surrey's blank verse into rhyming couplets),
which ought to be a climactic moment in the play, is merely rather dull:

> Meanwhile the skies 'gan thunder, and in tail
> Of that fell pouring storms of sleet and hail.
> The Tyrian lords and Troyan youth, each where
> With Venus' Dardan nephew, now in fear
> Seek out for several shelter through the plain,
> Whilst floods come rolling from the hills amain.
>
> (5.2.56–61)

In *Dido, Queen of Carthage* Marlowe is more attractive, but not necessarily more Virgilian, substituting glittering single-line lyric jets for Virgil's
deeper-driven music and mastery of paragraphing:

> I would have given Achates store of gold,
> And Ilioneus gum and Libyan spice,
> The common soldiers rich embroidered coats,
> And silver whistles to control the winds,
> Which Circe sent Sichaeus when he lived . . .
>
> (4.4.7–11)

Not even the finest poetic moments in the play give much sense of Virgil's
Latin:

> Heaven, envious of our joys, is waxen pale;
> And when we whisper, then the stars fall down
> To be partakers of our honey talk.   (4.4.52–4)

Shakespeare, even when the subject matter is Virgilian, seemingly does not
try to reproduce the style of Virgil (except perhaps in the case of Marcus'
speech in *Titus*). The sack of Troy seems to represent an ancient story in
Hamlet, associated with an old-fashioned and to some tastes (though not
Hamlet's) bombastic mode of writing. Scholars often see it as a parody

of a version of epic style – suggestions for the target include Lucan's
Pharsalia, Marlowe's *Dido*, and Phaer's *Aeneid*.[46] But if Shakespeare, 'a kind
of language sponge, a picker-up of specialized lexicons from every conceivable stratum of his society',[47] had wanted to parody something particular,
he could have done so more convincingly. Rather the design – or at any
rate the effect – is to make the verse of the main play seem, by comparison
with this *retardataire* epic mode, modern, naturalistic, and fluent.

Thirdly, Shakespeare is opportunistic in his use of his sources, taking
what he needs for the moment and ignoring the rest. Many of his readers,
even those who have thought him the greatest poet of all, have noted his
unevenness, and comparative lack of concern with formal perfection and
consistency (see David Hopkins' chapter in this book). In other words he
is a different sort of poet from Virgil, who laboured endlessly for perfection. The *Metamorphoses*, with its multiple stories ripe for purloining and
its unclassical form, better suits such a temper than the carefully balanced
structures of the *Aeneid*. Perhaps too Shakespeare preferred Ovidian flexibility to the more rigid models of imperial epic. It has recently been argued that
the iconoclastic Marlowe deliberately adopted a counter-Virgilian *cursus*
in opposition to Spenser who had ostentatiously modelled his career on
Virgil's,[48] and Shakespeare was in many ways Marlowe's heir. Tudeau-
Clayton shows how, in *The Tempest*, Shakespeare cunningly subverts the
Virgilian 'grammar of nature', the analogies between politics and the natural world which we find in a particularly pure form in Jonson's court
masques (as Shakespeare's boatswain says, 'What cares these roarers for the
name of king?', *Tempest* 1.1.16–17).[49] She argues that in Jonson's *Poetaster*
Virgil is a symbol at once of poetic perfection and of stasis, the community
of the same, whereas Ovid stands for adaptability, the possibility of change.
One can see why Shakespeare's preferences might have gone the other way.
And indeed Shakespeare's use of Virgil seems characteristic of his classicism
in general: a matter of complex, fragmentary refraction more than a fully
organised, head-on response in Jonson's manner.

There is a passage in *Henry VIII*, Cranmer's prophecy of the future reign
of Elizabeth, which can be seen as somewhat more Virgilian and Augustan,
both in its politics and in its style:

> In her days every man shall eat in safety
> Under his own vine what he plants, and sing
> The merry songs of peace to all his neighbours.
>   (5.4.33–5)

Interestingly, though, the scholars tend to assign it to Fletcher.

NOTES

1. Charles and Michelle Martindale, *Shakespeare and the Uses of Antiquity: An Introductory Essay* (London and New York 1990), p. 53.
2. For this text ('Upon Master William Shakespeare, the Deceased Author, and his Poems', 11–14) see Commendatory Poems and Prefaces in the *Oxford Shakespeare*, ed. Stanley Wells and Gary Taylor (Oxford 1988), p. xlviii.
3. For an admirable brief introduction to the topic see Stuart Gillespie, *Shakespeare's Books: A Dictionary of Shakespeare Sources* (London and New Brunswick, NJ 2001), pp. 495–506. Still fundamental is T. W. Baldwin, *William Shakspere's Small Latine and Lesse Greeke*, 2 vols. (Urbana, IL 1944) (vol. II, pp. 456–96 on Virgil). Less plausible, though sometimes suggestive, is Robert S. Miola, 'Vergil in Shakespeare: From Allusion to Imitation', in John D. Bernard, ed., *Vergil at 2000: Commemorative Essays on the Poet and his Influence* (New York 1986), pp. 241–59. Two interesting recent studies that emphasise the importance of Virgil to Shakespeare, both New Historicist in character, are Heather James, *Shakespeare's Troy: Drama, Politics, and the Translation of Empire* (Cambridge 1997), and Margaret Tudeau-Clayton, *Jonson, Shakespeare, and Early Modern Virgil* (Cambridge 1998); I am considerably indebted to both. Among the more important Virgilian loci are the following, the first three deriving from *Aeneid* 2: *Rape of Lucrece* 1,366–526 (ecphrasis of the sack of Troy); *Comedy of Errors* 1.1.31–139 (Aegeon's travels); *Hamlet* 2.2.436–521 (the Player's speech); *Tempest* passim. In *2 Henry VI* 2.1.24 Gloucester quotes a famous hemistich from the beginning of the *Aeneid* (1.11): *tantaene animis caelestibus irae?* (of course Shakespeare might have found the line in a text-book, or had it supplied by a friend). It has been claimed that 'fatal engine' in *Titus* 5.3.85 must show knowledge of Virgil's Latin (*fatalis machina*, *Aen.* 2.237), but contemporary parallels include Marlowe, *Dido* 2.1.176 'fatal instrument'. It is rather the pervasiveness of the allusions, as well as the nature of Tudor education, that is persuasive for direct influence.
4. Robert Kilburn Root, *Classical Mythology in Shakespeare*, Yale Studies in English 19 (New York 1965; first published 1903), p. 3.
5. A. D. Nuttall, 'Virgil and Shakespeare', in Charles Martindale, ed., *Virgil and his Influence* (Bristol 1984), pp. 71–93, 73.
6. Leonard Barkan, 'What did Shakespeare Read?', in Margreta de Grazia and Stanley Wells, eds., *The Cambridge Companion to Shakespeare* (Cambridge 2001), pp. 31–47, 43. On this topic see also Robert S. Miola, *Shakespeare's Reading* (Oxford and New York 2000).
7. The others are: *Shrew* 1.1.152; *2 Henry VI* 3.2.117; *Titus* 2.3.22 and 5.3.82; *Dream* 1.1.173; *Romeo and Juliet* 2.3.43; *Merchant* 5.1.10; *Hamlet* 2.2.449; *Tempest* 2.1.76 ff. For Shakespeare and Dido see Roger Savage, 'Dido Dies Again', in Michael Burden, ed., *A Woman Scorn'd: Responses to the Dido Myth* (London 1998), pp. 3–38, 14–18. I have not seen Adrianne Roberts-Baytop, *Dido, Queen of Infinite Literary Variety: The English Renaissance Borrowings and Influences*, Elizabethan and English Renaissance Studies (Salzburg 1974).

8. 'What is a Classic?', in *On Poetry and Poets* (London 1957), pp. 53–71, 62. Eliot returned to the scene again in 'Virgil and the Christian World', ibid., pp. 121–31, 129.

9. Dryden had already tacitly – and tactfully – corrected the 'mistake' in *All For Love*: 'While hand in hand we walk in groves below, / Whole troops of lovers' ghosts shall flock about us, / And all the train be ours' (5.395–7). The editor Theobald cited *Two Noble Kinsmen* 4.3.13–15, where Palamon is imagined as drawing Dido from Aeneas in the next world – but the author is probably Fletcher.

10. Barbara J. Bono, *Literary Transvaluation: From Vergilian Epic to Shakespearean Tragicomedy* (Berkeley 1984), p. 187. See also James, *Shakespeare's Troy*, p. 130.

11. Bono, *Literary Transvaluation*, p. 219.

12. So Harold Bloom, *Shakespeare: The Invention of the Human* (London 1999), p. 550: 'love is justified only as an aesthetic value'.

13. See Diane Perkiss, 'The Queen on Stage: Marlowe's *Dido, Queen of Carthage* and the Representation of Elizabeth I', in Burden, ed., *A Woman Scorn'd*, pp. 151–67. Roy Strong (*Gloriana: The Portraits of Queen Elizabeth I* (London 1987), pp. 101–7) argues that the portrait portrays Elizabeth's single-minded espousal of an imperial mission and thus that she corresponds wholly to Aeneas, who rejected the passionate allurements of Dido for Rome. Possibly that was the intention of whoever devised the iconographic scheme, but, given the association of Eliza and Elissa, the ramifications of the imagery can hardly be kept under quite such easy control.

14. James, *Shakespeare's Troy*, p. 18.

15. Matthew Arnold, 'On the Study of Celtic Literature', in R. H. Super, ed., *Lectures and Essays in Criticism* (Ann Arbor 1962), p. 380 (vol. III of *The Complete Prose Works*). C. S. Lewis (*English Literature in the Sixteenth Century Excluding Drama* (Oxford 1954), pp. 83–4) argued that Virgil is really less 'classical' than many of his admirers have supposed. On that story Chaucer and Shakespeare may have got Virgil 'right'. For an interesting discussion of the issue see Kenneth Haynes, 'Dryden: Classical or Neoclassical?', in Stuart Gillespie, ed., *John Dryden: Classicist and Translator* (Edinburgh 2001), pp. 67–77 (= *Translation and Literature* 10 (2001)).

16. Father M. Owen Lee, 'Unanswered Questions', *Amphora* 1 (2002), 1–3.

17. Pointed out by James, *Shakespeare's Troy*, p. 249, n. 18.

18. See Ann Moss, *Printed Commonplace-Books and the Structuring of Renaissance Thought* (Oxford 1996).

19. John H. Betts, 'Classical Allusions in Shakespeare's *Henry V* with Special Reference to Virgil', *Greece and Rome* 15 (1968), 147–63; James C. Bulman, 'Shakespeare's Georgic Histories', *ShS* 38 (1985), 37–47.

20. Jasper Griffin, 'The Fourth *Georgic*, Virgil and Rome', ch. 8 in *Latin Poets and Roman Life* (London 1985), pp. 163–82.

21. Baldwin, *Shakespeare's Small Latine*, vol. II, pp. 472–8.

22. William Empson, *Seven Types of Ambiguity*, rev. 3rd edn (London and Toronto 1953), p. 113 (first published 1930).

23. The classic essay is E. M. Waith, 'The Metamorphosis of Violence in *Titus Andronicus*', *ShS* 10 (1957), 39–49. See also Leonard Barkan, *The Gods Made Flesh: Metamorphosis and the Pursuit of Paganism* (New Haven and London 1986), pp. 243–51; Martindale, *Shakespeare and the Uses of Antiquity*, pp. 47–56; Jonathan Bate, *Shakespeare and Ovid* (Oxford 1993), pp. 100–17.
24. Root, *Classical Mythology in Shakespeare*, p. 15. Root thought the use of mythology in *Titus* out of line with Shakespeare's normal practice, and used this as an argument against Shakespearean authorship. (Indeed, Brian Vickers has recently restated the argument in favour of Peele's involvement.) Currently the consensus favours the authenticity of the whole of *Titus*, but fashions in these matters change. For Virgil in *Titus* see also Andrew V. Ettin, 'Shakespeare's First Roman Tragedy', *ELH* 37 (1970), 325–41; James, 'Blazoning Injustice: Mutilating Titus Andronicus, Vergil, and Rome', in *Shakespeare's Troy*, ch. 2, pp. 42–84. I am also grateful to students of mine Nancy Alsop, Amanda Hurley, and especially Zenobia Talati for their insights on this topic; also to Professor Niall Rudd for an instructive lecture on the play (see also his essay '*Titus Andronicus*: The Classical Presence', in *ShS*, forthcoming).
25. T. J. B. Spencer, 'Shakespeare and the Elizabethan Romans', *ShS* 10 (1957), 27–38, 32.
26. For the former see Ronald Broude, 'Roman and Goth in *Titus Andronicus*', *ShS* 6 (1970), 27–34.
27. *The Prose Works of Sir Philip Sidney*, ed. Albert Feuillerat, 4 vols. (Cambridge 1968), vol. III, p. 25.
28. So Miola, 'Vergil in Shakespeare', pp. 247–8. In *2 Henry VI* 5.2.61–5 Young Clifford carrying the body of his dead father compares himself to Aeneas; there is an emphasis on the lack of congruence of *exemplum* and event (in Virgil, father Anchises is alive).
29. So Grace Starry West ('Going by the Book: Classical Allusions in Shakespeare's *Titus Andronicus*', *SP* 79 (1982), 62–77) regards the play as an attack on Roman education, while others see rather a critique of education in Tudor England.
30. For an excellent discussion, though without much mention of Virgil, see Edward Berry, *Shakespeare and the Hunt: A Cultural and Social Study* (Cambridge 2001), ch. 3, pp. 70–94; also James, *Shakespeare's Troy*, pp. 55–8.
31. Berry, *Shakespeare and the Hunt*, p. 83.
32. Ibid., p. 94.
33. Robert S. Miola, *Shakespeare's Rome* (Cambridge 1983), p. 204.
34. The case is argued *in extenso* by Donna B. Hamilton, *Virgil and 'The Tempest': The Politics of Imitation* (Columbus, OH 1990). See also Jan Kott, 'The *Aeneid* and *The Tempest*', *Arion* 3 (1978), 425–52; John Pitcher, '"A Theatre of the Future": The *Aeneid* and *The Tempest*', *Essays in Criticism* 34 (1984), 194–215; Robert Wiltenburg, 'The *Aeneid* in *The Tempest*', *ShS* 39 (1986), 159–68; James, *Shakespeare's Troy*, ch. 6; Tudeau-Clayton, *Jonson, Shakespeare, and Early Modern Virgil*, ch. 6.
35. The most certain are as follows: the storm in 1.1 (which recalls, among other storms, that in *Aen.* 1); Ferdinand's greeting of Miranda in 1.2.424 (patterned

on Aeneas' words to Dido, *Aen.* 1.326–34); the discussion of 'widow Dido', 2.1.72 ff.; the Harpies and the banquet, 3.3.18 ff. (which corresponds to an episode in *Aen.* 3.209 ff.; in particular the stage direction 'claps his wings upon the table' translates *quatiunt alas*, 226); elements in the masque in 4.1 (where there is *contaminatio* with Ovid) e.g. 102 'Great Juno comes; I know her by her gait' which translates *Aen.* 1.405, perhaps by way of Marlowe, *Dido, Queen of Carthage* 1.241 'I know her by the movings of her feet'.

36. Pitcher, 'A Theatre of the Future', p. 196. For the Harpies see Baldwin, *Shakspere's Small Latine*, vol. II, pp. 481–4.

37. Hamilton, *Virgil and 'The Tempest'*, p. 40.

38. One example: Hamilton argues that Ferdinand swimming to shore recalls the serpents on their way to destroy Laocoon and his sons (pp. 23–5) – but what conceivable point could there be in such an echo?

39. Frank Kermode, *Shakespeare's Language* (London 2000), p. 295.

40. Pitcher, 'A Theatre of the Future', p. 197. Among his examples is the possible lurking presence of Virgil's Salmoneus who stole Jupiter's fire (*Aen.* 6.585–6) in Prospero's renunciation speech, 5.1.44–6.

41. Hamilton, *Virgil and 'The Tempest'*, p. x.

42. So Bate, *Shakespeare and Ovid*, pp. 239–63.

43. I owe this thought to Colin Burrow, who suggests *per litteras* that Shakespeare is reprising an association between Virgil, memory, and revenge present in *Hamlet*. In both plays the questions 'How do you remember?' and 'How do you re-enact the past?' are replicated in the treatment of Virgil.

44. Spenser was frequently likened to Virgil by Shakespeare's contemporaries; certainly Spenser shares the larger national vision and something of the musicality, but there is a world of difference between his stanzaic form and Virgil's hexameter paragraphs.

45. See *Poetaster*, ed. Tom Cain (Manchester and New York 1995), especially 5.1.75 ff.; Tudeau-Clayton, *Jonson, Shakespeare, and Early Modern Virgil*, pp. 42–3.

46. There is no proof that Shakespeare used Phaer; see Root, *Classical Mythology in Shakespeare*, p. 77 for a possible echo.

47. Barkan, 'What did Shakespeare Read?', p. 45.

48. Patrick Cheney, *Marlowe's Counterfeit Profession: Ovid, Spenser, Counter-Nationhood* (Toronto 1997).

49. Tudeau-Clayton, *Jonson, Shakespeare, and Early Modern Virgil*, ch. 6.

Several people have assisted me in writing this essay: Colin Burrow, Stuart Gillespie, David Hopkins, Tony Nuttall, Liz Prettejohn, Vanda Zajko – to all of them my thanks.

PLAUTUS AND TERENCE

CHAPTER 6

Shakespeare's reception of Plautus reconsidered

Wolfgang Riehle

It has long been recognised that Elizabethan playwrights took many suggestions concerning comic characters, intrigue, and other structural elements from the comedies of Plautus and Terence;[1] Terence is justifiably considered to be the more refined dramatist, to have invented the double plot, and to have made dramaturgic changes so as to create suspense, yet Plautus deserves the greater attention since he stimulated Shakespeare's imagination in many ways.[2] It is not mere chance that he used two of his plays, his *Menaechmi* and *Amphitruo*, as the basis for *The Comedy of Errors*. During the Renaissance Plautus' reputation was great; performances of his works were outstanding events, especially those of the *Menaechmi*. It is possible that as a grammar school pupil Shakespeare himself took part in a performance of one of Plautus' comedies and that as a schoolmaster during his 'lost years' he translated the *Menaechmi*.[3] There is no reason to maintain the old prejudice that Plautus is merely the author of knockabout farces. It is true that in most of his plays he is sceptical about including serious topics of general import, and he prefers to present 'a "Saturnalian" inversion of normal values'.[4] This aspect was first extensively demonstrated by E. Segal[5] who took up suggestions from C. L. Barber's study on the saturnalian element in Shakespeare.[6] That there are serious topics in Plautus, too, can, for example, be clearly seen in his *Captivi*; there a slave, who, in favour of his master, momentarily denies his own identity, pretends to be his master himself. This produces the astonishingly subversive result that the difference between master and slave seems to become irrelevant.[7]

Among the numerous aspects which would merit a closer study from a comparative perspective is, for instance, the role which music is assigned by Plautus and Shakespeare, because Shakespeare must have known that Plautine plays were originally performed as a kind of musical comedy, that soliloquies were sung as *cantica*, and that dialogues were accompanied by a *tibicen* (flute-player), who occasionally even participated in the action (for example in *Stichus*, 713 ff.). This classical model may well have contributed to the great importance of music in Shakespeare's comedies; above all it is the songs which come to mind, and which in *As You Like It* are sung by different characters.[8] In *Hamlet* it can also be seen how well he was informed about even minute Plautine details. The 'Mousetrap', the play within the play performed for Claudius and Gertrude, is ironically called a 'comedy' (3.2.280);[9] since flute-players took part in the performance of a Plautine comedy, the actors about to perform the 'Mousetrap' are accompanied by recorders: 'Come, some music, come, the recorders, / For if the King like not the comedy . . .' (280 ff.). There is no other reason why there should be recorders in this scene. The essential musical quality of Plautus' plays reinforces his stylising tendency by which he sets them one remove from reality. As a master of fiction he takes delight in manipulating characters and situations, and he plays with and suspends dramatic illusion in many ways. As has recently been shown by T. J. Moore, direct rapport with the audience is a fundamental feature of Plautus' comic strategy, and to this end he uses a number of anti-illusionist devices.[10]

In Plautus' plays, a marked distinction can be discerned between the actor's role-playing and his presence as an *actor*: 'Plautus seldom lets his audience forget the position of the actor as actor. The characters who so desire rapport with the spectators are also actors who want their perfor-mance to be noticed and appreciated . . . the spectators are encouraged to respond simultaneously to both actors and characters . . .'[11] The actors have to ensure that the audience understands the action, and a 'real or imagined heckler who professes not to follow' may be teased by playing on the double meaning of a word.'[12] Such wordplay with double mean-ings or with the literal sense of a word as used graphically is common in Plautus.[13]

This obviously has some bearings on the opening of *Romeo and Juliet* where Sampson and Gregory, two servants of the Capulets, engage in a verbal game with puns and quibbles and establish a close rapport with the audience. Their associating metaphoric expressions soon assumes sexual connotations ('maids . . . head – maidenhead; naked sword,' etc., 1.1.20 ff.). When Sampson announces: 'I will be civil with the maids – I will cut off their heads' (21 f.), he, by way of a paradox, indicates that he does not want to use violence; nevertheless his language contains an aggressive potential. The initial verbal game in *Romeo and Juliet* seems to establish the atmosphere of comedy, whilst at the same time it prepares for the ending where the young Juliet will really die. Gregory takes Sampson's punning literally and thus misunderstands (mis-takes) the phrase, which Sampson expressly permits him to do: '*take* it in what sense thou wilt' (22 ff.;

italics mine). Similarly, in *The Two Gentlemen of Verona* Launce understands a metaphor used by Speed in its literal sense, and Speed replies: 'your old vice still, mistake the word . . .' (3.1.279). In an influential essay on this play R. Weimann some decades ago examined the linguistic wordplay of these servants and their close relationship with the audience; he argued that Launce and Speed take their performing energy by which they succeed in making the audience laugh with them solely from the native English popular performance: 'If the comedy of laughing with the audience were to be fitted into a typological scheme . . . it would certainly not be classed among what has traditionally been called "New Comedy"'. In this tradition 'the audience, if indeed it laughs at all, definitely laughs at but never with the comic figure'.[14] Therefore Weimann feels justified in considering 'the clowning figure in the popular drama of the eighties and early nineties . . . the immediate predecessor of Launce'.[15] Launce, he says, is not only played by an actor who is performing this role, but who also as an actor personally establishes contact with the audience. To Weimann all this was achieved by the great popular Clowns, such as Richard Tarlton.[16] Yet, there is evidence that in 1590, a contemporary could, even in the case of Tarlton, be reminded of the *classical* actor Roscius, who was famous for his comic gestures and who is expressly mentioned in *Hamlet* (2.2.391).[17] As we have seen, this supposedly native English, performative, anti-illusionist play is paralleled in Plautine comedy, whose dialogues sometimes culminate in violence. Segal has reminded us recently that the 'shattering of the dramatic illusion' and of the 'actor calling attention to his own theatricality' can even be traced back as far as Aristophanes.[18] Weimann then goes on to pay special attention to Speed's reply quoted above: 'your old vice still, mistake the word . . .' (3.1.279). He argues that with this remark Speed here expressly refers to the popular and very theatrical Vice figure, the tempting character of the native medieval Morality Plays; in his opinion '[t]he allusion . . . is unmistakable'.[19] But are we justified in concluding that Speed here employs the technical term 'Vice' as familiar to theatre historians? Surely there is no indication that Speed uses the word 'vice' in any other than its neutral sense of 'bad habit', his habit of taking a metaphor literally, just as Sampson, in the comic dialogue at the beginning of *Romeo and Juliet*, allows his dialogue partner to do ('take it in what sense thou wilt', 1.1.25). Moreover, Speed's wordplay is different to that for which the Vice is famous, namely playing with two contrasting meanings of one word in order to deceive his victim, as Richard Gloucester claims to do when he converts his grim *aside* on Prince Edward's intelligence into its opposite meaning:

RICHARD GLOUCESTER (*aside*) So wise so young, they say, do never live long.
PRINCE EDWARD What say you, uncle?
RICHARD GLOUCESTER (*aside*) I say, 'Without characters fame lives long.'
   Thus like the formal Vice, Iniquity,
   I moralize two meanings in one word.   (*Richard III* 3.1.79–83)

The most powerful Shakespearean character who is frequently associated
with the Vice-figure is, of course, Iago. Interestingly enough, he fulfills his
destructive work within a tragedy which adopts a number of elements
from comedy, all of them recalling the classical tradition.[20] The play
reverses the fact that '[i]n New Comedy, the wife, not the husband, is the
jealous spouse'.[21] 'Othello is a tragic inversion of the *miles gloriosus*'.[22]
Whereas Iago's decision to destroy his victim by tempting him through
deceptions is initially reminiscent of the Vice, he also exhibits strong connections with the Roman cunning slave; for example, like Pseudolus he is
a brilliantly deceiving liar. Furthermore, it makes good sense to compare
Shakespeare's tragedy with the Plautine play *Miles Gloriosus* because in a
sense 'the situation is the same in both'.[23] In both plays a great soldier is
tricked and conquered by a clever servant; Iago resembles the slave Palaestrio
who wins over the soldier Pyrgopolynices, the great difference being that
Palaestrio remains a comic slave throughout.

   Even a minor detail establishes a significant link. On one occasion
Palaestrio starts a thinking process which he underlines with appropriate conventional gestures. Since his dialogue partner who is watching him
comments on these gestures and thus 'foregrounds' them, we notice them
all. Palaestrio first addresses Periplectomenus: *Paulisper tace, / dum ego mihi
consilia in animum convoco et dum consulo / quid agam* (2.2.196–8; 'Keep
still a moment, sir, while I call my wits to council and confer as to what to
do'), and then his partner comments on what he sees:

> . . . *Illuc sis vide,*
> *quem ad modum adstitit, severo fronte curans cogitans.*
> *pectus digitis pultat . . .*
> *ecce avortit: nixus laevo in femine habet laevam manum,*
> *dextera digitis rationem computat . . .*
> *concrepuit digitis: laborat . . .*
> *ecce autem aedificat: columnam mento suffigit suo . . .*
> *euge, euscheme hercle astitit et dulice et comoedice . . .*
> *habet opinor.*[24] (ll. 200–15)

Just look at him, how he stands there with bent brow, considering and cogitating.
He's tapping his chest with his fingers . . . Aha! Turns away! Rests his left hand on

his left thigh, and reckons on the fingers of his right hand . . . Snaps his fingers!
He's in distress . . . Look, though! . . . He's building – supporting his chin with a
pillar . . . Glorious! A graceful pose, indeed! Just like the slaves in the comedies! . . .
He's got it, I do believe!

This is interesting because when Iago in his soliloquies in the first two
acts is engaged with hatching his intrigue against Othello, he very clearly
assumes the thinking posture of the Roman slave, as Honigmann has already
observed:[25]

>   . . . I hate the Moor,
> And it is thought abroad that 'twixt my sheets
> He has done my office . . .
>   He holds me well:
> The better shall my purpose work on him.
> Cassio's a proper man. Let me see now . . .
>   Let's see . . .
> I ha't. It is ingendered . . .   (1.3.378–96)

Moreover, in all of Iago's soliloquies in the first two acts there is a marked
dichotomy between his consciousness of the spectators, whom he addresses,
and his concentration on himself until he has generated the plan for his
intrigue. This, too, is paralleled in the Roman slaves who may also change
within a single soliloquy between addressing the audience and momentarily concentrating entirely on themselves, forgetting the presence of the
audience, as Moore has shown in his analysis of a soliloquy of the slave
Epidicus.[26] It is, therefore, surprising how distinct the links between the
cunning slave and the dramatic character of Iago really are. Little remains,
then, of the long contested *formal* influence of the dramatic figure of the
Vice on Iago, although in the end Othello recognises in this 'cursèd, cursèd
slave' (5.2.283) 'a devil' (293) with cloven feet.[27]

    The whole question of the role played by classical comedy in the forming
of Elizabethan 'popular' characters acting in close contact with the audience
needs to be freshly reconsidered. Light can be shed by taking a new look at
an important transmitting 'link' between Plautus and Shakespeare, which
has so far been insufficiently examined. For the first time in the history
of English drama, the humanist Nicholas Udall with his comedy *Ralph
Roister Doister* succeeded in writing an English comedy in the classical
style by transforming the Latin 'paradigm' to English conditions. Critical
attention has so far concentrated mainly on the central braggart Roister
Doister, who is a vainglorious fool and thinks every woman who catches
sight of him dotes on him, something, however, that never happens. He

is usually compared with Plautus' Miles Gloriosus in his eponymous play, and with Thraso of the Terentian *Eunuchus*. Here it is his Parasite Matthew Merrygreek who deserves our closer attention. Because of his vitality and playful activity he is generally compared with the medieval Vice; according to W. Tydeman, he is 'less the traditional parasite . . . than a descendant of the medieval Vice . . . whose genius is for the manipulation and temptation of the leading character into imperilling his immortal soul. . . . Merrygreek . . . performs his trickery with the same pert smartness, the same relish for his own cleverness, the same conspiratorial intimacy with the audience'.[28] But does Merrygreek really act as the typical medieval tempter in a morality play or interlude? Certainly not. He supports and later perverts Roister Doister's folly and simply acts jestingly without causing him any real harm. It is true that he reads Roister Doister's love-letter to Dame Christian Custance with the wrong punctuation, thereby absurdly converting its content into an insult (a comic device which Shakespeare imitated with Quince's nonsensical delivery of the Prologue to the artisans' playlet in *A Midsummer Night's Dream*), and, feigning to attack Dame Christian Custance, he hits Roister Doister instead; but these actions are just small practical jokes directed against Roister's boastfulness; and they are used to fulfil the comedy's *corrective* function of exposing the central character's social depravity to ridicule.

The really remarkable thing is that in his comedy Udall himself, as it were, subtly includes a hint concerning a major origin of Merrygreek. This intimation has, however, been totally ignored; Udall adopts the name of Harpax for a minor character from Plautus' *Pseudolus*, a particularly brilliant comedy with regard to '[p]lot, structure, and character',[29] and he seems to have been fascinated by the cunning slave Pseudolus. Like Merrygreek he knows how to enjoy life; he is skilful and nimble in conceiving devices intended for deceptive purposes. He promises Calidorus, who is enamoured of the avaricious and intriguing pimp Ballio's girl Phoenicium, that he will fulfil his desire, which he achieves by cunningly deceiving the pimp. Merrygreek at first pretends to help Roister Doister to a successful wooing of his desired lady; then Merrygreek, as it were, performs mock-actions (including the purposeful mis-reading of Roister Doister's love-letter) in order to prevent Dame Custance and Roister Doister from becoming a married couple. His deceptive activity is surely comparable to Pseudolus' notorious insincerity and cunning. Thus Merrygreek, who is usually defined as a figure in the 'Vice'-tradition, instead owes much to the undiminished vitality of the classical slaves and parasites.

Merrygreek's activity, like that of the Shakespearean servants, often assumes the same improvisatory quality which characterises the Roman slaves. As has recently been recognised, the texts of Plautus' comedies contain a strong popular, 'extempore' element, since he had integrated suggestions from the folk tradition, the *fabulae Atellanae* of his own time and country. This is prominent, for example, in Pseudolus' verbal gaming exuberance which aids him in outdoing Ballio ('*Ballionem exballistabo*', 585). The play *Menaechmi*, too, abounds in situations in which the slave of the traveller twin and the Parasite enjoy what look like improvisatory language games: on some occasions the dialogue seems to deny logical progress because ad hoc thoughts and ideas are played with by what appears as 'ad-libbing', and sometimes a metaphor is continued and extended (*metafora continuata*)[30] by way of association – these in particular are techniques of the popular play acting tradition. Shakespeare took up such linguistic game-playing of the popular tradition for his Dromios; he provides them with ample opportunities for extempore games, for example in act 2 scene 2 the play on 'beat', 'sconce', 'dry basting', as it develops by way of association. Much of what so far has been attributed to a native English popular and 'oral' tradition of performing vitality must now be seen to have been transmitted through a 'literary' reception of the printed texts of the Plautine comedies, as they had preserved a very old Italian popular dramatic energy in *written* form.[31] This is of course not to deny the fact that the Dromios also in various ways perform their comic activities along individual lines of their native dramatic forebears, and that there are some parallels between the Dromios and the zany characters of the *commedia dell'arte* which continued the old Italian popular tradition *in the theatre*. What we have is an amalgamation of different influences,[32] yet the classical contribution to the development of Shakespearean comedy has been considerably underrated.

It is therefore advisable to reconsider the theory fashionable today that the entire *Comedy of Errors* is to be understood in terms of the native medieval and Christian tradition.[33] Does Shakespeare himself not suggest a Christian interpretation by introducing an Abbess, who replaces the goddess Diana in the *Apollonius of Tyre*, the source for the framing action, and who is essential for the resolution of the plot? The answer to this must be that this change cannot be taken as a deliberately Christian emphasis because it had already been made in the version by which Shakespeare became familiar with this source, Gower's *Confessio Amantis*. It is true that in *The Comedy of Errors* we hear of Satan, Adam and Eve, beads, the medieval image of hell, etc., yet these motifs, so familiar to the audience, become part of the comic play: for example, Dromio of Syracuse integrates the figure of Satan into his comic performance when he encounters the Courtesan (4.3.49 ff.),[34] and when Dr Pinch 'exorcizes' Satan from Antipholus, the audience knows, of course, that there is no spirit to be exorcised. Does this kind of playfully incorporating Christian themes not signify a remarkable freedom in their treatment?[35]

A close examination of this play shows that, rather than presenting medieval and specifically Christian aspects, Shakespeare on various levels combined them with classical elements in his play. This also applies to Ephesus as the locality of *The Comedy of Errors*. If we bear in mind that it suggested itself through the romance of *Apollonius of Tyre*, and that it occurs in the Plautine *Miles Gloriosus* as well, we cannot agree with Greenblatt and many others that Shakespeare's choice of Ephesus as the locality of the action is 'highly revealing'.[36] It is more important to point out that here, too, Shakespeare seems to follow Plautus who preserves the Greek setting of New Comedy for his own fictional world of the *fabulae palliatae*, the plays in Greek dress. Yet the audience of a Plautine comedy is also occasionally made aware of parallels to their own lives in *Rome* or of specifically *Roman* conditions,[37] a dramaturgy not to be found in Terence.[38] To a certain extent Shakespeare's strategy is strikingly similar to Plautus. As is well known, almost all his comedies take place in a distant locality. *A Midsummer Night's Dream* prefers Athens and thus alludes to the very origins of the New Comedy tradition, and yet the audience is reminded of their own reality.

In *The Comedy of Errors* the fact that Shakespeare's audience was familiar through St Paul with Ephesus as a city replete with sorcerers and exorcists was ideal for Shakespeare because it served his artistic intention of simultaneously 'engaging' as well as 'detaching' the audience; they had some familiarising information about this city, yet it was basically pagan, with the temple of Diana at its centre. The assumption that Shakespeare used the locality of Ephesus as a special allusion to St Paul's teaching on marriage in his *Letter to the Ephesians*, namely that the wife has to submit herself to her husband, is not very convincing because it is of course valid for the patriarchal society in Roman comedy, too; and the reactions of the Roman Matrona and the Elizabethan wife in our two texts are comparable. Whereas in *Menaechmi* the Parasite Peniculus advises the jealous Matrona to use her husband in such a way that he feels miserable (569), the jealous Adriana has maltreated her Antipholus by constantly keeping him from sleeping at night because of her reproaches and suspicions. Adriana's allusion to the idea of marriage as a bodily union of husband and wife is indeed a Pauline concept, yet Shakespeare's comedy confines itself to a secularising allusion to it, since nowhere does it mention St Paul's Christian sanctification of the marriage union by symbolising Christ's love for his Church: 'Husbands, love your wives, even as Christ also loved the church, and gave himself for it' (*Letter to the Ephesians* 5.25).[39] Furthermore, the Abbess' invitation to a 'gossips' feast' (5.1.408) is not given any significance as a sacramental baptism or a Christian rebirth, and the twins retain their names, whereas one of the Plautine Menaechmi regains his original name Sosicles. We therefore have to conclude that the alleged new Christian elements in *The Comedy of Errors* seem to agree fairly well with the nature of Roman comedy, which by no means appears to be 'cold at heart',[40] if performed. It would be wrong to claim that Shakespeare refined his source, the classical comedy of identity, because *The Comedy of Errors* contains, for example, a much stronger element of violence; it is therefore nearer the truth to state that he enormously *intensified* it by providing it with a far greater complexity.

The really significant theme in *The Comedy of Errors* is the experience of two pairs of twins that human identity can only be maintained through its acceptance by society. Renaissance dramatists, including Shakespeare, obviously not only realised the comic *and* the tragic potential contained in the subject of a mis-identification of twins, they may also have felt its immediate impact for an age in which the theme of the singularity of the human individual became so important. In Greek New Comedy there are at least three plays in which twins are among the *dramatis personae*,[41] and this is important because it was Plautus who for the first time introduced into world literature the theme of the loss of human identity,[42] and who in his wonderful *Amphitruo*, which may be an entirely original creation,[43] even doubled the problem of lost identity by repeating it in Sosia, Amphitruo's popular servant. He thus succeeded in making the play interesting for a wide and mixed audience, as is also familiar to us from the structure of Shakespeare's comedies. In order that he may enjoy Alcumena sexually, Jupiter and his 'servant' Mercury take the shape of Amphitruo and his slave Sosia. This develops into a climax of confusions; Sosia is in danger of losing himself, Amphitruo feels deprived of his identity, and Alcumena experiences moments of tragic intensity when she is suspected by her husband of having committed adultery, whereas she 'only' enjoyed Jupiter in Amphitruo's shape.[44] Such mistakings of identity could only happen in a distanced and un-real world, yet a world in which these confusions appear to be at least credible and conceivable, that is, a world of art. Plautus' brilliant slave Pseudolus articulates this artistic principle, when on one occasion he compares his own deceiving activity with the work of the poet: both, he says, are fiction and therefore lies; yet he nevertheless claims that the poet has to construct his fictional world according to the law of credibility: *Facit illud veri simile, quod mendacium est.* (*Pseudolus*, 401; '(the poet's weaving) makes a lie look like the truth').[45] Since in *Amphitruo* the confusion of identity almost develops into tragedy, things have to be redressed and a comedic closure has to be arranged by Jupiter's epiphany. Plautus dares to break through the conventional borders of genre as he realises the advantage of a mixed genre, what he rightly calls *tragicomoedia* (59). No matter how we interpret this much discussed term, it is clear that the play *Amphitruo* must have had a deep impact on Shakespeare and that this new term *tragicomoedia*, along with specific Italian influences, encouraged a tendency within him to which he was always inclined right up to the end of his career – the tendency to reach beyond and transcend the narrow confines of a single dramatic genre.

In *The Comedy of Errors* things happen which indeed go far beyond the realm of farce. As in *Amphitruo* we are confronted with a world which is not 'real' but utopian and nevertheless 'possible'. Egeon has to prepare himself for impending death before he is given a new life. Adriana, who realises that her marriage is in danger, suspects her husband of adultery, and he, having constantly been denied his identity by the sequence of confusions, is on the point of breaking down and of losing himself, much like the major characters in *Amphitruo*. Antipholus of Syracuse as well as his Dromio also become estranged from and in conflict with reality;[46] the Antipholi are even afraid of going mad, a prime theme in Shakespeare, and one that also produces great dramatic moments both in *Menaechmi* and *Amphitruo*.[47] In a way comparable to *Amphitruo*, the play dramatises the questions: 'What is the self? What are the guarantees of identity?'[48]

If in *Amphitruo* a *deus ex machina* is required for the prevention of tragedy, *The Comedy of Errors* needs the appearance of an entirely unexpected character – the Abbess; yet there is nothing which would suggest that she functions as a *dea ex machina* by personifying the specific providence of the Christian God.[49] The idea of providence is only vaguely suggested, the Abbess herself twice refers to the 'worldly' concept of fortune (5.1.363, 398), which she also has been subject to, and furthermore it has to be considered that divine providence is a theme not unknown in classical comedy (for example in the Plautine *Rudens*). For the characters in the play the real authority is the 'secular' Duke who had brought Adriana and Antipholus together. It is interesting that he knows his *Odyssey*, because, like Plautine characters,[50] he indirectly alludes to it when he thinks that the confusions have been caused by a drink 'of Circe's cup' (271). When he identifies one of the twins as the other's 'genius', a nice parallel is opened up with the situation when in *Menaechmi* Peniculus exuberantly calls his master his *genius* (138). The Duke thinks in classical images as well as concepts: when he begins to realise that it is more commendable to react to guilt with mercy than by exerting justice, he does not adopt a specifically Christian perspective, but follows the advice of Cicero and Seneca to men in power that they should exert clemency.[51]

Shakespeare's *Comedy of Errors*, which fascinates the audience with increasingly turbulent action, terminates in an unspectacular, though beautiful '*coda*'. The two Dromios, as popular twin servants, are the only remaining characters on stage in close contact with the audience; they now playfully decide to 'cast lots' in order to solve the comic 'problem' of who has the prior claim to enter the priory. Shakespeare couldn't have invented a closing situation more appropriate to his 'classical' play, because with their intended little game of casting lots the Dromios, who have much in common with the Roman comic slaves, jestingly allude to Fortune or *Tyche*, who 'generates' the action of classical comedy; for example, in the Plautine *Casina*, based on a Greek New Comedy play by Diphilus, a casting of lots is given central importance because it is to decide which of the two wooing slaves shall have the girl Casina (268). The real conclusion of *The Comedy of Errors* is, however, brought about by the Dromios changing their minds: instead of casting lots they leave the stage hand in hand, thus suggesting with a final gesture familial and general human solidarity. In this play it is the Roman virtue of familial *pietas* as well as favourable Fortune or *Tyche* which have brought about the family reunion. Thus, the very end of this play impressively documents Shakespeare's deep understanding of the nature of classical comedy.

NOTES

1. For studies of Plautus and Terence, see, for example, G. E. Duckworth, *The Nature of Roman Comedy: A Study in Popular Entertainment* (Princeton, 1952, 2nd edn Bristol 1994); E. Segal, *Roman Laughter: The Comedy of Plautus* (Cambridge, MA 1968); N. Zagagi, *Tradition and Originality in Plautus* (Göttingen 1980); D. Konstan, *Roman Comedy* (Ithaca 1983); R. L. Hunter, *The New Comedy of Greece and Rome* (Cambridge 1985); N. W. Slater, *Plautus in Performance: The Theatre of the Mind* (Princeton 1985); S. M. Goldberg, *Understanding Terence* (Princeton 1986); M. v. Albrecht, *Geschichte der römischen Literatur*, 2 vols. (München 1994), vol. I.
2. See especially W. Riehle, *Shakespeare, Plautus, and the Humanist Tradition* (Woodbridge 1990), and Robert S. Miola, *Shakespeare and Classical Comedy: The Influence of Plautus and Terence* (Oxford 1994).
3. This is suggested by A. Burgess, *Shakespeare* (London 1996), p. 45.
4. E. Segal, *The Death of Comedy* (Cambridge, MA 2001), p. 189.
5. See Segal, *Roman Laughter*.

6. C. L. Barber, *Shakespeare's Festive Comedy* (Princeton, NJ 1959).

7. See Albrecht, *Geschichte*, vol. i, p. 162.

8. See, for example, J. H. Long, *Shakespeare's Use of Music: A Study of Seven Comedies* (Gainesville 1955).

9. All Shakespeare quotations are taken from *The Complete Oxford Shakespeare*, ed. S. Wells and G. Taylor (Oxford 1987).

10. See T. J. Moore, *The Theatre of Plautus: Playing to the Audience* (Austin, TX 1998).

11. Ibid., p. 49.

12. Ibid., p. 17.

13. See Albrecht, *Geschichte*, vol. i, p. 154; for more examples see Duckworth, *Roman Comedy*, p. 350 ff.

14. Weimann, 'Laughing with the Audience: *The Two Gentlemen of Verona* and the Popular Tradition of Comedy', *ShS* 22 (1969), 35–42, esp. 35; see also his book, *Shakespeare and the Popular Tradition in the Theatre*, trans. R. Schwartz (Baltimore 1978).

15. Ibid., p. 39.

16. Ibid., p. 38.

17. Roscius is also mentioned in the Anonymous *Tarltons Newes out of Purgatorie (1590)* (Cambridge 1997): 'after his death mourned in conceit, and absented my selfe from all plaies, as wanting that merry Roscius of Plaiers, that famozed all Comedies so with his pleasant and extemporall inuention' (p. 2 f.). I am obliged to Dr Hugo Keiper for suggesting this text to me.

18. Segal, *Death of Comedy*, p. 52.

19. See Weimann, 'Laughing with the Audience', p. 39.

20. S. Snyder, *The Comic Matrix of Shakespeare's Tragedies* (Princeton, NJ 1979), pp. 70–90.

21. F. Teague, 'Othello and New Comedy', in *Acting Funny: Comic Theory and Practice*, ed. F. Teague (Rutherford 1994), p. 32.

22. Ibid., p. 34.

23. Ibid., p. 36.

24. *Plautus*, ed. and trans. P. Nixon, 5 vols. (Cambridge, MA 1970), vol. iii.

25. E. A. J. Honigmann, ed., *Othello* (London 1996), p. 160 ff., ns. 391, 402.

26. Moore, *Theatre of Plautus*, p. 37.

27. B. Spivack already admitted that there is 'no longer the coarse hilarity of the Vice of old', *Shakespeare and the Allegory of Evil* (New York 1958), p. 434.

28. W. Tydeman, ed., *Four Tudor Comedies* (London 1984), p. 25; cf. also Spivack: Merrygreek 'is sharply modified by the very English quality of the Vice . . . he is the Vice transferred to farce' (*Shakespeare*, pp. 319 and 321).

29. Moore, *Theatre of Plautus*, p. 96.

30. See E. Stärk, *Die Menaechmi des Plautus und kein griechisches Original* (Tübingen 1989), pp. 83 and 75.

31. See J. Blänsdorf, quoted by W. Hofmann, ed., *Plautus: Truculentus* (Darmstadt 2001), p. 9. It must be admitted that this new approach of the Freiburg school

of classical scholars now sometimes tends to overemphasise the presence of the improvisatory element in Plautus.

32. Cf. Miola, *Shakespeare and Classical Comedy*, pp. 14 ff.

33. For example by A. F. Kinney, 'Shakespeare's *Comedy of Errors* and the Nature of Kinds', *SP* 85 (1988), 29–52.

34. See also Riehle, *Shakespeare, Plautus and the Humanist Tradition*, pp. 198 ff.

35. The fact that on one occasion Antipholus of Syracuse speaks of himself as a 'Christian' (1.2.77) certainly cannot be given any significance, since he obviously uses the term for the sake of emphasis.

36. S. Greenblatt, in his interpretation of the play in *The Norton Shakespeare*, ed. S. Greenblatt *et al.* (New York 1997), p. 685.

37. Moore, for example, *Theatre of Plautus*, p. 143; Albrecht, *Geschichte*, vol. 1, p. 158.

38. See Segal, *Death of Comedy*, p. 223.

39. See Greenblatt, who points out that 'there seems to be no particularly uplifting lesson to be learned' (p. 687).

40. Greenblatt, in *Norton Shakespeare*, p. 684.

41. See Segal, *Death of Comedy*, p. 191.

42. See Stärk, *Menaechmi*, p. 128.

43. On this point cf. T. Baier, ed., *Studien zu Plautus' Amphitruo* (Tübingen 1999).

44. See Albrecht, *Geschichte*, p. 135.

45. See Moore, *Theatre of Plautus*, p. 98.

46. See Greenblatt, in *Norton Shakespeare*, p. 684.

47. See Stärk, *Menaechmi*, p. 105.

48. Greenblatt, in *Norton Shakespeare*, p. 684.

49. See ibid., p. 687.

50. See, for example, *Epidicus*, vol. 11, p. 604.

51. See, for example, Cicero, *De Re Publica* 2.14 (27) or Seneca's tract *De Clementia*.

My thanks are due to Sarah Mercer for valuable suggestions.

CHAPTER 7

Shakespeare, Plautus, and the discovery of New Comic space

Raphael Lyne

At Melania, every time you enter the square, you find yourself caught in a dialogue: the braggart soldier and the parasite coming from a door meet the young wastrel and the prostitute; or else the miserly father from the threshold utters his final warnings to the amorous daughter and is interrupted by the foolish servant who is taking a note to the procuress. You return to Melania after years and you find the same dialogue still going on; in the meanwhile the parasite has died, and so have the procuress and the miserly father; but the braggart soldier, the amorous daughter, the foolish servant have taken their places, being replaced in their turn by the hypocrite, the confidante, the astrologer.[1]

> haec urbs Epidamnus est, dum haec agitur fabula;
> quando alia agetur, aliud fiet oppidum.
> sicut familiae quoque solent mutarier:
> modo hic habitat leno, modo adulescens, modo senex,
> pauper, mendicus, rex, parasitus, hariolus.
>
> (72–6; vol. II, p. 370)[2]

(This city is Epidamnus, during the presentation of this play; when another play is presented it will become another town. It is quite like the way in which families, too, are wont to change their homes: now a pimp lives here, now a young gentleman, now an old one, now a poor man, a beggar, a king, a parasite, a seer.)

Calvino's character types are recognisably those of Greek and Roman New Comedy; his image of a city landscape that remains constant while the people within it change within strict limits is even anticipated by Plautus' Prologue to *Menaechmi*. In both cases there is a sense that the variety of human actions is played out within a fixed location that in some way determines a restricted range of possibilities. Shakespeare's versions of this New Comic cityscape owe a great deal to Plautus, and are remarkably varied: the Ephesus of *The Comedy of Errors*, the Illyria of *Twelfth Night*, and the non-urban island of *The Tempest*.[3] He encounters the complexity of what seems like a straightforward world – a city street, one or two houses, perhaps a shrine – and sees the implied processes, artistic and political, by which such a world is created. It is a world defined by theory (in Aristotle and post-Aristotle) and by practice (in classical tragedy as well as comedy): yet in neither case is the rationale straightforward. Its characteristics are summed up in the three traditional 'Unities', of which two, the Unity of Time and the Unity of Place, set out that the drama can only cover approximately one day, or a few hours, and only one location. (The third Unity, of Action, defines the need for a single complete story, and is therefore somewhat different.)

Plautine stage space is confined but within it there is room to manoeuvre, overhear, spy, etc.; it also has large horizons. Characters leave the visible area purposefully, heading to the forum or often to the harbour (and of course they can come back). Not only in *Rudens*, a sea-shore shipwreck play, is the sea visible to the onstage characters – in *Trinummus*, for example, Charmides addresses his thanks to *multipotenti* and *saltipotenti Neptuno* ('omnipotent and salt-ipotent Neptune') while looking back to the harbour (820–36; vol. v, pp. 176–8). In *Menaechmi* Sosicles reflects, as he walks onto the stage:

> voluptas nullast navitis, Messenio,
> maior meo animo, quam quom ex alto procul
> terram conspiciunt.   (226–8; vol. ii, p. 388)

(There is no pleasure sailors have, in my opinion, Messenio, greater than sighting from the deep the distant land.)

The imagined viewpoint takes in a huge vista, yet the character is entering the confined land-space. In addition, the unseen architecture is not as fixed as that which is seen, as in *Miles Gloriosus*:

> nam unum conclave, concubinae quod dedit
> miles, quo nemo nisi eapse inferret pedem,
> in eo conclavi ego perfodi parietem,
> qua commeatus clam esset hinc huc mulieri.
> (140–3; vol. iii, pp. 134–6)

(You see the soldier gave his girl one room in which no one but herself was to set foot, and I dug a hole through the wall of this room, so providing a secret passage for her from this house into that one.)

This is a handy way of deceiving the swaggering soldier Pyrgopolynices, but it also indicates the potential of the Plautine world. The plays represent their small-scale scenes in dynamic positions, between city affairs and foreign travel, and liable to redefinition and alteration. There is one aberration of Plautine time and space, incidental here though meaningful to later theorists. It comes in *Captivi*, when Hegio's trip from Aetolia to Elis and back takes an implausibly short time.

Rudens represents an expansion of the usual horizons in Plautus: the setting is a rocky shore where key characters are shipwrecked. Their precarious situation is matched by a marginal location, the home of an exile. Ampelisca's first reflection on her plight sets up this unusual quality:

> ita hic sola solis locis compotita sum.
> hic saxa sunt, hic mare sonat,
> neque quisquam homo mihi obviam venit.
> hoc quod induta sum, summae opes oppido.
> nec cibo nec loco tecta quo sim scio:
> quae mihist spes, qua me vivere velim?
> nec loci gnara sum, nec vidi aut hic fui.
> saltem aliquem velim qui mihi ex his locis
> aut viam aut semitam monstret, ita nunc
> hac an illac eam, incerta sum consili;
> nec prope usquam hic quidem cultum agrum conspicor.
>
>   (205–14; vol. IV, p. 306)

(Oh, to be alone in this lonely place! Nothing but those rocks and that roaring sea, and not a living soul in sight! These clothes that I have on are absolutely everything that I own, and where to go for food and shelter I can't see. What have I left to live for now? I don't know this place, never saw it, never came here. If there was someone at least to show me a road or a path out of here! As it is now, I can't tell whether to go this way, or that. And there's no land about here anywhere that looks cultivated, either.)

The stage turns out to be less empty than she thinks; it includes the house of Daemones, and both a temple and an altar dedicated to Venus. Ampelisca here conjures up an unfamiliar space, protesting too much perhaps, but nevertheless asserting the danger of an environment she cannot comprehend. Reading *Rudens* after several other Plautus plays can create the impression of a dramatist moving into a less constrained medium, but some of his characters have a negative experience of that change.

The unusual combination of comedy and romance in *Rudens* has been seen by critics as important to Shakespeare's treatments of Plautus.[4] Its special character may contribute to the extra notes of anxiety and disorientation in *Comedy of Errors*, in comparison with its more direct source *Menaechmi*. It may also explain Viola's swift decision to dress as a eunuch (or boy) in *Twelfth Night* as a sharp intertextual connection with her predecessor Ampelisca: the shipwrecked woman opts (with a speed of insight that resists easy explanation) to remove herself from the sexual danger that afflicts Plautine predecessors.[5] In Shakespearean romance the hints from *Rudens* are just as telling as in comedy. There are similarities most of all with *The Tempest* in plot (shipwreck, lost children, exiled father) and in mood (loss, confusion, strangeness).[6]

Shakespeare's use of the New Comic space in his experimentation with the Three Unities is evident in three plays: *The Comedy of Errors*, *Twelfth Night*, and *The Tempest*. Only the first truly emulates the limits of Plautine drama, but the others repeat plot features that show Shakespeare working within a version of its stage world, but uncovering, as his characters are discovering, the way such a world works. In *The Comedy of Errors* Shakespeare brings the limits of the drama to the surface. In his framing story, the limit of the performance is corroborated by a defined stay of execution:

> DUKE Therefore, merchant, I'll limit thee this day
> To seek thy health by beneficial help.
> Try all the friends thou hast in Ephesus:
> Beg thou or borrow to make up the sum,
> And live. If no, then thou art doomed to die.
> Jailer, take him to thy custody.
> JAYLOR I will, my lord.
> MER. Hopeless and helpless doth Egeon wend,
> But to procrastinate his lifeless end.
> (*CE* 1.1.150–8)

The Duke's verdict is conventional and convenient enough, but Egeon's reaction puts an interesting stress upon it. 'Procrastinate' literally means, of course, to put off until tomorrow – but it is not only used of a single fixed tomorrow. Here the word is used with an ironic accuracy, as the word means precisely what it says. Shakespeare seems to savour the Latin etymology (*cras* is tomorrow) and thereby to sharpen the presence of the play's timescale. This sharpening can be seen elsewhere:

> MER. This very day a Syracusian merchant [. . .]
> Dies ere the weary sun set in the west.
> There is your money that I had to keep.
> ANT. Go bear it to the Centaur, where we host,
> And stay there, Dromio, till I come to thee.
> Within this hour it will be dinner-time.
> Till that, I'll view the manners of the town.
> (*CE* 1.2.3, 7–12)

Now the execution might happen the same evening, rather than tomorrow: even precise procrastination could be denied to Egeon. More important,

here, is the decision of Antipholus to mark out the same timescale in his
inquisitive wandering. The scope of the drama is given a greater presence, as the pressing sense of time of the father is contrasted with the
leisurely approach of his son. The temporal structure of the play has its
final emphasis when the Abbess (the lost wife and mother) addresses the
two slaves named Dromio as 'calendars' of her sons' 'nativity' (5.1.407).
The Abbess is conscious of the scope of the unfolding of the action and
stresses the day of the play's duration. So the characteristic time and space
of New Comedy become the focus of attention here, as they do in Shakespeare's other examinations of those same proportions. In all cases the
stage space is not a familiar one for key characters: they experience it not
as a predictable city world, but as something very strange, dreamlike, or
magical.

Robert Miola sees *Twelfth Night* as a development, along New Comic
lines, from *The Comedy of Errors*. In particular, he sees a further enrichment
of the significance of the constrained scope of time and space: 'The conventional setting of Roman comedy thus suggests in *Twelfth Night* interior
states of characters. Orsino and Olivia are locked-in, entrapped in self-
absorbed vanities.'[7] A contemporary observer, John Manningham, made
the connection when he recorded in his diary for February 1602 that the
play was 'much like the commedy of errors or Menechmi in plautus', and
also like 'that in Italian called Inganni'.[8] In *Twelfth Night* the scope of the
play again becomes an issue, though here there is an interesting discrepancy
between the feeling of Unity in Time and Place and the fact that Viola's
stay in Illyria lasts three months, though much of the action is compressed
in the New Comic style. As in the earlier play, time-schemes are overlaid
on one another: Antonio complains about 'the danger of this adverse town'
(5.1.84) and how what was familiar 'not half an hour before' (92) can so
quickly become 'a twenty years removed thing' (89). This contrast is an
exaggeration of the real situation:

DUKE When came he to this town?
ANT. Today, my lord, and for three months before,
    No int'rim, not a minute's vacancy,
    Both day and night did we keep company.
                          (*TN* 5.1.90–3)

This double time-scheme in Antonio's encounter with the mysteries of
Illyria helps emphasise the compressed strangeness of the action. His reaction is to feel wronged and hurt, a rather different reaction from that of

Viola. Her reaction to Antonio's anger shows a characteristic combination
of perceptive practicality and whimsical dreaminess:

> Methinks his words do from such passion fly
> That he believes himself. So do not I.
> Prove true, imagination, O prove true,
> That I, dear brother, be now ta'en for you!
>
> (*TN* 3.4.365–8)

Viola's encounter with Illyria tends to be carried out with both resourceful-
ness and perplexity. The distraction of her very first lines, however, contrasts
with her usual sharp engagement with the world of New Comedy:

> VIO. What country, friends, is this?
> CAP. This is Illyria, lady.
> VIO. And what should I do in Illyria?
>   My brother, he is in Elysium.
>   Perchance he is not drown'd. What think you sailors?
> CAP. It is perchance that you yourself were saved.
> VIO. O my poor brother! – and so perchance may he be.
>
> (*TN* 1.2.1–6)

Her first question is a simple one, for information, but her response to the
answer is complex. She asks rhetorically what is a genuine question; she
then plays on the names Illyria/Elysium; then the wordplay continues as she
and the Captain quibble on the positive or negative potential in the word
'perchance'. She comes across as having a kind of generic self-consciousness,
a reluctance to enter but also a skilfulness in exploiting the New Comic
setting.

The exploitation of a version of the New Comic setting by a character is
seen in *The Tempest*, where Prospero manipulates the boundaries of space
and time by means of his magical power. In *The Tempest* it becomes clearer
than in *The Comedy of Errors* or *Twelfth Night* that the nature of such a
location, like any location, can be attributed to political processes. The
role of power in defining the interactions between characters and their
worlds, however, is an issue in the earlier comedies too. Elliot Krieger's
Marxist reading of *Twelfth Night* sees Illyria and its mood to be created
by the ruling ideology and the privileged fantasy of a drifting existence.
As he says, the assertion that 'all is fortune' works against social change
by denying, falsely, humans' ability to shape their social world.[9] Krieger's
analysis is aimed against an idealised image of Shakespeare's 'second-world'
comedies, in which these worlds are seen to liberate all characters from

social constraints. Servants and other subordinates are all too often tied to 'everyday demands and restrictions of time, space, and degree'.[10]

The Plautine locations of *The Comedy of Errors*, *Twelfth Night*, and *The Tempest* are not second worlds in so clear a sense as the forests of *As You Like It* or *A Midsummer Night's Dream*, yet they do all involve a discrepancy in different characters' ability to explore and adapt. Krieger's most important point in this context is that dramatic settings can be read as being produced by social and political dynamics, rather than as having some kind of insulation from such real concerns. This ties in usefully with an idea Douglas Bruster has about the different balances of power in Shakespeare and Plautus:

Changing the social relationships of the comedic model which he inherited, Shakespeare consistently pushed agency upwards on the social scale. In the politics of this revision, Shakespeare stresses a deference to political authority that goes far beyond a merely aesthetic transformation of his dramatic sources.[11]

The character who holds most agency and flexibility in Plautus is often the *servus* (slave); in Shakespeare things are different. The slaves of *The Comedy of Errors* are as beleaguered as anyone; in *Twelfth Night* it is Viola who manoeuvres with greatest skill, and the servant Malvolio who acts rigidly; in *The Tempest* it is Prospero, a refraction of another Plautine character type, the *senex* (old man), who is most effective. Ariel and Caliban, functionaries with opposite strengths, are remnants of the power of the *servus*, but they are thoroughly controlled by their master. Indeed, it is possible to see *The Tempest* as a play with many New Comic plot features which are radically distorted by the power of the *senex*. Prospero causes the shipwreck, keeps the lovers and servants (most of the time) under tight control, and indeed orchestrates all the solutions. This distortion is neither simply negative nor simply positive, nor is it straightforwardly conservative: Prospero's power defies easy moral evaluation.

In *The Tempest* in particular Shakespeare's version of the New Comic world is an openly contrived and engineered location that owes its origin to artistic contrivance and to power structures represented or implied within the play. This can be understood both in relation to Marxist and post-modern ideas of space, and in relation to Renaissance theory of dramatic location.[12] David Riggs is one of the few modern critics to deal with the elusive issues surrounding the Unities.[13] For him, the key theorists are Aristotle, Horace, and Lodovico Castelvetro, the sixteenth-century commentator on the *Poetics*. Riggs is alive to the strangeness of the doctrine and the fact that the main exponents do not provide a thorough rationale, nor one which seems to have dominated practice. Most importantly of all, Riggs sees the fact that the Unities can appear as something produced within the play, rather than preceding its action: 'Prospero's artificial day [. . .] is the medium in which he exhibits mastery over that reality'.[14] *The Tempest* is a play in which the Unities are more about mastery than about reality; yet the theory of the Unities that would have been available to Shakespeare approaches these conventions as innocent practicalities. Indeed, theory provides almost disappointing justifications and rationales for the dramatic Unities of Time and Place. Hence the usefulness of analysing it in combination with modern theories of space.

It is well established (as in Riggs) that the specifics of the theory, though usually thought of as Aristotelian, derive from Castelvetro's reading of the *Poetics* rather than from the *Poetics* themselves. Castelvetro believed his model was an unfinished work, and therefore in need of expansion and clarification. Accordingly he adds specificity:

La tragedia la quale conuiene hauere per soggetto vn' attione auenuta in picciolo spatio di luogo & in picciolo spatio di tempo, cio è in quel luogo & in quel tempo doue & quando i rappresentatori dimorano occupati in operatione, & non altroue, ne in altro tempo.[15]

(Tragedy works best when it has for its subject an action that happens in a small space and over a short time – that is, in a space no larger than the stage occupied by the actors, and for a duration no longer than the time for which they occupy the stage.)

The detail of this restriction is not an abuse of the *Poetics* but it is not in its idiom as it survives. Aristotle emphasises sensible proportion with some of the same goals as Castelvetro: credibility and memorability. However, when emphasising beauty as an equally valid motivation for dramatic conventions, he offers bolder yet more opaque limits:

ἔτι δ' ἐπεὶ τὸ καλὸν καὶ ζῷον καὶ ἅπαν πρᾶγμα ὃ συνέστηκεν ἐκ τινῶν οὐ μόνον ταῦτα τεταγμένα δεῖ ἔχειν ἀλλὰ καὶ μέγεθος ὑπάρχειν μὴ τὸ τυχόν· τὸ γὰρ καλὸν ἐν μεγέθει καὶ τάξει ἐστίν, διὸ οὔτε πάμμικρον ἄν τι γένοιτο καλὸν ζῷον (συγχεῖται γὰρ ἡ θεωρία ἐγγὺς τοῦ ἀναισθήτου χρόνου γινομένη) οὔτε παμμέγεθες (οὐ γὰρ ἅμα ἡ θεωρία γίνεται ἀλλ' οἴχεται τοῖς θεωροῦσι τὸ ἓν καὶ τὸ ὅλον ἐκ τῆς θεωρίας), οἷον εἰ μυρίων σταδίων εἴη ζῷον.[16]

(Besides, a beautiful object, whether an animal or anything else with a structure of parts, should have not only its parts ordered but also an appropriate magnitude: beauty consists in magnitude and order, which is why there could not be a beautiful animal which was either minuscule (as contemplation of it, occurring in an almost imperceptible moment, has no distinctness) or gigantic (as contemplation of it has no cohesion, but those who contemplate it lose a sense of unity and wholeness), say an animal a thousand miles long.)

Like his successor Horace in the *Ars Poetica* Aristotle insists, in a genial tone, on proportion, aiming to avoid two similar undesirable outcomes, incredulity and disgust. These two classical writers are a vital influence in this area, yet their writings do not give exact definition of the Unities (though the texts they approve do conform to strict conventions). This fuels the tetchiness of Castelvetro as he quibbles with Aristotle's more sweeping points, as he does when commenting on the previous passage:

Il che è falso essendo molto piu ageuol cosa il tenere o il mandare a mente le cose picciole, o brieui, che le grandi, o le lunghe. Senza che ancora la misura dell' animale che è grande oltre il conueneuole no ha interamente quella proportione verso l'occhio, che ha la misura della fauola grande verso la memoria, conciosia cosa che se la grandezza dell'animale non puo tutta essere compresa in vno sguardo, si possa comprendere in due o in piu presso che in vn tempo.[17]

(This is wrong, because it is much easier to see and remember small or short-lasting things than large or long-lasting. Furthermore, a visual appreciation of an unfeasibly large animal is not really the same as a memorial appreciation of a long plot, because if the size of the animal is such that it cannot all be taken in by one glance, it can be taken in by two or more glances as if at one moment.)

Castelvetro is almost impatient with the casual tone of his text; he is impatient also with the failures of writers to obey the rules, as he is with the short-cut in Plautus' *Captivi*, mentioned above.[18] Sir Philip Sidney seems to react to this passage when he says, in the *Defence of Poetry*, 'though Plautus have in one place done amiss, let us hit with him, and not miss with him'.[19] This may hint at an English attitude to this neo-classical theory, one generated by practice. In retrospect Dryden seems to share this feeling, when, in the person of Neander, he sums up one response to such debates: 'Now what I beseech you is more easie then to write a regular *French* Play, or more difficult then to write an irregular *English* one, like those of *Fletcher*, or of *Shakespeare*?'[20] There is an argument here between two ideas of nature: one sees the practice of English drama and the occasional noddings to the classics as a way of being natural. The other sees the constraints of the dramatic Unities as the best way of achieving *mimesis*, of representing nature. Nevertheless neither side truly manages to make drama and its rules seem natural.

Modern philosophers have developed energetic ideas about space that can help resolve this impasse, by viewing the location of drama not as some pre-existing natural state but as something created and developed. Michel de Certeau views 'spaces' as refined versions of geographical places, where practices and tactics have created something new:

> Space occurs as the effect produced by the operations that orient it, situate it, temporalize it, and make it function in a polyvalent unity of conflictual programs or contractual proximities. [. . .] In short, *space is a practiced place*. Thus the street geometrically defined by urban planning is transformed into a space by walkers.[21]

The important logical step here is to see location as something that is created by people within it, rather than something that precedes them. This parallels the observation of Jean Baudrillard that a map can precede the territory it describes, an idea expanded upon by Geoff King.[22] Modern studies of early modern geography often focus on the ways writers and mapmakers in this period, too, sought to shape the physical world through mapping and interpretation.[23] All this could be seen to parallel a movement in Shakespeare's work towards a sense that the presumed natural space for drama, within the Unities of Time and Place, may be a situation manipulated by power. The most fertile text for considering Shakespeare and the Unities is rather different. Henri Lefebvre's *The Production of Space* describes a specific set of historical conditions, yet its definition of 'social space' shadows Shakespeare's awareness, by defining locations that are determined by ideological constraints. These can work covertly, and they are hidden by 'a double illusion' which seems rather appropriate to a dramatic context:

> Each side of [this 'double illusion'] refers back to the other, reinforces the other, and hides behind the other. These two aspects are the illusion of transparency on the one hand and the illusion of society, or 'realistic' illusion, on the other.[24]

The first illusion, that of transparency, derives from a way of looking at the world but also points, perhaps, to a way of looking at the stage:

> The illusion of transparency goes hand in hand with a view of space as innocent, as free of traps or secret places. Anything hidden or dissimulated – and hence dangerous – is antagonistic to transparency, under whose reign everything can be taken in by a single glance from that mental eye which illuminates whatever it contemplates.[25]

The social production of space is unseen thanks to the illusion that everything is visible. Drama, Plautus and Shakespeare included, might enable a more energetic version of the illusion of transparency, in that it can both perpetrate such an illusion in its simple panoptic settings (as in the frontage and streets of New Comedy) but it can also hint at spaces beyond. The second, 'realistic' illusion also pertains to drama:

This is the illusion of natural simplicity – the product of a naïve attitude long ago rejected by philosophers and theorists of language, on various grounds and under various names, but chiefly because of its appeal to naturalness, to substantiality.[26]

The idea of natural simplicity may be more elusive in the theory of the dramatic Unities than one might have expected, but still the idea persists that such limits of location can create a more straightforwardly efficacious *mimesis*. Lefebvre advocates a deeper perception of society's spaces; Shakespeare obliges something similar, alerting the audience that the world of a play cannot simply be taken as just itself, or as the only way things could be.

In *The Tempest* the bearing of power on space is a pressing issue, whether moral or immoral, and whether in relation to English or colonial social dynamics.[27] It uses a location that is strictly limited to the dramatic Unities, a single island and a single day – but it explores these limits by making them illusory. The island is a single location but it has secret spaces that are controlled by Prospero; the single day of action is not bounded by characters' sleeps, as they sleep at the magician's command. There is one thing that exists outside the Unities, and that is the storm of act 1, scene 1. However, the appearance of Prospero and Miranda in 1.2 watching this storm marks it as a separate, enclosed scene; it is also a false storm, an illusion, which therefore occupies a less substantiated space than the rest of the action. In addition, this separate scene itself observes dramatic Unity: it represents the deck of the ship, and events and voices offstage are outside its primary scope. The noises from beyond the visible action add to the realism of the scene in their depiction of varied suffering, and their externality is also part of the necessary constraint of *mimesis*.[28]

The special characteristic of the space of *The Tempest*, then, is that the contrivance, rather than naturalness, of its space is brought to the surface, and thus it dispenses with Lefebvre's illusions of transparency and realism. (This is true at least from the perspective of the audience, but the audience can also see how characters are still deceived.) As well as an unusually clear depiction of the operation of 'social space' in drama, we see the possibility of resisting Prospero's definition of space. Within *The Tempest* there are characters who wilfully see the world differently; their action could be construed, after Lefebvre and indeed de Certeau (their approaches are very different, but the intersections with Shakespeare's Unities are relatively close), as a version of political resistance (whether in the cause of liberty or tyranny):

GON. Here is everything advantageous to life.
ANT. True, save means to live.
SEB. Of that there's none, or little.
GON. How lush and lusty the grass looks! How green!
ANT. The ground indeed is tawny.
SEB. With an eye of green in't.
ANT. He misses not much.
SEB. No; he doth but mistake the truth totally.

(*Tempest* 2.1.54–62)

This exchange could mark a difference in character: idealism meets infected cynicism. But moral judgements of character do not provide the most energetic means of approaching this schematic exchange. Instead it could be viewed in terms of models of power and space, under which circumstances Sebastian and Antonio seem purposeful, deploying resistant tactics. Gonzalo is more wrong than they are in believing in the innocence of this space; though they have no idea who created it, they respond to the strategies of power. The exchange rebounds instead on Prospero, as it maps out his manipulation of space, and this rebounds further onto the audience's interaction with this space, and how its sense of space is affected by power.

Elsewhere in the play Prospero's control, and perhaps abuse, of space helps validate resistance – it is not necessary to take a moral position on the Duke's methods to appreciate how the play demonstrates both his control over space and the opposition it elicits. This takes a straightforward form in the case of Ferdinand, whom Prospero threatens to imprison (1.2.463–7). The case of Caliban is more complex. He participates in a conspiracy that Prospero lets slip, and demonstrates a different kind of resistance when he appreciates the island in more complexity than necessarily fits his social role, hearing its 'noises' and 'twangling instruments' (3.2.138–40), and finding mysterious 'scamels' on its rocks (2.2.172).[29] Caliban's dream-like appropriation of the island redefines its space and diminishes Prospero's control over it. The other servant, Ariel, participates in the definition of the island's time and space, but also encounters his own powerlessness – and does so within the same scene. He shares his master's pleasure in their freedom from the constraints they apply to others:

PRO.   Of the King's ship,
  The mariners, say how thou hast disposed,
  And all the rest o'th' fleet?
AR.   Safely in harbour
  Is the King's ship, in the deep nook where once

> Thou calledst me up at midnight to fetch dew
> From the still-vexed Bermudas, there she's hid;
> The mariners all under hatches stowed,
> Who, with a charm joined to their suffered labour,
> I have left asleep [. . .]
> PRO.   Ariel, thy charge
> Exactly is performed; but there's more work.
> What is the time o'th' day?
> AR.   Past the mid season.
> PRO. At least two glasses. The time 'twixt six and now
> Must by us both be spent most preciously.
>   (*Tempest* 1.2.225–33, 238–42)

In this exchange the characters discuss marshalling the time and space of the drama, ironically proposing their own exclusion from its limits. 'The time 'twixt six and now' is the duration of the play and of Prospero's opportunity. The 'deep nook' is a space beyond the vision of the audience, where he can exercise a dramatist's ability to determine who is present on stage. It is also the cause of a reminiscence that combines both Prospero's usually panoptic awareness of his island and Ariel's ability to transcend the limits of the play, heading for the 'still-vexed Bermudas'. Soon after, when the servant reminds the master of a promise of liberty, the mood changes:

> Refusing her grand hests, she [Sycorax] did confine thee
> By help of her more potent ministers,
> And in her most unmitigable rage,
> Into a cloven pine; within which rift
> Imprisoned thou didst painfully remain
> A dozen years, within which space she died
> And left thee there, where thou didst vent thy groans
> As fast as mill-wheels strike. [. . .]
> If thou more murmur'st, I will rend an oak,
> And peg thee in his knotty entrails till
> Thou hast howled away twelve winters.
>   (*Tempest* 1.2.275–82, 295–7)

Ariel's past and threatened punishments are a travesty of dramatic time and space. The space shrinks from the already confined island to the impossible restriction of the inside of a tree, whether a pine or an oak. Conversely, the duration of the punishment, twelve years, is a vast expansion of the plot's one-day duration.

The Tempest, then, reveals its conventional Unities of Time and Place to be a constrained and manipulated product of power, against which certain characters strive. The play takes on other elements of New Comedy, but it shows them all distorted by the control of one character, whether he is to be admired or not. The presence of power in the determination of temporal and spatial limits, however, is not only found here. The end of *Twelfth Night*, for example, sees the Duke assert himself:

> Cesario, come –
> For so you shall be while you are a man;
> But when in other habits you are seen,
> Orsino's mistress, and his fancy's queen.
>
> (*TN* 5.1.381–4)

In *Twelfth Night* the high-born characters spend some of the time allowing fortune to determine events, but (as was discussed above) this is not a universal privilege. When the moment to reintegrate with quotidian time comes, at the end of the play, the Duke makes manifest his own particular authority. He takes control of time and the relationship between costume and identity, two facets of the dramatic process, and at the last, without hurrying, prepares to reveal the underlying ideological nature of the space of the play. The most explicit parallel in *The Comedy of Errors* faces the issues from another angle – from the perspective of women who move less freely through the world of the play:

> LUC. Perhaps some merchant hath invited him,
>   And from the mart he's somewhere gone to dinner.
>   Good sister, let us dine, and never fret.
>   A man is master of his liberty.
>   Time is their mistress, and when they see time
>   They'll go or come. If so, be patient, sister.
> ADR. Why should their liberty than ours be more?
> LUC. Because their business still lies out o' door.
> ADR. Look when I serve him so, he takes it ill.
> LUC. O, know he is the bridle of your will.
> ADR. There's none but asses will be bridled so.
> LUC. Why, headstrong liberty is lash'd with woe.
>   There's nothing situate under heaven's eye
>   But hath his bound in earth, in sea, in sky.
>
> (*CE* 2.1.4–17)

This is a curious speech, launching into a grand vision despite a mundane prompt – the absence of a husband from meal-time. The complaint about liberty, and the ironic paean to 'Man, more divine' that follows, have a spatial aspect in that they stem from the contrast between domesticity and public life, which equates to the difference in men's and women's ability to leave the stage-space and control their encounters with the wider world. This conversation between Adriana and Luciana is more explicit than it needs to be, but that counterbalances the parallel complaints of the Dromios, which are less explicit than they might be. The New Comic space of this play, as of *Twelfth Night* and *The Tempest*, is not represented as natural or automatic: Shakespeare shows characters finding it strange, and shows the methods by which it is sustained, and in doing so both revives and criticises the conventions of the genre.

NOTES

1. Italo Calvino, *Invisible Cities*, trans. William Weaver (London 1997), pp. 80–1.
2. *Plautus*, trans. Paul Nixon, 5 vols. (London 1916–38). The speaker is the Prologue to *Menaechmi*; line and volume/page references will be given in the text.
3. See Wolfgang Riehle, *Shakespeare, Plautus and the Humanist Tradition* (Woodbridge 1990), pp. 14–23 on the Elizabethan preference for Plautus over Terence. Terence's characters are richer, while Plautus has greater dramatic energy: it seems Shakespeare responded to the latter.
4. Robert S. Miola, *Shakespeare and Classical Comedy* (Oxford 1998), pp. 20–38 on *The Comedy of Errors*, sets out elements of comedy and romance with regard to the influence of *Menaechmi* and *Amphitruo*; see Niall Rudd, *The Classical Tradition in Operation* (Toronto 1994), pp. 32–60 on how romance elements are incorporated. See also Leo Salingar, *Shakespeare and the Traditions of Comedy* (Cambridge 1974), pp. 76–88; Riehle, *Shakespeare, Plautus, and the Humanist Tradition*, pp. 23–31; John Arthos, 'Shakespeare's Transformation of Plautus', *Comparative Drama* 1 (1967–8), 239–53; Anne Righter, *Shakespeare and the Idea of the Play* (London 1964), pp. 43–63.
5. At *TN* 1.2.52–61 Viola plans to disguise herself as a eunuch, but at 1.4.15 Orsino addresses her as a 'good youth'.
6. See Bruce Louden, '*The Tempest*, Plautus, and the *Rudens*', *Comparative Drama* 33 (1999–2000), 199–23: again the combination of comedy and romance is central. See also Riehle, *Shakespeare, Plautus, and the Humanist Tradition*, pp. 262–8, and James Svensden, 'The Fusion of Comedy and Romance: Plautus's *Rudens* and Shakespeare's *The Tempest*', in *From Pen to Performance: Drama as Conceived and Performed, III*, ed. Karelisa V. Hartigan (New York 1983), pp. 121–35.
7. Miola, *Shakespeare and Classical Comedy*, p. 41, and pp. 38–61. See also Riehle, *Shakespeare, Plautus and the Humanist Tradition*, pp. 230–4.
8. Quoted in *Twelfth Night*, ed. J. M. Lothian and T. W. Craik (London 1975), p. xxvi. See Louise George Clubb, 'Italian Comedy and *The Comedy of Errors*', *Comparative Literature* 19 (1967), 240–51, and T. W. Baldwin, *On the Compositional Genetics of 'The Comedy of Errors'* (Urbana 1965), pp. 200–14 on relationships with Plautus' *Menaechmi* and *Amphitruo*. See also Jack D'Amico, 'The Treatment of Space in Italian and English Renaissance Theater: The Example

of *Gl'Ingannati* and *Twelfth Night*, *Comparative Drama* 23 (1989–90), 265–83, and Salingar, *Shakespeare and the Traditions of Comedy*, pp. 175–218.

9. Elliot Krieger, *A Marxist Study of Shakespeare's Comedies* (London 1979), p. 130.
10. Krieger, *A Marxist Study of Shakespeare's Comedies*, pp. 2–3.
11. Douglas Bruster, 'Comedy and Control: Shakespeare and the Plautine *Poeta*', *Comparative Drama* 24 (1990–1), 217–31, 230.
12. Bearing in mind the *caveat* of Salingar, *Shakespeare and the Traditions of Comedy*, p. 1, that comic practice is rarely defined well by comic theory.
13. David Riggs, 'The Artificial Day and the Infinite Universe', *Journal of Medieval and Renaissance Studies* 5 (1975), 155–85 mainly concerns the Unity of Time, though the Unity of Place almost always accompanies it in classical and Renaissance theory and practice: they are, indeed, largely interdependent.
14. Riggs, 'The Artificial Day', p. 172.
15. Lodovico Castelvetro, *Poetica d'Aristotele Vulgarizzata et Sposta* (Vienna 1570), fol. 60*v*.
16. Aristotle, *Poetics*, ed. and trans. Stephen Halliwell (Cambridge, MA 1995), 1450b.33–1451a.3.
17. Castelvetro, *Poetica d'Aristotele Vulgarizzata et Sposta*, fol. 92*r*.
18. Ibid., fol. 96*r*.
19. Sir Philip Sidney, *A Defence of Poetry*, in *Miscellaneous Prose*, ed. Katherine Duncan-Jones and Jan Van Dorsten (Oxford 1973), p. 113.
20. John Dryden, *An Essay of Dramatick Poesy*, in *The Works of John Dryden*, ed. H. T. Swedenberg, vol. XVII, *Prose, 1668–1691* (Berkeley 1971), p. 53.
21. Michel de Certeau, *The Practice of Everyday Life*, trans. Steven Rendall (Berkeley 1984; originally *Arts de Faire*), p. 117.
22. See Geoff King, *Mapping Reality: An Exploration of Cultural Cartographies* (Houndmills 1996), and Baudrillard's *Simulations* (1981), trans. Paul Foss, Paul Patton, and Philip Beitchman (New York 1983). See also *Thinking Space*, ed. Mike Crang and Nigel Thrift (London 2000), and Edward W. Soja, *Postmodern Geographies: The Reassertion of Space in Critical Social Theory* (London 1989), p. 79, on 'the distinction between space *per se*, space as a contextual given, and socially-based spatiality, the created space of social organization and production'.
23. See Frank Lestringant, *Mapping the Renaissance World: The Geographical Imagination in the Age of Discovery*, trans. David Fausett (Berkeley 1994), first published as *L'atelier du cosmographe* (Paris 1991); John Gillies, *Shakespeare and the Geography of Difference* (Cambridge 1994); Bernhard Klein, *Maps and the Writing of Space in Early Modern England and Ireland* (Houndmills 2001); Andrew Gordon and Bernhard Klein, eds., *Literature, Mapping, and the Politics of Space in Early Modern Britain* (Cambridge 2001); David Buisseret, ed., *Monarchs, Ministers, and Maps: The Emergence of Cartography as a Tool of Government in Early Modern Europe* (Chicago 1992); and Jerry Brotton, *Trading Territories: Mapping the Early Modern World* (London 1997).
24. Henri Lefebvre, *The Production of Space*, trans. Donald Nicholson-Smith (Oxford 1991) – originally *La production de l'espace* (Paris 1974), p. 27.

25. Ibid., p. 27.

26. Ibid., p. 29.

27. See Crystal Bartolovich, '"Baseless Fabric": London as a "World City"', pp. 13–26, and Roland Greene, 'Island Logic', pp. 138–45, both in *'The Tempest' and its Travels*, ed. Peter Hulme and William H. Sherman (London 2000).

28. The scripted 'confused noise within' at 1.1.61–2 is given to Gonzalo in Folio, though editors are right to recognise the unusual scripted nature of the offstage clamour.

29. The Oxford Shakespeare has 'sea-mews' for Folio's 'scamels' here, which has the benefit of discovering an interpretable word within Caliban's obscurity – but it loses the obscurity.

I am grateful for the help and advice offered by Charles Martindale, Christopher Burlinson, Carolyn Twigg, and John Kerrigan.

SENECA

CHAPTER 8

'Confusion now hath made his masterpiece': Senecan resonances in Macbeth

Yves Peyré

'We . . . have no indication that Shakespeare read Seneca's plays in the original. Nor do I find any evidence worth repeating that Shakespeare had read English Seneca,' Baldwin wrote sceptically in 1944.[1] Not everyone agreed. John W. Cunliffe, Jakob Engel, Cornell M. Dowlin, and Kenneth Muir collated parallel phrases which suggest that *Macbeth* teems with echoes from Seneca's plays[2] – whether from the Latin original or Elizabethan translations.[3] Conversely, when Frank Justus Miller translated *dubio consilio* (*Agamemnon* 50) as 'doubtful of purpose', echoing 'infirm of purpose',[4] *peractum est* (*Agamemnon* 901) as 'the deed is done', perhaps remembering 'I have done the deed', or *Infandos procul / averte sensus* (*Hercules Furens* 973–4) as 'Have done with these horrible imaginings', inspired by Macbeth's 'Present fears / Are less than horrible imaginings' (1.3.136–7), he was rediscovering Seneca in the light of Shakespeare.[5] This cross-fertilisation may not be merely rhetorical. It reflects similitudes of a deeper kind that reach well beyond formal echoes. The purpose of this chapter is not to assess any direct, clearly provable influence, although Kenneth Muir's theory that Shakespeare reread Seneca while working on *Macbeth* is not only tempting but plausible,[6] and might account for the diffuse nature of Senecan features in the play. Analogies in thought, phrase, or situation become meaningful when considered not in isolation, but as elements of shared imaginative structures. The cohesiveness of their interaction constitutes one of the 'musical lines' in the dissonance between the classical and Christian traditions that Robert S. Miola has persuasively traced[7] in what appears to be 'the most Senecan of all of Shakespeare's plays'.[8]

Seneca's *nefas*, or most sacrilegious crime, transgresses fundamental rules insofar as it challenges both *fas* (divine will) and *pietas*, the personal sense of parental, social, and religious duties. Clytemnestra kills her husband, Hercules his own sons, Medea stains herself *caede cognata* (*Medea* 523; 'with kindred blood'). Macbeth is aware of the 'impiety' of his crime:

> He's here in double trust;
> First, as I am his kinsman and his subject,
> Strong both against the deed; then as his host,
> Who should against his murderer shut the door,
> Not bear the knife myself.   (1.7.12–16)

Duncan's first address to Macbeth as 'worthiest cousin' (1.4.14) emphasises the family relationship, which Lady Macbeth reinforces when she recoils from committing *impietas* herself because of the resemblance she imagines between the king and her father. Aristotle had remarked that 'if a man injures his enemy, there is nothing pitiable either in his act or in his intention . . . nor is there if they are indifferent to each other'. But the tragic feeling arises 'when the sufferings involve those who are near and dear to one another, when for example brother kills brother, mother son, or son mother'.[9] 'The nea'er in blood, / The nearer bloody' (2.4.133–4), Donalbain perceptively comments. By imposing on allies the relations that usually obtain between enemies, such crimes sap the most basic distinctions on which social organisation is felt to rest. The crimes Hippolytus declines with horror all pertain to *nefas*:

> . . . nullum caruit exemplo nefas.
> A fratre frater, dextera nati parens
> Cecidit, maritus coniugis ferro iacet
> Perimuntque fetus impiae matres suos.
> . . .
> sed dux malorum femina; haec scelerum artifex
> obsedit animos   (*Hippolytus* 553–60)

(. . . no impious deed lacked precedent. Brother was slain by brother, father by the hand of son, husband lay dead by the sword of wife, and unnatural mothers destroyed their own offspring . . . But the leader of all wickedness is woman; 'tis she, cunning mistress of crime, besets our minds.)

Not only does Hippolytus' speech provide an ethical context for the delineation of such characters as Macbeth and Lady Macbeth, it goes on to suggest that, beyond distorting all bonds within families and nations as well as between men and gods, the crimes it lists affect the very structure of the universe: *terras cruor / infecit omnes fusus et rubuit mare* (*Hippolytus* 551–2; 'streams of blood stained all lands and the sea grew red').[10]

When he pretends to kill Duncan's guards 'in pious rage' (3.6.12), Macbeth, 'mock[ing] the time with fairest show' (1.7.81), disguises *nefas* as an act of *pietas*. Theseus belatedly discovers the deceptive indistinctness of the tragic world:

> o vita fallax, abditos sensus geris
> animisque pulchram turpibus faciem induis:
> pudor impudentem celat, audacem quies,
> pietas nefandum.   (*Hippolytus* 918–21)

(O two-faced life, thou keepest thy true thoughts hidden and dost clothe foul purpose with an aspect fair – chaste bearing hides unchastity; meekness effrontery; piety, sin unspeakable.)

In Seneca, the confusion between foul and fair obliterates the distinctions between *pietas* and *nefas*,[11] *fides* and *infidus*,[12] and even *fas* and *nefas*, in Atreus' paradoxical equation, *fas . . . est nefas* (*Thyestes* 220; 'Whate'er is wrong . . . is right'). When Atreus kills his brother's sons, murder parades under the guise of religious ceremony: *Seruatur omnis ordo, ne tantum nefas / non rite fiat* (*Thyestes* 689–90; 'The accustomed ritual is all observed, lest so great a crime be not duly wrought'); this confusion between murder and sacrifice, frequent in Seneca, is explored by Shakespeare in *Titus Andronicus* and recalled in *Julius Caesar* and *Othello*.

In *Macbeth*, a similar principle of confusion associates murder with the social ritual of the banquet. It is the ghost of Thyestes who, with appropriate irony, announces the tragic proximity of massacre and festivity in *Agamemnon*:

> iam scelera prope sunt, iam dolus, caedes, cruor –
> parantur epulae.   (47–8)

(Now crimes are near, now treachery, slaughter, gore – feasts are being spread.)

Clytemnestra and Aegisthus plot Agamemnon's death with a complicity not unlike Macbeth and Lady Macbeth's: Aegisthus' *Tu nos pericli socia* (234; 'Thou partner of my peril') announces Clytemnestra's *Consors pericli pariter ac regni mei* (978; 'Thou partner equally in my perils and my throne'), which reverberates in Macbeth's 'my dearest partner of greatness' (1.5.9–10).[13] In much the same way as Macbeth plots Duncan's death while the feast is going on, with noise of music and laughter from within and busy servants carrying dishes (1.7) to and fro, Cassandra announces a similar juxtaposition of feast and slaughter:

> sanguinem extremae dapes
> domini videbunt et cruor Baccho incidet.
> (885–6)

(The banquet's close shall see the master's blood, and gore shall fall into the wine.)

The cloying saturation that Atreus sardonically attributes to Thyestes[14] is felt by Macbeth, who has 'supped full with horrors' (5.5.13). Thyestes, ironically, had taken the pose of the modestly contented wise man; in Jasper Heywood's translation,

> We nothing fear, the house is safe without the hidden knife. (3.1.64)[15]

Macbeth, in contrast, must 'eat [his] meal in fear' (3.2.17) and Malcolm will have to 'Free from our feasts and banquets bloody knives' (3.6.35). Macbeth's banquet is disrupted by Banquo's ghost, who may owe something to Seneca's apparitions[16] and be imagined, as Paul A. Jorgensen suggests,[17] like Laius' shadow in *Oedipus* (624–5). What horrifies Macbeth most is that murdered men 'rise again' (3.4.80), as if there were no longer any clear distinction between the worlds of the living and the dead, since funerary rites are ignored: the Chorus' fear that corpses be given 'to the birds to feed upon' (*Thyestes* 750) threatens to become reality in *Macbeth*, where 'our monuments / Shall be the maws of kites' (3.4.71–3).

This regression towards pre-cultural times is a consequence of tyranny,[18] which also perverts the powerful symbol of the hand[19] as a sign of faithfulness and concord. 'Give me your hand', says Duncan to Lady Macbeth (1.6.29) in token of loyal amity. *Datas fidei manus* (*Thyestes* 764; the hand 'that is given in pledge of faith') is the hand that stabs. Signs thus become unreliable and unreadable; 'imperfect speakers' (1.3.70) 'That palter with us in a double sense' (5.8.20) create an ambiguous world similar to that of Oedipus, with its *nodosa . . . verba et implexos dolos* (101; 'intricate, guile-entangled words'), or of Hippolytus, where the nurse's *Perplexa . . . verba* (858; 'riddling words') echo Phaedra's *verba perplexa* (639; 'Words of doubtful meaning'). One loses one's bearings and everything becomes uncertain: *Responsa dubia sorte perplexa iacent* (*Oedipus* 212; 'Doubtful lies the answer and involved the doom'); *ambiguus ut me sortis ignotae labor* (*Hippolytus* 840; 'dubious battling with an unknown fate'). Seneca's *dubius* is Shakespeare's 'doubtful', which significantly opens the tragedy as the Captain reports, 'Doubtful it stood . . .' (1.2.7), and eventually poisons Lady Macbeth's 'doubtful joy' (3.2.11).

As has often been noted, night symbolises moral blindness. *Ne quid obstaret pudor, / dies recessit* (*Thyestes* 891–2; 'That shame may not hold me back, day has departed') exclaims Atreus, in anticipation of Macbeth's call to the stars to hide their fires (1.4.50–2) and Lady Macbeth's appeal to 'thick night' to prevent heaven from crying 'Hold, hold!' (1.5.48–52). Yet, more than the deepest obscurity, it is the doubtful moment between day and night that symbolises the loss of certainties as distinctions blur and collapse: *dum lux dubia est* (*Hippolytus* 41, 'while the light is still dim') and the night is 'Almost at odds with the morning, which is which' (3.4.127), or when 'The west yet glimmers with some streaks of day' (3.3.5). This, in *Hercules Furens*, defines the entrance of hell:

> non caeca tenebris incipit primo via;
> tenuis relictae lucis a tergo nitor
> fulgorque dubius solis adflicti cadit
> et ludit aciem. Nocte sic mixta solet
> praebere lumen primus aut serus dies.
>
> (668–72)

(Not in utter darkness does the way first begin; a slender gleam of the light left behind and a doubtful glow as of the sun in eclipse falls there and cheats the vision. Such light the day mingled with night is wont to give, at early dawn or at late twilight.)

Macbeth is played out at the entrance of hell, in dubious light that 'cheats the vision'. In *Troades, premitur … dubius nocte vicina dies* (1,142; 'the uncertain daylight is dimmed by the approach of night'), or, in Jasper Heywood's translation, 'When starres againe with night at hand oppress the doubtful day' (fol. 118*r*). Medea's invocation, *nox condat alma lucem* (876, 'let friendly darkness veil the light'), is expanded by John Studley into 'let groueling light with *Dulceat* nyght opprest / In cloking Cloudes wrapt vp his muffled Face' (fol. 136*v*). The overtranslation of *condere* by 'oppress', which echoes Heywood's choice of the same word in a similar context, creates the setting for a cosmic fight between light and darkness, with, however, a domestic, familiar tone intruding, suggested by 'cloking' and 'muffled', which is not unlike Lady Macbeth's 'blanket of the dark' (1.5.51) or Macbeth's call for 'seeling night' to 'Scarf up the tender eye of pitiful day' (3.2.46–7). A transformation even more fearful than Heywood's change of 'veil' into 'oppress' occurs if that cosmic scarf is imagined projecting murder into heaven, when 'dark night strangles the travelling lamp' (2.4.7). The cosmos reflects the transformation of epic bravura into scheming treachery that occurs in act 1. Ominously, as if heeding Lady Macbeth's invocation to 'make thick my blood', 'light thickens', seemingly engendering its own destruction; 'So from that spring whence comfort seemed to come, / Discomfort swells' (1.2.27–8).

Ultimately, indistinction threatens to pull the world back into the primary Chaos, a perspective which delights Medea (426–7); John Studley's

Hercules calls for 'filthy fogges' (205v) and wishes 'Heaven frames should here & there be brast';[20] Macbeth would rather see 'the frame of things disjoint' (3.2.16), and have his way

> though the treasure
> Of nature's germen tumble altogether
> Even till destruction sicken.
>
> (4.1.57–9)

until weariness finally drives him to wish 'th'estate o' th' world were now undone' (5.5.49). Oedipus similarly calls for Chaos in *Phoenissae*: *miscete cuncta, rapite in exitium omnia* (342; 'confound all things, hurry all to destruction'), or, in Thomas Newton's translation, 'a hurly burly make / Confusedly of eu'ry thinge' (*Thebais* fol. 48r). It is the 'hurly-burly' the Witches have announced (1.1.3), a state of primeval confusion. In his edition, Kenneth Muir expounded 'hurly-burly' as 'uproar, tumult, confusion, especially the tumult of sedition or insurrection', and pointed to a close parallel in Studley's translation of *Agamemnon*, 'One hurly burly done, another doth begin' (notes to 1.1.3 and 5.3.45). Studley also uses 'hurly-burly' in partial translation of *nefas* in *Medea*: Seneca's *quodcumque vidit Pontus aut Phasis nefas, / videbit Isthmos* (44–5; 'Whatever horror Pontus has beheld, or Phasis, Isthmus shall behold') thus becomes 'What euer hurly burly wrought doth Phasis vnderstand, / What mighty monstrous bloudy feate I wrought by Sea or Land: / The like in Corynth shalbe seene in most outragious guise' (fol. 120v). What the Weird Sisters announce seems to start as mere insurrection (the hurly-burly in *Agamemnon*), but it is not unconnected with Macbeth's 'mighty monstrous bloudy feate' (the hurly-burly in *Medea*) and finally degenerates into social, mental, and universal chaos (the hurly-burly in *Thebais*).

Shakespeare's word for this hurly-burly can also be 'confusion', with two meanings that tend to overlap. Macbeth is drawn on 'to his confusion' (3.5.29), or ruin; suggestions of universal chaos are never far: with Duncan's murder, which is accompanied by 'dire combustion and confused events' (2.3.50), 'Confusion now hath made his masterpiece' (2.3.59). It is in a context of imagined chaos that 'the yeasty waves / Confound and swallow navigation up' (4.1.52–3). Dissociating himself from Macbeth by pretending to resemble him, Malcolm threatens to 'Uproar the universal peace, confound / All unity on earth' (4.3.99–100). Less ambiguously, Seneca repeatedly uses the verb *miscere, miscete cuncta*, 'confound all things'. More specifically, the word often refers to the kinds of crime that bring on Chaos.

Phaedra's intended and Oedipus' unintentional incests, Thyestes' banquet,
result in a confusion between the generations.[21] Thyestes recalls it at the
beginning of *Agamemnon*:

> versa natura est retro;
> avo parentem, pro nefas! Patri virum,
> natis nepotes miscui – nocti diem.
>
> (34–6)

(Nature has been confounded; father with grandsire, yea, monstrous! Husband
with father, grandsons with sons, have I confused – and day with night.)

''Tis unnatural', ''Gainst nature still' (2.4.10, 27), Ross and the Old Man
might say, not only because the confusion between generations is analo-
gous to the confusion between night and day, but also because this *nefas*,
like other Senecan crimes, ignores the usual cultural distinctions whereby
human beings try to define what constitutes human nature.

Some of these perversions may consist in indifferentiation between man
and woman. Clytemnestra condemns Electra's *Animos viriles* (*Agamemnon* 964; 'mannish soul'). Macbeth admiringly sees similar qualities in
his wife, whose 'undaunted mettle should compose / Nothing but males'
(1.7.72–4). As Inga-Stina Ewbank has shown, Lady Macbeth is partly
modelled on Medea.[22] Creon's remark, *tu malorum machinatrix facino-
rum, / feminea cui nequitia ad audendia omnia, robur virile est* (266–8;
'thou contriver of wickedness, who combinest woman's wanton reck-
lessness and man's strength'), could apply to Lady Macbeth as well as
Medea, and this transgression of sexual differences is grotesquely and grimly
echoed, in *Macbeth*'s world, by the Weird Sisters' appearance: 'you should
be women, / And yet your beards forbid me to interpret / That you are so'
(1.3.43–5).

The perversion of human nature culminates in Lady Macbeth's powerful
depiction of infanticide:

> I have given suck and know
> How tender 'tis to love the babe that milks me:
> I would, while it was smiling in my face,
> Have plucked my nipple from his boneless gums
> And dashed the brains out, had I so sworn
> As you have done to this.   (1.7.54–9)

In a globally Senecan context, it may be Ovid who inspired the image of
a parent brutally dashing out the brains of the child smiling in her or his
face. In the *Metamorphoses*, Athamas suddenly grasps his young son:

deque sinu matris ridentem et parva Learchum
bracchia tendentem rapit et bis terque per auras
more rotat fundae rigidoque infantia saxo
discutit ora ferox . . .   (4.516–19)[23]

And lyke a Bedlem boystouslie he snatched from betweene
The mothers armes his little babe Læarchus smyling on him
And reaching foorth his preatie armes, and floong him fiercely from him
A twice or thrice as from a slyng: and dasht his tender head
Against a hard and rugged stone untill he sawe him dead.[24]

While Shakespeare's 'smiling in my face' and 'dashed the brains out' seem
closer to Golding's 'smyling on him' and 'dasht his tender head' than
to Ovid's *ridentem* and *discutit ora*, it is Ovid's *deque sinu matris*, rather
than Golding's 'from betweene / The mothers armes' which may have
suggested the image of giving suck. In *Gorboduc*'s fourth dumb show, Ino
and Athamas appeared in a series of infanticides, after two Senecan figures,
Tantalus[25] and Medea. Similarly, if Shakespeare's imagination blends, in
Lady Macbeth's speech, the Latin and the English versions of Athamas'
murder in the *Metamorphoses*, it also fuses them with reminiscences of
Senecan murderers. It is not impossible that Seneca, who alludes to Ino's
suicide in *Oedipus* (22–6), himself remembered Ovid when he described
Hercules' murder of his son:

> dextra precantem rapuit et circa furens
> bis ter rotatum misit; ast illi caput
> sonuit, cerebro tecta disperso madent.
> (*Hercules Furens* 1,005–7)

(With his right hand he has caught the pleading child, and, madly whirling him
again and yet again, has hurled him; his head crashed loudly against the stones;
the room is drenched with scattered brains.)

Echoes between *rapuit* and *rapit*, *bis ter rotatum*, and *bis terque . . . rotat*,
put Seneca's text in resonance with Ovid's. Like Ino running away with her
second child, Megara tries to protect her younger son against the criminal
fury of his own father:

> at misera, parvum protegens natum sinu,
> Megara furenti similis e latebris fugit.
> (1,008–9)

(But Megara, poor woman, sheltering her little son within her bosom, flees like a
mad creature from her hiding-place.)

Andromache is just as helpless as she attempts to protect her son in *Troades* (792–8), and so is Lady Macduff in *Macbeth*. Like Andromache and Megara, Lady Macduff illustrates the naturally protective function of a mother, so that Lady Macbeth's *impietas*, which reverberates in the 'birth-strangled babe' (4.1.30), in the sow 'that has eaten / Her nine farrow' (4.1.63–4) and Scotland, no longer 'our mother, but our grave' (4.3.168), appears all the more horrific.

In Lady Macbeth's invocation to the Spirits that tend on mortal thoughts (1.5.39–49) and in her denial of maternity (1.7.54–9), Inga-Stina Ewbank pointed to several parallels with Studley's translation of *Medea*, which are not to be found in the Latin text. Seneca's reference to Medea's motherhood, *maiora iam me scelera post partus decent* (50; 'greater crimes become me, now that I am a mother') is developed by Studley into a concrete 'sith my wombe hath yeelded fruict', more akin to Lady Macbeth's 'I have given suck'.[26] What seems to be an essential imaginative nexus, however, the association of, and near confusion between, motherhood and crime, appears more clearly in the Latin:

> parta iam, parta ultio est:
> peperi.   (25–6)

(Already borne, borne is my vengeance! I have borne children!)

The echo between *post partus* (50) and *parta . . . est* (25), relayed by *peperi*, confusing life and death, closely associates motherhood with the engendering of crime. So does the couple, in *Macbeth*, give birth not to life, but to murder, which monstrously engenders new crimes, until the act of giving birth is ultimately transferred from Lady Macbeth to Macbeth, when he decides that 'The very firstlings of my heart shall be / The firstlings of my hand' (4.1.146–7).

Read in the context of Lady Macbeth's taunts at her husband's virility in 1.7 and of the porter's prattle about the effects of drink in 2.3, crime appears as the fruit of perverted sexual energy. Murder seen as rape, in the image of Tarquin (2.1.55), answers the sexualised language, conflating murder and intercourse in the verb 'to do'. Because of this perversion, 'the swelling act' (1.3.127) of the imperial theme, perceived as a conflation of tumescence and pregnancy, cannot be dissociated from its malignant version, when 'Discomfort swells' (1.2.28). What a good king cures – carbuncles 'All swoll'n and ulcerous' (4.3.153), evil brings forth. Seneca refers to those sickly swellings with the adjective *tumidus*, which he also applies to 'the swelling act of the imperial theme': *Pelasgo tumidus imperio Creo* (*Medea*

178; Creon, 'puffed with Pelasgian power'), or Agamemnon, addressed as *O tumide* in *Troades* (301; 'O thou swollen with pride') and characterised by *spiritus tumidos* in *Agamemnon* (248; '[swollen] pride'). The word also refers to poisonous swellings (*Hercules Furens* 221, 935–6; *Medea* 689), and finally brings together the swellings of empire, poison, and monstrous pregnancy, with *tumidum . . . monstro pelagus* (*Hippolytus* 1,016; 'the sea, swollen with a monstrous birth'): *nescio quid onerato sinu / gravis unda portat* (1,019–20; 'some strange thing in its burdened womb the heavy wave is carrying'). So does crime 'swell', *tumet* (*Thyestes* 266–7) in Atreus' soul.

Unlike Seneca's murderers, though, Macbeth and Lady Macbeth do not find pleasure in committing murder. Atreus gleefully anticipates Thyestes' dismay (903–7), and Medea gloats at Jason's grief:

> voluptas magna me invitam subit,
> et ecce crescit   (991–2)

(Great joy steals on me 'gainst my will, and lo, it is increasing.)

But Shakespeare's murderers only find 'doubtful joy' in the act:

> Nought's had, all's spent
> Where our desire is got without content.
>   (3.2.5–6)

Never does Macbeth, like Atreus, complacently view human disaster as *fructus hic operis mei* (*Thyestes* 906; 'the fruit of all my toil'). In Shakespeare's play, the *voluptas magna* of Seneca's murderers shrivels into disillusion.

Through the perversions of human nature that confound murder and pleasure, motherhood and manslaughter, Shakespeare's and Seneca's heroes fashion themselves into monsters. The transformation, however, is difficult, and persuasiveness is required; the Nurse's encouragements to Phaedra, *quid dubitas? dedit / tempus locusque casus* (*Hippolytus* 425–6; 'Why dost thou hesitate? Chance has given thee both time and place'), anticipate the way in which Lady Macbeth sets to work on her husband:

> Nor time, nor place
> Did then adhere, and yet you would make both.
> They have made themselves and that their fitness now
> Does unmake you.   (1.7.51–4)

Lady Macbeth's 'th'attempt and not the deed / Confounds us' (2.2.10–11) can be paralleled with Phaedra's *honesta quaedam scelera successus facit* (*Hippolytus* 598; 'Success makes some sins honest'). Such objurgations need to be all the stronger as most Senecan criminals hesitate. Even Clytemnestra has to brace herself: *Accingere, anime* (192, 198; 'Now gird thee up, my soul!').

Thyestes echoes her: *anime, quid rursus times / et ante rem subsidis? auden-dum est, age!* (*Thyestes* 283–4; 'O soul, why dost shrink back in fear and halt before the deed? Come! thou must dare it!'). An image twisted out of its original context in Seneca, *saepe in magistrum scelera redierunt sua* (*Thyestes* 311; 'often upon the teacher have his bad teachings turned'), gives words to Macbeth's doubts: 'we but teach / Bloody instructions, which being taught, return / To plague th'inventor' (1.7.8–10).[27] Not only does Macbeth share with Hippolytus and Hercules his dismay at blood-stained hands,[28] his hallucinatory uncertainty about reality was already Oedipus', who won-ders *an aeger animus falsa pro veris videt?* (204; 'does my sick fancy see false for true?'). The 'mynd opprest with care' (Alexander Nevile's translation of *aeger animus*, fol. 81*v*) makes night oppressive,[29] so that 'the benefit of sleep' and 'the effects of watching' (5.1.9) are undifferentiated. The body is violently affected: on the verge of crime, Atreus is aware that *tumultus pectora attonitus quatit / penitusque volvit* (*Thyestes* 260–1; 'A frantic tumult shakes and heaves deep [his] heart'). Deianira is similarly affected: *erectus horret crinis . . . cor attonitum salit* (*Hercules Oetaeus* 707–8; '[her] hair starts up in horror . . . [her] heart leaps wildly in fear').[30] So does Macbeth yield 'to that suggestion / Whose horrid image doth unfix [his] hair / And make [his] seated heart knock at [his] ribs / Against the use of nature' (1.3.133–6). Yet with time, Macbeth almost forgets the taste of fears:

> The time has been, my senses should have cooled
> To hear a night-shriek and my fell of hair
> Would at a dismal treatise rouse and stir
> As life were in't.   (5.5.10–13)

This new indifference is the result of accumulated crimes,[31] which create 'hard use' (3.4.143), a progressive toughening that implies becoming all muscle and no soul, like 'the rugged Russian bear, / The armed rhinoceros, or th'Hyrcan tiger' (3.4.100–1), or animated stone. Macbeth's desperate attempts to become 'Whole as the marble, founded as the rock' (3.4.21) harden him up as though he were trapped in the gaze of 'a new Gorgon' (2.3.66) of evil. While Seneca's characters are often petrified in fear and woe,[32] in *Macbeth*, the transformation of man into stone is the work of evil, which inverts God's promise, 'I will take away the stony heart out of your flesh, and I will give you an heart of flesh' (Ezekiel 36. 26).

While Atreus remains unmoved, *flevit in templis ebur* (*Thyestes* 702; even 'the ivory statues in the temples weep'). Insensitive statue that he has become, Macbeth cannot weep at his wife's death. Old Siward, satisfied that his son bravely died fighting, stoically refuses to shed a tear. But Mal-colm rebukes him: 'He's worth more sorrow' (5.9.17). We are far, at the end of the play, from the epic battlefields on which it opened, when men were qualmlessly 'unseamed . . . from the nave to th' chaps' (1.2.22). In between, Malcolm has been taught a lesson. When Macduff, still under the shock of his family's massacre, stayed prostrate, wordless, as if petrified, Malcolm first tried to console him with a Senecan tag,

> Give sorrow words; the grief that does not speak,
> Whispers the o'erfraught heart and bids it break.
> (4.3.211–12)[33]

He then appealed to his manliness: 'Dispute it like a man' (4.3.222). Macduff's answer, 'I shall do so; / But I must also feel it as a man' (4.3.223–4), reintegrates feeling in the definition of 'man'. While Seneca's monsters remain unchallenged, *Macbeth* sets against each other two types of human beings, those who deliberately stifle or crush their human nature, and those who reassert it. In the Gorgon's realm, milk dries up and whether in fear, grief, or evil, the distinctions between man and stone no longer obtain. On the way to battle, Macduff reinstates them, by reassociating action and emotion.

Shakespeare transported Holinshed's chronicle into a Senecan universe reinterpreted from a Christian point of view. Some scenes in *Macbeth* partially illustrate some of Seneca's maxims, like Amphytrion's *ius est in armis, opprimit leges timor* (*Hercules Furens* 253; 'might is right and fear oppresses law') or Lycus' *rapta . . . trepida manu / sceptra obtinentur* (*Hercules Furens* 341–2; 'usurped sceptres are held in anxious hand'). As the Chorus remarks in *Thyestes*,

> rex est qui posuit metus
> et diri mala pectoris.
> (348–9)

(A king is he who has laid fear aside and the base longings of an evil heart.)

Like Seneca's tragic heroes, Macbeth and Lady Macbeth ignore his precepts in the moral treatises, according to which man finds equanimity when freed from the enslavement of passions, desire, and fear. Seneca's idea, however, that man may elevate himself above his condition, even in serenity, had been severely rebuked by Montaigne at the end of his 'Apologie of Raymond Sebond':

'Oh what a vile and abject thing is man (saith [Seneca]), unlesse he raise himselfe above humanity!' Observe here a notable speech and a profitable desire; but likewise absurd. For to make the handful greater than the hand, and the embraced greater than the arme, and to hope to straddle more than our legs length, is impossible and monstrous: nor that man should mount over and above himselfe or humanity;

for he cannot see but with his owne eyes, nor take hold but with his owne armes. He shall raise himself up, if it please God extraordinarily to lend him his helping hand. He may elevate himselfe by forsaking and renouncing his owne meanes, and suffering himselfe to be elevated and raised by meere heavenly meanes.[34]

Montaigne's text offers an enlightening background to images of Macbeth as a 'dwarfish thief' in 'a giant's robe' (5.2.20–1) and to his initial reflection that 'If chance will have me king, why chance may crown me / Without my stir' (1.3.142–3) – chance, here, being substituted for God. This thought immediately follows Macbeth's feeling that unreality is displacing reality: 'nothing is but what is not' (1.3.140–1), a phrase that acquires a blasphemous resonance when read in the context of Montaigne's definition of God (echoing Exodus 3.14) as 'who is the only one that is', so that 'there is nothing that truly is but he alone'.[35] Montaigne's rebuttal of Seneca points to moral issues in Shakespeare's play. Macbeth had at first refused to step beyond the pale of humanity:

> I dare do all that may become a man;
> Who dares do more is none.
>
>   (1.7.46–7)

But, like Atreus, his criminal swelling soon transports him, not above, but outside humanity, *supra fines moris humani* (*Thyestes* 267; 'beyond the bounds of human use'), not towards equanimity but, through agonizing torture, towards insensitivity. Read in this light, *Macbeth* dramatises the shortcomings and distortions of Stoicism as well as the curdling effects of Senecan criminality within the Christian soul.

In the process, Shakespeare's imagination seems to be set ablaze by fundamental images on which the play concentrates, infanticide and monstrous pregnancy, a bloody banquet, night at odds with day. In such cases, literary creation does not necessarily imply direct borrowing or conscious allusion. Wrenched out of their original context, images blend, so that Ovid and Seneca, Seneca and the Bible, suddenly fuse, Athamas, Hercules and Medea merge. This process of coalescence is often accompanied by a process of expansion, creating complex reverberations, as broken banquets and devouring mothers multiply. Thus reworked or reimagined, Senecan images seem to contribute to *Macbeth*'s tragic vision, through the collapse of most of the distinctions that help to define human identity. In this respect, *Macbeth* is in deep resonance with Seneca's tragedies, and several themes of destructive confusion fuel what might be called Shakespeare's own creative 'confusion' – in the original sense of *confundere*, or pouring together: the coalescing and expanding powers of poetic imagination.

NOTES

1. T. W. Baldwin, *William Shakspere's Small Latine and Lesse Greeke*, 2 vols. (Urbana, IL 1944), vol. II, p. 560.
2. John W. Cunliffe, *The Influence of Seneca in Elizabethan Tragedy* (London 1893); Jakob Engel, 'Die Spuren Senecas in Shakspseres Dramen', *Preussische Jahrbücher* 112 (1903), 60–81; Cornell M. Dowlin, 'Two Shakespeare Parallels in Studley's Translation of Seneca's *Agamemnon*', *Shakespeare Association Bulletin* 14 (1939), 256; Kenneth Muir, 'A Borrowing From Seneca', *N&Q* 194 (1949), 214–16; 'Seneca and Shakespeare', *N&Q* 201 (1956), 243–4.
3. Throughout this chapter quotations will be from Seneca, *Tragedies*, ed. and trans. Frank Justus Miller, 2 vols. (Cambridge, MA 1917; repr. 1998). Jasper Heywood's translation of *Thyestes* is quoted from Joost Daalder's edition (London 1982). All the other Elizabethan translations are quoted from Thomas Newton's *Seneca His Tenne Tragedies* (London 1581, repr. Amsterdam 1969). The Elizabethan translations are given only when their phrasing seems nearer to Shakespeare's play.
4. In the same play, *consilii impotens* (126), translated by Miller as 'ungoverned in thy purpose', was even closer to 'infirm of purpose', which could almost translate it literally.
5. Similarly, *Macbeth* 5.5.18–19 may have inspired his translation of *tempus te tacitus subruit horaque / semper praeterita deterior subit* (*Hippolytus* 775–6) as 'Time is silently undermining thee and an hour, worse than the last, is ever creeping on.'
6. Kenneth Muir, 'Shakespeare and the Tragic Pattern', *Proceedings of the British Academy* 44 (1958), 145–62.
7. Robert S. Miola, *Shakespeare and Classical Tragedy: The Influence of Seneca* (Oxford 1992).
8. Henry N. Paul, *The Royal Play of 'Macbeth': When, How, and Why it was Written by Shakespeare* (London 1948, repr. 1950), p. 48.
9. Aristotle, *On the Art of Poetry* §14, in *Classical Literary Criticism*, ed. T. S. Dorsch (Harmondsworth 1965), p. 50.
10. The same concatenation occurs in *Thyestes* 40–4.
11. Also in *Agamemnon* 158–70; *Phoenissae* 260–1; *Hercules Oetaeus* 985; *Medea* 261. It is a major theme in *Troades,* where Astyanax's murder/sacrifice (1,101–9) answers Iphigenia's (246–9).
12. *Oedipus* 686.
13. Robert S. Miola points to the similitudes in situation and atmosphere between *Macbeth* and *Agamemnon*, in *Shakespeare and Classical Tragedy,* p. 97, n. 46.
14. *Non novi sceleris tibi / conviva venies* (*Thyestes* 62–3; 'To no novel feast of crime wilt come as banqueter').
15. This version is closer to Shakespeare than to the Latin, which says *non timemur, tuta sine telo est domus* (468; 'I am not feared, safe without weapons is my house').
16. See F. W. Moorman, 'Shakespeare's Ghosts', *MLR* 1 (1906), 192–201.
17. Paul A. Jorgensen, *Our Naked Frailties: Sensational Art and Meaning in Macbeth* (Berkeley 1971), p. 123.

18. Allan H. Gilbert, 'Seneca and the Criticism of Elizabethan Tragedy', *PQ* 13 (1934), 370–81; W. A. Armstrong, 'The Influence of Seneca and Machiavelli on the Elizabethan Tyrant', *RES* 24 (1948), 19–35.
19. For a full analysis of Seneca's and Shakespeare's focus on hands see Miola, *Shakespeare and Classical Tragedy*, pp. 114–17.
20. Also: *hinc et hinc compagibus / ruptis* (*Hercules Oetaeus* 1,135–6; 'this side and that should heaven's frame be burst').
21. *Miscere thalamos patris et nati apparas / uteroque prolem capere confusam impio?* (*Hippolytus* 171–2; 'Dost purpose to share thy bed with father and with son, and receive in an incestuous womb a blended progeny?').
22. Inga-Stina Ewbank, 'The Fiend-Like Queen: A Note on *Macbeth* and Seneca's *Medea*', *ShS* 19 (1966), 82–94, reprinted in *Aspects of Macbeth*, ed. Kenneth Muir and Philip Edwards (Cambridge 1977), pp. 53–65.
23. Ovid, *Metamorphoses*, ed. Frank Justus Miller, rev. G. P. Goold, 2 vols. (Cambridge, MA 1916, 3rd edn. 1999), vol. 1. The author of *Alphonsus, Emperor of Germany* (1594?) had also been struck by this episode and reworked it into a threat: 'Like Athamas first will I seize upon / Thy young unchristen'd and despised son / And with his guiltless brains bepaint the stones' (4.3.61–3), in *The Plays and Poems of George Chapman, The Tragedies*, ed. T. M. Parrott (London 1910).
24. *Shakespeare's Ovid being Arthur Golding's Translation of the Metamorphoses*, ed. W. H. D. Rouse (London 1904, repr. 1961), 4.636–40.
25. Tantalus killed his little son who was running to kiss him, *Thyestes* 144–5.
26. Ewbank, 'The Fiend-like Queen', p. 64, n. 9.
27. Joost Daalder pointed to the parallel in his edition of Jasper Heywood's *Thyestes*, n. to 2.136–8, p. 42. Also Howard Jacobson, *ShQ* 35 (1984), 321–2.
28. On the well-known possibility that *Macbeth*, 2.2.59–62 blends *Hippolytus* 715–18 and *Hercules Furens* 1,323–9, see Muir's edn., pp. 57–58. Miola persuasively argues for *Hercules Furens* as a source, in *Shakespeare and Classical Tragedy*, pp. 112–14.
29. 2.2.39–43 is traditionally compared with *Hercules Furens* 1,065–81.
30. Also *Medea* 926–7, *Octavia* 735–6, *Oedipus* 224, 585.
31. 'Things bad begun make strong themselves by ill' (3.3.55). The parallel with *Agamemnon* 115 is a commonplace.
32. For example: *metu corpus rigens* (*Thyestes* 634; 'numbing fear'); *ut spiritu expulso stupens / corpus rigescat* (*Thyestes* 905–6; 'how his body, breathless with the shock, grows stiff'); *torpens malis rigensque sine sensu fero* (*Troades* 417; 'I bear, benumbed with woe, stony, insensible'), or, in Jasper Heywood's words, 'But me (alas) amaseth most the fearful heauines / That all astonied am for drade, and horrour of the sight' (fol. 108r).
33. The frequently quoted *Curae leves locuntur, ingentes stupent* (*Hippolytus* 607; 'Light troubles speak; the weighty are struck dumb').
34. *The Essayes of Michael Lord of Montaigne translated by John Florio*, ed. Henry Morley (London 1894), 2.12, p. 310.
35. A few lines above in the 'Apologie of Raymond Sebond', p. 310.

CHAPTER 9

'These are the only men': Seneca and monopoly in Hamlet 2.2

Erica Sheen

When Polonius arrives to announce the arrival of the Tragedians of the City, he describes them as 'the best actors in the world':

Seneca cannot be too heavy, nor Plautus too light. For the law of writ and the liberty, these are the only men. (*Hamlet* 2.2.382–4)[1]

The idea that there is a relation of influence between classical and early modern drama is fundamental to any account of the English Renaissance. But Polonius inadvertently provides a clue to something a little less obvious, something we might adapt his own words to describe as a writ of theatrical liberty:[2] the summoning up of classical writers such as Seneca and Plautus by practitioners of the Elizabethan professional theatre, and the suggestion that the appropriate frame of reference for this mutually emancipatory embodiment of authorship might be a conception of freedom within the law that increasingly characterised the economic and political culture of Elizabethan and Jacobean England. It is thus not surprising that the Players' Scene has long been recognised as a peculiarly intense, and intensely peculiar, engagement with classical sources, even though there is no real consensus as to what the nature of that engagement is. What *is* surprising is that no one has yet taken Polonius at his word and considered the possibility that the embodiment in question here is not Virgil or Ovid, as most commentators suggest, but Seneca. In this essay I propose not only a Senecan influence, but also a hitherto unrecognised source. More importantly, however, I seek to place the relation between Seneca and Shakespeare in *Hamlet* in the context of sixteenth-century legal, political, and economic debates about monopoly and the Senecan discourse of benefits.

An approach of this kind constitutes something of a re-embodiment for Shakespearean source studies itself. Since the early years of New Historicism, when Stephen Greenblatt famously described them as 'the elephant's graveyard of literary history', source studies have been in a state of neglect.[3]

Writing of the connection between *King Lear* and Samuel Harsnett's *A Dec-laration of Egregious Popish Impostures*, Greenblatt asserted that the relation between the two texts

has . . . been known for centuries, but the knowledge has remained almost entirely inert, locked in the conventional pieties of source studies.[4]

Almost from that precise moment, Shakespeareans dutifully diverted their attention from the diachronic study of influence to a synchronic study of context. Greenblatt commemorated this epistemic shift by announcing a new programme of study, 'cultural poetics', and identified its central concern as the 'institutional economy' within which both Shakespeare and Harsnett circulated. From such a perspective, source studies were exposed as an approach in which 'a freestanding self-sufficient disinterested art work produced by a solitary genius . . . has only an accidental relation to its sources' – as opposed to one in which 'the protective isolation' of such works 'gives way to a sense of their interaction with other texts and hence to the permeability of their boundaries'.[5]

Since then, much work has been done to correct the New Historicist bias in favour of contemporary over classical context. Over the interven-ing years, as Renaissance scholars have refined their account of the agency of early modern authorship, one of our most important insights into the early modern period has been an understanding of the political use to which it put its rediscovery of the classics. But there remains something of a methodological aporia in our account of Shakespeare, precisely because there is no agreed account of what in his case the agency of authorship is – or rather perhaps because the range of accounts we have map out the institutional economy of contemporary Shakespearean studies rather than that of Shakespearean theatre. Work on Shakespeare and the classics still takes place largely under the rubric of source studies, and still to some extent confirms Greenblatt's reservation, despite the fact that it has under-gone its own internal programme of transformation. Writing in 1990, Robert Miola distinguished between a 'traditional' approach that 'privi-leges the author as the central intelligence who reads or watches sources and reshapes them, consciously or unconsciously, into a new text' and an 'alternative' understanding that 'the source is an intermediated text' rather than an imitated text. This perspective privileges 'not the author but the text itself'.[6] It

provides more spacious perspectives in which to work, a methodology that opens discussion to the various routes of influence, direct and indirect, and to the various forms influence can take, verbal and non-verbal.[7]

For Miola, this post-structuralist perspective has 'a serious potential limitation: it can succumb to a vague impressionism that timorously avoids committing itself to any single text as a source'.[8] Weighing up these alternatives, Miola embraced a middle way, a combination of the two that presents 'a view of texts as historical artefacts with partially recoverable etiologies – *with, in other words, a specific source that an author transforms*'.[9] Here again is Greenblatt's 'conventional piety', but I suggest that such an approach – or at least the version of it I propose in this chapter – has a more important part to play in post-New Historicist criticism than that dismissive description implies. What classical source studies can offer the contemporary study of Shakespeare is not – or at least not necessarily – an unthinking critical conservatism, but a conceptual paradigm that can explain why and how the early modern period was so productive of authors and authorship, a paradigm whose object of study is a cognitive schema that worked historically to configure what Pocock has referred to as textual 'events' in terms of an author, a source, and a dynamic of transformation between the two.[10]

From this perspective, what source studies address is the *source relation*, a term I conceive in analogy to the Saussurean notion of the sign relation. Just as the sign relation selects a signifier from the paradigm, and gives it meaning within a text by linking it with a signified, so the source relation embodies authorship in textual events by linking a present moment of production to a past author. Approached in this way source studies reveal themselves not so much as a problem for the notion of an 'institutional economy' of Shakespearean theatre, as the basis of an account of its fundamental dynamic of production. In this chapter I pursue this institutional economy in Shakespeare's source relation to Seneca in the Player's Speech, and argue that such an analysis requires us to combine a diachronic account of the relation between Shakespeare and Seneca's plays with a synchronic account of the situation of Shakespearean theatre within a contemporary economic culture pervaded by the Senecan discourse of benefit. And I am going to propose that the appropriate historical frame of reference for this analysis of the relation between the transforming author and his single source is the common law account of the origin of personal property in the creation or manufacture of a new thing, the principle which was taken as an exception to the voidance of monopolies in Edward Coke's Statute of Monopolies of 1624, and which remains today the basis on which a derivative work can be copyrighted as an 'original work'.

We might begin by explaining what the word 'original' means in contemporary media law, because it helps us get a perspective on the difficulties we experience as soon as we try to use it to discuss Shakespeare. As Rhonda Baker glosses it,

The sense in which this word is used . . . is that the work must represent the end result of a sufficiently substantial amount of skill, knowledge or creative labour on the part of the author. The work can be derived from someone else's work (so not original in that sense) but if sufficient skill and labour have been put into making the new work . . . it will be original for the purposes of copyright law and is capable of being protected.[11]

Given the utter clarity of this definition, it is paradoxical that the history of copyright is precisely the reason why there are so many problems involved in discussing Shakespeare as what he actually is: the author of derivative works. It is widely accepted that the kind of author-figure Miola wishes to retain and Greenblatt sought to jettison is a post-copyright invention. Mark Rose has outlined the process by which what he calls the proprietary author emerged as a back-formation from the booksellers' resistance to the imposition of copyright term in the Copyright Act of 1709. Noting that Shakespeare, Bacon, and Milton were 'the perennials of the book trade' whom 'the booksellers had been accustomed to treat as if they were private landed estates', Rose shows how Lockean arguments about the origin of property in individual acts of appropriation from the general state of nature were used to advance the idea that authors were actually already owners of their own work (and consequently that the transfer of this property to booksellers gave the booksellers a legitimate title to it).[12] He suggests that a crucial element of this process of authorisation is the development of an idea of style based on the concept of originality, since style came to be recognised as the basis of an author's property in his or her own work.

This argument provides us with the basis of a very adequate account of the way the derivative work constitutes itself as 'original', according to which the author who wishes to appropriate other people's work strategically treats source texts as part of the general state of nature rather than property in its own right; and stylistic innovation is seen as the process by which he or she converts the source text into his or her own property. But historians of intellectual property have been reluctant to apply this argument to writers of the sixteenth and seventeenth centuries, particularly Shakespeare.[13] Thus, according to Laura Rosenthal, 'For Shakespeare, the story of Lear had no particular owner or specific textual origin.'[14] Note the implications of this statement: 'Shakespeare . . . treats the old *Leir* as if it belongs in the public domain':[15] an assertion which betrays the underlying contradictions of her position, since the public domain is what authored works enter after the expiry of copyright term and is fundamentally a property-based concept.[16] Rosenthal refers to the process at work here as 'intertextuality', and it is significant how frequently this term emerges in discussions of this kind – with the effect, as here, of dematerialising the process of transfer from one author to another.[17] Implicitly, she agrees with Rose, who suggests that before the proprietary author could come into being there had to exist

an adequate theory of property, or more precisely an adequate discourse about property, a language in which the idea of the proprietary author could be elaborated. This discourse developed under the sign, as it were, of John Locke . . .[18]

This assertion makes it obvious why accounts of literary property that work backwards from 1709 are so uncomfortable with Elizabethan and Jacobean writers. The 'adequate discourse about property' exploited by the booksellers in the early eighteenth century was fundamentally the sixteenth-century discourse of monopoly, which became prominent in debates about patents throughout the 1580s and 90s, and came to a head in the eventual confrontation between Elizabeth and Parliament in 1601. In fact, the Lockean discourse of property is based on sixteenth-century common law debates about the origins of property in labour. As early as 1520, lawyers in Filoll v. Asshelleygh, a dispute concerning the ownership of a stray bloodhound, asserted the logical connection between the principle of 'occupation' as the basis on which wild things or raw material are taken into possession and made tame by one's labour, and monopoly as an activity defensible on the grounds of the expertise involved in that labour.[19]

David Harris Sacks has shown that the Senecan discourse of benefits pervaded the Elizabethan patents debates.[20] Significantly, an interest in the publication of Seneca's moral works spanned the precise period of those debates, from Arthur Golding's 1578 translation of Seneca's *De Beneficiis* – 'The work of the excellent philosopher L. A. Seneca concerning benefits, that is to say the doing, receiving and requiting of good turns' – to the 1607 collection, *Seneca's Morals*, and Thomas Lodge's translation of the complete moral works in 1614. As Sacks demonstrates, Elizabeth herself drew on the discourse of benefits in her description of the grant of patents as 'a priuate benefitt' 'by way of recompense for . . . service done'.[21] Monopoly may have been seen as a grievance by those excluded from its privileges, but it played a large part in the theory of the mutuality that underpinned the Elizabethan commonwealth. According to Seneca, a system of reciprocal benefit, the interchange of skill and industry, is the very fabric of human society. He figures this analysis in his account of the Three Graces, whose roles embody the process encapsulated in Golding's title:

Why do the sisters dance hand in hand in a ring that returns upon itself? For the reason that a benefit passing in its course from hand to hand returns nevertheless to the giver; the beauty of the whole is destroyed if the course is anywhere broken, and it has most beauty if it is continuous, and maintains an uninterrupted succession.[22]

The Senecan dance of benefits is, I suggest, a far more useful point of departure for an account of authorial transfer in the 1590s and 1600s than the concept of intertextuality. If an aesthetic of originality underpins the proprietary author, an account of a mode of authorial agency that figures its subsumption of other people's labour into its private symbolic capital as a benefit 'passing in its course from hand to hand' can provide us with the basis of an aesthetic of monopoly. It is within such an aesthetic that I propose to situate the development and consolidation of Shakespearean theatre, and what follows is a case study for this proposal as applied to the Player's Speech of Aeneas' Tale to Dido in *Hamlet* 2.2.

Completed in 1601, two years after the Chamberlain's Men moved into their permanent home at the Globe, *Hamlet* registers in a very full way the edgy assertiveness of its political and economic context. Editorial commentary on the Player's Speech characteristically approaches its distinctive style in terms of parody,[23] but Shakespeare's concerns are, I suggest, more material than formal. The question of property emerges as soon as the players enter:[24]

We'll e'en to't like French falc'ners, fly at anything we see. We'll have a speech straight. Come, give us a taste of your quality. (2.2.412–14)

The hawking metaphor is indicative: unlike a straying bloodhound, when a tamed bird of prey was let fly at a quarry, not only did the bird remain the property of its owner, its quarry also became his.[25] But the question of exactly whose quarry this is remains for the present unclear. Shakespeare does not tell us about the writer; indeed he makes a point of not doing so. But we *are* told about the style: 'an honest method, as wholesome as sweet, and by very much more handsome than fine' (424–6), and we proceed from that to what turns out to be a covert investigation of the 'lost' play's author. At the outset, Hamlet's conspicuous failure of memory draws our attention to the speech's first allusion to a source text:

> – let me see, let me see:
> The rugged Pyrrhus, like th'Hyrcanian beast –
> 'tis not so. It begins with Pyrrhus –   (429–31)

This 'accidental' reference to the Hyrcanian beast is generally recognised as the first reference in this speech to Marlowe and Nashe's *The Tragedie*

of Dido Queene of Carthage, where Dido uses the word to describe Aeneas'
decision to leave her and sail for Italy:

> Thy mother was no Goddesse, periurd man,
> Nor *Dardanus* the author of thy stocke:
> But thou art sprung from *Scythian Caucasus*,
> And Tygers of *Hircania* gave thee sucke:
> (5.1.1, 564–7)[26]

Dido was published in 1594 with a title page that claims it was acted by
the Chapel Children, the children's company that became so fashionable
in London at the turn of the century and which Hamlet discusses with
Rosencrantz and Guilderstern earlier in this scene. There is thus already
much at stake when Shakespeare alludes to *and dismisses* this source in a
speech intended to vindicate the superior quality of a company of adult
players who have lost their audience to the 'little eyases'.

But the allusion also glances back to Robert Greene's famous attack
on Shakespeare himself, probably dating from 1592, an attack that draws
unmistakeably on the contemporary idiom of grievance against monopoly:

for there is an upstart Crow, beautified with our feathers, that with his *Tyger's heart
wrapt in a Players hide, supposes he is as well able to bumbast out a blanke verse as
the best of you: and being an absolute Johannes fac totum*, is in his owne conceit the
only Shake-scene in a countrie.[27]

Greene's denunciation parodied a line from *Richard Duke of York (3 Henry
VI)*, directed at Queen Margaret by Richard of York: 'O tiger's heart
wrapped in a woman's hide!' (1.4.138), which was itself followed by an earlier
borrowing from *Dido*: 'But you are more inhuman, more inexorable, / O,
ten times more than tigers of Hyrcania' (155–6). Since Greene's attack on
Shakespeare is generally held to be addressed to Marlowe, Nashe, and Peele,
it is clear that what we are looking at in *Hamlet* is not just an appropriation
of a source: it is a reflection on that process of appropriation as it institu-
tionalises across time into a monopolistic mode of production. From his
innocent first borrowing in *3 Henry VI*, to Greene's accusation of theft and
this subsequent act of outright expropriation, Shakespeare's 'occupation'
of his source gains momentum across the eight years that passed between
Greene's resentful snipe at a fledgeling dramatist and his own now assured
status as the leading writer for the leading theatre company, permanently
established at the Globe: 'the best actors in the world'.

As Aeneas' story moves towards the death of Priam, Shakespeare's engagement with Marlowe–Nashe gathers in intensity. Editors have noted two

main points of contact. First, lines 453–4: 'But with the whiff and wind of his fell sword / Th'unnervèd father falls'. Harold Jenkins describes this as

> seemingly a reminiscence (the likeliest one) of Marlowe and Nashe's *Dido*, 'He . . . whisk'd his sword about, And with the wound thereof the King fell down' (ii.i.253–4), where accordingly *wound* is often emended to *wind*.[28]

But as Jenkins points out, it reverses the order of events: in *Dido*, Priam's confrontation with Pyrrhus is a response to an attack on Hecuba; in *Hamlet*, it is itself the subject of a response by Hecuba, which, in its turn, is the subject of the Player's response to her, and of Hamlet's response to him. This in itself would be a significant alteration: the more conspicuous the reference to his competitors' play, the more conspicuously Shakespeare seems to insist on rewriting it, and to associate that rewriting with the defining formal features of his own work. But then we reach Pyrrhus' famous 'pause', conventionally read as a parallel to Hamlet's continuing inability to kill Claudius:

> For lo, his sword
> Which was declining on the milky head
> Of reverend Priam, seemed i'th'air to stick.
> So, as a painted tyrant, Pyrrhus stood,
> And like a neutral to his will and matter,
> Did nothing.   (457–62)

According to editorial tradition, this is another Marlowe–Nashe allusion. Jenkins comments, 'Leech supposes this to derive from *Dido*, II.i.263: "he stood stone still"'.[29] As such, it constitutes another reversal: as Jenkins points out, in *Dido* Pyrrhus' pause comes after Priam's death; in *Hamlet* it comes before it, and as such serves to focus the subsequent all-important introduction of Hecuba. But Jenkins thought the parallel was 'dubious', and he was right, though only in so far as the recognition, once again, that *Dido* is *not* the text we should be trying to remember prepares us for the revelation of a hitherto unrevealed source, a revelation that radically reinterprets the process of rewriting to which Marlowe and Nashe have been subject since the beginning of the speech. That source is Seneca's *Troades*, translated by Jasper Heywood as *Troas* and published in 1581 in Thomas Newton's collection of 'Englished' Senecas.[30]

Seneca's play is set in the aftermath of the fall of Troy. Anxious to return home after ten years of siege, the Greeks are becalmed on the Trojan coast. To appease the ghost of Achilles, they agree to sacrifice his erstwhile-betrothed Polyxena, one of the two surviving children of Priam and Hecuba.

As she is led out to death at the hands of Achilles' son Pyrrhus, a crowd
gathers to witness her death:

> Some with her beauty moved were, some with her tender yeares:
> Some to behold the turnes of chaunce, and how each thing thus wears.
> But most them moves her valiant minde, and lofty stomacke hie,
> So strong, so stout, so ready of hart and wel prepard to dye.
> Thus passe they forth and bold before King Pirrhus goeth the mayde,
> They pitty her, they marvel her, their hartes were all affrayde.
> As sone as then the hard hil top (where die she should) they trode,
> And hie upon his fathers tombe the youthful Pyrrhus stoode.
> The manly mayd she never shronke one foote, nor backward drew,
> But boldly turnes to meete the stroke, with stoute unchanged hew,
> Her corage moves eche one, and loe a strange thing monstrous like,
> That *Pyrhus even himselfe stood stil for dread, and durst not strike.*[31]

Here, then, is Pyrrhus' pause: 'So as a painted tyrant, Pyrrhus stood /
And like a neutral to his will and matter / Did nothing.' It is, I suggest, a
clear and direct parallel, and it presides over a network of similarities and
differences that would repay the attentions of any scholar of source studies,
conventionally pious or otherwise. But my concern here is above all with
this remarkable counterpoint of contrasting source relations: on the one
hand, a ruthless expropriation of contemporary competition, on the other,
a beneficial return to the classical tradition. It is also, increasingly, with
the institutional implications of the focus on women that is beginning to
emerge from Shakespeare's rewriting of Marlowe–Nashe.

   To understand this, we might ourselves pause, as Shakespeare may have
done, over Heywood's address 'To The Reader', and notice its thoughtful
gloss on the way a writer transforms a classical source and embodies himself
as a contemporary author in the process. Pointing out 'how hard a thing it
is for mee to touch at ful in all poynts the authors mynd', Heywood has, he
says, 'sondrye places augmented and some altered in this my translation':

First forasmuch as this worke seemed unto mee in some places unperfite, whether
left so of the Author, or parte of it loste, as tyme devoureth all thinges . . . I have . . .
with addition of myne owne Penne supplied the wante of some thynges . . .[32]

This account contrasts strongly with the by now obviously inadequate
suggestion that sixteenth-century writers had no sense of textual origins.
Heywood's analysis, with its complex temporality of authorial loss and
retrieval, inserts into the source relation a kind of prototypical sense of
copyright term, and a strong corrective to Rosenthal's problematic notion
of a pre-authorial public domain. Note that the process is described as one

of 'perfecting', with its dual senses of completing and improving. An area of meaning that begins to 'perfect' itself as this text passes in its course from Seneca to Heywood to Shakespeare is that of theatre itself: according to the messenger that brings the news of Polyxena's death, a crowd came 'as if thronging to a theatre': *crescit theatri more concursus frequens* (1,125).[33] Their response is unmistakeably that of a tragic catharsis: *omnium mentes tremunt / mirantur ac miserantur* (1,147–8) – as Heywood puts it, 'They pitty her, they marvel her, their hartes were all affrayde'.[34] Neither Seneca's play nor Heywood's translations were written for performance. As such, what they offered Shakespeare was an idea of theatre in which female characterisation goes beyond the limitations of existing conventions, beyond even the conventions that Shakespeare himself had hitherto observed. Like *Troas*, but unlike *Dido*, it is focused completely on Hecuba: she is its point of view. Shakespeare places her at the centre of a complex network of spectatorship both inside the speech and outside it, in Hamlet's response to the Player who is responding to her. As such she also presides over what has been seen as the play's prevailing critical concern: the question of delay. Here too it is hard not to believe that Shakespeare took his cue from Seneca–Heywood. As Seneca's play begins, the Greeks are ready to sail, but their ships are becalmed. This situation is described over and over again as *mora*, translated by Heywood as 'delay'. Like *Hamlet*, its salient concern is the nature of the agency that asserts itself in the 'interim' between the beginning of an action and its completion. This concern provides a template for a play in which the action as a whole spans the freeze-frame effect of a single arrested moment of violence, but within which that single moment is also embedded as the explanation of its own arrest. Once we realise that what 'really' happens at the point at which the descending blade 'seemed i'th'air to stick' is not the death of a man but a woman, once we see that this all but subliminal image completely reorganises our understanding not just of the action of the play but of the kind of theatre that is capable of presenting it, we have, I think, plucked out the heart of *Hamlet*'s 'mystery'. On a local basis, Polyxena's subliminal presence in *Hamlet* provides a dramatic key to Ophelia: her problematic position within the overall structure of the play; the ambiguous agency of her death; the critical misconstruction to which she has notoriously been subject. *Globally*, she provides the institutional key to the innovative female characterisation that would become so dominant a feature of Shakespearean theatre in the years that followed.

   The Player's Speech records a precarious moment in the history of Shakespearean theatre. Arising from and responding to the immediate threat of unemployment, it makes an ambitious claim for the Chamberlain's Men,

but the claim was amply vindicated in their elevation to the status of King's
Men in 1603, and in the plays that followed in the subsequent years. In
1601, 'Aeneas' Tale to Dido' served the short-term need to overcome the
challenge of the fashionable children's companies; in the longer term, it signalled stylistic and generic changes in Shakespeare's plays that would help
his company consolidate their status as the 'best actors in the world'. With
their massive debt to Seneca, Shakespeare's later tragedies would stand as a
fitting recompense for service done in *Hamlet*.

NOTES

1. All references to *Hamlet* are from S. Greenblatt, W. Cohen, J. E. Howard, and
   K. E. Maus, eds., *The Norton Shakespeare* (New York 1997).
2. *Habeas corpus* – the writ by which judges order imprisoned persons to be
   brought into court to determine if they are being legally held – is also commonly
   called 'the writ of liberty'.
3. See e.g. S. Greenblatt, 'Shakespeare and the Exorcists', in Patricia Parker and
   Geoffrey Hartmann, eds., *Shakespeare and the Question of Theory* (London
   1985), p. 163.
4. Ibid., p. 165.
5. Ibid., p. 165.
6. Robert S. Miola, 'Othello furens', *ShQ* 41 (1990), 49.
7. Ibid., p. 50.
8. Ibid., p. 49.
9. Ibid., p. 50 (*my italics*).
10. J. G. A. Pocock, 'Texts as Events: Reflections on the History of Political
    Thought', in Kevin Sharpe and Steven N. Zwicker, eds., *Politics of Discourse:
    The Literature and History of Seventeenth-Century England* (California 1987).
11. Rhonda Baker, *Media Law: A User's Guide for Film and Programme Makers*
    (London 1995), p. 23.
12. Mark Rose, 'The Author as Proprietor: *Donaldson v. Becket* and the Genealogy
    of Modern Authorship', *Representations* 23 (1988), 53.
13. For work that has begun to correct this tendency, see Joseph Loewenstein's
    chapter, 'Upstart Crows and other Emergencies', in his recent study, *Ben Jonson
    and Possessive Authorship* (Cambridge 2002), pp. 50–103.
14. Laura Rosenthal, '(Re) Writing Lear: Literary Property and Dramatic Author-
    ship', in John Brewer and Susan Staves, eds., *Early Modern Conceptions of
    Property* (London 1996), p. 324.
15. Ibid., p. 327.
16. Ibid.
17. Ibid., See also Louise Scheinler, 'Latinized Greek Drama in Shakespeare's
    Writing of *Hamlet*', *ShQ* 41 (1990), 29–48, for a Kristevan reading of Shake-
    spearean intertextuality.
18. Rose, 'Author as Proprietor', p. 56.

19. *Reports del Cases*, T.12.H8 3–5 pl.3. Although the last yearbook was printed in 1535, the *Reports* were frequently reprinted in the Elizabethan period, first as single-year volumes and then between 1590 and 1610 as collections.

20. David H. Sacks, 'The Countervailing of Benefits: Monopoly, Liberty, and Benevolence in Elizabethan England', in Dale Hoak, ed., *Tudor Political Culture* (Cambridge 1995), pp. 272–91.

21. Ibid., p. 285.

22. *Moral Essays*, trans. John W. Basor, 3 vols., The Loeb Classical Library (London 1928–35), vol. III, p. 13.

23. See Harold Jenkins' 'Longer Note on the Player's Speech', in the Arden edn *Hamlet* (London 1982), pp. 478–9 for a summary of this argument.

24. For a discussion of this speech from a contrasting but complementary perspective, see Loewenstein, 'Upstart Crows', pp. 84–103.

25. J. H. Baker, 'Introduction' in Baker, ed., *The Reports of Sir John Spelman*, 2 vols. (London 1977), vol. I, p. 210.

26. *The Tragedie of Dido Queene of Carthage*, in *The Works of Christopher Marlowe*, ed. C. F. Tucker Brooke (Oxford 1966).

27. Cited in Greenblatt, Cohen, Howard and Maus, *Norton Shakespeare*, pp. 3,321–2 (*their italics*).

28. Jenkins, 'Longer Note', pp. 479–80.

29. Ibid., p. 480. In Tucker Brooke, ed., *Tragedie of Dido*, these lines occur at 2.1.558–9.

30. For other accounts of Shakespeare's use of the Englished Senecas, see Miola, 'Othello furens', and Erica Sheen, 'The Agent for his Master: Political Service and Professional Liberty in *Cymbeline*', in Gordon McMullan and Jonathan Hope, eds., *The Politics of Tragicomedy: Shakespeare and After* (London 1992), pp. 55–76.

31. Jasper Heywood, *The Sixte Tragedie of the Most Grave and Prudent Author Lucius Annaeus Seneca Entituled Troas with Divers Sundrye Additions to the Same*, in Thomas Newton, *Seneca His Tenne Tragedies Translated into English*, in Charles Whibley, ed., *Newton's Seneca*, 2 vols. (London 1927), vol. II, p. 51 (*my italics*).

32. Ibid., pp. 3–4.

33. L. A. Seneca, trans. F. J. Miller, *Troades*, The Loeb Classical Library (London 1968), p. 218.

34. Ibid., p. 220.

I acknowledge with thanks a British Academy Overseas Conference award that supported the early development of this work, and the Renaissance Studies Society for an invitation to present it in Oxford in November 2002.

PART III

'LESSE GREEK'

PLUTARCH

CHAPTER 10

'Character' in Plutarch and Shakespeare: Brutus, Julius Caesar, and Mark Antony

John Roe

JULIUS CAESAR

Nothing in Plutarch's Life of Julius Caesar or of Marcus Brutus quite prepares us for those extended soliloquies with which Shakespeare equips Brutus when he considers the justification for conspiring against the former enemy, who in Plutarch (but not in Shakespeare) has spared his life:

> It must be by his death, and for my part,
> I know no personal cause to spurn at him,
> But for the general: he would be crown'd.
> How that might change his nature, there's the question.
> It is the bright day that brings forth the adder,
> And that craves wary walking. Crown him – that!
> And then, I grant, we put a sting in him
> That at his will he may do danger with.
>
> (*Julius Caesar* 2.1.10–17)[1]

Shakespeare makes no mention of the events that had previously set Brutus and Caesar against one another, but he emphasises the situation, which Brutus here addresses, and which is beginning to alarm others, whereby Caesar threatens to become more than 'but a man'.[2] These words, spoken later by the younger Pompey, naturally reflect that character's sense of grievance; none the less they state a viewpoint that was common enough, as Plutarch's pages demonstrate. Those pages, however, show themselves to be subject to variation, depending on which particular narrative we consult, for, as in Shakespeare, different arguments produce a different emphasis.

T. J. B. Spencer is right to surmise that Plutarch on the whole preferred his Greeks to his Romans: 'he drew his ideals from the Hellenic past, not from the Roman world, past or present'.[3] The projected comparison between Caesar and Alexander has been lost but judging, for example, from the clear preference Plutarch expresses for Alcibiades over Coriolanus, it is

likely that it would have favoured Alexander.[4] Notwithstanding, there is
little doubt that Brutus emerges the better from the comparison between
himself and Dion. We may compare accounts of Caesar from within the
Lives by contrasting what Plutarch says about him in his own life and in
that of Brutus. Tellingly, in the Life of Caesar, he makes this assertion:

the chiefest cause that made him mortally hated, was the covetous desire he had to
be called king: which first gave the people just cause, and next his secret enemies,
honest colour to beare him ill will. (Plutarch, 5.337)

Does Shakespeare make it clear that Caesar harboured this ambition?
Brutus' thoughtful speech (above) seems to assume as much – 'he would be
crown'd' – and Brutus shows concern not so much with the ambition itself
but with what it might augur in terms of further threat to the common
good. As for his ambition, Plutarch, a page or two before he gives the cause
of Caesar's mortal hatred, says:

Caesar being borne to attempt all great enterprises, and having an ambitious desire
besides to covet great honors: the prosperous good successe he had of his former
conquestes bred no desire in him quietly to enjoy the frutes of his labours, but
rather gave him hope of things to come. (5.335)

Those 'things to come' Plutarch describes, in the main, as foreign conquests, but the effect at home soon registers itself in the form of general
anxiety, as Plutarch cites first Cicero's ironic remark that the star Lyra 'will
rise . . . at the commaundement of Caesar' (5.337), and then refers to the
populace's detestation of his desire for the kingship. Geoffrey Bullough
notes that Shakespeare borrows this detail for the tribune Flavius' cautionary observation at the end of the first scene,[5] but it also formed the basis
for Brutus' speech quoted above.

Shakespeare, if anything, deepens the 'mystery and opacity' in Plutarch's
portraits, while keeping his dramatic lines open and clear. To take an early
example: Casca's indignant recounting of Caesar's refusal of the crown
and his disgust at the ease with which play-acting can cast a spell on the
ignorant multitude (1.2) derives some of its details clearly from Plutarch,
but the scene as Shakespeare constructs it leaves itself open to interpretation, an effect mainly of dramatic as compared to narrative exposition.
Shakespeare seamlessly fuses together elements which Plutarch keeps separate and distinct. According to Casca, Caesar falls to the ground, overcome
by the 'stinking breath' of the gullible populace, who themselves have
just fallen for the cheap trick performed (as Casca sees it) by Caesar and
Antony:

> Marry, before he fell down, when he perceiv'd the common
> herd was glad he refus'd the crown, he pluckt me ope his
> doublet, and offer'd them his throat to cut.
>
> (*JC* 1.2.262–4)

All this seems part of the same dramatic moment, Caesar adopting the classic posture of selfless heroism in offering his life to the people, only for them to assure him that he must live. Plutarch orders the narration of incident quite differently. The throat-cutting offer is made not to the people as part of a spectacle of wooing but privately and in a spirit of furious irony to his 'frendes'. Caesar has just refused the senate's offer of honours (somewhat short of the kingship) but in an arrogant manner that has caused general anxiety:

> But he sitting still in his majesty, disdaining to rise up unto them when they came in, as if they had bene private men, aunswered them that his honors had more neede to be cut of, then enlarged. This did not only offend the Senate, but the common people also ... Thereupon also *Caesar* rising, departed home to his house, & tearing open his doblet collar, making his necke bare, he cried out alowde to his frendes, that his throte was readie to offer to any man that would come and cut it. (Plutarch, 5.337–8)

Plutarch, as we have seen above, distinguishes carefully between the response of the people and that of the senate to Caesar's ambition. While both groups are united in their hostility to any attempt by Caesar to become king of Rome, the smaller group ('his secret enemies') prepares (as Caesar well knows) to take particular advantage of his discomfort, finding 'honest colour to beare him ill will'. The word 'colour' carries a particular paradiastolic significance, in that it shows how an action or motive can be described so as to seem better than it might first appear.[6] With this phrase Plutarch distinguishes clearly between good and bad motives for the collective 'hatred' of Caesar. The falling sickness, which Casca witnesses with derision, gains only a mention in Plutarch's narrative, and then as an explanation by Caesar's followers for his failure to rise from his chair. Plutarch is duly sceptical of the excuse, and remarks that Caesar was in reality restrained from rising by his friend Cornelius Balbus, who flatteringly reminded him to insist on his dignity (5.338). In other words, Plutarch's narrative does not, unlike the dramatic narrative of Shakespeare, show Caesar's epilepsy occurring before the people. All such elements Shakespeare refashions as part of play-acting to the multitude, as reported by Casca. This has the effect of making Caesar, in Shakespeare's account, curiously oblivious of the patrician enmity which in Plutarch he senses keenly, and with good reason. (The exception to this, in Shakespeare, is the figure of the 'lean and hungry' Cassius who clearly makes him ill at ease.)

Whether Plutarch dislikes Caesar, as he seems to dislike some other Romans, is a perplexing question, and doubtless the missing comparison with Alexander would have made matters clearer. Sidney Homan argues that Shakespeare made use of the comparative lives where he could find them, and accordingly consults the comparison of Demetrius with Antony and that of Dion with Brutus.[7] Plutarch finds against Antony, in the one comparison, on the grounds that he intended to 'deprive his countriemen of their libertie and freedom' (6.402), an offence similar to that which made Caesar 'mortally hated'. For Plutarch this is clearly a serious vice (he often refers to other, lesser vices, with a degree of equanimity), and it brings Antony and Caesar, as offenders, together under the common failing of ambition, a debasement, according to moralists such as Cicero, of the noble quality of magnanimity.[8] (Shakespeare, if he had this part of the *Lives* in mind, appears, as I shall argue, less keen to condemn Antony.) As for Caesar, it seems clear that Plutarch thinks that he was bent on imposing himself on the people in a manner counter to the spirit of republicanism, and that furthermore everyone knew what he was up to. Hence the general alarm which determined the conspirators on their course of action. Plutarch, summarising the Life of Caesar, remarks:

So he reaped no other frute of all his raigne and dominion, which he had so vehemently desired all his life, and pursued with such extreame danger: but a vaine name only, and a superficiall glory, that procured him the envy and hatred of his contrie. (Plutarch, 5.348)

This hardly looks like a lament for Caesar. What, then, of the ultimate failure of the conspiracy and the unhappy fate of all those who had joined it? In explaining this, Plutarch distinguishes between the point that Caesar's conduct was rightly castigated and the fact that fortune in some sense always (or nearly always) favoured him, even after death:

But his great prosperitie and good fortune that favored him all his life time, did continue afterwards in the revenge of his death. (5.348)

Plutarch attributes the successful acquisition of 'revenge' to the gods, no less: 'But above all, the ghost that appeared unto *Brutus* shewed plainly, that the goddes were offended with the murther of *Caesar*' (pp. 348–9). Clearly, while acknowledging the power of Caesar's name, Plutarch is determined that the original judgment which brought about his downfall (i.e. that he was too ambitious) should stand. What the gods decree is one thing, but what men require in terms of government is another, more serious matter.

Alan Wardman suggests that in the circumstances in which the Romans found themselves, Caesar's rule was not (for Plutarch) such a bad thing.[9] He bases this observation on a statement that comes earlier in the life, according to which monarchy alone could cure the diseases of the state.[10] However, the context in which this occurs, the rivalry between Caesar and Pompey, reveals that in such a case the majority favoured Pompey (pp. 301–2). And even so, it is seen as a partial and temporary solution, which hardly endorses the principle of monarchy. Wardman's view finds better support in the comparison of Dion with Brutus, where speaking of Caesar's 'power and government' (i.e. his period as dictator), Plutarch says:

> there never followed any tyrannical nor cruell act, but contrarilie, it seemed that he was a mercifull Phisition, whom God had ordeyned of speciall grace to be Governor of the Empire of Rome, and to set all thinges againe at quiet stay, the which required the counsell and authoritie of an absolute Prince. And therefore the Romanes were marvellous sorie for Caesar after he was slaine, and afterwardes would never pardon them that had slaine him. (7.169–70)

The concerns that make *Julius Caesar* an enigmatic, teasing play may be found more evidently in the Life of Brutus than in that of Caesar himself. Plutarch presents Brutus from the beginning as a man who 'me thinkes was rightly made of virtue'. An intimation of how he intends to regard him throughout the life comes in the next sentence (which clearly provided Shakespeare with his cue for Antony's final tribute):

> So that his verie enemies which wish him most hurt, bicause of his conspiracy against *Julius Caesar*: if there were any noble attempt done in all this conspiracie, they referre it whollie unto *Brutus*, and all the cruell and violent actes unto Cassius, who was *Brutus* familiar frend, but not so well geven, and condicioned as he. (7.106)

If anybody's motives come under question in Plutarch's account of the conspiracy, then they are those of Cassius who, though fervently opposed to tyranny, had personal reasons for disliking Caesar, one of these being Caesar's preference for Brutus over himself in the matter of the Praetorship of the city (7.112). Plutarch spends some of his early pages on the subject of Caesar's close friendship with Brutus, as well as on the question of his sparing Brutus' life following the overthrow of Pompey, whom Brutus had supported. Almost none of this appears in Shakespeare, who seems to take care (in *Julius Caesar* at least) to avoid the related topic of whether Brutus was Caesar's illegitimate son (7.109).[11] The famous but slightly enigmatic, 'Et tu, Brute', delivered at the moment of his death, might be Shakespeare's way of alluding to the particular intimacy which, according to Plutarch, they had shared. Whether this is a poignant moment, and whether it should sear Brutus' conscience, as some commentators have argued, nonetheless

remains an open question. Throughout the life Plutarch repeatedly extols
Brutus' clemency, and insists on his purity of motive, in contrast to Cassius,
'a chollericke man, and hating Caesar privatlie, more than he did the
tyrannie openly' (7.113).

Sidney Homan, turning attention once more to the comparison between
Brutus and Dion, finds evidence not only that Plutarch *impugns* Brutus but
that Shakespeare seems to follow his lead:

> Plutarch also comments that whereas Brutus always referred friendship to matters
> of justice and equality, he nevertheless slew the man who had saved his life (7.171).
> This paradox in the 'Comparison', a paradox also sustained by the play when
> we consider Brutus' anguished reaction to Caesar's ghost, is raised by classical,
> medieval, and Renaissance commentators.[12]

Nothing, in fact, could be further from the truth of Plutarch's account,
whatever other commentators say. Plutarch (and here is an interesting
example of a Roman overcoming a Greek) accords the moral superiority to
Brutus over Dion:

> For wherein their chiefest praise consisted, to witte, in hating of tyrannies and
> wicked men: it is most true that *Brutus* desire was most sincere of both. For having
> no private cause of complaint or grudge against *Caesar*, he ventred to kill him,
> onely to set his contrie at libertie. Where if *Dion* had not received private cause of
> quarrell against *Dionysius*: he woulde never have made warre with him. (7.170–1)

Shades of Cassius in the judgment on Dion. Plutarch then repeats the
judgment of Brutus, shared even by his enemies, which he gives in the Life
of Brutus:

> But for *Brutus*, his verie enemies them selves confessed, that of all those that
> conspired *Caesars* death, he only had no other ende and intent to attempt his
> enterprise, but restore the Empire of ROME againe, to her former state and gov-
> ernment. (7.171)

Plutarch then makes clear to the reader why he has just previously, in the
comparison, established a picture of a Caesar much loved by the Romans.
Whereas it was easy enough for Dion to rise against his despicable former
friend, it took particular fortitude of mind for Brutus to do the same against
the revered Caesar:

> But to have undertaken to destroy *Julius Caesar*, and not to have shronke backe for
> feare of his greate wisdom, power, and fortune, considering that his name only was
> dreadfull unto everie man . . . this could not come but of a marvelous noble minde
> of him, that for feare never fainted, nor let fall any part of his courage. (7.171–2)

Despite the claims of Homan and others, neither Plutarch nor Shakespeare gives any evidence that Brutus suffers an 'anguished reaction' when confronted with his 'evill spirit' (Plutarch) or ghost of Caesar (Shakespeare):[13]

So *Brutus* boldly asked what he was, a god, or a man, and what cause brought him thither. The spirit answered him, I am thy evill spirit, *Brutus*: and thou shalt see me by the citie of PHILIPPES. *Brutus* being no otherwise affrayd, replyed againe unto it: well, then I shall see thee agayne. (7.147)

Shakespeare heightens the mood of fear, a natural enough dramatic effect, but does not interpret Brutus' reaction as one of 'anguish'; we only have to think of a comparable moment in *Macbeth* (incidentally, the play which follows *Julius Caesar* in the Folio) to appreciate both how close Shakespeare is to Plutarch, and how far Brutus is from conscience-stricken remorse:

> BRU.   Art thou any thing?
>   Art thou some god, some angel, or some devil,
>   That mak'st my blood cold and my hair to stare?
>   Speak to me what thou art.
> GHOST Thy evil spirit, Brutus.
> BRU. Why com'st thou?
> GHOST To tell thee thou shalt see me at Philippi.
> BRU. Well; then I shall see thee again?
> GHOST Ay, at Philippi.
> BRU. Why, I will see thee at Philippi, then. [*Exit Ghost*]
>   Now I have taken heart thou vanishest.
>   Ill spirit, I would hold more talk with thee.
>   (*JC* 4.3.276–86)

Brutus' initial fear does not differ significantly from the coolness he shows in Plutarch. Clearly he is more agitated, for Shakespeare would be a fool not to exploit the frisson of terror such a moment theatrically provides; but no reflective guilt follows from the encounter, only the beginnings of a sense that the gods are offended with him – a point Plutarch makes both in the comparison (7.169) and in the Life of Caesar (5.348–9), where he says that Caesar's fortune, in life *and* in death, was such that nobody could withstand its force.

We come then to the all-important question of the assassination. That Brutus acts from principled motives is, for Plutarch, beyond doubt (hence the continual comparison with both Cassius and Dion). Brutus is also more virtuous than Caesar, whom Plutarch finds to be corrupt, though generous, and rather less corrupt than those who have taken advantage of his authority and friendship, as Brutus himself observes following Caesar's death (7.146). Shakespeare, for his part, does not represent Caesar as a martyr figure any more than Plutarch, while he more than sufficiently follows Plutarch in developing a portrait of Brutus as a man of conscience, 'rightly made and framed unto vertue' (Plutarch, 7.106). The play-acting with Antony (see above) hardly reflects well on Caesar; and his behaviour in the senate shortly before his death smacks of arrogance ('I could be well mov'd, if I were as you', 3.1.59), as well as showing insensitivity, of another sort, to the mood deepening around him. But it is Brutus and not Caesar who finally wields the knife, so if we are to test the play's ethics, we must do so through him.

Shakespeare several times explores the question of conscience in regard to homicide, and mostly either condemns it or shows those responsible as remorseful. Murderers such as Henry IV, who seem to be ultimately exonerated by providence, suffer notwithstanding from an uneasy conscience which persists till their death. Macbeth sees his action as irredeemably stained with blood. Even a figure who appears to have good reason to kill, a revenge hero like Hamlet, finds it all but impossible to perform the act in a deliberate manner. Yet this is precisely what Brutus does, and he attempts, furthermore, to make his action answerable to conscience, which for him means preferring universal freedom over personal loyalty or friendship, as both Plutarch, in the comparison with Dion, and Shakespeare, in the speech from which I have quoted ('It must be by his death'), make clear. In this connection, Plutarch mentions Brutus' republican lineage, noting at the very opening of the life his descent from Lucius Junius Brutus, who had 'valliantly put downe the TARQUINES from their kingdom of ROME' (7.105). Brutus' ancestor did not have to kill anyone to do that, but he was helped in his revolutionary quest by somebody who did take a life, and that is the ravished and subsequently 'self-slaught'red' Lucretia, who took her own.[14] The situations in *Julius Caesar* and *Lucrece* produce an instructive parallel: on each occasion a body is placed on public view, each time its significance is 'read' by an interpreter, who in each case takes the side of the victim against the perpetrator. Although Lucrece has killed herself, Brutus manages to use the occasion to turn opinion against the Tarquins, who are seen effectively as murderers as well as ravishers. Antony, who concentrates attention on 'dead Caesar's wounds' and on his 'sacred blood' (3.2.132), similarly turns opinion against the conspirators, though, only shortly before his intervention, the crowd had ironically desired to make a Caesar of Brutus: 'Let him be Caesar!' (3.2.50). The difference perhaps rests on this: while the act of suicide may (for Shakespeare's audience) be regarded sympathetically, despite its breach of Christian ethics, that of homicide produces unease, however just the cause for which it is performed. This is a point which, as I have suggested, Shakespeare bears keenly in mind in his representation of Hamlet as an avenger.[15]

Notwithstanding, the revulsion at Caesar's death does not persist for very long in Shakespeare's play, for the simple reason that Antony's appropriation of it, and his rhetorical triumph over Brutus, shortly inspire another murder (this time the word is fully apt), that of Cinna the poet: a brutal mob attack which arguably goes some way towards displacing the image of Caesar's killing in the minds of the audience. Much naturally depends on how the two events are performed dramatically, but the text makes clear that the first is at least answerable to principle, whereas the second is merely frenzied. Shakespeare follows Plutarch's lead in depicting the murder of Cinna as resulting from Antony's intervention, and shows it proceeding immediately from Antony's brilliant speech beginning, 'If you have tears, prepare to shed them now' (3.2.169 ff.). However, he differs notably from Plutarch in making Antony much more instrumental in inciting the mob:

> O masters, if I were disposed to stir
> Your hearts and minds to mutiny and rage . . .
> (3.2.121–2)

which is precisely what happens. Though some commentators are disposed to place the responsibility for the eruption of violence in the city on the conspirators, it is surely Antony who sets it off. His speech is a masterpiece in the oratory of blood, a word he uses three times to calculated effect, along with 'stab', 'rent', 'dagger', 'steel', and their variants.[16]

Because *Julius Caesar* is a play that enacts the events of an earlier culture within the ethical consciousness of a later one, it inevitably produces in performance a tension which a commentator belonging to the former culture, Plutarch, would not feel. Notwithstanding, Shakespeare gives little impression that he views matters differently from his predecessor. If we think in terms of Christian remorse, Brutus is hardly a forerunner of Macbeth, even though the one play furnishes parallels for the other. In other respects the motivation of the central protagonists is reversed: Brutus is determined to put an end to ambition with Caesar's death, whereas in killing Duncan Macbeth succumbs to his own 'vaulting ambition'. Brutus does not feel regret, let alone remorse, for what he has done, nor does the play produce any strong compulsion for him to do so. If, then, we insist on understanding his action in the terms of later morality, we must interpret him, somewhat awkwardly, as a tragic hero who wants the self-recognition that only a later ethic can provide.[17] Yet Brutus does not lack self-knowledge. What he lacks is tactical awareness, which is why he surrenders the initiative to Antony, who in turn pays for his success by acquiring the bloodlust (i.e. inciting the violence that kills Cinna) that had attached itself previously to the conspirators.

In *Julius Caesar* Shakespeare seems to enjoy some relief at not having to invoke the Christian terminology that haunts some of his other heroes. The circumstances of pagan Rome give him an ethical freedom that is otherwise difficult, if not impossible, to attain. Coming at a significant juncture in Shakespeare's career, that is, after he had completed the second history tetralogy, and just as he was embarking on the first of the major tragedies, *Julius Caesar* is more than usually sensitive to themes and preoccupations in other of the dramatist's plays. Yet in this play action and consequence follow one another to diverse overall effect, as if he were exploring other ethical perspectives than the ones to which he is normally subject. The killing of the monarch in *Richard II* immediately induces a degree of guilt which takes an entire tetralogy fully to absolve. Later, in *Macbeth*, the guilt that comes with the killing of another monarch can only be absolved by the death of the protagonist. In *Julius Caesar*, accordingly, he explores themes in a way that provides other of his plays with their bearings. Brutus is guilty of 'murder', yet his cause remains just, and even his enemies regard him as admirable at the end. He is both noble and doomed, a paradoxical condition, which has proved determinedly resistant to modern ethical interpretation. In contriving this, Shakespeare enjoys the freedom to explore the circumstantial dynamics that govern action; how, for example, so much depends on straightforward error (the decision to spare Antony) as well as on the incalculable role of chance and opportunity (or opportunism in Antony's case). It is the nearest he comes to a Machiavellian free play of mind.[18] The drama works out like a perfect mathematical equation, relatively unburdened by the kind of moral concern that Shakespeare must confront in the later tragedies. The freedom to experiment that this pagan treatment of homicide gives nonetheless indicates to him what limits he must observe when he returns to themes embedded in his own culture, and instructs him in what he may, and may not do in *Hamlet* and *Macbeth*.

ANTONY AND CLEOPATRA

It is often observed how little the Antony of the great, mature love tragedy resembles the manipulative, opportunistic Antony of *Julius Caesar*. Only on the two funereal occasions in the earlier play, first when he weeps privately over the body of his slain friend, and next when he pays tribute to his dead foe, does he show that generosity of spirit which characterises the lover of Cleopatra. Plutarch insists, nonetheless, that as a consequence of avenging Caesar's death he managed to 'deprive his countriemen of their libertie and freedom' (comparison with Demetrius, 6.402). Although Shakespeare takes a good deal from Plutarch for this play, he borrows mainly incidental detail – most famously the words of the celebrated description of Cleopatra on her barge – which does not affect fundamental questions of interpretation. In shaping Antony's character he seems to take his cue almost exclusively from Plutarch's emphasis on his liberality which, like Brutus' virtue, seems to have been a family characteristic (6.298–9). Shakespeare fashions a hero who, whatever his faults, is characterised by what the ancients call 'greatness of soul' (magnanimity). While the modern meaning of magnanimity is positive, for moralists such as Cicero it could carry two opposed senses, 'greatness of soul' being the positive one, the negative one signifying ambition (specifically vainglory).[19] In observing this latter application of the term in Antony's nature and conduct, Plutarch gives a harsher, more abrasive portrayal than does Shakespeare.

Plutarch also surveys the earlier part of his life, including the conspiracy, Caesar's death, and its immediate aftermath, whereas Shakespeare turns immediately to the love-affair with Cleopatra. This means that Shakespeare omits a vivid example of cruelty in Antony, and one which exercises Plutarch to a degree, his treatment of Cicero and his glee following the latter's demise. Plutarch paints a grisly picture:

So when the murthrers brought him *Ciceroes* head and hand cut of, he beheld them a long time with great joy, and laughed hartily, and that oftentimes for the great joy he felt. Then when he had taken his pleasure of the sight of them, he caused them to be set up in an open place, over the pulpit for Orations (where when he was alive, he had often spoken to the people) as if he had done the dead man hurt, and not bleamished his owne fortune, shewing himselfe (to his great shame and infamie) a cruell man, and unworthie the office and authoritie he bare. (6.320)

Cruelty to adversaries, unworthiness of office, inclination towards tyranny, as well as the more personal vices of drunkenness and concupiscence, are the chief charges which Plutarch lays at Antony's door. Of these Shakespeare retains three, dropping the first and the third, and those that remain are all capable of being transformed by paradiastole into their opposite and better selves, just as magnanimity can be applied in a good or bad sense. Plutarch himself acknowledges that Antony's drinking is not always injurious: he earns the good will of his soldiers by fraternising with them in the camps (6.305), without risking discipline by his familiarity:

all were . . . so earnestly bent to esteeme *Antonius* good will and favor, above their owne life & safety: that in this point of marshall discipline, the auncient ROMANES could not have done any more. (6.350)

Plutarch also acknowledges the care Antony had for his soldiers, especially the wounded, under the duress of the Parthian campaign (a lengthy section of the life, which Shakespeare all but ignores), which won him their devotion (pp. 349–50). On the other hand, familiarity may still be a vice, especially when it is practised on other men's wives (p. 305). More ominously, however, Plutarch names Antony among those who were responsible for blackening the name of Caesar by taking advantage of his protection while in office:

Caesars friends that governed under him, were cause why they hated *Caesars* government (which in deede in respect of him selfe was no lesse than a tyrannie) by reason of the great insolencies and outragious parts that were committed: amongst whom *Antonius*, that was of greatest power, and that also committed greatest faultes, deserved most blame. (7.305–6)[20]

The more serious charges, and this last one is very grave, Shakespeare chooses to omit, and builds up a picture of Antony as one who, though given to vice, may ultimately redeem himself. Hence, those brief, occasional allusions to dissolute behaviour as recorded by Plutarch ('the bellows and the fan / to cool a gypsy's lust', 1.1.9–10; 'keep the turn of tippling with a slave', 1.4.19) need not be the last word; indeed they are countered elsewhere as the play goes on by more positive descriptions of the same impulse to gratify instinct. Drinking is integrated with the theme of valour, as Antony calls about him all his 'sad captains' (3.13.184), and also love, as he determines not only to make 'the wine peep through their scars' (190) but also to include Cleopatra in the ritual:

> Come on, my queen,
> There's sap in't yet. The next time I do fight
> I'll make death love me; for I will contend
> Even with his pestilent scythe.   (190–3)

Enobarbus closes the scene on a sceptical note, putting down such bravery to bravado (another form of paradiastolic redescription); yet the victory that follows is Antony's. Notwithstanding the fact that circumstances are gradually reducing around Antony, his spirit remains capable of expansion. Indeed, the above quotation strikes an appealing transcendental note. Whether or not Antony is merely deluding himself, a question that hangs over much interpretation of the play, Shakespeare seems deliberately to have selected from Plutarch those traits which are redeemable rather than those which no amount of excusing can properly justify – the cruelty shown towards Cicero being perhaps the chief of them.

Antony's major redeeming characteristic is his generosity ('liberalitie'), which of course some commentators both inside and outside the play dismiss as licentiousness. However, liberality, like magnanimity, can be divided into both bad and good: prodigality – capable of turning nasty and cruel – and charitableness. Plutarch distinguishes both elements in Antony, yet can never forget the ruthlessness that made him an ally of Caesar's and an enemy to universal freedom, as the comparison with Demetrius shows:

The desire of Demetrius was unblameable and just, desiring to raigne over people, which had been governed at all times, and desired to be governed by kings. But *Antonius* desire was altogether wicked and tyrannical; who sought to keepe the people of ROME in bondage and subjection, but lately before rid of *Caesars* raigne and government. (6.402)

Similarly, he seems unwilling to see anything redemptive in Cleopatra, even though he commends her strength of purpose in confronting death at the end. Plutarch introduces the subject of Cleopatra's effect on Antony into his discussion of his vulnerability to flattery, Antony being disposed by nature to her seductive charm:

Antonius being thus inclined, the last and extreamest mischiefe of all other (to wit, the love of *Cleopatra*) lighted on him, who did waken and stirre up many vices yet hidden in him, and were never seene to any: and if any sparke of goodnesse or hope of rising were left in him *Cleopatra* quenched it straight, and made it worse than before. (6.325)

Shakespeare departs radically from these two judgments, eliminating the first from all discussion, and extracting from the second Antony's charitable treatment ('goodnesse') of those who have deserted or betrayed him (Enobarbus and Cleopatra especially). The mercenary wrangling over property, which threatens to diminish the tragic beyond recovery in the concluding act, finds redemption in Cleopatra's description of Antony's 'bounty' – all the more pertinent in that it is set against Caesar's false promise of generous treatment:

> an autumn 'twas
> That grew the more by reaping. His delights
> Were dolphin-like: they show'd his back above
> The element they liv'd in.   (5.2.87–90)

Significance turns on the interpretation of 'delights', which is usually glossed as pleasures. However, it has a more active sense, 'pleasing gifts', as in Sonnet 102.12: 'And sweets grown common lose their dear delights' (i.e. power to please).[21] Understanding the word in this application prevents us from rejecting Antony's generosity as a mere version of his debilitating hedonism, which would undermine Shakespeare's attempt to establish him (for all his botches and embarrassments) as noble and heroic at the close. That nobility is partly achieved by being expanded to embrace the concept of humility, a point which is true of Cleopatra also, who is willing to forswear her regal status for that of 'the maid that milks / And does the meanest chares' (4.13.74–5).

In *Antony and Cleopatra*, Shakespeare proves selective in his reading of the Life of Antony, carefully ignoring aspects that Plutarch deplored, and that would damage any effort at sympathetic portrayal. To retain that sympathy he concentrates on, and exploits, the concept of magnanimity, a word that is capable of being bent various ways. Ultimately the way of selflessness and generosity prevails. Both Antony and Cleopatra behave in a manner that induces scepticism, but never to such a degree as to put their conduct beyond recovery. In *Julius Caesar*, I have argued, Shakespeare seems happy to maintain the pagan ethic relatively unchallenged, and that is because it suits him temporarily to treat the subject of homicide in a manner that is free from either the obligations of English history or the dictates of Christian conscience. In *Antony and Cleopatra*, an ethic more familiar to his own time and culture reasserts itself in the play's final, redemptive movement: within and despite its pagan, herculean frame the pulse of charity continues to beat forcefully.

NOTES

1. All quotations from Shakespeare are taken from *The Complete Works*, ed. Peter Alexander (London 1951).
2. *Antony and Cleopatra* 2.6.19.
3. *Shakespeare's Plutarch* (Harmondsworth 1964), p. 8.
4. The 1603 edition of North's Plutarch does contain a comparison of Caesar and Alexander, but this was an Elizabethan addition.
5. See Geoffrey Bullough, *Narrative and Dramatic Sources of Shakespeare*, 8 vols. (London 1957–75), vol. v, p. 79.
6. The rhetorical tactic is described aptly by Puttenham: 'as when we make the best of a bad thing, or turne a signification to the more plausible [i.e. worthy of applause]'. See *The Arte of English Poesie*, ed. G. D. Willcock and Alice Walker (Cambridge 1936; repr. 1970), pp. 184–5.

7. Sidney Homan, 'Dion, Alexander, and Demetrius – Plutarch's Forgotten *Parallel Lives* – as Mirrors for Shakespeare's *Julius Caesar*', *ShSt* 8 (1976); 195–210.

8. '*In maximis animis . . . exsistunt honoris, imperii, potentiae, gloriae cupiditates*' ('In the greatest souls . . . we find ambitions for civil and military authority, for power, and for glory, springing up'). See *De Officiis* 1.8.26, Loeb Classical Library, trans. Walter Miller (London and Cambridge, MA 1913), pp. 26–7.

9. See Alan Wardman, *Plutarch's Lives* (London 1974), pp. 112–13.

10. See Plutarch, *Caesar* 28.4, Loeb Classical Library, ed. and trans. Bernadotte Perrin (London and Cambridge, MA 1914–26), vol. vii (1919), pp. 512–13.

11. A suggestion of it comes in *2 Henry VI*: 'Brutus' bastard hand / Stabb'd Julius Caesar' (4.1.136–7).

12. Homan, 'Dion, Alexander, and Demetrius', pp. 203–4.

13. Consider, for example, Cynthia Marshall's recent Freudian, and markedly Oedipal, assumption that Brutus is 'gripped with guilt', in her essay, 'Shakespeare, Crossing the Rubicon', *ShS* 53 (2000), 82.

14. See *The Rape of Lucrece*, l. 1,733.

15. Philip Edwards' edition of *Hamlet* has two instructive pages on the relationship of the hero's dilemma vis-à-vis murder in each play. See *Hamlet* (Cambridge 1985), pp. 5–6.

16. For a view that the conspirators rather than Antony are to blame, see Robert S. Miola, *Shakespeare's Rome* (Cambridge 1983), p. 105.

17. See, for example, J. L. Simmons, *Shakespeare's Pagan World* (Brighton 1974), pp. 107–8.

18. I develop this consideration in the chapter on *Julius Caesar* in my *Shakespeare and Machiavelli* (Woodbridge, Suffolk 2002).

19. See above, n. 8.

20. See p. 179, above; also Life of Brutus 7.146.

21. See Roe, *Shakespeare and Machiavelli*, pp. 202–5.

CHAPTER II

Plutarch, Shakespeare, and the alpha males

Gordon Braden

In the Folio text of *Coriolanus*, a recitation of the title character's family tree seems to have a lacuna:

> Of the same House *Publius* and *Quintus* were,
> That our best Water, brought by Conduits hither,
> And Nobly nam'd, so twice being Censor,
> Was his great Ancestor.[1]

The transition between the second and third lines does not quite make sense, but help is to hand on the opening page of Plutarch's Life of Coriolanus in Sir Thomas North's translation: 'Of the same house were Publius, and Quintus, who brought Rome their best water they had by conducts. Censorinus also came of that familie, that was so surnamed, bicause the people had chosen him Censor twise' (2.143; *Coriolanus* 1.1).[2] A nineteenth-century German, Nicolaus Delius, retrieved from North's phrasing the pentameter now recognised as the missing line:

> Of that same House *Publius* and *Quintus* were,
> That our best Water brought by Conduits hither,
> And *Censorinus* that was so surnam'd,
> And Nobly named so, twice being Censor,
> Was his great Ancestor.   2.3.241–5[3]

Emendation is rarely so blessed with evidence that the critic is retracing the footsteps of the author. Geoffrey Bullough calls Shakespearean source study 'the best, and often the only, way open to us of watching Shakespeare the craftsman in his workshop';[4] the passage from *Coriolanus* is part of the ballast for that generalisation, which taken to some extremes can seem dubious but in particulars like these is all but incontrovertible.

This example is not especially consequential, but it is only one of many. Some of Shakespeare's closest appropriations of North are among the most famous moments in their respective plays: Portia's conversation with Brutus, Volumnia's final meeting with Coriolanus, Cleopatra on her barge. The information has been familiar for a long time, but can still be startling to look at:

Antonius, I dare assure thee, that no enemie hath taken, nor shall take Marcus Brutus alive: and I beseech God keepe him from that fortune. For wheresoever he be found, alive or dead: he will be found like him selfe. (6.233; *Brutus* 50.5–6)

> Safe *Antony, Brutus* is safe enough:
> I dare assure thee, that no Enemy
> Shall ever take alive the Noble *Brutus*:
> The Gods defend him from so great a shame,
> When you do finde him, or alive, or dead,
> He will be found like *Brutus*, like himselfe.
>
> (*Julius Caesar* 5.4.20–5)

With no other book – not even Golding's Ovid – does Shakespeare show such sustained intimacy.

He appears to have first looked into North's Plutarch by the mid-1590s. The catalogue of Theseus' erotic conquests in *A Midsummer Night's Dream* (2.1.77–80) appears to derive from the Life of Theseus;[5] modern editors regularly emend two of the names (Perigenia and Eagle) to match the forms found in North (Perigouna, Aegle). Nine characters in *Titus Andronicus* have names found in the non-Plutarchan Life of Scipio Africanus that North includes.[6] *Theseus* and *Scipio* come first and last in North's earlier editions – a circumstance which suggests one way in which a newcomer might well approach a 1,200-page volume. By 1599 Shakespeare is no newcomer; the use of North in *Julius Caesar* is of a different order. With the now quite extensive verbal borrowings comes a new version of classical Rome: not the fantasia of *Titus*, but the disciplined recreation of a particular historical moment, populated with specific historical characters whose demeanour involves a well-articulated attempt to imagine what being 'Roman' in the high classical sense might be like. When Shakespeare returns to ancient Rome about a decade later, in *Antony and Cleopatra* and *Coriolanus*, he returns to the same kind of close involvement with North's Plutarch – in some regards, an even closer involvement. (He also spins yet another classical play, *Timon of Athens*, out of a brief passage in the Life of Antony.) The phenomenon has attracted some expansive claims about the turning point that Plutarch marked in Shakespeare's career. J. A. K. Thomson, fifty years ago: 'I believe that it was from Plutarch that Shakespeare learned how to make a tragedy of the kind exemplified in *Hamlet* and *Othello*, *Macbeth* and *Lear*. It was, I think, in the course of writing *Julius Caesar* that he learned it.'[7] Cynthia Marshall has recently recast Thomson's thesis in new terms; the encounter with Plutarch in *Julius Caesar* is the key event in Shakespeare's developing, historically momentous sense of dramatic character: 'What happens . . . in Shakespeare's conversion of [Plutarchan] narrative into drama, is the establishment of our culture's prevailing model of character as one that is at once intensely performative and putatively interiorized.' Marshall calls this Shakespeare's crossing of the Rubicon: 'marking off the richly inventive but largely plot-driven plays of the 1590s from the deeply characterological dramas that follow, in order to take possession of his territory as a dramatist'.[8]

The best resource for absorbing the relevant evidence here is still M. W. MacCallum's book.[9] It harvests a century or so of scholarship, and not much basic information has been added since. Arguments have been made for the relevance of passages in the *Lives* outside the obvious ones,[10] and the conviction has grown that Plutarch's *Isis and Osiris*, from his *Moralia* (translated by Philemon Holland in 1603), was on Shakespeare's mind when he wrote *Antony and Cleopatra*.[11] The stately phrase 'remembrance of things past' (Sonnet 30.2) has a multiple Plutarchan pedigree.[12] More may come to light, but further canvassing is not necessarily a priority; the impressive characteristic of most of Shakespeare's connections with North is their obviousness, and MacCallum displays that obviousness with extensive quotations in a generous format that remains unmatched. He also has the leisure to analyse points of contact, almost one by one, with enlightened respect both for the closeness of the parallel (what Richard Farmer saw as plagiarism) and for the differences that the closeness makes visible. The general picture is of a kind of professional collaboration, Shakespeare as script-doctor to Plutarch's very promising first draft; he 'rejects all that is otiose or discordant in speech or situation, and adds from other passages in his author or from his own imagination, the circumstances that are needed to bring out its full poetic significance. He always looks to the whole, removes discrepancies, establishes the inner connection'.[13]

The trail of influence is simplified by the lack of evidence that Shakespeare had recourse to the French translation of Jacques Amyot from which North worked, let alone to Plutarch's Greek. When Shakespeare has Antony make Cleopatra 'Of lower Syria, Cyprus, Lydia, / Absolute Queene' (*Antony and Cleopatra* 3.6.10–11), he is rearranging North – 'of Cyprus, of Lydia, and of the lower Syria' (6.57; *Antony* 54.4) – but scrupulously honouring a misprint: 'Lydia' should be 'Libya'. At times, North's eccentricities can be a serious benefit. When Volumnia tells her son that her death will be one of the consequences if he persists in his campaign, Plutarch has her imagine him 'treading underfoot the corpse of her who bore you' (*Coriolanus* 35.3). In Amyot he walks on her *corps*, but North elevates a subtext to startling explicitness: 'thy foote shall treade upon thy mothers wombe, that brought thee first into this world' (2.184). Shakespeare makes sure the moment does not pass without emphasis:

> thou shalt no sooner
> March to assault thy Country, then to treade
> (Trust too't, thou shalt not) on thy Mothers wombe
> That brought thee to this world.
>
> (*Coriolanus* 5.3.123–6)

Here he breaks the speech, recognising that it has reached one of its high points; we can almost no longer imagine the scene without it.

Shakespeare will sometimes duplicate one of North's mistakes even when the result is unmistakably confusing. Brutus' inconsistent attitude toward suicide follows from the text as Shakespeare found it in North: 'Brutus aunswered him [Cassius], being yet a young man, and not overgreatly experienced in the world: I trust, (I know not how) a certaine rule of Philosophie, by the which I did greatly blame and reprove Cato for killing of him selfe . . . but being nowe in the middest of the daunger, I am of a contrary mind' (6.222; *Brutus* 40.7–8). In the original, Brutus contrasts a position he held many years ago with the position he holds now: 'And Brutus answered: "When I was a young man, Cassius, and without experience of the world, I was led, I know not how, to speak too rashly for a philosopher. . . . In my present fortunes, however, I am become of a different mind."' At the very least, the punctuation in North is misleading as to where Brutus begins speaking, though the tense of 'trust' suggests that the translator actively misread his source and thought 'being yet a young man' was the narrator's characterisation of the forty-year-old Brutus.[14] Shakespeare omits any reference to youth and makes Brutus' opposition to suicide if anything more ringing:

> CASSIUS What are you then determined to do?
> BRUTUS Even by the rule of that Philosophy,
>   By which I did blame *Cato*, for the death
>   Which he did give himselfe, I know not how:
>   But I do finde it Cowardly, and vile,
>   For feare of what might fall, so to prevent
>   The time of life, arming my selfe with patience,
>   To stay the providence of some high Powers,
>   That governe us below. (*Julius Caesar* 5.1.99–107)

Yet Brutus will commit a classically Roman suicide – part of what would have attracted Shakespeare to his story – and is about to say as much.

Dealing with the contradiction leads Shakespeare to correct a more substantive mistake in North. Breaking Brutus' speech up helps make the inconsistency dramatic rather than just perplexing:

> CASSIUS   Then, if we loose this Battaile,
>   You are contented to be led in Triumph
>   Thorow the streets of Rome.
> BRUTUS No *Cassius*, no:
>   Thinke not thou Noble Romane,
>   That ever *Brutus* will go bound to Rome,
>   He beares too great a minde. But this same day
>   Must end that worke, the Ides of March begun.
>   And whether we shall meete againe, I know not:
>   Therefore our everlasting farewell take.   (107–16)

MacCallum congratulates Shakespeare on making capital out of North's confusion: 'He got over it, and produced a new effect and one very true to human nature, by making Brutus' latter sentiment the sudden response of his heart, in defiance of his philosophy, to Cassius' anticipation of what they must expect if defeated.'[15] But as Paul Cantor points out,[16] Shakespeare is also making Brutus more authentically pagan, repairing a slide toward Christianity which North induced at the end of his speech:

> For if it be not the will of God, that this battell fall out fortunate for us: I will looke no more for hope, neither seeke to make any new supply for warre againe, but will rid me of this miserable world, and content me with my fortune. For, I gave up my life for my contry in the Ides of Marche, for the which I shall live in another more glorious worlde. (6.222; *Brutus* 40.8)

God is there in Plutarch, but not the future tense or what sounds very much like an anticipation of heaven. North, following Amyot's lead, spins that anticipation from what is originally a reference to the classical cult of earthly fame: 'on the Ides of March I gave my own life to my country, and since then, for her sake, I have lived another life of liberty and glory'. If Shakespeare had had recourse to the Greek, he might well have restored something like this original sense; as it was, his feel for antiquity seems to have told him something was wrong, and led him to replace a whiff of Christian hope with a stern implication of finality. Such stringent worldliness was part of the alterity that Shakespeare was trying to capture in his Roman characters; that effort brought with it an intuition that could take him beyond even the most treasured of his source materials.

Usually that intuition worked with North rather than against him. Key elements in Shakespeare's conception of the Roman character can be seen germinating in almost subliminal tricks of translation on North's part. Reuben Brower noted North's particular fondness for the word 'noble', an adjective whose adhesion to 'Roman' is a famous part of the legacy of Shakespeare's plays.[17] More recently, Geoffrey Miles has drawn attention to the way in which a number of different Plutarchan terms having to do with admirable qualities appear in North as 'constant' or similar words.[18] In Brutus' speech on suicide, for example, 'accepting fearlessly whatever befalls' becomes 'constantly and paciently to take whatsoever it pleaseth him to send us'. The observation that Antony 'was most like a good and true man when he was unfortunate' becomes 'the heavier fortune lay upon him, the more constant shewed he him selfe' (6.17; *Antony* 17.2). It would be extreme to speak of mistranslation, but in the systematic repetition of his key terms North is perceptibly at odds with the original.

He is closest to the mark in passages such as the description of the conspirators' inscrutability just before killing Caesar: 'any one who knew what was about to happen would have been above all things astonished at the indifference and composure of the men on the brink of this terrible crisis' (*Brutus* 14.6). North sharpens the focus on his key term: 'here is to be noted, the wonderfull assured constancie of these conspirators, in so daungerous and waightie an enterprise as they had undertaken' (6.195). A marginal note highlights 'the wonderfull constancie of the conspirators'. Apathy and constancy diverge in modern usage, but align closely in Stoic philosophy, where they are both important desiderata: it is by withdrawing your emotional investments in external reality that you attain true steadiness. The later sixteenth century saw a revived interest in that philosophy, both as one of the commanding achievements of classical antiquity and as a potential guide to modern life; within that revival, the term *constantia* looms if anything larger than in the original classical texts. North's translation, probably without much conscious thought on his part, is Plutarch seen through neostoic lenses.

More than that, according to Miles, the Stoic tinting brings out a latent diagram of serious consequence: 'an Aristotelian pattern of virtue as a mean between excess and defect: Brutus embodying the virtue of constancy, Antony its defect, inconstancy, and Coriolanus its excess, wilful obstinacy'.[19] In other words, this is how Shakespeare selected and organised the subjects for his three Plutarchan plays. The reading of the plays in this perspective is a strong one, handsomely responsive to Shakespeare's own choice of words. North's description of the impassivity of the conspirators

on the Ides of March becomes in Shakespeare an injunction from Brutus
on the night before – one linked, no less, to the craft of acting:

> Let not our lookes put on our purposes,
> But beare it as our Roman Actors do,
> With untyr'd Spirits, and formall Constancie.
>
> (*Julius Caesar* 2.1.224–6)

Cleopatra aspires to the same virtue:

> My Resolution's plac'd, and I have nothing
> Of woman in me: Now from head to foote
> I am Marble constant: now the fleeting Moone
> No Planet is of mine.
>
> (*Antony and Cleopatra* 5.2.234–7)

Facing defeat, she targets one of the defining values of classical Rome as
Shakespeare imagined it from the evidence before him.

The result is not exactly a misrepresentation of Plutarch, but it does
involve a bias that Plutarch would have found uncongenial. There is nothing programmatically Stoic about the *Lives*. Within the sectarian categories
of classical philosophy, Plutarch was a professed Platonist and hostile to
Stoicism; three essays in his *Moralia* are devoted to refuting Stoic doctrine.
This hostility is not implacable, and not particularly evident in the *Lives*;
and neostoic *constantia* has enough congruence with the general classical
ethos of self-control that no significant harm is done to Plutarch's narratives by shading the latter into the former. Those narratives, however,
have a somewhat different focus of attention, one obscured in Renaissance
translation but which nevertheless shows signs of registering with Shakespeare, particularly in his choice of subjects for *Antony and Cleopatra* and
Coriolanus. The pattern here – not inconsistent with the schema traced by
Miles but still different – was first suggested by Bullough: Shakespeare's last
two Roman heroes 'exemplified the two complementary aspects of human
nature defined by many ethical writers since Aristotle; for if Antony was a
slave to the "concupiscible" forces, Coriolanus was at the mercy of the "irascible" elements in his personality'.[20] This suggestion has been expanded by
Paul Cantor as a contrast between *eros* and a 'complex of austerity, pride,
heroic virtue, and public service' that he calls 'spiritedness'.[21] The latter
term is offered as the least unsatisfactory English equivalent for *thymos*, a
word of general use in classical Greek and of specific importance in the
theoretical model on Cantor's mind: the Platonic tripartition of the human
soul.

A primary sense of *thymos* is simply anger – it is often interchangeable with *orgê* – but it is also used for the part of the self from which anger comes. The term enters the *Republic* when Socrates considers the qualities needed in those who will defend the state in war; the initial comparison is with a horse or a dog who is *thymoeidês* (2.15/375A). As the analogy between the state and the individual is worked out, *to thymoeides* becomes one of the parts of every person's soul. Without satisfactory cultivation the *thymos* can become erratic and hostile to reason (3.18/411), and initially it is spoken of as simply one of the irrational appetites, like those for food and pleasure, that the rational part of the soul must control. But in an important turn (4.14–15/439E–41C), Socrates draws attention to the way anger can take reason's side against the lower appetites in, as he calls it, the party-politics of the soul; if the *thymos* is irrational, its irrationality is different from that of the other irrational drives, and to understand how the soul operates we must think of it as having three distinct parts. In due course, Plato's conceptualisation of this alternate irrationality becomes clearer: the second part of the soul is *philonicon* and *philotimon*, in love with winning and in love with *timê*, insignia of public honour granted to a victor (9.7/581B).[22] The irrational appetite with this special place for itself in the scheme of things is competitiveness.

Plato is well disposed to this form of irrationality; he is so taken with the capacity of the second part of the soul to make men indifferent to pain, deprivation, and the baser forms of desire that he spends little time on its abuses. In the *Phaedrus*, the *thymos* is the good white horse in the soul's harness (253D). The events of Plato's time made others less forgiving. Thucydides links the internecine savageries of wartime party politics to unbridled *philotimia* (3.82.8); Pindar laments the manifest pain it brings to cities.[23] Euripides has a despairing Jocasta cry out to her son Eteocles: 'τί τῆς κακίστης δαιμόνων ἐφίεσσαι / Φιλοτιμίας, παῖ; μὴ σύ γ᾽· ἄδικος ἡ θεός' (*Phoenissae* 531–2; 'Why do you follow Philotimia, the most evil of spirits, child? Do not, she is an unjust god'). A half a millennium later, Plutarch hears both intonations. Plato's model for the soul is approvingly summarised in his *Moralia*;[24] *thymoeidês* is a recurring term of characterisation in the *Lives*, often in company with *philotimia* and *philonicia*: e.g. of Alexander: 'the high spirit [*to thymoeides*] which he carried into his undertakings rendered his ambition [*philoneician*] finally invincible' (*Alexander* 26.14).[25] But such characterisation does not merely celebrate success; Plutarch quotes the passages from Pindar and Euripides as well (he is our source for the former),[26] and is far more willing than Plato to explore the pathology of the soul's second part. Plutarch in his *Moralia* makes uncharacteristic common cause with the Stoics and against Plato (and Aristotle) in adopting the 'absolutist' position against anger, the identifying emotion of the soul's second part; immediately after quoting Pindar, he delicately makes his disagreement clear:

> from the pain and suffering of the soul, caused generally by weakness, there arises the outburst of passion [*thymos*] which is not, as someone has said, like 'sinews of the soul', but like the strainings and convulsions of the soul when it is stirred too vehemently in its impulse to defend itself.[27]

'Someone' is Plato, offering a metaphor for the role of the *thymos* at its most vital (*Republic* 3.18/411B). In the *Lives* an explicit reference to the tripartite soul comes in the diagnosis of Coriolanus' disorder as a morbid excess of the second part:

> He had indulged the passionate and contentious part of his soul [τῷ θυμοειδεῖ καὶ φιλονείκῳ μέρει τῆς ψυχῆς], with the idea that there was something great and exalted in this, and had not been imbued, under the influence of reason and discipline, with that gravity and mildness which are the chief virtues of the statesman. (*Coriolanus* 15.3)[28]

The proud white horse in this case draws the charioteer to his destruction.

Coriolanus is not the only cautionary example. Agesilaus, a king of Sparta, is *philoneicotatos* and *thymoeidestatos*, 'contentious and high-spirited beyond his fellows' (*Agesilaus* 2.1); even in those superlatives he is merely fulfilling the social design of his city: 'the Spartan lawgiver [Lycurgus] seems to have introduced the spirit of ambition and contention into his civil polity as an incentive to virtue, desiring that good citizens should always be somewhat at variance and in conflict with one another' (5.3). But Agesilaus' story is repeatedly one of civic dangers generated by this contentiousness – a pointless rivalry with Lysander whose destructive potential is only forestalled by Lysander's death (7–8), military and diplomatic blunders on Agesilaus' part (18.2, 23.6, 26.3) whose baleful effect is counteracted only when he goes against his own nature: 'all agree that the salvation of Sparta at this time was due to Agesilaus, because he renounced his inherent passions of contentiousness and ambition, and adopted a policy of safety' (33.1). Even this is not enough to repair Sparta's standing (or to save Agesilaus from a humiliating death as a mercenary in Egypt), and the dominant tone is admonitory: 'ambitious natures in a commonwealth, if they do not observe due bounds, work greater harm than good' (8.4). Looming over such examples is a perspective revealed in one of the Roman lives, an acerbic thesis as to why the Greek world lost its ascendancy: 'Greece has fought all her battles to bring servitude upon herself, and every one of her trophies stands as a memorial of her own calamity and disgrace, since she owed her overthrow chiefly to the baseness and contentiousness of her leaders' (*Flamininus* 11.3).

Distant history here has strong links to the reality of Plutarch's own time. In 67 AD Nero proclaimed Greece free from direct Roman rule – a happy event which Plutarch also recalls in his *Flamininus* (12.8) – but the resulting instability led Vespasian to revoke the decree in 70. Even under the enforced peace of Roman rule, the scramble for *timê* was a defining feature of aristocratic life. J. E. Lendon argues that it was one of the central challenges and resources of imperial governance; the men of Plutarch's class 'had the competitive outlook of Homeric heroes, but no Trojan War to settle who was the best of the Achaeans'.[29] An immense amount of attention was accordingly consumed by an infinitely ramifying network of honorific precedence reaching from the imperial throne into the intimate corners of local life; Plutarch's alarmingly detailed account of the politics of seating people at a dinner party is an especially vivid piece of evidence.[30] His *Lives* are shaped not just by his study of the sources but also by his own experience in this milieu.

Individual narratives repeatedly become stories of the main character's quite specific rivalry with someone else, often a fellow countryman; the example of Agesilaus and Lysander is mirrored in that of Pericles and Cimon, Aristides and Themistocles, the elder Cato and Scipio Africanus, Crassus and Pompey. Sometimes these rivalries fade without reaching any decisive crisis; sometimes they structure a whole life. The collection as we have it opens with an example of the latter. Theseus from his early years measured himself against Heracles, and that emulation informs the key decision of his young manhood, to go by land rather than sea from Troezen to Athens. The competitiveness here is presented in an entirely positive light, a spur to heroism without any invidious backwash. Eventually Theseus meets his role model and 'the interview passed with mutual expressions of honor, friendliness, and generous praise' (*Theseus* 30.4); when Heracles later rescues Theseus from imprisonment, Theseus handsomely recognises that he has been bested and rededicates to Heracles the sacred precincts at Athens that had been set aside in his own honour. Often, however, the consequences are more destructive; upon Cimon's death, his kinsman Thucydides continues the rivalry with Pericles and the result is a severe enhancement of social divisions at Athens:

Now there had been from the beginning a sort of seam hidden beneath the surface of affairs, as in a piece of iron, which faintly indicated a divergence between the popular and the aristocratic program; but the emulous ambition of these two men cut a deep gash in the state, and caused one section of it to be called the *People*, and the other the *Few*. (*Pericles* 11.3)

Modern historians resist such personalised explanations for major political conflicts, and Plutarch's account has been brusquely rejected;[31] but a bias toward seeing things as he does comes with the very enterprise of writing, as he puts it, lives rather than history – and within that predilection the model of the rivalrous pair is one of his most favoured paradigms, a powerful guide to making sense of the record. Even someone who has seemingly transcended all rivalries replicates them on another plane; so Julius Caesar after defeating Pompey: 'What he felt was . . . nothing else than emulation of himself, as if he had been another man, and a sort of rivalry between what he had done and what he purposed to do' (*Caesar* 58.5). Caesar dies before the consequences of this disposition reveal themselves; Plutarch does not take the matter any further, but we can extrapolate what his explanation might be for one of the major facts in the Roman history of his own time, the psychopathology of emperors such as Nero and Domitian.[32]

An Aristotelianised version of the tripartite soul is formulated by Thomas Aquinas, who codifies the terms 'irascible' and 'concupiscible' (*Summa Theologica* 1.81); it is primarily in this form that the theory passes into Renaissance psychology. In the process the irrational appetites blend back into each other, with reason being set in some general way against all the passions, and the instinct of the soul's second part to make common cause with the first against the third – the phenomenon in which Plato was so interested – often gets ignored. Tasso uses the Thomist terminology to formulate an impressively Platonic allegory for *Jerusalem Delivered*, with the knight Rinaldo representing 'the irascible faculty': 'just as it is the soldier's duty to obey his captain, who exercises the art and skill of command, and to fight the enemy, so it is the duty of the irascible part of the soul, warlike and robust, to arm itself with reason against the desires'.[33] Thomas More's *Utopia* – where, among other startling features, the citizens avoid military service themselves and wage war through mercenaries – may be understood as an attempt to recast Plato's *Republic* with the second part of the soul surgically excised. But such engagements with Plato's theory are rare – certainly not enough to induce translators to make the complex of Greek words particularly visible. In the characterisation of Alexander quoted above, North translates *to thymoeides* simply as 'noble corage' (4.329); Coriolanus under the same Greek rubric is 'a man to full of passion and choller' (2.159–60). The description of Agesilaus as *philoneicotatos* and *thymoeidestatos* exemplifies the pattern Miles detects: 'having better spirite, and being more constant' (4.160; *Agesilaus* 2.1). When Agesilaus acts *hypo thymou philoneicias*, it is 'of a noble corage to shew his valliantnes' (4.179; 18.2); when later he is thought to be speaking *thymôi tini cai philoneiciai*, it is 'for very spite and private malice of his owne' (4.189; 26.3); when he finally transcends *philoneicia* and *philotimia*, he is 'leaving his ambition and selfe will' (4.197; 33.1). The clear focus of the Greek terminology is smeared into something generalised and unsystematic; insofar as there appears to be a trend, it is to obscure the sense of competitiveness with implications of solitary self-sufficiency.

The operations of the soul's second part, however, are sufficiently embedded in Plutarch's storytelling that the cloudiness of North's lens does not keep Shakespeare from engaging his source on just this point; there seems to have occurred an important leap of imaginative sympathy across the gap that the translator had opened. In the last two decades there has been notable attention to the role of male competitiveness in Shakespeare; Coppélia Kahn, in the most ambitious recent attempt to treat his Roman works as a group, argues for the centrality in them of

the agon, that 'zero-sum game' of rivalry through which the hero wins his name by pitting himself against his likeness or equal in contests of courage and strength. . . Shakespeare's Roman heroes strive to prove themselves men not in relation to women, but against a rival whom they emulate in two senses – by imitating as the mirror-image of an ideal self, and by competing against with the aim of excelling and dominating.[34]

Cogent analyses of *Julius Caesar* and *Antony and Cleopatra* support this claim; *Coriolanus* is clearly part of the same picture (though Kahn's own discussion takes another tack, focusing on Volumnia rather than Aufidius). Looking at the plays on this sight-line makes, for instance, excellent sense of the actions of Brutus, and yields a political lesson that Plutarch does not specifically draw but that closely resembles some that he does:

At precisely those points at which he fulfills his function as the voice of republican purism . . . he also pursues a not-so-subtle one-upmanship against Cassius. . . In each instance . . . Brutus makes a tactical error. This succession of blunders marks the ideological fault line of *Julius Caesar*, the point at which republican idealism and emulation meet and clash.[35]

Brutus' missteps are like those of Agesilaus, without the late recovery. Kahn comes to her thesis primarily by way of contemporary feminist theory, but what the theory here detects in Shakespeare is already significantly articulated in his source material. Shakespeare's concern with such things was not of course dependent on his source material; there is, for instance, nothing in Holinshed to suggest the circling rivalry between Hal and Hotspur that is central to the plotting of *1 Henry IV*.[36] But when Shakespeare did, at about this time, open North for serious study, part of what was waiting for him and secured his long-term interest was a wealth of skilfully shaped stories about the occasional successes and characteristic missteps of, as one classicist has recently called them, Plutarch's 'alpha males'.[37]

The most complicated and provocative case here is the Life of Antony. Plutarch provides textual warrant for the schema that Bullough and Cantor put forward; Antony's story is that of the catastrophic dominance of the soul's third part:

the dire evil which had been slumbering for a long time, namely, his passion [*erôs*] for Cleopatra, which men thought had been charmed away and lulled to rest by better considerations, blazed up again with renewed power as he drew near to Syria. And finally, like the stubborn and unmanageable beast of the soul, of which Plato speaks, he spurned away all saving and noble counsels . . . (*Antony* 36.1)

Antony's Greek precedent is Demetrius Poliorcetes, a man of similar weaknesses, who uses the Acropolis as a brothel and eventually dies 'through inactivity and a surfeit of food and wine' (*Demetrius* 52.3); Plutarch sets these two lives off as explicitly negative examples, 'ample testimony to the truth of Plato's saying that great natures exhibit great vices also' (1.7). Yet though the portrait of Demetrius is largely coloured within these lines, that of Antony becomes an instance of one of Plutarch's most significant narrative patterns: 'crude initial statement and progressive redefinition'.[38] Nobody remembers his biography as a pathetic and sordid story of manly ambition ruined by lust. By the end, the author's disapproval has become part of a famously nuanced awareness of the interrelation of Antony's strengths and failings – and astonishingly, a comparable enrichment of sympathy is granted to the agent of his downfall. There are still ten chapters to go after Antony's death – a continuation without parallel in the *Lives* – and they are mostly devoted to Cleopatra's final actions, which do more than anyone expected to redeem both her own reputation and that of the love-story of which she was part. Caesar is left amazed at her nobility (*eugeneia*) and orders that she and Antony be buried together 'in splendid and regal fashion' (*Antony* 86.4).

Shakespeare's play has the same post mortem space as Plutarch's biography – Antony dies at the end of act 4 – but it subtends an even stronger redemptive arc. Plutarch never really articulates the proposition – there is no reason to think he would – that sexual love itself can lay claim to heroic status. Shakespeare, however, seems to allow his Antony and Cleopatra knowledge of their future reputation; their confidence in that possibility inflects their worldly behaviour. As Cantor puts it, 'the love of Antony and Cleopatra seems to be not an alternative to the Roman quest for public eminence, but rather an alternative path to a new kind of public eminence itself'; Cantor devotes a final chapter of his book to just this subject, since it represents a significant twist in his schema:

> pride and eros are ordinarily two separate forces, working against each other and thus moderating each other. But for Antony and Cleopatra pride and eros have become united: since they take pride in their love, their pride only serves to increase the force of eros in their lives. Once Antony and Cleopatra derive their sense of achievement from their status as lovers, they begin to demand a great deal more from love than most men and women do, and they also allow love to assume an importance for them that goes well beyond its usual role.[39]

In other words, the second part of the soul has made an alliance different from that which Plato endorsed: it has invested the appetites of the body with the aspirations of the *thymos*.

Kahn, focused on the more traditionally Plutarchan competition between Antony and Caesar, does not discuss this new psychic alliance; but it has important consequences against the traditional grid of gender roles. The alphas here in play are not exclusively male. Plutarch himself is not rigid in excluding women from the motivations of the soul's second part; among his surviving works is an admiring compilation, *Bravery of Women*, which includes some quite militant examples ('the women, suddenly possessed of fierce and savage spirit [*thymon*] . . . hastened to mount the walls, both bringing stones and missiles, and exhorting and importuning the fighting men'; *Moralia* 245B–C). But the reconfiguration evident in Shakespeare's play is of a different order; his reading of Plutarch is overlaid with four centuries of vernacular love-poetry, the legacy of the troubadours passed on through Petrarch and others to the rest of European literature, in which what we now call romantic love is treated as something it never really is in classical antiquity, a source of competitive and public prestige: *pretz e valor* in the troubadours' language.[40] Cantor is not sentimental about the political consequences of the new dispensation as displayed in Shakespeare's play – 'a trait that seems acceptable in a lover . . . is unacceptable in a ruler, where the same trait appears as selfishness, arbitrariness, and willful blindness to reality'[41] – but I think his way of formulating it does justice to its momentousness.

It is of course most memorable and compelling in the wake of political failure. On the verge of suicide, Shakespeare's Antony breaches the rule that his Brutus had so scrupulously observed of not looking to the consolation of an afterlife; the promise of erotic celebrity feels too sweet not to be true:

> Where Soules do couch on Flowers, wee'l hand in hand,
> And with our sprightly Port make the Ghostes gaze:
> *Dido*, and her *Aeneas* shall want Troopes,
> And all the haunt be ours.
>
> (*Antony and Cleopatra* 4.15.51–4)

After his death, Cleopatra's great profession of love is an imperial vision knowingly contrary to fact –

> I dreampt there was an Emperor *Anthony*.
> Oh such another sleepe, that I might see
> But such another man.   (5.2.75–7)

– linked to a bold assertion of the rights of the imagination: 't'imagine / An *Anthony* were Natures peece, 'gainst Fancie, / Condemning shadowes quite' (97–9). Dolabella, her audience of one, does not believe a word of it, but knows she has made the point that really counts: 'Your losse is as your selfe, great; and you beare it / As answering to the waight' (100–1). In obedient respect for the dignity which she has successfully claimed, he betrays to her his emperor's secret intent.

None of these speeches is in Plutarch, though they blossom in the soil he laid down.

NOTES

1. *The First Folio of Shakespeare*, ed. Charlton Hinman (New York 1968), p. 630.
2. I quote North's translation from *Plutarch's Lives of the Noble Grecians and Romans Englished by Sir Thomas North*, intro. George Wyndham, The Tudor Translations, 6 vols. (1895, repr. New York 1967), with reference to volume and page in this edition; I attach references to the Greek text as I find it in *Plutarch's Lives*, ed. and trans. Bernadotte Perrin, 11 vols., Loeb Classical Library (Cambridge, MA 1914–26), with reference to chapter and subsection within the individual *Life*. The modern translation of the *Lives* occasionally quoted below is Perrin's, with minor adjustments. Plutarch's other works are cited from *Moralia*, ed. and trans. Frank Cole Babbitt *et al.*, 15 vols., Loeb Classical Library (Cambridge, MA 1927–69), with reference to the Stephanus pages for the collection as a whole.
3. The text as printed in Shakespeare, *The Complete Works: The Original-Spelling Edition*, ed. Stanley Wells and Gary Taylor (Oxford 1986). Except as noted, other citations of Shakespeare's plays are from this source, with normalisation of i/j and u/v to modern usage; I give act-scene-line references consistent with those in the Wells–Taylor modernised text.

4. Geoffrey Bullough, ed., *Narrative and Dramatic Sources of Shakespeare*, 8 vols. (London 1957–75), vol. VIII, p. 346.

5. North 1.36, 45–8, 55; *Theseus* 8, 19–20, 26.

6. See Robert Adger Law, 'The Roman Background of *Titus Andronicus*', *Studies in Philology* 40 (1943), 145–53.

7. J. A. K. Thomson, *Shakespeare and the Classics* (New York 1952), p. 242.

8. Cynthia Marshall, 'Shakespeare, Crossing the Rubicon', *ShS* 53 (2000), 73, 80.

9. M. W. MacCallum, *Shakespeare's Roman Plays and their Background* (1910, repr. London 1935). *Shakespeare's Plutarch*, ed. T. J. B. Spencer (1964, repr. Harmondsworth 1968), prints modernised texts of the four principal lives with the major Shakespearean parallels at the bottom of the page and a brief introductory essay.

10. For instance: Sidney Homan, 'Dion, Alexander, and Demetrius – Plutarch's Forgotten *Parallel Lives* – as Mirrors for Shakespeare's *Julius Caesar*', *ShSt* 8 (1975), 195–210; E. A. J. Honigman, 'Shakespeare's Plutarch', *ShQ* 10 (1959), 25–33.

11. See most recently Janet Adelman, *Suffocating Mothers: Fantasies of Maternal Origin in Shakespeare's Plays, 'Hamlet' to 'The Tempest'* (London 1992), pp. 183–8, 337–40; an impressive piece of evidence for the specific impress of Holland's translation on Shakespeare's text was first noted by John Adlard, 'Cleopatra as Isis', *Archiv für das Studium der neueren Sprachen und Literatur* 212 (1975), 325.

12. See Kenneth Muir, 'Blundeville, Wyatt, and Shakespeare', *N&Q* 206 (1961), 293–4; and Ralph Aiken, 'A Note on Shakespeare's Sonnet 30', *ShQ* 14 (1963), 93–4.

13. MacCallum, *Shakespeare's Roman Plays*, p. 166. For a fresh discussion in a similar spirit, see C. B. R. Pelling, ed., *Plutarch: Life of Antony* (Cambridge 1988): 'There is no danger of minimising [Shakespeare's] transformation of his source . . . But it is also noticeable how often his transformation can be seen as a dramatic turning or equivalent of a Plutarchan idea, or a different response to a similar dramatic problem; and how often it is the *distinctive* Plutarchan touches which [Shakespeare] selects to elaborate' (p. 45).

14. See MacCallum, *Shakespeare's Roman Plays*, pp. 184–5. Amyot handles the passage correctly. In his modernisation of North, Spencer, *Shakespeare's Plutarch*, pp. 154–5, muddies the trail by putting quotation marks where the sense demands ('Brutus answered him: "Being yet but a young man" ').

15. MacCallum, *Shakespeare's Roman Plays*, p. 185.

16. Paul A. Cantor, 'Shakespeare's Parallel Lives: Plutarch and the Roman Plays', *Poetica* (Tokyo) 48 (1997), 71–2.

17. See Reuben A. Brower, *Hero and Saint: Shakespeare and the Graeco-Roman Heroic Tradition* (New York 1971), pp. 205–11.

18. Geoffrey Miles, *Shakespeare and the Constant Romans* (Oxford 1996), pp. 110–22.

19. Ibid., p. 111.

20. Bullough, *Narrative and Dramatic Sources*, vol. v, pp. 454–5.

21. Paul A. Cantor, *Shakespeare's Rome: Republic and Empire* (Ithaca 1976), p. 37.

22. My periphrastic handling of the latter term is meant to distinguish it from its usual English translation, 'ambitious', which can cover acquisitiveness as well as the desire for official recognition; Plutarch's Life of Crassus hinges precisely on a conflict between *philoplousia*, love of wealth, and *philotimia*. Etymologically, *philonicos* is distinct from *philoneicos*, in love with strife, and Plato appears to insist on the former; but in general usage the two are almost interchangeable, and my quotations follow the edition at hand.

23. Fragment 210 in the new Loeb edition of Pindar, ed. and trans. William H. Race, 2 vols. (Cambridge, MA 1997).

24. *On Moral Virtue*, *Moralia* 441F–42A; the charioteer metaphor from the *Phaedrus* is cited at 445C.

25. On *thymoeidês* as the pivotal term in Plutarch's characterisation of Alexander, see A. E. Wardman, 'Plutarch and Alexander', *Classical Quarterly* n.s. 5 (1955), 96–107. On the prominence of this complex of terms in the *Lives* generally, see Tim Duff, *Plutarch's Lives: Exploring Virtue and Vice* (Oxford 1999), pp. 83–9.

26. *On the Control of Anger*, *Moralia* 457B; *Sulla* 4.4.

27. *On the Control of Anger*, *Moralia* 457B–C. 'Absolutist' in this sense is William V. Harris' term, from his *Restraining Rage: The Ideology of Anger Control in Classical Antiquity* (Cambridge, MA 2001); on Plutarch's place in this tradition, see pp. 118–20.

28. See at greater length Duff, *Plutarch's Lives*, pp. 208–15.

29. J. E. Lendon, *Empire of Honour: The Art of Government in the Roman World* (Oxford 1997), p. 191.

30. *Table-Talk* 1.2; *Moralia* 615C–19A; see Lendon, *Empire of Honour*, p. 61.

31. With particular vigour by A. Andrewes: 'Plutarch's description . . . of the conflict between Thoukydides and Perikles . . . is worthless and has seriously distorted our picture of this period and of Athenian attitudes to the empire'; 'The Opposition to Perikles', *Journal of Hellenic Studies* 98 (1978), 1.

32. See my *Renaissance Tragedy and the Senecan Tradition: Anger's Privilege* (New Haven 1985), pp. 8–15. Plutarch lived through the reign of Nero and was in Rome during the reign of Domitian. He understandably has little to say about either, and Nero's kindness to Greece clearly made a difference to him; but he recognised the monstrosity of both men. See C. P. Jones, *Plutarch and Rome* (Oxford 1971), pp. 18–9, 22–5.

33. Torquato Tasso, *Jerusalem Delivered*, ed. and trans. Anthony M. Esolen (Baltimore 2000), p. 418.

34. Coppélia Kahn, *Roman Shakespeare: Warriors, Wounds, and Women* (London 1997), p. 15.

35. Ibid., p. 95.

36. It has in fact been argued that this and other features of the *Henry IV* plays were significantly influenced by Shakespeare's reading of Plutarch; see Judith Mossman, 'Plutarch and Shakespeare's *Henry IV parts 1 and 2*', *Poetica* (Tokyo) 48 (1997), 99–117.

37. Robert Lamberton, *Plutarch* (New Haven 2001), p. 73 and elsewhere.

38. Pelling, *Life of Antony*, p. 42.
39. Cantor, *Shakespeare's Rome*, p. 187.
40. See my discussion in *Petrarchan Love and the Continental Renaissance* (New Haven 1999), pp. 47–50. In his *Dialogue on Love* Plutarch discusses the potential of male homosexual love to inspire military prowess, but has no heterosexual examples to offer (*Moralia* 760D–61D).
41. Cantor, *Shakespeare's Rome*, p. 203.

GENERAL

CHAPTER 12

Action at a distance: Shakespeare and the Greeks

A. D. Nuttall

Ben Jonson successfully persuaded the centuries which followed that Shakespeare had many virtues but that classical learning was not among them. Jonson's poem of commendation, prefixed to the First Folio of Shakespeare's plays, is a psychologically tormented affair, masquerading, as is usual with Jonson, as bluff benevolence. The opening words splinter as we read them.

> To draw no envy (Shakespeare) on thy name
> Am I thus ample to thy book, and fame

'Envy' here bears the old sense, 'ill will', 'hostility'. Before he has got under way Jonson hastens to reassure us: 'I am not hoping to sow the seeds of hostility here.' It is a strange way to begin, so strange as to provoke at once a shrewd unbelief in the reader. The words instantly become an inadvertent *occupatio* – that figure of rhetoric in which the speaker negates or denies things which he knows will nevertheless lodge in the hearer's mind ('I shall pass over the fact that my honourable friend has been stealing from central funds for years'). So here we think, 'Hah, so there is a case for hostility is there?' But Jonson is not in clear command of this effect. Within a few lines he is eagerly distancing himself from those who 'pretend' praise and 'think to ruin, where it seemed to raise' (11–12). The impression somehow grows stronger with each denial that something in Jonson wishes to do exactly this. This in its turn has a semantic effect, retroactively, on 'envy' in line 1. The sense, we said, was 'ill will'. But if Jonson's own psyche is covertly complicit with the offence here disclaimed, 'envy' can take on, as a subaudition, the other meaning (well established in Jonson's time), 'resentment of some supposed superiority in another'. This, surely, is the key. Jonson found it very hard to bear the success of Shakespeare. The one place in which he could clearly score over the sweet swan of Avon was the field of learning. Of course this is not the whole picture. When we reach the line, 'He was not for an age, but for all time!', genuine, generous praise really does blow all the cobwebs away. But the cobwebs were there, before

209

they were dispersed. Such is the context of the famous parenthetic twitch, 'Though thou hadst small Latin, and less Greek'.[1] The judgement behind these words has hardened, over the years, into something like Gospel. But should we believe Jonson?

In the world of learning of course standards are variable. It is pretty clear that Jonson was a better classicist than Shakespeare. T. W. Baldwin in his magisterial book, *William Shakspere's Small Latine and Lesse Greeke* showed that Shakespeare nevertheless read huge quantities of Ovid, for example, in the original language. It looks as if he never read beyond the first six books of Virgil's *Aeneid* but, even so, he covered far more ground than young persons who describe themselves as classicists in universities today. All this Baldwin can show on the Latin side of the equation. On the Greek, however, he comes up with a virtual zero (Shakespeare *may* have had a brief engagement with New Testament Greek). At the end of his book Baldwin confesses, in effect, that a better (though less catchy) title might have been 'Shakespeare's Considerable Latin and Non-existent Greek'. Suddenly it looks as if grudging Jonson may actually have erred on the side of generosity, at least with reference to Greek. Baldwin writes, 'Jonson's statement is still our strongest warrant that Shakespeare had any Greek at all'.[2] But the thought need not detain us long. It is easy to imagine Jonson growling '– and less Greek!' with a glint in his eye (meaning 'and I'm putting it mildly!').

That Shakespeare was cut off from Greek poetry and drama is probably a bleak truth we should accept. A case can be made – and has been – for Shakespeare's having some knowledge of certain Greek plays, such as Aeschylus' *Agamemnon*, Euripides' *Orestes*, *Alcestis*, and *Hecuba*,[3] by way of available Latin versions, but this, surely, is an area in which the faint occasional echoes mean less than the circumambient silence. When we consider how hungrily Shakespeare feeds upon Ovid, learning from him or extending him at every turn, it becomes the more evident that he cannot in any serious sense have found his way to Euripides. In *Richard II* Shakespeare broke new ground in the dramatic presentation of psychological interiority, linking it to a mannered Narcissism in the subject.[4] Euripides achieved a strikingly similar transformation of dramaturgy in his *Hippolytus*. Shakespeare, had he read the *Hippolytus*, would surely have found it electrifying. It might be said indeed that the *Hippolytus* is actually *too* 'proto-Shakespearean' to be pleasing to Shakespeare. There are occasions when writers are thrown by too close a coincidence of method and deliberately shut their eyes, in order to safeguard the separate integrity of their own work. For this reason poets desire imperfect predecessors rather than great. Milton did not feel himself to be fortunate in following Shakespeare; his genius was not quickened but petrified: 'Dost make us marble with too much conceiving'.⁵ Yet, for all that, Milton's engagement with Shakespeare is clear in his earlier poems. If the *Hippolytus* was too close, then, surely, the great Euripidean women, Medea, Electra, Phaedra, Agave, would have laid hold on Shakespeare's imagination. The thought obstinately persists: Shakespeare simply did not know this material in any intimate way.

The old view that Shakespeare had no sense whatever of history or cultural difference – the idea that his Romans, for example, are just Elizabethans with grand names – is no longer tenable. Certainly they did not have lavishly illustrated teaching aids at Stratford grammar school and this means that Shakespeare may well have been hazy about the appearance of an ancient temple; he seems not to have known what a pyramid was. Notoriously clocks chime in *Julius Caesar* and people wear spectacles in *Coriolanus*. But he read intelligently. This means that a suicide in a Roman play is quite different from a suicide in one set in later times. Moreover, within the field of 'Roman-ness' he can distinguish rising republican political mechanisms (*Coriolanus*) from their later decay (*Julius Caesar*). It is now fashionable to trace hidden reference to English contemporary politics in the Roman plays, but such reference is acknowledged to exist in negotiation with the overt depiction of an alien polity. Thus Heather James in her *Shakespeare's Troy* (Cambridge 1997) investigates the poet's 'use of the political and literary tradition derived from imperial Rome to legitimate the cultural place of the theatre in late Elizabethan and early Stuart London' (p. 1); when she turns to *Troilus and Cressida* she finds a work in which 'the matter of Troy' is no longer simply authoritative but is rife with ambiguity, a site of subversion and dissolution. Meanwhile the battle for the essential Roman-ness of Shakespeare's Romans has been won.

But what of the Greeks? Are they distinctively Greek? *Timon of Athens* is a Plutarchan play (as is *Julius Caesar*) and its protagonist is Greek. In *Julius Caesar* we find an intense engagement with concrete Roman events and with Roman ideology. The picture of an aristocratic republican misjudging the mood of a populace which is in fact drifting towards monarchy is *historically* shrewd. Although I have said that current criticism must allow significant reference to earlier cultures even as it argues for contemporary events determining the text, it must be acknowledged that this sort of skill in history shown by the playwright is not congenial to present day historicists. They are happier where literature can be seen as betraying certain assumptions, rather than as showing understanding of the distinct assumptions of another time. It is felt to be mildly scandalous to suggest that the dramatist might prove capable of cognitive behaviour, of ceasing to be material for analysis and becoming an analyst in his own right; Shakespeare is history (Jonson was monumentally wrong to suppose that he was for all time) – not, surely, a historian! Of course he is primarily a playwright. But moments of historical insight do occur in Shakespeare. The notion that Stoic *apatheia* might find itself fused with a Narcissism very different from that of Richard II is, again, brilliant. But *Timon of Athens* gives us no sense of a different culture. The play on gentlemanly obligation versus legal indebtedness, central to the drama, is wholly Jacobean. *The Comedy of Errors* is notionally Graeco-Mediterranean (Syracuse and Ephesus) but there is no sense of deliberate distinction in the giving of Greek names to some (Aegeon, Antipholus) and Latin to others (Emilia, Luciana), and the schoolmaster is named, unclassically, 'Pinch'. There is indeed a sense of cultural distinctness in this play but it is attached to Ephesus (an urban labyrinth populated by tricksters and magicians, a little like the Morocco visited by Bob Hope, Bing Crosby, and Dorothy Lamour in the *Road to-* film). *A Midsummer Night's Dream* is set in ancient Attica but Hermia and Helena are nice English girls; Bottom and his friends, like Luce and Pinch in the earlier play, do not even have Greek names. The wood near Athens could as easily be a wood near Warwick. Nowhere do we receive any impression of Greek history as a developing, complex phenomenon. The hegemony of Athens, the Peloponnesian war, the transcendent Forms of Plato or the immanent forms of Aristotle, the Parthenon, the sculpture of Phidias, Athenian democracy – none of these appears to have registered with him. We may find in Shakespeare stray references to Aristotle (especially to the *Nicomachean Ethics*) or to Pythagoras, but these are not integrated by him in a perceived historical process as, say, Stoicism and Epicureanism are integrated in a Roman process in *Julius Caesar*.

We may seem, then, to have drawn a blank, much as Baldwin drew a blank, in his investigation of the poet's education, on Shakespeare's 'less Greek'. There may however be a response in Shakespeare to the Greeks of a kind which will be especially elusive to those who confine themselves to verbal reminiscence and the historiographical perspective – a response which is unscholarly, irresponsible – and aesthetically alert.

In *The Winter's Tale* Florizel says to Perdita,

> The gods themselves,
> Humbling their deities to love, have taken
> The shapes of beasts upon them. Jupiter
> Became a bull, and bellowed; the green Neptune
> A ram, and bleated; and the fire-robed god,

> Golden Apollo, a poor humble swain,
> As I seem now   (4.4.25–31)

One incarnation is central to Christianity. But the ubiquitous incarnations of Greek religion are utterly different. These amorous gods in bestial form belong to another world. Florizel's speech is commonly compared with certain lines in Marlowe's *Hero and Leander*:

> There might you see the gods in sundry shapes,
> Committing heady riot, incest, rapes . . .
> Jove, slyly stealing from his sister's bed,
> To dally with Idalian Ganimed:
> And for his love Europa, bellowing loud,
> And tumbling with the Rainbow in a cloud . . .
>   (1.143–4, 147–50)

It is likely that Shakespeare remembered these lines as he wrote his speech for Florizel (notice the word 'bellow' in both). These are Greek gods transmitted by a Roman poet, Ovid, and Shakespeare shares with Marlowe the prize for freeing Ovid from the moralising commentary which had encrusted his writings by the end of the sixteenth century. 'It's really all about sex!' they joyously pointed out. We must however acknowledge a difference between the two poet-dramatists. Marlowe's lines are marvellously unfettered but at the same time they are consciously naughty ('sister's bed', 'slyly', 'dally'). Shakespeare's gods are august, even in their animal transformations. Shakespeare's bull-Jupiter bellows as does Marlowe's but Shakespeare avoids the riotously rococo 'tumbling in a cloud'. It is a nice question which of the two passages is truer to the spirit of Ovid. Ovid followed – and refused to follow – Virgil, the author of the great, moralised, historical Roman epic. The *Metamorphoses*, contrariwise, is a *carmen perpetuum* (1.4), a timeless 'perpetual song', made not out of teleologically conceived history but out of the old Greek endlessly ramifying myths,[6] those things which, in the words of the neoplatonist Sallustius, 'never happened and always are'.[7] There is in this enterprise a conscious delinquency which Marlowe catches and Shakespeare ignores. It is as if the Stratford poet has passed through the half-Roman medium to the Greek material on the far side. In these shining epiphanies there is a faint intuition of the (entirely Greek) awe which Apollonius describes when Apollo appears to the Argonauts (*Argonautica* 2.681). I say 'half-Roman' because Ovid indeed lived on uneasy terms with his own society. We learn without surprise that he was banished. Meanwhile, if Shakespeare got his Greek mythology via a Roman, let us not forget that he got the concrete Roman history of which we have

made so much from a Greek, Plutarch. Indeed, just as Ovid may have been
sharply aware of the Hellenism of his material *because* he was a Roman,
Plutarch may have had a Greek's special awareness of the macho militarism
and rigidity of the Romans.[8] Florizel speaks as he does to Perdita from
an anxiety which is entirely of Shakespeare's own time and culture. He
is worried that Perdita will think it deeply wrong that a lower-class girl
should have an upper-class lover. The stories of the gods descending to animal shapes is intended, so to speak, to cheer her up: 'Other grand persons
have been even more condescending than I am being now.' If we pause to
reflect we may find the sentiment lacking in gallantry. But the occasion of
the speech is oddly unimportant. The words naturally detach themselves
from their context and linger separately in our minds after the play is over.
Recent critics tirelessly despise those older editors like William Dodds who
excerpted 'Beauties of Shakespeare' – especially fine passages to be read in
isolation. Yet Shakespeare seems sometimes to invite exactly this. Mercutio's
Queen Mab speech is somehow *written* as an-anthology-piece-before-the-
anthologists. So with Florizel and the ancient gods. We pass from the
dramatic action through a magic casement which opens on a remote sunlit
world.

I am suggesting that Shakespeare had a faculty for driving through the
available un-Greek transmitting text to whatever lay on the other side. At
the end of the seventeenth century Isaac Newton scandalised the Cartesians
with his theory of gravity: the sun acts upon the earth from far away, with
no mediating physical system of pulleys, cogwheels, ropes. It is mysterious,
Newton agreed, and yet it is so: 'I frame no hypotheses'.[9] I have argued
elsewhere[10] that both in *The Comedy of Errors* and in the late Romances
Shakespeare was straining towards a mythical nexus involving children lost
and found, which is more Greek than Roman. Roman Comedy is clearly the
'source' of *The Comedy of Errors*, but Roman Comedy emphasises gulling,
clever servants and the like. In the Greek New Comedy from which Roman
Comedy derived we find the mythic resonance Shakespeare sought – and we
find it still more in those strange Euripidean 'happy-ending tragedies' (*Ion,
Alcestis*) from which New Comedy itself developed.[11] In *The Tempest* the
source for Ferdinand's meeting with Miranda is obviously Virgilian: Aeneas'
meeting with his goddess mother in *Aeneid* 1. Virgil in his turn drew on
the Homeric meeting of Odysseus and Nausicaa (*Odyssey* 6.149–52). This,
it is generally agreed, Shakespeare never read. But although tracking verbal
reminiscences in Shakespeare will take us immediately to Virgil, the more
general character of the encounter (human meets human – not human
meets goddess – and male person gallantly pretends that the female person

could be divine) brings the *Tempest* episode far closer to the remote Greek original than to the available Latin. The link to Homer is strengthened by the magic island context in both. Phaeacia is a kind of paradise where the fruit never decays in the garden of Alcinous (*Odyssey* 7.117); the shimmering island of *The Tempest* is intermittently Edenic. But the setting of *Aeneid* 1 is simply North Africa, *terra cognita*.

If we stand back, as it were, from the usual business of tracing echoes and look at larger, more diffuse structures, we may well begin to think that it is simply inaccurate to say that there are no Greek effects in the work of Shakespeare. So far I have avoided discussion of one play with Greek persons in it – *Troilus and Cressida*. This work, probably written for Shakespeare's sharpest, best-educated audience (the Inns of Court)[12] brilliantly entwines Chaucerian chivalric codes with a desolate Greek brutalism (quite unlike the 'virilism' of *Coriolanus*). Here Chapman's translation of Homer (or whatever Chapman had completed by this date) has clearly left its mark on the text. Moreover it appears that Shakespeare was a penetrative rather than a docile reader of Chapman. In his accompanying commentary Chapman strains every nerve to turn Homer into a high moral Stoic, but the Homeric material, violent, raw, erotically pre-chivalric, will come through.[13] Roughly speaking, Shakespeare's Trojans are more Chaucerian, his Greeks more Greek, reflecting the line which links Troy, not Athens, to King Arthur and British history (a sequence variously exploded and subverted by Shakespeare's time but still mythically potent).[14] Shakespeare makes sure that we feel the alien quality of this ancient matter by giving his opening Prologue a language on stilts, studded with strange words, 'the princes *orgillous*', '*immures*', '*corresponsive*', and Chapmanesque compound-words. This, Shakespeare's 'Trojan style', was used in *Hamlet* (2.2.446–91) to register the space between the player's narrative of Priam's death and the main, Danish action.[15] Here it is developed symphonically, chivalric Gallicisms played against classicism. The whole is indeed complex. The Greeks are themselves characterised simultaneously by a reductive intellectualism and a gross (oddly abstract) physicality. Act 1, scene 3 is studded with phrases which are relishingly physical: 'nerve and bone of Greece' (54), where 'nerve' means 'muscle'; 'his mastic jaws' (72); 'give me ribs of steel' (177); 'large Achilles on his pressed bed lolling / From his deep chest . . .' (162–3), 'blockish Ajax' (375), 'sinew' at 136 and 143 (compare 2.1.101, 3.1.150, 5.3.33, and especially 4.7.10–11: 'the sinews of this leg / All Greek'). These expressions compose a Mannerist picture – exaggerated musculature, turbulent graphic panache, a classicism close to grotesquerie – which is akin to that displayed by Giulio Romano in his Sala de' Giganti at Mantua. The final result is a work which hovers, in a wholly controlled manner, between horrified fascination and burlesque; the play itself becomes a killing field of high traditions.

It is time to think about structures. Shakespeare sets us thinking about Greek ideas of plotting 28 lines into the play with the words, 'Beginning in the middle'. Homer famously did not begin his *Iliad* with the egg from which Helen was hatched but instead plunged *in medias res*, into the middle of the story. What will become apparent only later is that Shakespeare out-Homers Homer by *staying* in the middle, by refusing to take his story to any kind of satisfying conclusion. As Dryden put it, 'The chief persons, who give name to the tragedy, are left alive.'[16] He might have said, 'are left remorselessly alive'.

The source-hunters have sought to relate 1.2, the scene in which Cressida first sees Troilus, to Chaucer's *Troilus and Criseyde*; Criseyde sees Troilus pass by, wounded, at 2.647 and she sees him again from her window as he rides by, at 2.1,247. That these are source-passages I do not dispute. But if, once more, we step back and apprehend the dynamics of Shakespeare's scene we shall find that it is really a *teichoskopia*. I borrow the word from the ancient scholiast on Euripides, *Phoenissae* 88.[17] It is the ancient scholarly critical term for the episode in *Iliad* 3 in which Helen watches from the wall as the Greek heroes pass to and fro, within view: 'the looking-from-the-wall'. The essence of the episode is a comparative display of figures. Agamemnon passes, taller than the rest, then Odysseus, shorter but broader, then the gigantic Ajax (3.161–229). In Shakespeare's play Aeneas passes before Cressida, then brave Hector with his splendid 'countenance', then Paris, and later Troilus. Cressida wickedly asks, 'What sneaking fellow comes yonder?' (1.2.223) and Pandarus, as unofficial master of ceremonies, affects to believe she means Deiphobus and hastily points out how Troilus' helmet is more deeply hacked than Hector's. One suspects that the faintly gossipy, excited character of the Homeric sequence, with its Greek interest in male beauty (they are like models on a catwalk) would have seemed undignified to Virgil. There is no parallel passage in the *Aeneid*. But the undignified element is exactly what Shakespeare wants, and he heightens it. Most importantly, in the Chaucerian passages there is no parade of figures within which Troilus appears, no awarding of points. Once more, this episode, with all its savage burlesque, is at bottom more Homeric than Chaucerian.

We commonly assume that Homer, the first and grandest of the epic poets, is also the most uniformly elevated. The truth is that to early modern readers brought up on Virgil Homer himself, unaltered, could look very like burlesque. At *Iliad* 9.558–65 the huge Ajax is wonderfully compared with a donkey which has broken into a cornfield; small boys beat it with sticks but can scarcely shift it. Marco Girolamo Vida was appalled by the simile: he allows that the comparison is exact but just can't take the donkey itself – *sed turpe pecus,* 'but the animal is base!'[18] All this is alien to our age, yet even I can feel that there is something Cervantic about the donkey simile. At *Iliad* 24.621–2, Achilles, with the air of one offering a guest a cup of coffee, casually rises and slaughters a sheep. One thinks of Johnson's shocked reaction to the word 'knife' in *Macbeth* as 'the name of an instrument used by butchers and cooks in the meanest employments'.[19]

If *Troilus and Cressida* 1.2 is a *teichoskopia,* then, still more clearly, the later part of *Timon of Athens* is Greek in form. Here the pattern is: the hero, humiliated, in a wild place; to him come, in succession, persons who, despite his humiliation, solicit his aid. This is the pattern of Aeschylus' (?) *Prometheus Bound* and, more powerfully, of Sophocles' *Philoctetes,* where the hero, now offensive to society, is approached by Neoptolemus and Odysseus. It is there again in *Oedipus Coloneus.* There the blinded protagonist, filthy and in rags, is visited by Theseus, Creon, and Polynices. Timon becomes the hater of mankind and retreats to the wilderness; he is visited by Alcibiades and then by a succession of senators who seek his help. When Milton wrote his drama, 'never intended' for the stage, in proud contradistinction to the English theatrical tradition, he followed this Greek pattern: Samson humiliated; to him come Manoa, Dalila, Harapha. No one doubts the Hellenism of *Samson Agonistes,* but Shakespeare – he of the 'native wood-notes wild'[20] – got there first.

If Shakespeare knew no Greek, how did he bring off this feat, this accurate identification of shapes of thought, modes of drama, other than his own? If we suppose what is simply probable, that he talked in pubs to Ben Jonson and others, knew a little of academic Latin drama, had already become alert to Romano-Greek negotiations within the work of Ovid, it becomes intelligible that he should have scented Greek forms behind Plautus, Terence, and Seneca (though there is no Senecan *Philoctetes* or *Oedipus Coloneus*). As for the *teichoskopia,* Chapman's translation of *Iliad* 3 had not been published but Chapman, like Jonson, is a person to whom Shakespeare may have talked. There were Latin versions of the *Iliad* and Arthur Hall had covered *Iliad* 3 in his English.[21] Hall's version is in no sense a burlesque but, equally certainly, gives the reader a counter-Virgilian picture, a world of 'massy' shields, 'stiff' heroes, in which splendour co-exists with a strange grossness in the diction ('his bigge and bumpishe targe therewith in pieces brast' and the like).[22]

Robert Greene's *Euphues His Censure to Philautus* (1587) contrasts Greeks and Trojans in a manner which clearly set Shakespeare's thoughts racing. The brilliant sentence in which Hector exposes the moral dubiety of fighting a war for Helen, "Tis mad idolatry to make the service greater than the god' (2.2.55–6), may have been prompted by two passages in Greene. His Cressida marvels that the Greeks should 'bear arms in her defence whose dishonesty ruinates both their fame and their country' and his Bryses later calls Helen 'an idol'.[23] Greene's Trojans are chivalrous, his Greeks philosophical, but their philosophy is basely utilitarian. Polyxena says, 'Do we not know our enemies are Grecians, taught in their schools amongst their philosophers that all wisdom is honest that is profitable, that their heads are as full of subtlety as their hearts are of valour?'[24] The editor of the older Arden edition of *Troilus and Cressida* has pointed out that it is the Trojans who talk about fundamental questions in ethical philosophy: Is Helen worth keeping? What does 'worth' mean? Is value simply something which we assign – to anything we randomly choose – in an unconstrained manner? Or are we *not* free to decide, for example, that the maiming and killing of thousands for the sake of one is a virtuous thing? This is real philosophy and will return, as is the way of real philosophy, in different forms in different centuries. G. E. Moore's dispute with C. L. Stevenson over the suggestion that 'This is good' might be fairly reducible to 'I like this'[25] is a twentieth-century re-run of Hector versus Troilus in 2.2. The Arden editor goes on to observe that the Greeks on the other hand talk only about means, not ends.[26]

Although many would say the Greeks have right on their side, they are given a style of reasoning which smells of sophistry, in the technical meaning of the term. Ulysses is given a speech of astonishing philosophical sophistication when he says, 'No man is the lord of anything . . . / Till he communicate his parts to others' (3.3.110–12). The thought here is that the very fabric of language forces us to construe individual persons relationally. I suspect that the word 'lord' was prompted by thoughts about the word 'property' in the sense 'attribute of a person or thing', with its strong connotation of ownership. This then generates the paradox: 'That which is yours is not private to you but is logically shared.' 'The property of rain is to wet' (*As You Like It* 3.2.26); the inmost character of rain shows only as it acts upon other things. We may suppose for a moment that a relation holds between two things which must exist prior to the relation and that we should therefore be able to say something about these things in themselves, before we proceed to the relation. If we say, 'Jane is a generous person' we are saying that Jane gives to others. If we say, 'John is a recluse' we are saying that John noticeably absents himself from the company of others. The supposed prior substance, where we thought true identity inhered, dissolves before our eyes. We are close to the Structuralist intuition that context is not posterior to identity but on the contrary confers identity. Of course Ulysses as he speaks is really just trying to sting Achilles into action ('If you do no brave action you cannot think "But I am Achilles" because "Achilles" is now nothing'). This is all very clever. The general drift, which is to resolve substance into relation, can be felt as obscurely chilling, more chilling even than the 'volitional value' upheld by Troilus. The Trojan debate has ethical warmth; the Greek exchange has none. The Sophists were feared because they could through words make the worse appear the better cause,[27] as Gorgias did in his arrogant 'Praise of Helen'. Robert Greene's notion that the Greeks confine ethics to low profit (which is as much as to say that they abolish ethics) comes through strongly in Shakespeare's play.

I have said that *Timon of Athens* is socially and economically English and yet its plot structure, considered abstractly, is strikingly Greek. Abstraction is perhaps the key. As long as we go on looking for the kind of concrete engagement with a past culture that we find in Shakespeare's Roman plays we shall continue to conclude that Greek culture is simply absent. But if we are willing to entertain the thought that 'Greekness' to Shakespeare *means* abstraction – play of schemata, ramifying myth rather than determinate history, irony rather than *praxis* – everything changes.[28] Rome is matter, Greece is form. Hellenism is after all present, but more as a series of experimental opportunities than as an object of investigation. I have indeed suggested that Shakespeare actually saw a kind of starkness which is really there in Homer, but of course the perception is immediately heavily ironised, though never to the point where we can settle in the easy presumption that the play is pure burlesque – it is too sad, too terrible for that. This irony, it will be said, is un-Homeric. Yes, but meanwhile irony is itself very Greek. Rome is not an ironic culture. Consider the way we in England think of Americans as possessed of great military strength but amazingly short on irony. *Timon* is not just an oddly schematic play. It is an essay in abstraction. The movement from giving to hating is Euclidian. At the same time the piece is laced with an irony which can be traced back to Lucian. Euclid was one kind of Greek writer, Lucian another. *The Tempest* is a sea-play; the *Odyssey* is a sea-epic, and from the *Odyssey* there sprang, not only Roman epic but Greek Romance. Heliodorus is more involved with air and water than with earth. In *Timon of Athens* a servant says, 'We must all part / Into this sea of air' (4.2.21–2). Troilus and Cressida were left alive, Timon's death at the end is not presented; rather it is presumed, indistinctly. William Poole has pointed out that Timon wishes to be buried παραπόντιος, between land and sea, exactly like the Greek invective poet Archilochus.[29] Shakespeare never looks steadily at the Greeks, but he does, on occasion, look with Greek eyes.

I have argued throughout from the presumption that Shakespeare did not read Greek literature in the original language. I have set aside old-fashioned source-hunting and the quest for verbal reminiscence as inappropriate in the present case. Yet I am haunted by the language applied by Shakespeare to the six gates of Troy: 'with massy staples / And corresponsive and full-filling bolts' (Prologue, 17–18). What is startling about this is the accuracy with which it catches Homer's fascination with the way gates are put together. Take for example,

> ὡς Ἕκτωρ ἰθὺς σανίδων φέρε λᾶαν ἀείρας
> αἵ ῥα πύλας εἴρυντο πύκα στιβαρῶς ἀραρυίας
> δικλίδας ὑψηλάς· δοιοὶ δ᾽ ἔντοσθεν ὀχῆες
> εἶχον ἐπημοιβοί, μία δὲ κληῒς ἐπαρήρει.
> *(Iliad* 12.453–6)

(So Hector lifted the stone and bore it straight at the doors which defended the gate, stoutly fitted, double-folding, lofty – and, within, double bars, interchanging, held them and a single bolt fastened them.)

'Corresponsive', it might be said, is actually a better translation than my 'interchanging' of Homer's ἐπημοιβοί. Virgil did not pick up this manner and repeat it in the *Aeneid*. Hall did not translate this passage. In Spondanus' parallel Greek and Latin *Homer* (the book Chapman worked from) the word is rendered by the Latin *mutui*;[30] this is not wrong, but it fails to capture the craggily technical effect of Homer's tetrasyllabic word. Perhaps after all, with Chapman sitting at his elbow, Shakespeare did hack his way through some of Homer's Greek?

NOTES

1. 'To the Memory of My Beloved, the Author Mr William Shakespeare', 31.
2. T. W. Baldwin, *William Shakspere's Small Latine and Lesse Greeke*, 2 vols. (Urbana, IL 1944), vol. II, p. 661.
3. See Douglas B. Wilson, 'Euripides' *Alcestis* and the Ending of Shakespeare's *The Winter's Tale*', *Iowa State Journal of Research* 58 (1984), 345–55; Emrys Jones, *The Origins of Shakespeare* (Oxford 1977), pp. 91–7; Louise Schleiner, 'Latinized Greek Drama in Shakespeare's Writing of *Hamlet*', *ShQ* 41 (1990), 29–48.

4. See Geoffrey Miles, *Shakespeare and the Constant Romans* (Oxford 1996), pp. 14–17.

5. 'On Shakespeare', 14.

6. I was unpersuaded by Brooks Otis' original presentation (1966) of Ovid as a second Virgil, glorifying Augustus but I applaud his later retreat from this position in the 2nd edn of *Ovid as an Epic Poet* (Cambridge 1970), see esp. pp. vii, 306–74.

7. *Concerning the Gods and the Universe*, ed. A. D. Nock (Cambridge 1926), p. 8.

8. See Gary B. Miles, 'How Roman are Shakespeare's Romans?', *ShQ* 40 (1989), 257–83 at p. 273, and Hermann Heuer, 'From Plutarch to Shakespeare: A Study of *Coriolanus*', *ShQ* 10 (1957), 50–9.

9. *Principia*, General Scholium to book II, trans. F. Cajori, 2 vols. (Berkeley 1962), vol. II, p. 547.

10. A. D. Nuttall, 'Two Unassimilable Men', in *Shakespearean Comedy*, ed. Malcolm Bradbury and David Palmer (London 1972), pp. 210–40, at 217–24 (Stratford-upon-Avon Studies 14).

11. See Satyrus, *Life of Euripides*, Oxyrhynchus Papyri 1,176, ed. A. S. Hunt, part IX (London 1912).

12. Well documented and persuasively linked to the burlesquing of Homer by W. R. Elton, in his *Shakespeare's 'Troilus and Cressida' and the Inns of Court Revels* (Aldershot 2000).

13. G. K. Hunter wrote of 'the bleak ferocity' of the *Iliad*, of the great difference between this bleakness and the medieval tradition and the consequent (fruitful) shock to Shakespeare's sensibility in his '*Troilus and Cressida*: A Tragic Satire', *ShSt* (Tokyo), 13 (1974–5), 1–23, 7. My concern is not to stress the contrast of Homer with Chaucer (which is indeed inescapable) so much as the contrast with Virgil, *within* the classical tradition. Like Geoffrey Bullough – see his *Narrative and Dramatic Sources of Shakespeare*, 8 vols. (London 1957–75), vol. VI (1966), pp. 87–8 – Hunter is confident of the influence of Chapman on Shakespeare, and I think that he is right. Robert K. Presson, in his *Troilus and Cressida and the Legends of Troy* (Madison 1953) said (p. 9) that it would be very odd indeed if Shakespeare did not avail himself of Chapman's translation. But not all agree. Kenneth Palmer in the Arden edition of 1982 (pp. 33–4) guardedly acknowledges the close correspondence of acts 1–4 with the published portions of Chapman's version but insists that this is not enough to demonstrate influence. Stuart Gillespie in his *Shakespeare's Books: A Dictionary of Shakespeare's Sources* (London and New Brunswick 2001) observes on pp. 252–3 that no one has ever been able to prove that Shakespeare used Chapman's *Homer*.

14. See Heather James, *Shakespeare's Troy*.

15. On discordant neologisms in *Troilus and Cressida* see T. McAlindon, 'Language, Style, and Meaning', in *Shakespeare's Troilus and Cressida*, ed. Priscilla Martin (London 1976), pp. 191–218, at 191–2.

16. Preface, 'The Grounds of Criticism in Tragedy', prefixed to Dryden's adaptation of *Troilus and Cressida* (1679), in John Dryden, *Of Dramatic Poesy and Other Critical Essays*, ed. George Watson, 2 vols. (London 1962), vol. I, p. 240.

17. *Scholia in Euripidem*, ed. E. Schwarz, 2 vols. (Berlin 1887), vol. I, p. 260.

18. *De Arte Poetica* (1517?), 2.299, text with a translation and commentary by Ralph G. Williams (New York 1976), p. 62.

19. *Rambler* 168, in the Yale edition, *The Prose Works of Samuel Johnson*, 16 vols. (New Haven 1958–90), vol. V (1969), p. 128.

20. Milton, 'L'Allegro', 134.

21. Arthur Hall, *Ten Books of Homers Iliades*, translated from the French (London 1581).

22. Ibid., p. 128 (I have preserved Hall's spelling, which contributes to the effect).

23. In *The Life and Complete Works . . . of Robert Greene*, ed. Alexander B. Grosart, 15 vols. (London and Aylesbury 1881–6), vol. VI, pp. 166 and 170.

24. Greene, *Euphues His Censure*, in *Life and Works*, vol. VI, p. 162.

25. See G. E. Moore, *Principia Ethica* (Cambridge 1903), p. 16; C. L. Stevenson, 'Moore's Arguments against Certain Forms of Ethical Naturalism', printed in P. A. Schilpp, ed., *The Philosophy of G. E. Moore* (Evanston and Chicago 1942), pp. 71–90.

26. *Troilus and Cressida*, ed. Kenneth Palmer, Arden Shakespeare (London and New York 1982), p. 45.

27. See e.g. Plato, *Apology* 23D.

28. Sara Hanna gets it exactly right: 'While history (and historical sources) to a large extent dictate action in the Roman works . . . the Greek works offer the dramatist the opportunity to explore worlds of fable, myth and fantasy', in her article, 'Shakespeare's Greek World: The Temptations of the Sea', in John Gillies and Virginia Mason Vaughan, eds., *Playing the Globe: Genre and Geography in English Renaissance Drama* (London 1998), pp. 107–29, at p. 114. This brilliant essay begins with a proposal to focus on ancient geography but almost at once takes to the water, to the fluid sea; geography becomes thalassography. I read Sara Hanna after I had virtually completed the present piece. I am delighted that we agree.

29. William Poole, 'All At Sea: Water, Syntax, and Character Dissolution in Shakespeare', *ShS* 54 (2001), 201–12, at p. 209. See also *Palatine Anthology* 7.71.

30. Joannes Spondanus, *Homeri Quae Extant Omnia* (Basle 1583), p. 238.

GREEK ROMANCES

CHAPTER 13

Shakespeare and Greek romance: 'Like an old tale still'

Stuart Gillespie

Since this discussion will not be pausing much to examine individual texts, and since examples of early modern English versions of the Greek romances are not universally familiar, I start with a specimen of one. The beginning of Heliodorus' *Aethiopica* is a passage frequently cited in treatments of the Greek narratives: it is both striking and characteristic. It was most familiar to the Elizabethans in Thomas Underdowne's prose translation or paraphrase, done from the Latin of Warshewiczki and printed two or three times down to 1587. But readers around the end of the sixteenth century could also have found the *Aethiopica*'s opening Englished in 235 hexameter lines in Abraham Fraunce's compilation *The Countess of Pembroke's Ivychurch*, 1591. This rendering, of which I give a segment here, seems not to have been noted as a possible form in which Shakespeare could have known the passage.[1]

> As soone as Sun-beames could once peepe out fro the mountayne
> And by the dawne of day had somewhat lightned Olympus,
> Men, whose lust was law, whose life was stil to be lusting,
> Whose thryuing theeuing, conueyd themselues to an hil-top,
> That stretched forward to the Heracleotical entry
> And mouth of Nylus: looking thence downe to the maine-sea
> For sea-faring men; but seeing none to be sayling,
> They knew 'twas booteles to be looking there for a booty:
> Soe that straight fro the sea they cast theyr eyes to the sea-shore;
> Where they saw, that a ship very strangely without any shipman
> Lay then alone at roade, with cables tyde to the maine-land,
> And yet full-fraighted, which they, though farr, fro the hil-top,
> Easily might perceaue by the water drawne to the deck-boords.
> But men on euery side lay scattred along by the sea-shore,
> Some dead, some dying, some whose corps heauily panting
> Shewed a late fighting, though noe iust cause of a fighting:
> Onely a man might gesse, there had been some bloody banket
> Which to the guests quaffing gaue such vnfortunat ending . . .
> But, notwithstanding for a time they stood thus amazed,

225

Yet for greedy desire of gaine they hastened onward
And drew nere to the place, where men lay all to bemangled,
And ship-full-fraughted; thinking themselues to bee victors.
But good God, what a sight, what a strange sight, yea, what a sweet sight,
And yet a woeful sight, to the theeues vnlookt-for apeared?
There was a maide soe made, as men might thinck her a Goddesse,
There was a sweete-fac't maide, that sate on a rock by the sea-shore,
Sate on a rock full sad to behold this desperat outrage,
Sad, yet not dismaid to behold this desperat outrage,
For that a maidens face was there well matcht with a mans-hart.
Lawrel crowned her head, but her head gaue grace to the lawrell:
Left hand arm'd with a bow, and back with a quyuer adorned,
Right hand held vp her head; her thye was a stay to the right hand:
Head neuer mouing, eyes euer fixed on one thing,
Fixed on one yong man sore wounded downe by the sea-shore . . .
Sore-wounded yongman for grief now closed his eye-lidds
And yet he causd this mayd very steedily stil to behold him,
Stil to behold his wounds and face very steedily, soethat
Whosoe lookt to the mayd must alsoe looke to the yongman;
Whoe, when he came t'himself, these woords very faintly vttred:
And art thou yet saulf, thou sweetest soule of a thousand,
Or by thy death hast thou augmented this bloody slaughter?
Whether death doe triumph, or whether life be prolonged,
Whom Loue hath ioyned, noe death shall cause to be seu'red.
In thee alone doe I ioy, and for thee alone am I liuing,
On thee alone doe I see my wealth to be wholly depending.

Displayed here are a number of features both of narrative content and formal presentation that are characteristic of the tales with which this chapter is concerned. Among them may be noted, for example: shipwreck and violence; the mutual faith of youthful lovers; the juxtaposition of distant and close-up perspectives; and an alternation in mode between detached *ekphrasis* and pathetic lament. Fraunce also manages to suggest in some sort his original's elaborate, self-conscious, somewhat euphuistic language and style.

Of some of these features, more shortly. First I turn from the narratives themselves to the ways in which they have been understood or constructed by their readers over the years. In his long-standard study *The Greek Romances in Elizabethan Prose Fiction* (1912), Samuel Lee Wolff saw discontinuity between Renaissance and modern ideas of what constitutes the 'classical':

Hardly any other kind of fiction . . . could appeal more strongly to the sixteenth century novel-reader and novel-writer than the ornate, spectacular, rhetorical, sentimental, fortuitous medley [of the Greek romance] . . . The Renaissance, in its uncritical acceptance of everything Greek and Roman as *ipso facto* classical, felt at liberty to choose according to its own unquiet taste, and thus established and for centuries maintained among the canons of classicism the late works of Alexandria and of the Hellenized and Romanized Orient – works which today are perceived not to be classical at all.[2]

The present seems a good time to reconsider some of these points. In the near-century since Wolff wrote, scholars of the ancient world have begun to enlarge their notions of what can be considered to lie within 'the canons of classicism', and indeed to ask whether the notion of any such canon should be kept up at all; and recently neglected works now being studied less as repositories of timeless values than as products of their age include the Greek romances.[3] English literary historians, for their part, have become aware that the dividing-line usually drawn in modern times between the novel and the romance may be based on ideology as much as on any real differences in style or form.[4] That is to say, we can now begin to see why the spectacular, rhetorical, sentimental sort of fiction which is my subject here need not be thought of as an inferior kind of fiction superseded by the (ostensibly) true-to-life kind – the kind which claimed for itself the newly privileged label of the novel.

Both shifts are undoubtedly related to larger historical changes. In the nineteenth and early twentieth centuries it was taken for granted in the imperial nations of the West that the most significant feature of the early centuries of our era was the Roman empire, and the Greek world of the same period attracted less attention. Today we tend towards more critical analysis of the Roman empire's institutions and their effects, and the Greek period of Arrian, Marcus Aurelius, Galen, and Pausanias has acquired increased prominence. (This does not mean we are recapturing a Renaissance view of the classics: the enthusiastic eclecticism Wolff describes is quite different from our nervously self-conscious neutrality. But a range of attitudes is of course found today, just as there were 'classicising' critics, such as Jonson, in the Renaissance.) Equally, if the attractions of verisimilitude have seemed to pall in our time, bringing into sharper relief the claims of non-realistic fiction, the causes may naturally be sought outside the literary tradition itself. A simple example is Bernard Bergonzi's claim: 'we have no common sense of reality. We are saddled with all kinds of relativistic structures. We do not believe in there being "one reality" out there as Tolstoy undoubtedly did.'[5] Such contentions are standard in discussions of fiction, in which the rise of new modes is routinely ascribed to changes in sensibility. As history moves on, so too, it would seem (and in close relation), do the priorities of literary historians.

Because of the manifold uncertainties surrounding their context, attitudes to the Greek romances have always tended to embody the preconceptions of those expressing them in more transparent ways than is the case with traditionally canonical writing. At one end of the time-scale, the very late *editio princeps* of *Daphnis and Chloe* of 1598 had been long preceded by translations into French and English, as interest outpaced scholarly knowledge.[6] The title page of the English translator, Angel Day, clearly expresses his concerns, which today may seem almost comically inapt:

Daphnis and Chloe EXCELLENTLY defcribing the weight *of affection, the fimplicitie of love, the purport* of honeft meaning, the refolution of men, and difpofi*tion of Fate, finifhed in a Pastorall, and interlaced with the prafies* of a moft peerlefle Princeffe, wonderfull in Maieftie, and rare in perfection, celebrated within *the same Paftorall, and therefore* termed by the name of The Shepheards Holidaie.[7]

At our own end of the reception history, expert opinion on the development of the entire genre was being radically revised well into the twentieth century. We are familiar with the idea that Shakespeare's work has been an important determinant of what the West has constituted as the 'literary', and it is by no means unlikely that the twentieth-century application of the term 'romance' to a group of four late Shakespeare plays has been a factor in the growing interest in the Greek novels with which I am concerned.[8] Certainly, Shakespeare's Late Plays are now part of the meaning of the Greek romances. In any case, these Greek works are today being rated as highly as at any time since the late Renaissance, even if by a far smaller and more specialised readership, and the last thirty years have seen them rehabilitated as *literary* texts, of very considerable artistic sophistication. The five surviving showpieces include the three that were of importance for the English and European Renaissance, those by Achilles Tatius (*Leucippe and Clitophon*), Longus (*Daphnis and Chloe*), and Heliodorus (the *Aethiopica*); in considering Shakespeare's relation to this body of writing, we should add that later, textually unstable farrago probably based on a similar type of Greek tale, the *Apollonius of Tyre*.

On the whole, though, the Greek novels must be counted among the challenges to which students of the English Renaissance in general, and of Shakespeare in particular, have yet to rise. This is partly for a reason which works to conceal the relation between Shakespeare and certain other classical writers too: that the narrative ingredients of a Shakespeare play tend to be seen not as representing one point in a continuum of tales that is developing over a period of centuries, but as appropriations from proximate sources which are usually close to him in time. Today, Greene's *Pandosto* is regularly printed in whole or in part in connection with *The Winter's Tale*, but how often are Greene's own debts to the Greek novels drawn to our attention?[9] How many of those who have read the *Arcadia* as a Shakespeare source look beyond Sidney to his own narrative sources, or how widely is it realised that even where Sidney, or Greene, or Lyly have no primary debt to Greek romance material, they are often engaging with it at second hand through such later followers as Boccaccio?[10] In a word, the very considerable importance of the romances in the Elizabethan ocean of stories, that mackerel-crowded sea of translated, retold, recycled, summarised, excerpted tales that formed a pan-European storehouse for poets and dramatists, is little recognised.[11] Heliodorus, Longus, and Achilles Tatius may seem in many ways remote from Shakespeare, but it is easy to see how such blind spots help sustain (and are sustained by) the idea that, apart from Plutarch, ancient Greek literature makes little difference to him; that Greek and Latin texts appealed largely to an elite audience overlapping only minimally with London playgoers (compare Joseph Hall's remark of 1620, 'What Schole-boy, what apprentice knows not Heliodorus?'[12]); that Shakespeare's creative genius characteristically manifests itself as an ability to transform minor (and usually contemporary) source works into great art; that the Elizabethan theatre is very largely a native product. Our preference for such explanations where Shakespeare is concerned is matched by a predilection for simple, streamlined, often monoglot literary history ('the plot of *The Winter's Tale* is taken from Greene's *Pandosto*'), in the broader realm of which the Greek romances would seldom be correctly identified today as lying ultimately behind many of the core elements – heroines and love being only the most obvious – that we take for granted in the body of Western fiction.

Yet the principle behind the phenomenon I am describing is well understood. Samuel Johnson's 'Life of Dryden' provides a standard account of what happens when a literary influence becomes pervasive:

A writer who obtains his full purpose loses himself in his own lustre. Of an opinion which is no longer doubted, the evidence ceases to be examined. Of an art universally practiced, the first teacher is often forgotten. Learning once made popular is no longer learning: it has the appearance of something which we have bestowed upon ourselves, as the dew appears to rise from the field which it refreshes.[13]

An account of how the art of the romances was popularised might begin with Sidney's *Arcadia* (1580s), Guarini's *Pastor Fido* (1589), and Montemayor's *Diana Enamorada* (1559), all of which works were known to

Shakespeare either in translation or original.[14] It should be stressed that these are by no means the type of minor, almost provincial successes that largely populate Bullough's volumes of Shakespeare's 'narrative and dramatic' sources. But the many, diverse, and important ways in which these and other romance-inspired texts coloured Shakespeare's work are not the subject of the present discussion, though some of the dangers of compartmentalising their significance in a separate area from the subject of 'Shakespeare and the Classics' will by now be clear. My purpose here is rather to review recent scholarship and then propose some fresh suggestions as to what the Greek romance could have offered Shakespeare more directly, and what he may have discerned in it that differed from what Sidney, Greene, and the rest found.

One source of confusion should be noted first. The currently standard list of 'romance' features, the list usually deployed in connection with Shakespeare's Late Plays, has been derived more from the later English and European tradition than the ancient Greek, making it hard to see beyond lowest common denominators. One is told that romances include plot elements such as pastoral interludes, disguises, apparent deaths, and final reunions, together with particular types of heroes and heroines whose high birth is revealed only at a late juncture, and formal devices such as narrative frames. All this may (roughly speaking) be true of the Greek tales, but it tends to assimilate them to the modern narratives deriving from them, rather than revealing how they may be differentiated. When more or less faithful English versions, and in some cases also French, Italian, Spanish, and Latin renderings, of the Greek romances were obtainable,[15] it is unwise to think of Shakespeare, or indeed of his contemporaries generally, as unable to distinguish their qualities from those of the English narratives they were influencing. (And we need not, of course, suppose the translators themselves were capable of deep insight into the nature of the material before we may imagine that more perceptive readers could discern through their work its more 'foreign', more challenging, and perhaps less assimilable, qualities.)

Speculations about Shakespeare's direct use of romance material have always clustered around the Late Plays, on account of the obvious affinities which are most often ascribed to the effect of proximate sources. Speculations they must remain, since we have no proof Shakespeare knew any Greek romance at first hand (whether in Greek or, much more likely, in translation or paraphrase), as must my own suggestions here. The playwright's relationship to the story of Apollonius of Tyre (not in itself a Greek romance, but probably based on a lost one) is rather more immediate: he knew it in

Gower's fourteenth-century *Confessio Amantis*, giving him at least one route into the realm independent of his Elizabethan contemporaries. I shall refer in a moment to Gower's choric appearance in *Pericles*, but Shakespeare's relation to the *Confessio* narrative tends in certain important ways to place him at a further remove from the romances, because Gower's main generic inspiration, the saint's life, works against the Greek models to simplify and moralise the material.[16] The case for any Shakespearean echoes whatever of Chariton and Xenophon of Ephesus is untenable because of their unavailability to him, and only relatively less doubtful are signs of direct local echoes of the romances (in matters of plot, theme, character traits) in Shakespeare plays before *Pericles*: there seem always to exist better or at least equally plausible explanations.[17] Only one critic is known to me who has argued for more diffuse echoes in earlier plays: Martha Latimer Adams urges the Greek novels as the ultimate source of Shakespeare's emphasis on romantic love and 'superior' feminine roles, with special emphasis on the comedies, on *Antony and Cleopatra*, and *Romeo and Juliet*.[18] But this argument has not been taken up by other scholars, and Adams, in any case, does not press a claim for direct influence.

This leaves us with the Late Plays and the three novels *Daphnis and Chloe*, *Clitophon and Leucippe*, and the *Aethiopica*. Much evidence has been assembled on possible connections here, the standard work being Carol Gesner's *Shakespeare and the Greek Romance*, though in practice Gesner more often than not concedes that the romance features she discerns in the Late Plays could have been transmitted through the derived tradition.[19] The problem, other than some overstatement of the robustness of the connections, is that the elements her painstaking comparisons identify are very largely in pieces of plot material; sometimes in structural devices and other details such as character names. This means that while her work is of great interest as indicating the presence of the Greek novels behind a wide range of Shakespeare's source-materials, as well as, occasionally, Shakespeare's own possible first-hand awareness of the texts, Gesner devotes little attention to the question of how Shakespeare's response to these materials may be said to differ from those of his contemporaries. Yet his taste for them is sufficiently strongly implied; particularly notable in this regard is Gesner's observation that, as well as any direct debts he incurs, the Late Plays show an instinctive preference for materials which 'evolved from, or have an affinity to' Greek romances (p. 114).

My purpose in what remains is to add to previous suggestions as to how the late Shakespeare may have profited from the romances more directly and more individualistically. Two linked areas can be identified briefly and

tentatively in the form of questions. One of the features readers usually
identify in Greek romance is the 'distanciation' of the narrative events, the
way that human life becomes mere spectacle, as exemplified in the *theatron*
prepared for the pirates at the opening of the *Aethiopica*. In the medium of
drama, clearly, a similar effect can only be achieved by other means, perhaps
the most obvious being the employment of a chorus. As romance can move
out of single narrative voice into display, drama can travel in the reverse
direction from 'theatrical' mode to single voice. The Chorus in *Pericles* is
of course not the first example the Shakespeare canon supplies, but it is a
very different kind of thing from its predecessor in *Henry V*, whose epic
and patriotic energies generate ironic and subversive effects. The Gower
Chorus is also strongly identified with the content of the Prologue's 'song
that old was sung', the tale of *Apollonius of Tyre*. A chorus was (presumably) always an option for Shakespeare: is his decision to use one in fully
fledged structural form for only the second time in his career part of an
attempt to evoke the effect of the romances?[20] Some similar ambition may
lie behind the Time Chorus of *The Winter's Tale* and the modes resembling
the *theatron* – the range of masques, pageants, ekphrases, and dumbshows –
in *Pericles*, *Cymbeline*, and *The Tempest* as well. A second question concerns
the half-buried religious (gnostic and mystery cult) elements of the Greek
romance, especially the *Aethiopica*,[21] elements, in fact, which were evidently
wholly buried for most though not all sixteenth-century readers and inter-
preters, but Shakespeare's discovery of which could be mapped well enough
onto our understanding of his last phase. Some modern scholars would see
Heliodorus' tale as a continuous religious allegory, but this is not required
for it to be accepted that the spiritual climate of the *Aethiopica* and other
romances is one of transcendence, a dying from this world into another;
it is the soul's resultant freedom that allows the sublunary world to be
contemplated dispassionately.[22] These elements were partly assimilated to
Christianity in some imaginative Renaissance reworkings.[23] How far are we
here from the 'sea-changes' of *The Tempest*, the close of *The Winter's Tale*,
and *Pericles*' fifth-act divine revelations – or how near?

My final suggestions require slightly more elaborate sketching out. Terry
Comito's insufficiently well-known essay of 1975, 'Exile and Return in
the Greek Romances', sets me my example here. In her brief remarks
on Shakespeare, Comito's attention does not fall on plot elements or on
formal devices. While the romances may have led to new departures in
narrative form or material for a storyteller such as Sidney, she observes,
for a playwright such as Shakespeare their unique qualities could have
seemed to embody 'an intuition about the rhythms of experience itself'.

Particular significance may attach here to the spatial wanderings of the Late Plays:

> In his earlier plays, when Shakespeare considers how man's nature and his experience of the world impinge upon one another, he characteristically thinks of the mutability of time. One measure of the significance of the romances is the way these concerns are transposed to a new key in works composed under their influence. In the late plays, and especially in *Pericles* and *Cymbeline* – as in Heliodorus or Achilles Tatius – the emphasis is put on wandering in space.[24]

Comito's remarks on this point leave unclear quite how other Shakespearean plays can be accommodated to this pattern: for example, geographical space is very deliberately emphasised in the Histories, while *The Winter's Tale* gives considerable prominence to time as well as space. However, this is immediately attractive as an example of a *kind* of possibility to be entertained, not concerning narrative materials and devices that Shakespeare's romances share with the Greek ones (as also with Sidney and the rest), but the particular sensibility that finds expression in both the ancient and the Shakespearean works.

The Greek romances are remarkable for their self-consciousness and sometimes self-referentiality. Achilles Tatius seems to mark the point at which naive tale-telling turned into self-conscious narrative strategy: he 'broke down the conventions'.[25] Chariton clearly plays with his readers as well as with his genre, introducing his final book by announcing that they will find his ending most agreeable. Longus, though working on more than one level, has been seen as self-conscious to the point of 'deconstructing himself'.[26] Heliodorus, finally, is the most self-aware of all the Greek novelists, and the *Aethiopica* shot through with references to the theatre (often using abstruse theatrical vocabulary) which define 'the relationship between reader and text as one between spectator and spectacle' and 'self-referentially comment on . . . the theatrical and artificial nature of the novel's plotting'.[27] This quality is seldom found in early modern works that take their rise from the Greek novels, no doubt because of the comparative lack of sophistication or insight of some of the writers involved, and the different purposes of others. Could it be that Shakespeare was able to see his way through to this aspect of the romances and make use of it as his contemporaries did not? No very deep acquaintance with them need be postulated – only a coincidence of artistic purpose. Jonson famously called the *Pericles* story a 'mouldy tale'. In its own way, each of the Late Plays both acknowledges its narrative as an 'old tale' (as the Gentleman of *Winter's Tale* 5.2.61 calls it) and foregrounds its own equally self-aware theatricality. As Shakespeare justifies the improbabilities of his plots by acknowledging or half-acknowledging his artifice, Heliodorus makes his characters justify his strategies – 'Nor is it meet', Chariclea tells Theagenes at one point, 'to reveal in a moment that which hath been long a working'.[28] The art of *The Winter's Tale* is based, Anne Barton observes, on 'a desperate artistic honesty which [admits] to creating fictions, while making us understand why and how much we should like those fictions to be real'. Through the Gower Chorus, Peter Womack tells us, *Pericles* 'positively insists on its status as a kind of storytelling: it not only executes, but self-consciously dramatizes, the primacy of narrative'.[29] Such descriptions characterise the Greek romances better than perhaps any other works Shakespeare could have known (Ovid's *Metamorphoses* comes close, but Shakespeare's lifelong use of this poem is one factor making these comparatively sudden departures in the late romances harder to explain as a response to it). This does not constitute evidence of a relation, of course. But it reminds us that we ought not to identify Shakespeare's classicism exclusively with realistic narrative and dramatic modes, nor assume that the metatheatre of the Late Plays is unprecedented in ancient texts. The Late Plays are, indeed, one of the reasons we have discovered such effects in classical works, and one of the reasons why works in which such effects can be discovered are classical.

NOTES

1. Shakespeare's direct knowledge of Heliodorus remains to be established (see below); it is not claimed here that any evidence points to his use of Fraunce in particular, merely that Fraunce's rendering, like its immediate source, Underdowne's better-known version, is one of the forms in which the *Aethiopica* was available to the English reader of Shakespeare's time. Though unmentioned in discussions of Shakespeare's relation to Heliodorus, *The Countess of Pembrokes Yuychurch* (London 1591), Fraunce's idiosyncratic compilation of pastoral and mythological tales in translations from sources classical and modern, was popular enough to reach a third part published in the following year.
2. Samuel Lee Wolff, *The Greek Romances in Elizabethan Prose Fiction* (New York 1912), pp. 235–6. The large-scale recent treatment of the ancient novel in relation to later English and European literature is Margaret Anne Doody's controversial study *The True Story of the Novel* (New York 1996).
3. For an overview of twentieth-century developments in the study of the romances see Simon Swain, 'A Century and More of the Greek Novel', *Oxford Readings in the Greek Novel*, ed. Swain (Oxford 1999), pp. 3–35.
4. The novel/romance distinction is drawn as early as William Congreve in 1692, and the availability of the alternative terms has given it special force in English; for a full account of its history see Geoffrey Day, *From Fiction to the Novel*

(London 1987). With the Greek tales, the term 'romance' is as valid as 'novel', since the themes of the five major surviving works are those of romantic love; but for the ancient tradition more widely, including Latin texts, 'novel' is now often preferred.

5. Bernard Bergonzi, 'Realism, Reality, and the Novel', a Symposium, *Novel* 2 (1969), 200. Bergonzi's remarks are analysed by Raymond Tallis, *In Defence of Realism* (London 1988), pp. 9–20.

6. For a bibliographical survey of editions from the beginnings to the present, see Giles Barber, *Daphnis and Chloe: The Markets and Metamorphoses of an Unknown Bestseller* (London 1989).

7. *Daphous and Chloe*, trans. Angel Day (London 1587). The italics decoratively follow the line-divisions rather than the sense.

8. The 'romance' label is first applied to Shakespeare by Edward Dowden in his *Introduction to Shakespeare* of 1893.

9. The Greene text is printed, for example, in the Arden *Winter's Tale*, edited by J. H. P. Pafford (London 1966), and by Geoffrey Bullough in *Narrative and Dramatic Sources of Shakespeare*, 8 vols. (London 1957–75), vol. VIII. Greene's Greek sources were very fully documented, indeed somewhat exaggerated, by Wolff, *Greek Romances*, (n. 2), pp. 375 ff.

10. For Boccaccio's contact with Greek fiction in relation to Greene, see Wolff, *Greek Romances*, pp. 360–5; in relation to Lyly, pp. 248–61; and to Sidney, p. 364.

11. The first page of Carol Gesner's *Shakespeare and the Greek Romance: A Study of Origins* (Lexington 1970) contains the remark 'the whole question of the influence of Greek romance on Renaissance literature in England and on the continent has yet to be investigated' (p. vii). One is still waiting.

12. Quoted from Douglas Bush, *English Literature in the Earlier Seventeenth Century, 1600–1660* (Oxford 1945), p. 53.

13. 'Life of Dryden', *Lives of the English Poets*, ed. George Birkbeck Hill, 3 vols. (Oxford 1905), vol. I, p. 411.

14. For brief surveys of the significance of these three works to Shakespeare, with further references, see my *Shakespeare's Books: A Dictionary of Shakespeare Sources* (London 2001).

15. Heliodorus' *Aethiopica* alone had appeared in all these languages by 1591; Gesner, *Shakespeare and the Greek Romance*, pp. 154–62 supplies a full Renaissance publication history for this and the other romances.

16. For clashes and coalescences between saint's life and romance models in *Pericles*, see Peter Womack, 'Shakespeare and the Sea of Stories', *Journal of Medieval and Early Modern Studies* 29 (1999), 169–87.

17. *Apollonius of Tyre* figures in *The Comedy of Errors*, however: for a resume of the evidence see Elizabeth Archibald, *Apollonius of Tyre: Medieval and Renaissance Themes and Variations* (Woodbridge 1991), p. 61, and variously for other possible Shakespearean uses of *Apollonius*. Powerful arguments against any Shakespearean role for Chariton and Xenophon are advanced by Gerald N. Sandy, 'Ancient Prose Fiction and Minor Early English Novels', *Antike und*

Abendland 25 (1979), 41–55 (p. 55). For possible local uses of romance material in plays before *Pericles*, see Gesner, *Shakespeare and the Greek Romance*, ch. 3; Gesner includes references to the older commentary which is the main repository of these claims, as they are seldom revived.

18. Martha Latimer Adams, 'The Greek Romance and William Shakespeare', *University of Mississippi Studies in English* 8 (1967), 43–52.

19. Often overlooked as possible routes of transmission are the various forms in which romance material found its way into compilations and collections. Abraham Fraunce (above) is one kind of example; another is Brian Melbank's *Philotimus: The Warre betwixt Nature and Fortune* (1593), a series of *sententiae* and *exempla* useful for romantic suits. On Melbank see Gerald Sandy, 'The Heritage of the Ancient Greek Novel in France and Britain', in *The Novel in the Ancient World*, ed. Gareth Schmeling (Leiden 1996), pp. 735–73 (769–71).

20. Other explanations for the use of a chorus in *Pericles* have come and gone. The older hypothesis that Barnabe Barnes' play *The Devil's Charter* inspired it is frowned upon by the most recent editors, who propose that the narrator of the *Confessio Amantis* 'and his obvious enjoyment of storytelling surely suggested to Shakespeare the Chorus'. *Pericles*, ed. Doreen DelVecchio and Antony Hammond (Cambridge 1998), pp. 35, 5.

21. For a summary of current opinion on religious elements in Heliodorus, see J. R. Morgan, 'E. Heliodoros', in *The Novel in the Ancient World*, pp. 417–56 (446–54).

22. Such a spiritual climate is found even more clearly in a related work almost certainly known to Shakespeare, the *Golden Ass*. Apuleius' Latin novel lies outside the scope of this discussion, but see J. J. M. Tobin, *Shakespeare's Favorite Novel: A Study of the Golden Ass as Prime Source* (Lanham, MD 1984), which presents a comprehensive, if at times overstated, case for its wide influence on Shakespeare.

23. For one example see Walter Stephens, 'Tasso's Heliodorus and the World of Romance', in *The Search for the Ancient Novel*, ed. James Tatum (Baltimore 1994), pp. 67–87. Stephens writes for example that Heliodorus' Destiny 'would have appeared to Tasso and his contemporaries as a view of divine providence, the more so since they believed that Heliodorus had been an apostate Christian' (p. 70; Heliodorus was persistently identified with a Christian bishop of that name).

24. Terry Comito, 'Exile and Return in the Greek Romances', *Arion* n.s. 2 (1975), 59–80 (60).

25. R. M. Rattenbury, 'Traces of Lost Greek Novels', in *New Chapters in the History of Greek Literature III*, ed. J. U. Powell (Oxford 1933), pp. 256–7.

26. B. P. Reardon, 'Μυθος οὐ λόγος: Longus's Lesbian Pastorals', in *The Search for the Ancient Novel*, pp. 135–47 (146).

27. Morgan, 'Heliodorus', p. 437. Some commentators go further, reading the novel as a parable of what it is to read a novel: most influential has been J. Winkler, 'The Mendacity of Kalasiris and the Narrative Strategy of Heliodoros' *Aithiopica*', *Yale Classical Studies* 27 (1982), 93–158.

28. *Heliodorus: An Aethiopian Romance*, trans. Thomas Underdowne, rev. F. A. Wright (London [1928]), p. 281; 9.4 in the original Greek text.

29. Anne Barton, 'Leontes and the Spider: Language and Speaker in Shakespeare's Late Plays', in *Shakespeare's Styles: Essays in Honour of Kenneth Muir*, ed. Philip Edwards *et al.* (Cambridge 1980), pp. 131–50 (149); Womack, 'Shakespeare and the Sea of Stories' (n. 16), p. 182.

GREEK TRAGEDY

CHAPTER 14

Shakespeare and Greek tragedy: strange relationship

Michael Silk

Against all the odds, perhaps, there is a real affinity between Greek and Shakespearean tragedy. What there is not is any 'reception' in the ordinary sense:[1] any influence of Greek tragedy on Shakespeare; any Shakespearean 'reading' of the Attic drama. There is no reason to suppose that Shakespeare ever encountered any of the Greek tragedians, either in the original language or otherwise.[2] There were no English versions of Greek tragedy published in his time;[3] and any indirect influence from Euripides, Sophocles, or Aeschylus will have been mediated through classical Latin sources and those, in turn, through Renaissance culture in general.

Of these Latin sources, Senecan drama is much the most important[4] – albeit itself a form mediated through a more recent Continental tradition. Here, the sixteenth-century Italian tragedies of Cinthio and others play a special role. It is from this tradition that, as Marvin Herrick observed, Elizabethan drama derives its five-act structure, its 'close-knit complex plot', its 'emphasis on revenge, blood and lust, ghosts and supernatural characters, prophetic dreams, elaborate laments' – in short, its 'attempt to out-Seneca Seneca'.[5] For all that, Seneca himself, clearly, is a central presence. Seneca, for the Renaissance the 'most available and prestigious ancient tragedian', is cited in *Hamlet* by Polonius ('whose opinions are unlikely to be other than conventional') as 'the prime model for tragedy'; and, all in all, Seneca, however removed from (even) Euripides, is – as a Roman writer looking back to (in particular) Euripides – no doubt 'the closest Shakespeare ever got to Greek tragedy'.[6]

Of all the many Senecanisms in Shakespearean tragedy, one might reasonably ascribe a special significance, not to the more lurid features listed above, nor to the constructional presuppositions, important though those are, but to a rather different cluster: the grand rhetoric; the preoccupation with the inner torments of the psyche; and what T. S. Eliot once characterised as the 'attitude of self-dramatisation . . . at moments of tragic intensity'.[7] Without Seneca and the Senecan tradition, one can hardly

imagine such climactic moments as the end of *Othello*. Here is the hero
confronting his dead wife and himself and fending off the rest of the world
(5.2.268–90):

OTHELLO   I have seen the day
That, with this little arm and this good sword,
I have made my way through more impediments
Than twenty times your stop. But O, vain boast!
Who can control his fate? 'Tis not so now.
Be not afraid, though you do see me weaponed.
Here is my journey's end, here is my butt
And very sea-mark of my utmost sail.
Do you go back dismayed? 'Tis a lost fear.
Man but a rush against Othello's breast
And he retires. Where should Othello go?
(*To Desdemona*) Now, how dost thou look now? O ill-starred wench,
Pale as thy smock! When we shall meet at count,
This look of thine will hurl my soul from heaven,
And fiends will snatch at it. Cold, cold, my girl,
Even like thy chastity. O cursèd, cursèd slave!
Whip me, ye devils,
From the possession of this heavenly sight.
Blow me about in winds, roast me in sulphur,
Wash me in steep-down gulfs of liquid fire!
O Desdemon! Dead Desdemon! Dead! O! O!
LODOVICO Where is this rash and most unfortunate man?
OTHELLO That's he that was Othello. Here I am.

And then Othello killing himself as he killed his wife (5.2.348–69):

OTHELLO I have done the state some service, and they know't.
No more of that. I pray you, in your letters,
When you shall these unlucky deeds relate,
Speak of me as I am. Nothing extenuate,
Nor set down aught in malice. Then must you speak
Of one that loved not wisely but too well,
Of one not easily jealous but, being wrought,
Perplexed in the extreme; of one whose hand,
Like the base Indian, threw a pearl away
Richer than all his tribe; of one whose subdued eyes,
Albeit unusèd to the melting mood,
Drops tears as fast as the Arabian trees
Their medicinable gum. Set you down this,
And say besides that in Aleppo once,

> Where a malignant and a turbaned Turk
> Beat a Venetian and traduced the state,
> I took by th' throat the circumcisèd dog
> And smote him thus. (*He stabs himself*)
> LODOVICO O bloody period!
> GRAZIANO All that is spoke is marred.
> OTHELLO (*to Desdemona*) I kissed thee ere I killed thee. No way but this:
> Killing myself, to die upon a kiss. (*He kisses Desdemona and dies*)

Having said which, we should at once acknowledge the distinctive and very un-Senecan presence of the human Othello, alongside, or rather – some-how – through, all the distancing magniloquence of our hero's last speeches. New Historicist protests notwithstanding, Shakespeare is justly renowned for (in Leavis' phrase) 'the inwardness and completeness of his humanity';[8] and the artistic realisation of this 'humanity' in his stage figures[9] owes nothing to Seneca (or Seneca's Greek-tragic sources) – albeit something, no doubt, to two different currents of inherited Latinity, the 'subjective' empathisings of Virgil[10] and the ordinary-character contrasts of Terence.[11]

As this last line of thought suggests, the differences between Shake-spearean and Greek tragedy – irrespective of their (un)common origins – are themselves real and unmistakable. Even a passionate Deianeira (Sophocles' *Trachiniae*) or a neurotic Pentheus (Euripides' *Bacchae*) does not impinge as *human* in the way that Othello does, let alone Hamlet or Lear. Part of the difference is Shakespeare's much-discussed use of the stylistic spectrum, from grand formality ('O ill-starred . . . / Pale as thy . . .') to the simple everyday ('. . . wench / . . . smock'), to which there is no real counterpart in Greek tragedy, any more than there is in Racine. And part is his partic-ularising detail ('And say besides that in Aleppo once . . .'). All in all, as Samuel Johnson said (and his words sum up the characteristic distance of the people of, say, Sophocles from those of Shakespeare), 'Shakespeare has no heroes; his scenes are occupied only by men':[12] men, and women, made individually present (as Jonathan Bate suggests) by 'what Tolstoy called Shakespeare's "peculiarity"'[13] – the peculiarity (one might say) that makes Othello's 'speak of me as I am' a personal confidence as well as a formulary statement.

But this is only the beginning. If Shakespeare's 'men' differ from the 'heroes' of Greek tragedy, they do so not least because the ones are, literally, men and the others, most likely, heroes by mythic genealogy. Shakespeare's world is populated by a few characters with links to the supernatural, like the witches in *Macbeth*, but, for the rest, an array of strictly earthly figures, headed by princes, kings, and queens. In Greek tragedy, the servants, the functionaries, and the chorus too are, usually, earthlings, but the suffering characters belong to the realm of heroic mythology, whose many noble figures are, in one way or another, above the strictly human and in touch with the divine.[14] Agamemnon and Ajax, Helen and Ion, are descendants of gods;[15] Oedipus and Hippolytus are, in historic Greek religious cult, worshipped as the superhuman dead, as 'heroes', precisely, in a technical sense; and the canon of tragic figures includes demigods (like Heracles, suffering hero of Sophocles' *Trachiniae* and Euripides' *Heracles*) and even full divinities (like Prometheus, suffering hero of *Prometheus Bound*, ascribed to Aeschylus). No less important, in their mythological trials and tribulations even the more 'ordinary' heroes meet or confront divinities – as Oedipus meets the Sphinx in (or, strictly, before) *Oedipus Rex*, and Pentheus confronts Dionysus in *Bacchae* – while of course the great gods frequently appear *ex machina* on (or, strictly, above) the tragic stage. There are indeed great tragic figures, like Euripides' Hecuba, who are not demonstrably in any of these categories, but such characters consort with the many that are: they all breathe the same air. When the anguished Oedipus blinds himself, and gives Apollo the credit for prompting him to do it (Sophocles, *Oedipus Rex* 1,329–30), this is (literally) worlds away from Othello's appeal to 'ye devils' to 'whip me . . . / From the possession of this heavenly sight' (5.2.284–5). To a mythic sufferer, Apollo is not a creature of faith or superstition, but a reality and a presence. In line with the orthodoxies of Greek religious tradition, Attic tragedy assumes a hierarchical chain of gods, demigods, heroes, men – and its suffering figures are located along the chain, rather than at its purely human end. There is no counterpart to this in Shakespeare.

The personages of the two versions of tragedy are distinguishable in other terms as well. It was Hegel, two centuries or so after *Hamlet* was first staged, who saw in that play the epitome of 'modern' tragedy.[16] In Hegel's incisive analysis, the tragedies of Aeschylus and Sophocles centre on socio-cultural conflicts of 'moral' interest embodied in outward-looking characters, each of whom asserts one of the 'conflicting rights' in a kind of monotonic absoluteness. The strivings and the killings associated with Aeschylus' Clytemnestra and Orestes, Sophocles' Antigone and Creon (and the *Oresteia* and, especially, *Antigone* are Hegel's paradigms of tragic drama), are interpreted in this spirit. By contrast, 'modern' tragedy centres on inward feeling and private preoccupations. Othello kills Desdemona, not to assert the principle of marital fidelity, but out of the 'arbitrariness' of his jealous love. And Hamlet's tortured revenge on the murderous king is not (like the Aeschylean Orestes' revenge on his murderous mother) a cog in a cosmic wheel of Justice, to which the whole drama (in Aeschylus' case, the whole trilogy) is devoted. In Shakespeare's play, as Hegel puts it, 'the real issue is the subjective character of Hamlet, whose noble soul is not made for this kind of energetic action'.[17] Plausibly, too, Hegel sees the 'vacillating characters' of 'modern' tragedy as anticipated by the distinctive individuals of Euripides, in whom 'exceptional aspects of personal sensibility' are already a notable point of interest.[18] Yet if, indeed, the pathologies of a Pentheus or a Hippolytus are closer to the sensibility of a Hamlet (inversional, 'post-tragic' almost?)[19] than to the 'unified' purpose of an Antigone or an (Aeschylean) Orestes, the larger contrast between Shakespearean tragic drama and that of the Greeks remains clear.

And these are far from being the only meaningful differentiae between the two forms. There is Greek tragedy's minimalist design: contrast its three actors and single plot with the proliferation of characters and subplots in Shakespeare. There is Greek tragedy's formalised hierarchy of performative modes – speech, 'recitative', song – in professed imitation of which, Italian opera took shape in the first Shakespearean decade of the 1590s, but to which, plainly, Shakespeare's own dynamic of sporadic and unpredictable interruptions (prose or solo song) to a more or less consistent verse-speech norm is no equivalent. And, not least, there is the Greek chorus (the song of Greek tragedy, of course, is generally choral song). Fifth-century tragedy is constructed on a dialectic between determinate character and collective chorus, between the striving and the still, between the endangered individual and – unfashionable though it is to say so – the privileged voice. And the voice of the chorus *is* privileged. This is not because the chorus is always right: it is often partial (like the victim group of, say, *Trojan Women*), or elusive (like the elders of *Antigone*), or simply wrong (the elders of *Oedipus Rex* offer notorious examples). Nevertheless, the voice of the chorus is privileged, because its members alone are granted the striking combination of survival and (given the characteristic elaboration of Greek lyric song) the most impressive idiom.[20] In Shakespeare it is the fraught hero who has the richest lines – like Othello, with his 'journey's end' (5.2.274), his 'steep-down gulfs of liquid fire' (287), his 'perplexed in the extreme' (355). The concentration of such special discourse in an alternative voice, or voices, creates perspectives of an inimitable kind.

When one adds, to this tally, the well-known list of externals that help to make Greek tragic theatre what it is and to which, certainly, there is no Elizabethan–Jacobean equivalent – masks, open amphitheatre, religious context, state patronage, public competition – it may seem amazing that Shakespeare's tragedy should have anything significant in common with

Greek tragedy at all. And yet it does. There remains a profound affinity, in the shape of a common inner logic, between the two forms.

This affinity has nothing to do with random resemblances between this play and that – the triadic pattern of revenge deaths in the *Oresteia* and *Hamlet*, the use of oracles in *Macbeth* and *Oedipus Rex*.[21] Nor is it the kind of relationship disclosed, or created, by the imposition of some pre-existing common frame of reference. Here one thinks, in particular, of many ill-judged attempts to link the two traditions via Aristotle's *Poetics*,[22] which, though an absorbing document in its own right and more or less influential on Renaissance drama overall, is no sort of 'guide' to Shakespeare, nor indeed to fifth-century tragedy either; and one need only recall the *Poetics'* effective elimination of the chorus, the gods, and the socio-political to see why.[23] Among the more promising versions of this kind of linkage (Aristotle apart) are recent attempts to associate the Greeks and Shakespeare in terms of the 'mimetic desire' and 'scapegoating' of René Girard;[24] but then again, as Girard himself has made amply clear, there are too many examples of the societal functions of violence and victimage, in art as in life, for this version of the linkage to have any distinctive heuristic status.

To all intents and purposes, Shakespeare and Greece constitute the twin independent peaks of tragedy, with all other versions looking back to one, or both, of these. This is no new thought. It is already part of Ben Jonson's praise of Shakespeare in 1623 that, despite, or because of, his 'small Latin and less Greek', he is *both* a new beginning ('all the muses still were in their prime') *and* the equal of 'thund'ring Aeschylus, Euripides and Sophocles'.[25] We find the thought articulated with particular force within the extensive German tradition of theorising about tragedy, as by Hegel, and never more so than by Hegel's influential contemporary, August Wilhelm Schlegel. For Schlegel, Sophocles and Shakespeare constitute a classic contrasting pair, 'the Greek' and 'the Gothic', because 'the Pantheon is not more different from Westminster Abbey . . . than the form of a tragedy by Sophocles is from a play of Shakespeare's'.[26]

Thus elevated to parity with the Greeks, Shakespeare, remarkably, has exerted a multifarious interpretive pull over them: not affinity here, then, either, but a kind of reverse, Eliotian influence.[27] Features of Shakespeare, that is, have been read back into Greek tragedy; and here at least there is something for the student of 'reception' in the ordinary sense.

The earliest of these re-readings involves that most familiar ingredient of Renaissance drama, 'the tragic hero': the single, focal, striving and suffering figure around whom the action is structured, on whom the chief interest is centred, and with whom the drama is virtually co-extensive (not for nothing has the phrase '*Hamlet* without the Prince' become proverbial).[28] Shakespeare's tragedies characteristically have such a focal figure. So do some Greek ones: Aeschylus (?), *Prometheus Bound*; Sophocles, *Oedipus Rex*; Euripides, *Heracles*. Others, particularly those of an overtly Hegelian 'conflictual' shape, do not: Aeschylus, *Agamemnon* (or, indeed, the *Oresteia* as a whole); Sophocles, *Antigone*; Euripides, *Trojan Women*. In such plays, the suffering and the striving – without which, indeed, it is difficult to imagine any tragedy, Greek or other – is, so to speak, distributed over two or more participants, in a variety of patterns.

Under Shakespearean influence (with a bit of help from misreadings of Aristotle), expectation of the unitary-heroic matrix has been, often still is, imposed on Greek tragedy as a whole.[29] Since the time of Dryden, certainly, focal-hero tragedies like *Oedipus Rex* are seen as exemplary – and, not least, *Oedipus Rex* itself, partly because (again) Aristotle esteemed it, albeit for rather different reasons[30] – while one continues to find attempts to bring plays like *Antigone* into line with the pattern.[31] *Antigone* notwithstanding, it has been argued, 'the presentation of the tragic dilemma in the figure of a single dominating character seems . . . to be an invention of Sophocles';[32] and the type is undoubtedly more characteristic of Sophocles than of Aeschylus or Euripides. The result has been to help give Sophocles the role of canonical Greek tragedian – Schlegel's 'Sophocles and Shakespeare' is a representative pairing – in incidental contrast to Shakespeare's own age, in which Euripides was often more esteemed.[33]

Euripides himself is the beneficiary of a quite different re-reading. Since at least the age of Dr Johnson, Shakespeare has been praised for the cultivation of a tragicomic kind of tragedy. 'Shakespeare's plays,' declared Johnson in 1765, 'are not in the rigorous and critical sense either tragedies or comedies . . . Shakespeare has united the powers of exciting laughter and sorrow not only in one mind, but in one composition.'[34] Others in the neo-classical age had censured Shakespeare for the same (notably Voltaire, who in the Shakespearean tragicomic could only see 'monstrous farces, to which the name tragedy is given),'[35] but if, now, exploration of the tragicomic mode could be credited, without disparagement, to the one peak of tragedy, eventually it would be to the other. In recent decades, in particular, it has been shown that Aeschylus' *Oresteia* itself displays some features that, in one sense or another, might be regarded as 'comic',[36] and that a wide range of Euripidean manoeuvres – from the bitter-sweet reconciliation at the end of *Ion* to the sinister voyeurism and cross-dressing in *Bacchae* – are illuminated by a critical reorientation of the tendencies of Euripidean drama, especially his later drama, as a whole.[37]

The illumination is not in doubt. What is open to question, however, is
the proper weight to be attached to the mixed-mode experiments within
Euripides' entire *oeuvre*, lost as well as surviving (for Aristotle, who knew
more Euripides than we do, his version of tragic drama was the paradigm
of 'unhappy' endings),[38] and, equally, the actual generic affiliation of the
'comic' aspects of Euripides' surviving work (which have little enough in
common with the attested comic drama of his own day).[39] Whatever else,
Shakespearean 'precedent' has surely helped to dull critical anxieties about
the awkward loose ends that in fact confront us in the case of Euripides.

Such Shakespearean 'influence' on Greek tragedy can be seen to be operative on quite different levels too. The long-standing admiration for Shakespeare's astonishing power of imagery (*Othello* 5.2.274–5: 'here is my butt /
And very sea-mark of my utmost sail') and a particular preoccupation with
the thematic function of the imagery within individual plays ('sickness
images in *Hamlet*', 'the world of animals and plants in *Timon of Athens*'), ini-
tiated, or at least popularised, by Caroline Spurgeon and Wolfgang Clemen
in the 1930s,[40] helped to precipitate a similar awareness in respect of Greek
tragedy – most of all in Aeschylus, where such thematics are very evident
('the ship of state' in *Seven Against Thebes*, 'light and dark' in the *Oresteia*);[41]
least of all in Euripides, given that, whatever else, 'simile and metaphor . . .
does not seem to be his most natural element'.[42] More remarkably, these
preoccupations have stimulated a need to vindicate the aberrant Euripides
by finding, if not *this* kind of imagery in his work, at least *something* like
it, in the form, perhaps, of 'pictorial' or 'descriptive' language or, perhaps,
'the tropes of contemporary rhetoric'.[43]

And yet, when due allowance has been made for readings back from
Shakespeare onto one or other of the Greeks, and the, perhaps, problematic communality thereby in view; for any possible indirect influence,
of the ordinary kind, from Greek tragedy onto Shakespeare; for the substantive differences and the random resemblances between them: affinity
between the two versions of tragedy is still unmistakable,[44] irrespective
of their different cultural or institutional presuppositions and irrespective
of any theoretical scruples (Wittgensteinian or neo-historicist) that some
may have about invoking cross-cultural entities like Tragedy with a capital
'T'.[45]

As between Greek tragedy and Shakespeare, there are, to begin with,
shared dramatic presuppositions of concentrated action and cumulative
logic; and of more or less elevated and intensified language,[46] with the
elevation correlative to the high (heroic or royal) status of the significant
players, and in turn to the vastness of tragedy's concerns.

That 'vastness', in both cases, has a metaphysical scope to it. In the case of Greek tragedy, as befits its heroic-mythological matrix, metaphysics is overt: 'great deaths and sufferings unheard-of', reports the chorus at the end of Sophocles' *Trachiniae* (1,276–8), 'and all of it – Zeus'. In Shakespearean tragedy, it is notoriously more elusive. Among much else, and in an immensely delicate way, Shakespeare presupposes a Christian frame of reference ('But wherefore could I not pronounce Amen?')[47] without enacting Christian ideology or pursuing the mirage of 'Christian tragedy'.[48] Says one critic: 'Shakespeare's version of the Lear story is worryingly lacking in religious [i.e. Christian] sentiment and moral [i.e. Christian] order.'[49] Another, bent on finding cosmic 'resolution' and 'restoration of order' in *Hamlet*, has to acknowledge 'unsettling questions'.[50]

In fact, one of Shakespeare's many remarkable achievements is that, by an inimitable non-sectarian inclusiveness, he creates a cosmic amoralism within which an all-too-human, but simultaneously more-than-human, 'nature' is made operative. The symptomatic outcome is an un-Greek universe with a Greek-compatible shape, such that, if and when allusion to pagan godhead is contextually appropriate, as most obviously in the Roman plays, it seems (for lack of a better expression) spiritually appropriate too. There is, then, an effective continuum between Lady Macbeth's doomed aspiration (*Macbeth* 1.5.42–5),

> Make thick my blood,
> Stop up th' access and passage to remorse,
> That no compunctious visitings of nature
> Shake my fell purpose

and the explicit appeal from Marcus, in the early *Titus Andronicus* (4.1.58–9):

> O, why should nature build so foul a den,
> Unless the gods delight in tragedies?

Implicated in this remarkable re-creation – of the Greek-compatible, if not of the Greek[51] – is a distinctive affirmation, which Nietzsche, with the Greeks, above all, in mind, famously characterised as 'pessimism of strength', as 'saying yes to life even in its strangest and hardest problems; the will to life rejoicing at its own inexhaustibility in the very sacrifice of its highest types'.[52] It is characteristic that in the tragic closure, however painful it may be, this 'will to life' can be heard. In *Trachiniae* it is the surviving chorus that equates the recently experienced horrors of the play with 'Zeus'; in *Antony and Cleopatra* (to take an equally disconcerting

Shakespearean instance) it is the triumphant Caesar – though robbed of his final triumph by Cleopatra's suicide – who likewise calls up 'high order' (albeit no Christian, 'moral', order) as the necessary complement to her end (5.2.352–60):

> She shall be buried by her Antony.
> No grave upon the earth shall clip in it
> A pair so famous. High events as these
> Strike those that make them, and their story is
> No less in pity than his glory which
> Brought them to be lamented. Our army shall
> In solemn show attend this funeral,
> And then to Rome. Come, Dolabella, see
> High order in this great solemnity.

Above all, it is characteristic of Shakespearean and of Greek tragedy that the tragic suffering – the 'sacrifice' of the 'highest types', whether single focal 'heroes' or not – is associated with a distinctive nexus of determinative elements, which is operative at the most urgent level of tragic language.[53] The elements are threefold: compulsion, excess, identity. In linguistic terms, the tragic is seen to crystallise in terms of *must*, *too*, and the *name*.

It is characteristic also that these elements become most prominent at critical and climactic moments, as they do at the end of *Othello*. The Moor has murdered his wife, and now knows her innocence. Tragedy is all about choice; it is also all about compulsion. Desdemona had to be killed ('Yet she must die', 5.2.5), and, as he prepared to kill, Othello had to pity her ('I must weep', 5.2.20). Now, in the anguish of recognition, the *must* takes on, first, its most traditional external shape, with Othello's question, 'Who can control his fate?' (5.2.272), then translates itself into stylistic incantation with those last words of all (5.2.368–9),

> I kissed thee ere I killed thee. No way but this:
> Killing myself, to die upon a kiss

where a simple statement of necessity ('No way but this') is enacted by the coiled inevitabilities of verbal patterning that encompass it: 'kissed', 'killed'; 'killing', 'kiss'; and all within the inescapable rhyme ('... this', '... kiss'). No 'might', no 'can': the striving individual *must* assert himself, *must* create or destroy.

The striving individual knows no proportion, no sufficiency, no restraint. Where a Cassio, or indeed a Desdemona, 'never did / Offend' (5.2.63–4), a self-assertive Othello is excessive, goes *too* far. He has, inevitably, the cast

Of one that loved not wisely but too well,
Of one not easily jealous but, being wrought,
Perplexed in the extreme.   (5.2.353–5)

And this striving individual is a special someone with an identity, which must, by his or her striving, be lived up to, created, realised. He, or she, must, in Pindar's words, 'become what you are' and, as we say, live up to their name.[54] 'Speak of me as I am', says Othello (5.2.351) (a formulary statement, then, as well as a personal confidence), and to Lodovico's query, 'Where is this rash and most unfortunate man?', he answers, disconcertingly, 'That's he that was Othello. Here I am' (5.2.289–90). He *has* lived up to his name, but in the first shock of self-discovery can no longer live up to it; with subject and object now disjunct, he three times speaks of himself in the third person (5.2.277–8, 290).

In that living-up-to is all the compulsion to strive and all the risk or reality of excess. Lesser characters – the senators, the gentlemen, the clown, in *Othello* – are not striving individuals. On a tragic level they take no risks and so they have no name. And likewise the guard in *Antigone*, or the nurse in *Hippolytus*, or above all the tragic chorus – that 'collective and anonymous presence' from whose 'ordinary condition' the tragic individual is 'more or less estranged'.[55] And the estrangement is accompanied by compulsion, precipitated by excess, and symbolised by the name. For the striving individual – to vary the Shakespearean example – 'my lord is Antony again' (with all the attendant tragic entailment) and so (with the same entailment) 'I will be Cleopatra',[56] where that *will* implies decision and necessity as well (*Antony and Cleopatra* 3.13.188–9).

Among the Greek tragedians, the determinative role and the characteristic configurations of the three elements are remarkably in line with what we find in Shakespeare – notwithstanding the distinctive dialectic between character and chorus in Attic tragedy and, equally, the special significance of 'going too far' within a cosmic hierarchy of human, quasi-human, and divine. Dionysus' warning to Pentheus (*Bacchae* 795), not to challenge the limits of human possibility, 'mortal against god', has a representative status.

Out of a wealth of Greek examples of the tragic determinants in action,[57] *Bacchae* provides a short-list as good as any. This is a play that confronts us with alternative extremities: on the human side, Pentheus, obdurate, obsessive and 'painfully mad' in his hatred of the new cult of Dionysus (Tiresias' words, 326); on the divine, the god himself (his true identity at first concealed beneath his pose as a mysterious stranger), summed up by his own superlatives for himself, 'most dreadful but most gentle to mankind'

(861). The question, what *must* be done, is articulated according to a corresponding schema. Pentheus declares to the stranger, 'You must be punished for your sophistries'; Dionysus replies in kind, 'And you for ignorance and impiety to god' (489–90). Faced with the same choice of either opposing the new religion, like Pentheus, or joining its orgiastic worship, however half-heartedly and incongruously, the aged Cadmus (who, unlike his grandson Pentheus, survives) feels he 'has to join the dance, not fight the god' (324–5). Threatened with imprisonment by Pentheus, Dionysus shrugs: 'What must not be, I must not suffer' (515–16). Pentheus, for his part, insists, 'No hesitation must there be' (780); and having now decided on his fateful course of action – spying on the women worshippers in woman's costume – he asserts the same sense of compulsion: he 'must go on reconnaissance' (838).

Compulsion, meanwhile, has been suitably reified in the fetters through which Pentheus makes his futile attempt to constrain the stranger – just as his doomed identity takes scenic shape both with the fatal disguise and then when his mother, in a state of Dionysiac possession, having helped to kill and dismember him, now 'sees' her son's head as a lion's (1,277–84). The issue of Pentheus' identity has already been probed in the most ominous linguistic terms. The implication, latent in his name, that he is 'man of *grief (penthos)*' is spelled out by Tiresias (367) and restated by the stranger (506–8):

DIONYSUS You know not who you are . . .
PENTHEUS Pentheus, son of Echion and Agave.
DIONYSUS You have a name that means calamity.

Faced with death, the helpless son calls out, 'Mother, it is I, Pentheus, your son' (1,118–19), but now exposed to the anonymising frenzies of his killers, he is Pentheus only (as we say) nominally (1,135–6):

And one and all, blood all upon their hands,
Played catch-the-ball with bits of flesh of Pentheus.

Cadmus, confronting the horror, moralises it into insoluble cosmic paradox: 'The god has ruined us – justly but too much' (1,249–50). Dionysus' own final comment, to Cadmus and Agave, re-articulates the complaint of excess dismissively: 'Too late you knew me; when you had to, you knew me not' (1,345). The 'you' here is plural and, in effect, general, and the 'had to' is yet another version of the *must* that the striving Pentheus, in particular, construed in terms doomed to end his striving for ever.

In a striking variety of configurations, and guises, the three determinants sound and re-sound in Shakespeare, as in the Greeks. Here, more than anywhere, one can see the two versions of tragedy converge, amidst all their many differences of overt particularity and implicit context. Strange relationship.[58]

NOTES

1. Albeit the 'strange relationship' argued for here involves 'reception' in the extended sense advocated by, among others, Charles Martindale in *Redeeming the Text: Latin Poetry and the Hermeneutics of Reception* (Cambridge 1993).
2. On this issue, and some of the general questions concerning the relationship between Shakespearean and Greek tragedy, see Leonard Barkan, 'What Did Shakespeare Read?', in *The Cambridge Companion to Shakespeare*, ed. Margreta de Grazia and Stanley Wells (Cambridge 2001), pp. 31–47; U. Suerbaum, 'Shakespeare und die griechische Tragödie', in *Tragödie: Idee und Transformation*, ed. H. Flashar (Stuttgart 1997), pp. 122–41; Charles and Michelle Martindale, *Shakespeare and the Uses of Antiquity: An Introductory Essay* (London 1990), pp. 29–44.
3. Charles and Michelle Martindale, *Shakespeare and the Uses of Antiquity*, p. 30. There were also Latin versions of (e.g.) the *Oresteia*, *Hecuba*, *Iphigenia at Aulis*, which Shakespeare *could* have come across (L. Schleiner, 'Latinized Greek Drama in Shakespeare's Writing of *Hamlet*', *ShQ* 41 (1990), 29–48; Emrys Jones, *The Origins of Shakespeare* (Oxford 1977), pp. 90–105, 109–118), but there is nothing but speculation to suggest that he did.
4. See above, pp. 141–64, and Robert S. Miola, *Shakespeare and Classical Tragedy: The Influence of Seneca* (Oxford 1992).
5. M. T. Herrick, *Italian Tragedy in the Renaissance* (Urbana 1965), pp. 115, 292. The five-act structure derives in turn from Roman (Terentian) Comedy. Fifth-century tragedy is quite different. *Oedipus Rex*, for instance, consists of six sequences of spoken 'action', punctuated by five integral choral odes.
6. Charles and Michelle Martindale, *Shakespeare and the Uses of Antiquity*, pp. 30, 33, 44: *Hamlet* 2.2.401–3.
7. T. S. Eliot, 'Shakespeare and the Stoicism of Seneca', in *Selected Essays* (2nd edn, London 1934), p. 129.
8. F. R. Leavis, *Education and the University* (2nd edn, London 1948), p. 75, as against the arguments of e.g. A. Sinfield, *Faultlines: Cultural Materialism and the Politics of Dissident Reading* (Oxford 1992), pp. 52–79. Correctly noting that (a) it is only from the eighteenth century that this aspect of Shakespeare begins to be properly appreciated, and that (b) the overt ideology of Shakespeare's own age hardly yet caters for it, Sinfield and others infer that (c) it can't be there. In itself, such logic is worthless. It is precisely characteristic of exploratory literature to stretch or 'rupture' the dominant ideology: see e.g. Terry Eagleton, *Criticism and Ideology* (London 1976).

9. The point is unaffected by (post-modern or other) anxieties about any 'Bradleyan' hypostasising of character or the constructionality of 'character' *per se*: see briefly M. S. Silk, *Aristophanes and the Definition of Comedy* (corr. edn, Oxford 2002), pp. 212–14.

10. Cf. R. A. Brower, *Hero and Saint: Shakespeare and the Graeco-Roman Heroic Tradition* (Oxford 1971), pp. 84–119.

11. Via Shakespearean *comic* practice: K. Newman, *Shakespeare's Rhetoric of Comic Character* (New York 1985), pp. 49–56.

12. Samuel Johnson, 'Preface to Shakespeare' (1765), in *Johnson on Shakespeare*, ed. W. Raleigh (Oxford 1908), p. 14.

13. Jonathan Bate, *The Genius of Shakespeare* (London 1997), p. 175 referring to Tolstoy's 1906 essay, 'Shakespeare and the Drama'.

14. The human-historic figures of (e.g.) Aeschylus' *Persians* are exceptional.

15. Agamemnon's ancestor Tantalus and Ajax's ancestor Aeacus were sons of Zeus; Helen was herself a daughter of Zeus (and Leda), Ion a son of Apollo (and Creusa).

16. M. S. Silk and J. P. Stern, *Nietzsche on Tragedy* (rev. edn, Cambridge 1983), pp. 312–25, esp. 322–3. Hegel's theory of tragedy is expounded in various of his works, from the *Phenomenology of Spirit* (1807) to the lectures on *Aesthetics* of the 1820s.

17. Silk and Stern, *Nietzsche on Tragedy*, p. 323.

18. A. and H. Paolucci, *Hegel on Tragedy* (New York 1962), p. 86 (from *Aesthetics*).

19. 'Post-tragic': so E. Faas, *Tragedy and After: Euripides, Shakespeare, Goethe* (Kingston, Ontario 1984).

20. See M. S. Silk, 'Style, Voice, and Authority in the Choruses of Greek Drama', *Drama* 7 (1999), 1–26.

21. See respectively: Jan Kott, *The Eating of the Gods: An Interpretation of Greek Tragedy*, trans. B. Taborski and E. J. Czerwinski (New York 1973), pp. 240–67; R. W. Bushnell, 'Oracular Silence in *Oedipus the King* and *Macbeth*', *Classical and Modern Literature* 2 (1981–2), 195–204.

22. Among the more interesting attempts is A. D. Nuttall, *Why Does Tragedy Give Pleasure?* (Oxford 1996); interesting, but still problematic: see my review, *TLS* 4,907 (18 April 1997), 5–6.

23. See S. Halliwell, *Aristotle's Poetics* (London 1986), pp. 230–5, 238–52, and Edith Hall, 'Is there a *Polis* in Aristotle's *Poetics*?', in *Tragedy and the Tragic: Greek Theatre and Beyond*, ed. M. S. Silk (corr. edn, Oxford 1998), pp. 295–309.

24. See R. N. Mitchell-Boyask, 'Dramatic Scapegoating: On the Uses and Abuses of Girard and Shakespearean Criticism', in Silk, *Tragedy and the Tragic*, pp. 426–37.

25. Ben Jonson, 'To the Memory of My Beloved, the Author, Master William Shakespeare', 31, 44, 33–4. Jonson would 'Leave thee [Shakespeare] alone for the comparison / Of all that insolent Greece or haughty Rome / Sent forth, or since did from their ashes come.' No other English poet, from Chaucer (20) to Marlowe (30), can stand this comparison. Bate, *Genius of Shakespeare*,

p. 28, is surely wrong in reading this to mean that, for Jonson, 'the works of Shakespeare even outdid [sic] those of the ancients'.

26. A. W. von Schlegel, *Vorlesungen über dramatischen Kunst und Literatur* (2nd edn 1816), ed. G. V. Amoretti (Bonn 1923), vol. I, pp. 8–9.

27. T. S. Eliot, *Selected Essays*, p. 15 ('Tradition and the Individual Talent').

28. Albeit of obscure origin. *The Oxford Dictionary of Quotations*, ed. E. Knowles (5th edn, Oxford 1999), p. 652 ascribes the gist, but not the exact phrase, to Walter Scott's *The Talisman* (1825).

29. The concept of 'the hero' has been erroneously ascribed to Aristotle too: see J. Jones, *On Aristotle and Greek Tragedy* (London 1962), pp. 12–20, and cf. n. 30 below.

30. In 'Heads of an Answer to Rymer' (1677) Dryden assumes that 'in ancient tragedy' there is always a 'chief person', and in 'The Grounds of Criticism in Tragedy' (prefixed to *Troilus and Cressida*, 1679) he refers to 'the chief character or hero in a tragedy', implicitly associating Aristotle (cf. esp. *Poetics* 8) with this requirement ('tragedy . . . must not be a history of one man's life . . . but one single action *of theirs*' (my italics), where the italicised phrase, not in Aristotle, points towards the focal hero): Dryden, *Of Dramatic Poesy and Other Critical Essays*, ed. G. Watson (London 1962), vol. I, pp. 218, 250, 243. In the Preface to *All for Love* (1678) Dryden calls *Oedipus* 'the masterpiece of Sophocles', and in the Preface to *Oedipus: A Tragedy* (1679) declares that '*Oedipus* was the most celebrated piece of all antiquity', with Oedipus himself, of course, its 'hero' (vol. I, pp. 231–3). On Aristotle and *Oedipus*, cf. S. A. White, 'Aristotle's Favorite Tragedies', in *Essays on Aristotle's Poetics*, ed. A. O. Rorty (Princeton 1992), pp. 221–40.

31. 'In this play two characters [sc. Antigone and Creon] assume the heroic attitude, but one of them [sc. Creon] is in the end exposed as unheroic': B. M. W. Knox, *The Heroic Temper* (Cambridge 1964), p. 62. For a recent example, cf. F. Budelmann, *The Language of Sophocles* (Cambridge 2000), pp. 78, 189–90.

32. Knox, *Heroic Temper*, p. 1.

33. See e.g. Peter Burian, 'Tragedy Adapted for Stages and Screens: the Renaissance to the Present', in *The Cambridge Companion to Greek Tragedy*, ed. P. E. Easterling (Cambridge 1997), p. 232. In Italy, though, *Oedipus Rex* was already the 'unchallenged master text' by the 1560s: D. Javitch, 'On the Rise of Genre-Specific Poetics in the Sixteenth Century', in *Making Sense of Aristotle: Essays in Poetics*, ed. Ø. Andersen and J. Haarberg (London 2001), p. 133. By the age of Dryden (n. 30 above), Sophocles and *Oedipus* reign supreme.

34. Johnson, 'Preface to Shakespeare': Raleigh, *Johnson on Shakespeare*, pp. 15–16.

35. Voltaire, *Letters Concerning the English Nation*, ed. C. Whibley (London 1926), p. 125.

36. See Oliver Taplin, 'Comedy and the Tragic', and B. Gredley, 'Comedy and Tragedy – Inevitable Distinctions', in Silk, *Tragedy and the Tragic*, pp. 188–202, 203–16.

37. See esp. B. Seidensticker, *Palintonos Harmonia* (Göttingen 1982); Simon Goldhill, *Reading Greek Tragedy* (Cambridge 1986), pp. 244–64; Oliver Taplin,

'Fifth-century Tragedy and Comedy: A *Synkrisis*', *JHS* 106 (1986), 163–6. Faas' association of Euripides and Shakespeare as 'post-tragic' (n. 19 above) is related. The recognition that some Greek tragedies – including the *Oresteia* and Euripides' *Electra, Ion*, and *Helen* – have 'happy' endings is already there in J. C. Scaliger's *Poetics* (1561), but Scaliger is simply following Aristotle (*Poetics* 13). Scaliger notes, correctly but irrelevantly, that there is nothing very tragic about Euripides' satyr-play *Cyclops*, but neither he nor Aristotle before him raise any problem about the generic identity of Euripidean (or Aeschylean) tragedy.

38. *Poetics* 13. Of Euripides' (probable) 92 plays (tragedies and satyr-dramas), we possess 18 (discounting *Rhesus* as non-Euripidean, but including the satyric *Cyclops*). Among the Euripidean tragedies that Aristotle cites are some we know well and others now lost: so *Medea*, but also *Cresphontes*, in *Poetics* 14; *Orestes*, but also *Melanippe*, in 15.

39. Silk, *Aristophanes and the Definition of Comedy*, p. 51.

40. C. F. E. Spurgeon, *Shakespeare's Imagery and What it Tells Us* (Cambridge 1935); W. H. Clemen, *The Development of Shakespeare's Imagery* (London 1951, based on a 1936 study, *Shakespeares Bilder*). The quotations are from Spurgeon, p. 423 ('Chart VII'), and Clemen, p. 175.

41. See esp. E. Petrounias, *Funktion und Thematik der Bilder bei Aischylos* (Göttingen 1976). The first recorded acknowledgement of thematic imagery in Shakespeare in fact comes in a neglected work by W. Whiter of 1794, while the first equivalent diagnosis for Aeschylus is made, quite independently, by W. G. Headlam in 1900: on both, see M. S. Silk, 'Walter Headlam: Scholarship, Poetry, Poetics', in *The Owl of Minerva*, ed. C. A. Stray (Cambridge, forthcoming).

42. S. A. Barlow, *The Imagery of Euripides* (London 1971), p. 96.

43. Barlow, *Imagery of Euripides*, pp. vii–viii and *passim*, and S. Goldhill, 'The Language of Tragedy', in Easterling, *Cambridge Companion to Greek Tragedy*, p. 148.

44. Cf. variously: G. W. Kaiser, *The Substance of Greek and Shakespearean Tragedy* (Salzburg 1977); Adrian Poole, *Tragedy: Shakespeare and the Greek Example* (Oxford 1987); M. Ewans, 'Patterns of Tragedy in Sophokles and Shakespeare', in Silk, *Tragedy and the Tragic*, pp. 438–57. To what extent Shakespeare and Greek tragedy share an affinity that is not shared by – especially – the classicising Racine is a separate question.

45. For a fuller version of this argument, see Silk, *Tragedy and the Tragic*, pp. 2–10, and *Aristophanes and the Definition of Comedy*, pp. 61–71.

46. On the distinction between elevation ('O ill-starred . . .', *Othello* 5.2.279) and intensification ('here is my butt / And very sea-mark . . .', 5.2.274–5), see Silk, *Tragedy and the Tragic*, pp. 459–62. Of the four tragedians, Shakespeare is the least (consistently) elevated, Euripides the least intensified (cf. pp. 243, 245 above).

47. *Macbeth* 2.2.29.

48. 'The metaphysics of Christianity . . . are anti-tragic': George Steiner, *The Death of Tragedy* (London 1961), p. 324. How far the threat of censorship in Shakespeare's age helped to influence this outcome is an open question.

49. Bate, *Genius of Shakespeare*, p. 150.

50. T. McAlindon, *Shakespeare's Tragic Cosmos* (Cambridge 1991), pp. 124–5.

51. From the rather different context of *The Winter's Tale* and its Ovidian sources, Charles and Michelle Martindale are moved to ponder 'Shakespeare's ability to discern, behind the generally commonplace . . . materials he was directly using, the possibilities of patterns of action and emotion which had in fact resided in the great poetry of classical Greece which he had never read' (*Shakespeare and the Uses of Antiquity*, p. 82). M. Mueller's notion of an Orestean archetype behind *Hamlet* ('*Hamlet* and the World of Ancient Tragedy', *Arion* 5 (1997), 22–45) is comparable.

52. In, respectively, the 'Self-Criticism' prefaced to the 1886 edition of *The Birth of Tragedy* (1872), and *Twilight of the Idols* ('What I Owe to the Ancients', 5), repeated in *Ecce Homo* ('The Birth of Tragedy', 3) (both 1888). See Silk and Stern, *Nietzsche on Tragedy*, pp. 118–25.

53. I have argued what follows more fully in 'Tragic Language: The Greek Tragedians and Shakespeare', in Silk, *Tragedy and the Tragic*, pp. 458–96.

54. Pindar, *Pythians* 2.72 – and Nietzsche, *The Gay Science*, 270.

55. J.-P. Vernant in J.-P. Vernant and P. Vidal-Naquet, *Tragedy and Myth in Ancient Greece*, trans. J. Lloyd (Brighton 1981), p.10.

56. The timbre of such paradoxes, no doubt, owes something to Seneca: cf. esp., from his *Medea* 171, 'Medea – fiam' and 910, 'Medea nunc sum' ('Medea – I'll become', 'Medea I now am').

57. See Silk, 'Tragic Language', pp. 464–96.

58. My thanks, for helpful comments on this chapter, to Rosemary Barrow, Ingo Gildenhard, and Charles Martindale.

PART IV

THE RECEPTION OF
SHAKESPEARE'S CLASSICISM

CHAPTER 15

'The English Homer': Shakespeare, Longinus, and English 'neo-classicism'

David Hopkins

Discussions of 'Shakespeare and the Classics' have generally focused on the influence of classical literature and culture on Shakespeare's writing, whether by considering the general impact on his work of his humanist education, or his responses to particular classical authors and themes. Such, indeed, is the emphasis of the earlier chapters of this book. But 'Shakespeare and the Classics' is a topic which also has resonances for students of the afterlife and reception of Shakespeare's work. In 'Tradition and the Individual Talent', T. S. Eliot famously observed that

> No poet, no artist of any art, has his complete meaning alone. His significance, his appreciation is the appreciation of his relation to the dead poets and artists. You cannot value him alone; you must set him, for contrast and comparison, among the dead. I mean this as a principle of aesthetic, not merely historical, criticism.

Eliot's main concern was the way in which the appearance of a new work of art inevitably affects readers' appreciation of all the works of art which preceded it. 'What happens when a new work of art is created,' he argued,

> is something that happens simultaneously to all the works of art which preceded it. The existing monuments form an ideal order among themselves, which is modified by the introduction of the new (the really new) work of art among them.

A reader sympathetic to such ideas, Eliot believed, would 'not find it preposterous that the past should be altered by the present as much as the present is directed by the past'.[1]

Eliot's thoughts can, I believe, be usefully extended to encompass a further suggestion: that a significant revaluation of an 'older' work or author might substantially affect readers' responses to a 'newer' one. In this chapter, I shall consider the late seventeenth- and early eighteenth-century reception of Shakespeare in the light of that period's preoccupation with classical literature and literary criticism, a preoccupation which is widely believed to have seriously inhibited appreciation of Shakespeare's distinctive genius.

It was only, it is commonly supposed, when 'neo-classical' dogma began to
lose its authoritative hold that English readers came, for the first time, to
value the unique qualities of Shakespeare's art.

I shall argue, against such a view, that, at least in one notable respect, late
seventeenth- and early eighteenth-century writers' preoccupation with the
classics was a positively *enabling* force in their developing appreciation of
Shakespeare's distinctive artistic stature. During the period, I shall suggest,
Boileau's translation of Longinus' treatise *On the Sublime* (1674) was a
powerfully influential force in shaping a conception of Shakespeare as an
inspired, original, and 'fiery' poet of the Sublime, an 'English Homer'.

It is widely believed that responses to Shakespeare from the Restoration to
the mid-eighteenth century were seriously vitiated by a body of assumptions
which can be collectively characterised as 'neo-classical literary theory'. In
the introduction to the first volume of his comprehensive collection of early
Shakespeare criticism, Brian Vickers refers to the impact after the Restoration of the 'highly developed critical concepts of rules, decorum, propriety,
the unities, and so on – that amalgam of Aristotle and Horace borrowed
from the French seventeenth century (who had themselves borrowed it
from the Italian sixteenth century), which was to determine neo-classical
attitudes to Shakespeare for several generations'. And in his second volume
Vickers describes the period from the 1690s to the 1730s as 'one in which
the theoretical system of Neo-classicism was applied with energy and with
few reservations'.[2] Similar sentiments can be found in a number of influential specialist studies, and still persist in summary form in most handbook
accounts of post-Restoration literature and Shakespeare criticism.[3]

According to the received account, the tenets of neo-classical theory
placed a number of rigid restrictions on a dramatist's activity: the playwright
should observe the Unities of time and place; he should observe the laws
of decorum, according to which comedy must be strictly segregated from
tragedy; he should never confuse his characterisations of the high-born –
and the language which they are given to speak – with those of the 'vulgar',
or his depictions of the virtuous with those of the vicious; he must constantly
remember that the true purpose of his art is 'instruction'; consquently, his
plays should maintain Poetic Justice, according to which virtue is always
seen to triumph and vice to fail; he should eschew linguistic excesses, such as
puns, complex metaphors, extravagant conceits, and ambiguities; he should
avoid, wherever possible, the on-stage presentation of violent action.

On all these counts, it is claimed, Shakespeare's plays were found conspicuously wanting, and badly in need of 'correction'. With only a couple

of exceptions, they violated the Unities, sometimes to an extreme degree. Their language frequently seemed obscure or bombastic, and was riddled with indecorum, quibbling, and strained metaphors. Their action was often morally equivocal or ambiguous. They included blindings, assassinations, and mutilations, performed in full view of the audience. They manifested a disconcerting blend of comic and tragic action and language. As a consequence, the story goes on, they were regularly travestied in stage rewritings which reduced the nuanced subtleties of their language and the intricate ambiguities of their plot-construction to displays of studied elocution, stiff didacticism, sentimental melodrama, or bawdy farce. Editors of the period felt free to emend and abridge Shakespeare's texts according to their own canons of literary 'taste'. And discursive critics indulged in regular and prolonged litanies of his 'faults'. For many modern commentators, therefore, the period spanned by the writing careers of John Dryden and Alexander Pope constitutes something of a dark age in the history of Shakespeare interpretation.

But such an account is open to a number of serious objections. Chief among them is the awkward fact that it was precisely during the period between the Restoration and the mid-eighteenth century that Shakespeare was first decisively differentiated from Jonson and Fletcher – the contemporaries with whom he had previously been regularly lumped – and came to be clearly recognised as an English classic: 'the greatest English poet, perhaps the greatest poet of all time'.[4] Why, one might ask, should critics of the period have offered such a radically and daringly affirmative evaluation of Shakespeare when their theoretical principles militated so decisively and comprehensively against him? Why should the 'escape clauses' which, according to Brian Vickers, enabled them to offer high praise of Shakespeare while simultaneously castigating his faults, have been needed?[5] Recent scholarship has illuminated the processes whereby Shakespeare's works were 'appropriated' by various political and ideological interests in the period. But it has had considerably less to say about why Shakespeare should have been selected for appropriation in the first place.[6]

In exploring these issues, we might first consider the notorious Restoration stage adaptations of Shakespeare's plays. A survey of these versions reveals that, contrary to common belief, they were prompted by far more diverse considerations than slavish obedience to a set of rigid neo-classical rules.[7] In *Shakespeare Improved* Hazleton Spencer offered what is still widely regarded as the most scrupulous and detailed comparison of the adaptations with their originals. Very few of the redactions, Spencer's analyses show, are in fact driven by a dogmatic neo-classicism.[8] Despite contemporary disapproval of what Joseph Addison called 'that dreadful butchering of one another, which is so very frequent upon the *English* stage',[9] adaptations such as Nahum Tate's versions of *Coriolanus* and *King Lear* and Sir William Davenant's of *Macbeth* are conspicuous for their *non*-avoidance of on-stage violence. Like most of the original plays of the period, moreover, few of the Restoration adaptations of Shakespeare make any sustained or serious attempt to observe the Unities.[10] As Jean I. Marsden has recently pointed out, only the adaptations of John Dennis make any systematic attempt to 'regularise' their originals. Even then, the modification is not dogmatically effected. Dennis' versions, moreover, were not popular. And the regularising tendency of his adaptations co-exists with extravagant praise of Shakespeare in his critical writings.[11] The Restoration redactions, moreover, seldom effect the strict separation of tragic and comic elements demanded by neo-classical theory. Nor do most of them make any serious attempt to preserve Poetic Justice.

If the prime concern of the adapters was not to square Shakespeare with the neo-classical Rules, what, then, were their motives in altering Shakespeare's originals? Their prime intention, the evidence suggests, was to produce performing versions suited to the needs, expectations, and interests of contemporary audiences in a highly competitive, commercial theatre, at a time when, unlike today, there was no state support for, or academic pressure to attend, Shakespearean performances. Such versions clearly needed to be purged of linguistic archaism and obscurity, so that they would be immediately intelligible at the speed of theatrical delivery to audiences unfamiliar with the original texts, and lacking the annotated editions, synopses, and other aids which twenty-first-century readers and theatre-goers take for granted.

Considerations of clarity and intelligibility seem also to have been responsible for many of the adapters' alterations of Shakespeare's plots. Many of these changes seem designed to compensate for what they perceived as a lack of clarity both of moral focus and of psychological motivation in many of Shakespeare's dramatic designs. Nahum Tate, for example, provided an explanation of Cordelia's blunt refusal to indulge her father's request for flattery in the opening scene of *King Lear* by making her secretly in love with Edgar, and thus unwilling to marry Burgundy. Thomas Shadwell accounted for, and softened, Timon of Athens' sudden outburst of misanthropy by making it the result of his rejection by the coquette Melissa.[12] Sir William Davenant, in his *Law Against Lovers*, excused and explained Angelo's pardon at the end of *Measure for Measure* by depicting his intentions as having been always essentially honourable: he had only been pretending to seduce Isabella in order to to test her virtue, and had never intended to take Claudio's life.

Some of the redactors' reshapings of Shakespeare can be explained by their desire to exploit the new circumstances and scenic resources of the Restoration theatre: female actors, moveable scenery, bands of trained musicians.[13] The adaptations also sought to point up the 'relevance' of Shakespeare to the contemporary political situation. The earlier Restoration versions were often specifically tailored to celebrate the restored monarchy.[14] Two decades later, Shakespeare was extensively 'applied' to the modern situation during the period of the Popish Plot and Exclusion Crisis.[15] The majority of the adaptations from this period are firmly royalist in bias, a fact which – as much as any adherence to academic principles of Poetic Justice – explains the emphasis of such plays as John Crowne's versions of *1–2 Henry VI* and Edward Ravenscroft's *Titus Andronicus* on the benignity of providence and the destruction of socially or politically disruptive forces: the triumph of virtue is seen in such dramas as intimately connected with the protection and preservation of civic order.[16] Finally, the adaptations sometimes sought to accommodate Shakespeare to the philosophical debates, generic fashions, and sensibilities of their own day, incorporating, for example, touches of Hobbesian libertinage in the comic episodes of Shakespeare's 'serious' plays,[17] transforming some of Shakespeare's heroines into icons of suffering virtue,[18] and interpolating additional lascivious dialogue and low buffoonery to transform *The Tempest* into typical 1670s 'sex comedy'.

In all these respects, the Restoration and early eighteenth-century adapters can be seen not so much as neo-classical dogmatists but as practical men of the theatre, tailoring their presentations of Shakespeare – in a manner not dissimilar to the practice of modern stage and cinema producers – to the tastes, expectations, and interests of their audiences. This, of course (as with modern producers), often resulted in versions which were reductive, partial, modish, or downright silly. Few would probably wish to see many of the Restoration redactions revived on the modern stage. The discursive criticism of the period, moreover, contains its fair share of mundane, mechanical, and clichéd writing, much of it, indeed, deploying conventional neo-Aristotelian vocabulary and rhetoric, or displaying a merely snobbish aversion to the 'low' elements in Shakespeare's texts. But this should not lead us to assume that the impulses behind Restoration and early eighteenth-century responses to Shakespeare can always be confidently dismissed as mere Rules-bound aberrations. For some of them were prompted by features of Shakespeare's texts which have been found equally problematic by critics in very different contexts and from very different intellectual traditions.

Cordelia's rebarbative bluntness and the Duke's final distribution of justice (already mentioned as features of their respective plays which seem to have disturbed the Restoration redactors) have frequently proved stumbling-blocks in later accounts of *King Lear* and *Measure for Measure*. Even Hazleton Spencer – generally no admirer of the adaptations – acknowledged that Shadwell's *Timon of Athens* supplies psychological motivation and dramatic unity which is conspicuously lacking in Shakespeare's original.[19] G. F. Parker has argued convincingly that the infamous remarks about the 'horrible' and 'unnatural' aspects of *Othello* to be found in Thomas Rymer's *Short View of Tragedy* (1693) – often regarded as the acme of neo-classical obtuseness about Shakespeare – rest, in large part, not on Aristotelian dogma, but on an empirically grounded appeal to common readerly humanity which finds an echo in many later responses to deeply disturbing elements in Shakespeare's play: Iago's arbitrary malignity, the impotence of Cassio, Desdemona and Emilia in countering his villainy, Othello's seeming incapacity to comprehend or acknowledge the evil which is invading him.[20] And in another recent essay, A. D. J. Brown has demonstrated that Alexander's Pope's notorious emendations and excisions from Shakespeare's text in his edition of 1725 depend not on narrowly eighteenth-century canons of taste and decorum, but on a subtle and discriminating appreciation of Shakespeare's own stylistic practices, and on a shrewd (albeit incomplete) awareness of the material circumstances in which his texts were produced and transmitted.[21]

Many of the general reservations about Shakespeare voiced by the critics of the period have, significantly, found powerful echoes in the responses of later critics. A. C. Bradley, for example, an Edwardian Hegelian with (on the face of it) little sympathy for neo-classical aesthetics, substantially endorsed earlier critics' findings that Shakespeare's language is often 'obscure, inflated, tasteless, or "pestered with metaphors"', and offered a trenchant account of Shakespeare's inconsistent, hasty, negligent, and morally confused conduct of his plots which is substantially in accord with that current in the post-Restoration period.[22] More recently, George Steiner has drawn on the notes of the philosopher Wittgenstein to support his own feelings about the 'prolixity and repetitiveness' in many of Shakespeare's plays, 'the intrusion of vulgarity and waste motion into even the major texts (how many of us have ever seen a production of *Othello* which includes the wretched exchanges with the Clown)', and the elements in Shakespeare's comedies which are 'rancid or verbally witty rather than funny in any real sense'.[23]

It is not necessary to agree with such accounts to concede that the conception of Shakespeare as a profoundly flawed artist – both in his linguistic practices and in the coherence and intelligibility of his dramatic designs – is by no means a limitedly neo-classical phenomenon.[24] And it is equally clear that such descriptions have often been felt – both within and outside the neo-classical period – to be perfectly compatible with the highest general estimate of Shakespeare's genius.

Perhaps the most unfortunate consequence of the modern stress on post-Restoration neo-Aristotelianism is that it has distracted attention from another strand of critical thought in the period – one equally deserving of the label 'neo-classical' – which was of crucial importance in promoting a powerfully positive appreciation of Shakespeare's distinctive artistic qualities. I refer to the growing tendency to characterise Shakespeare as 'the English Homer', a tendency closely bound up with the intense revival of interest from the mid-1670s in the ancient treatise generally known as *On the Sublime* and attributed to 'Longinus'.

The names of Shakespeare and Homer had been occasionally linked from earliest times. In 1598 Francis Meres had affirmed that the English tongue had been 'mightilie enriched, and gorgeouslie invested in rare ornaments and resplendent abiliments' by Shakespeare, just as Greek had been 'made famous and eloquent by Homer'. An anonymous writer in 1651 had pronounced Shakespeare the 'Butler' in the realm of 'Eloquentia' where Homer was 'Master of the Wine-Cellars'. And in 1668 Dryden had referred to Shakespeare *en passant* as 'the Homer, or Father of our Dramatick Poets'.[25] But the association between the two writers became invested with an altogether new charge of significance after the appearance and rapid dissemination in England of Boileau's *Traité du Sublime ou du Merveilleux dans le Discours traduit du Grec de Longin*, published in Paris in 1674.[26]

Boileau is still often popularly thought of as the archetypal 'neo-classical' Rules critic, a 'Législateur du Parnasse' who laid down tyrannical and procrustean laws for literary composition. But as Jules Brody showed long ago,[27] such an account gives a quite misleading impression of the French writer's main critical principles and priorities. Boileau, Brody demonstrates, thought that the central imperative to which all other rules of literary composition should be subordinated was the capacity of literature to produce powerful and intense emotional effects on its readers – a quality found in its most concentrated and irresistible form in the Longinian Sublime.

The Sublime, in Boileau's reading, 'charms' and 'transports', producing 'a certain Admiration mingled with Astonishment and Surprize' (p. 13).[28] It is 'an invincible Force which ravishes the Souls of all that hear' it (p. 13). The 'Sublime and Pathetick, by their Violence and Impetuosity, naturally carry away every thing with them' and 'don't give the Hearer time to amuse himself, with cavilling at the Number of Metaphors; but throw him into the same Rapture with the Speaker' (pp. 65–6). The Sublime is not to be confused with 'Pompous and Magnificent' 'Bombast' (p. 15), or with the 'affected' 'Puerility' which 'wou'd continually say something extraordinary and Brillant [sic]' (p. 16). Its most intense effects, indeed, often come from extreme simplicity. It is 'a sort of Enthusiasm and Noble Fury, which animates' literary discourse, 'and gives it a Divine Fire and Vigour' (p. 23). The sublimity of the orator Demosthenes, for example, was visible in the 'Violence[,] Rapidity, and Vehemence, with which he bears down all before him' (p. 36). The sublime poet, similarly, 'carries the Reader along with him . . . making him rather see [the things he is describing] than read of 'em' (p. 59). He chooses 'Words, that give a sort of Soul and Life to things' (p. 64). Art reaches its perfection of sublimity when 'it so nearly resembles Nature, as to be taken for it: And on the contrary, Nature never succeeds better, than when the Art is hidden' (p. 54). The work of the sublime writer will inevitably contain faults, since

in the Sublime . . . the Riches of Discourse are Immense, every thing cannot be so Carefully look'd after, as it ought to be; and something, let the Orator or Poet be never so Exact, will be Neglected. On the Contrary, 'tis almost impossible for a mean and midling Genius to commit Faults; because, as he never ventures, never rises, he always, remains in a State of Safety: Whereas, the Great is of it self, and by its Character of Greatness, slippery and dangerous. (pp. 68–9)

The 'Fine Strokes and Sublime Thoughts, which are in the Works of . . . Excellent Writers', nevertheless, 'over balances [sic] all their Faults' (p. 74). And the supreme exemplar of the Sublime was Homer: the writer who, above all others, could, in his dramatic fictions, ravish and transport readers and rivet their attentions with his fiery intensity. Homer's 'Thoughts', according to Boileau's Longinus, were 'all Sublime' (p. 25). The 'whole Body' of his Iliad 'is Dramatick and full of Action' (p. 29), in the manner characteristic of the truly sublime poet.

   This praise of the Homeric Sublime was quickly taken up and applied to Shakespeare by a number of English writers, including some of the most influential poet–critics of the period. The rapid impact of Boileau's Longin can be seen with particular clarity in two critical prefaces of John

Dryden from the late 1670s. It is first evident in 'The Authors Apology for Heroique Poetry and Poetique Licence' prefixed to *The State of Innocence* (1677), where Dryden pointedly notes that '*Longinus*, who was undoubtedly, after *Aristotle*, the greatest Critique amongst the *Greeks* . . . has judiciously preferr'd the sublime Genius that sometimes erres, to the midling or indifferent one which makes few faults, but seldome or never rises to any Excellence'. Homer's faults, Dryden argues, 'are only marks of humane frailty: they are little Mistakes, or rather Negligences, which have escap'd his pen in the fervor of his writing; the sublimity of his spirit carries it with me against his carelessness'. Such thoughts have stylistic implications which cause Dryden to rethink some of his own earlier critical assumptions. 'The hardest Metaphors, and . . . the strongest *Hyperboles*', Dryden now argues, are justifiable if they contribute to a poet's capacity 'to sound the depth of all the Passions; what they are in themselves, and how they are to be provok'd'. 'Boldness of expression' which might otherwise seem merely bombastic or magniloquent is to be thought 'graceful' in the depictions of passion where it seems 'Natural' (*Works* XII.87–93).

These thoughts are applied specifically to Shakespeare two years later in 'The Grounds of Criticism in Tragedy' prefixed to Dryden's *Troilus and Cressida*. In the closing pages of this essay, Longinian arguments are vigorously deployed in defence of Shakespeare's mastery of the human passions (the unique preserve of 'a lofty Genius'), and his consequent capacity to kindle in his audiences the utmost 'concernment' for his characters. If 'the fury of [Shakespeare's] fancy,' Dryden declares, 'often transported him, beyond the bounds of Judgment, either in coyning of new words and phrases, or racking words which were in use, into the violence of a Catachresis', this should not be taken as an argument for the total elimination of metaphors in the expression of passion, 'for *Longinus* thinks 'em necessary to raise it'. If 'pompous words' and 'Bombast' are sometimes evident in Shakespeare's passionate speeches, he 'does not often thus', and Dryden goes on to offer examples from *Julius Caesar* and *Richard II* to illustrate Shakespeare's capacity to articulate 'thoughts . . . such as arise from the matter', and which are 'extreamly natural', their 'expression' not being 'viciously figurative' (*Works* XIII.244–7). The extravagance and obscurity which Dryden and his contemporaries had observed to be a recurrent characteristic of Shakespeare's writing are now seen as the inevitable price which has to be paid for the true Longinian sublimity of the dramatist's best work.[29]

The application to Shakespeare of the Longinian critique of Homer is also clearly evident in early eighteenth-century English translations of Longinus' treatise. In their versions of 1712 and 1739, Leonard Welsted and

William Smith offer many 'applications' of Longinus to English literature, and particularly to the works of Shakespeare.[30] Homer's mastery in the depiction of storms (praised by Longinus in 10.4) is paralleled, for example, by Welsted (pp. 169–70) with the description of the storm in *Julius Caesar* (1.3.4–8) and by Smith (pp. 138–40) with that in *King Lear* (*History of King Lear* 8.4–8; 9.13–15, 47–58). No one, says Smith (pp. 146–8) 'can enter into a Parallel with *Shakespeare*' in the 'affecting Horror' evoked by Longinus (15.1–6) when describing the distraction of Euripides' Orestes after the death of Clytemnestra, and cites in support the 'dagger' scene from *Macbeth* (2.1), a scene also invoked, along with that depicting Richard III's nightmares before the battle of Bosworth Field (*Richard III* 5.5), by Welsted (pp. 174–5).

Welsted's summing-up conveys vividly his conviction that the Homeric sublimity of Shakespeare's genius is both intimately bound up with, and also amply compensates for, any defects which his work might contain:

I am struck with Astonishment when I read *Shakespear*. Can one read him without the utmost Emotion? . . . At the same time it must be granted, that those Writers who excel so highly in the Grand and Lofty, are liable to numerous Failings, and those sometimes very gross ones; but how can one expect it should be otherwise. Human Spirit in such Works is wrought to its utmost stretch, and cannot, as our Critick observes, possibly support it self thro' the whole with equal Majesty: Nature asks a Breathing-time: He must trifle with *Homer*, who would rise to *Homer*'s Altitudes. (pp. 186–7)

Many of the Shakespearean parallels cited by Welsted and Smith significantly overlap with passages marked out for special approval in Alexander Pope's edition of Shakespeare,[31] and one can witness in Pope's writings on Homer and Shakespeare particularly striking evidence of the effects of the Longinian critique of Homer on the developing early eighteenth-century conception of Shakespeare's genius.

The Longinian provenance of Pope's celebration of Homer's poetic 'fire' is well established.[32] Near the beginning of the Preface to his *Iliad*, for example, Pope asserts that

No Man of a true Poetical Spirit is Master of himself while he reads [Homer]. What he writes is of the most animated Nature imaginable; every thing moves, every thing lives, and is put in Action. If a Council be call'd, or a Battel fought, you are not coldly inform'd of what was said or done as from a third Person; the Reader is hurry'd out of himself by the Force of the Poet's Imagination, and turns in one place to a Hearer, and in another to a Spectator. (*Prose Works*, vol. 1, pp. 224–5)

This passage, as Pope's early editor Gilbert Wakefield pointed out, clearly echoes Longinus' description of the effects of poetic sublimity, 'Wherein by an extraordinary Enthusiasm and Emotion of Soul, it seems as if we saw the things we speak of, and put them before the Eyes of those that hear us' (p. 40), and of the stylistic devices whereby the sublime poet convinces readers that they are 'not then in Narration but Action', and 'makes the Auditory often think themselves in the middle of the Danger' (p. 58).[33] Pope's account of Homer's ability to find out 'Living Words' (*Prose Works*, vol. I, p. 233) is similarly pre-echoed in Longinus' comments on Homer's genius for 'Words that give a sort of Soul and Life to things'. And his account of Homer's pre-eminence in 'the Grandeur and Excellence of his Sentiments' is indebted not merely to Longinus, but specifically to Boileau's version (p. 25), which at the appropriate place (9.4–5 in modern editions) fills out a lacuna in the original Greek text.[34]

There are also notable affinities between Pope's praise of Homer, and the general encomium with which Pope begins the Preface to his edition of Shakespeare. Pope's descriptions of the 'Fire' and 'Rapture' whereby Homer 'animates' his subject matter, overpowers criticism, and carries readers and audiences away in spellbound involvement, are closely paralleled in his remarks on Shakespeare's apparently effortless 'power over the passions':

The *Power* over our *Passions* was never possess'd in a more eminent degree, or display'd in so different instances. Yet all along, there is seen no labour, no pains to raise them; no preparation to guide our guess to the effect, or be perceiv'd to lead toward it: We are surpriz'd, the moment we weep; and yet upon reflection find the passion so just, that we shou'd be surpriz'd if we had not wept, and wept at that very moment. (*Prose Works*, vol. II, p. 14)

In the Preface to his *Iliad*, Pope had written in a similar vein of Shakespeare's 'Poetical Fire' which – just as powerfully as Homer's, albeit not so consistently or sustainedly – 'strikes before we are aware, like an accidental Fire from Heaven' (*Prose Works*, vol. I, p. 225). Precisely the same metaphor was, significantly, used by Anthony Blackwall when writing of the Longinian sublime:

The Sublime is a just grand, and marvellous thought. It strikes like lightning with a conquering and resistless flame . . . It carries all before it by its own strength; and does not so much raise persuasion in the hearer or reader, as throw him into an ecstacy, and transport him out of himself.[35]

The connections in Pope's mind between Homer and Shakespeare are equally evident when he voices his conviction that the sentiments spoken by Shakespeare's characters seem to flow from dramatically conceived creations, rather than appearing as general reflections, arbitrarily imposed on their speakers:

[E]very single character is *Shakespear* is as much an Individual, as those in Life itself; it is impossible to find any two alike; and such as from their relation or affinity in any respect appear to be most Twins, will upon comparison be found remarkably distinct. To this life and variety of Character, we must add the wonderful Preservation of it; which is such throughout his plays, that had all the Speeches been printed without the very names of the Persons, I believe one might have apply'd them with certainty to every speaker. (*Prose Works*, vol. II, pp. 13–14)

Here we may remember Pope's distinction in the Preface to his *Iliad* between the characterisation of Homer and Virgil:

In *Virgil* the Dramatic Part is less in proportion to the Narrative; and the Speeches often consist of general Reflections or Thoughts, which might be equally just in any Person's Mouth upon the same Occasion ... We oftner think of the Author himself when we read *Virgil*, than when we are engag'd in *Homer*. All which are the Effects of a colder Invention, that interests us less in the Action describ'd: *Homer* makes us Hearers, and *Virgil* leaves us Readers. (*Prose Works*, vol. I, p. 231)

'Invention', for Pope the distinguishing characteristic of Homer's genius, is, as Paul Hammond has reminded us,

a classical rhetorical term (*inventio*) for the first of the elements of composition, and its etymology implies that the writer does not make up but discovers material, which is thus thought to be there waiting to be used. Accordingly, Homer as the greatest poetic inventor is the writer who is closest to Nature.[36]

Pope's praise of Homer's 'Invention' is thus closely related to his celebration of Shakespeare's 'originality':

If any Author deserved the name of an *Original*, it was *Shakespear*. *Homer* himself drew not his art so immediately from the fountains of Nature, it proceeded through *Aegyptian* strainers and channels, and came to him not without some tincture of the learning, or some case of the models, of those before him. The Poetry of *Shakespear* was Inspiration indeed: he is not so much an Imitator, as an Instrument, of Nature; and 'tis not so just to say that he speaks from her, as that she speaks thro' him. (*Prose Works*, vol. II, p. 13)

These sentiments find a significant echo in the most important piece of Shakespeare criticism to appear in the second half of the eighteenth century, Johnson's great Preface of 1765. Johnson, we may recall, judged that

it would not be easy to find any author, except Homer, who invented so much as Shakespeare.[37]

He also echoed the terms of Pope's praise of the distinctively dramatic qualities of Homer and Shakespeare when comparing Shakespeare's *Othello* with a widely admired drama of his own century, Joseph Addison's *Cato*:

We find in *Cato* innumerable beauties which enamour us of its author, but we see nothing that acquaints us with human sentiments or human actions; we place it with the fairest and the noblest progeny which judgment propagates by conjunction with learning; but *Othello* is the vigorous and vivacious offspring of observation impregnated by genius. *Cato* affords a splendid exhibition of artificial and fictitious manners, and delivers just and noble sentiments, in diction easy, elevated, and harmonious, but its hopes and fears communicate no vibration to the heart; the composition refers us only to the writer; we pronounce the name of *Cato*, but we think on *Addison*. (p. 140)

And Johnson makes the Homeric parallel explicit when, commenting on Shakespeare's plots, he observes that

every man finds his mind more strongly seized by the tragedies of Shakespeare than of any other writer; others please us by particular speeches, but he always makes us anxious for the event, and has perhaps excelled all but Homer in securing the first purpose of a writer, by exciting restless and unquenchable curiosity, and compelling him that reads his work to read it through. (pp. 139–40)

Here Johnson stands in a direct line from Longinus (as translated by William Smith) who, commenting on a passage in which Homer addresses his readers directly about the deeds of Diomedes, observes:

By this Address you not only strike more upon his Passions, but fill him with a more earnest Attention, and a more anxious Impatience for the Event. (p. 65)

Shakespearean redaction and criticism of the late seventeenth and early eighteenth centuries, I have argued, is far less homogeneous, and far less pervasively and damagingly influenced by neo-Aristotelian neo-classicism than is usually supposed. Some of its criticisms of Shakespeare's faults are less pedantic and period-specific than might at first sight appear. And some of the most influential writers of the period developed a powerful and influential conception of Shakespeare as an author of 'fire', originality, and spellbinding dramatic power, whose very failings are an inevitable concomitant of his capacity to achieve the Longinian Sublime, and whose finest effects make him fully deserving of the title 'The English Homer'.

NOTES

1. T. S. Eliot, 'Tradition and the Individual Talent', in *Selected Essays* (2nd edn, London 1934), p. 15.
2. Brian Vickers, ed., *Shakespeare: The Critical Heritage*, 6 vols. (London 1974–81) (quotations from vols. I, p. 4 and II, p. 1).

3. See, e.g. T. R. Lounsbury, *Shakespeare as a Dramatic Artist, with an Account of his Reputation at Various Periods* (London and New York 1902); R. W. Babcock, *The Genesis of Shakespeare Idolatry, 1766–1799* (Chapel Hill 1931); George C. Branam, *Eighteenth-Century Adaptations of Shakespearean Tragedy* (Berkeley and Los Angeles 1956); for a popular summary account, see, e.g. Oscar James Campbell, ed., *A Shakespeare Encyclopedia* (London 1966), p. 6.

4. Jean I. Marsden, *The Re-Imagined Text: Shakespeare, Adaptation, and Eighteenth-Century Literary Theory* (Lexington 1995), p. 49.

5. Vickers, *Shakespeare: The Critical Heritage*, vol. II, p. 7.

6. For the 'appropriation' of Shakespeare, see Michael Dobson, *The Making of the National Poet: Shakespeare, Adaptation, and Authorship, 1660–1769* (Oxford 1992); Gary Taylor, *Re-Inventing Shakespeare: A Cultural History from the Restoration to the Present* (London 1990).

7. See Paulina Kewes, 'Shakespeare and New Drama', in David Womersley, ed., *A Companion to Literature from Milton to Blake* (Oxford 2000), pp. 575–88, 586.

8. Hazleton Spencer, *Shakespeare Improved* (Cambridge MA, 1927): Spencer's findings are fully endorsed by the latest commentator on the redactions. See Barbara A. Murray, *Restoration Shakespeare: Viewing the Voice* (Madison and London 2001), p. 19.

9. *The Spectator* 44 (20 April 1711).

10. Dryden's *All for Love*, often singled out as the most 'correct' and 'regular' of the Restoration versions, is an original play on a Shakespearean theme rather than an adaptation as such, and might be best thought of as a one-off, experimental attempt to revitalise serious drama in the mid-1670s by combining elements from the native English and French dramatic traditions. Dryden's adaptation of *Troilus and Cressida* certainly shows the influence of French criticism and drama. But his changes seem motivated not by any mechanically conceived Rules but by a desire to tighten the linguistic and dramatic coherence of a play which even Hazlitt thought 'the most loose and desultory' of Shakespeare's works. For further discussion, see Maximillian E. Novak's judicious commentary in H. T. Swedenberg *et al.*, eds., *The Works of John Dryden*, 20 vols. (Berkeley 1956–2000), vol. XIII, pp. 497–522.

11. Mardsen, *Re-imagined Text*, pp. 49, 55; Branam, *Eighteenth-Century Adaptations*, p. 23; E. N. Hooker, ed., *John Dennis: Critical Works*, 2 vols. (Baltimore 1939–43), vol. II, pp. 4, 168.

12. See Marsden, *Re-imagined Text*, pp. 26–7.

13. On actresses, see Elizabeth Howe, *The First English Actresses: Women and Drama, 1660–1700* (Cambridge 1992); on theatrical effects, see Jocelyn Powell, *Restoration Theatre Production* (London 1984); on music and musicians, see Curtis Price, *Music in the Restoration Theatre* (Ann Arbor 1979).

14. See Dobson, *Making of the National Poet*, ch. 1.

15. See Marsden, *Re-imagined Text*, pp. 40–2; Susan J. Owen, *Restoration Theatre and Crisis* (Oxford 1996); Dobson, *Making of the National Poet*, pp. 63–90.

16. See Marsden, *Re-imagined Text*, pp. 66–7.
17. See Kewes, 'Shakespeare and New Drama', p. 582.
18. See Marsden, *Re-imagined Text*, pp. 30–7.
19. Spencer, *Shakespeare Improved*, pp. 281–7.
20. G. F. Parker, 'Foul Disproportion: Rymer on *Othello*', *Cambridge Quarterly* 17 (1988), 17–27.
21. A. D. J. Brown, 'The Little Fellow has done Wonders', *Cambridge Quarterly* 21 (1992), 120–49; see also correspondence in 21 (1992), 260–1; and 22 (1993), 184–6.
22. A. C. Bradley, *Shakespearean Tragedy* (London 1904), pp. 73, 76.
23. George Steiner, 'A Reading Against Shakespeare', in *No Passion Spent* (London 1996), pp. 108–27, 127.
24. For a persuasive argument that Samuel Johnson's strictures on Shakespeare are less affected by neo-classical assumptions than is often assumed, see Philip Smallwood, 'Shakespeare: Johnson's Poet of Nature', in Greg Clingham, ed., *The Cambridge Companion to Samuel Johnson* (Cambridge 1997), pp. 143–60.
25. See J. Munro, ed., *The Shakespeare Allusion Book: A Collection of Allusions to Shakespeare from 1591 to 1700* (1909), with new Preface by E. K. Chambers, 2 vols. (Oxford 1932), vol. I, p. 46; vol. II, p. 18; Swedenberg *et al.*, eds., *Works of John Dryden*, vol. XVII, p. 58.
26. The English translations of Longinus' treatise which appeared in the ensuing decades were explicitly indebted to Boileau. John Pulteney's version of 1680 openly declared itself as 'now Translated out of the *French*', though 'Written Originally in *Greek* by *LONGIN*'. The anonymous translator of 1698 declared his version to have been 'Compar'd with the French of the Sieur Despreaux Boileau'. The first English translation of Boileau's collected *Works*, published in 1711–13, incorporated a third English version of the *Traité*, probably by John Ozell.
27. See Jules Brody, *Boileau and Longinus* (Geneva 1958). The received image of Boileau is also tellingly scrutinised in E. B. O. Borgerhoff, *The Freedom of French Classicism* (Princeton 1950).
28. Quotations from Boileau's *Longin* are taken from the 1711–13 English translation (see n. 26 above), cited in the text by page-references.
29. On this subject, see, further, Paul Hammond, 'The Janus Poet: Dryden's Critique of Shakespeare', in Claude Rawson and Aaron Santesso, eds., *John Dryden (1631–1700): His Politics, his Plays, and his Poets* (Newark and London 2004).
30. See Leonard Welsted, *The Works of Dionysius Longinus, On the Sublime; or, a Treatise Concerning the Sovereign Perfection of Writing, Translated from the Greek* (London 1712); *Dionysius Longinus on the Sublime: Translated from the Greek, with Notes and Observations . . . by William Smith* (London 1739). Since the divisions of Longinus' text differ both between Welsted's and Smith's translations and between both versions and modern editions, references to Longinus are keyed for convenience to the modern translation by D. A. Russell included in D. A. Russell and M. Winterbottom, eds., *Ancient Literary Criticism: The Principal Texts in New Translations* (Oxford 1972).

31. In Pope's edition 'some of the most shining passages are distinguish'd by comma's in the margin; and where the beauty lay not in particulars but in the whole, a star is prefix'd to the scene' (Norman Ault and Rosemary Cowler, eds., *The Prose Works of Alexander Pope*, 2 vols. (Oxford 1936–86), vol. II, p. 25).
32. For a modern analysis, see Kirsti Simonsuuri, *Homer's Original Genius: Eighteenth-Century Notions of the Early Greek Epic (1688–1798)* (Cambridge 1979), pp. 13, 60–4.
33. The second example is noted by Gilbert Wakefield, ed., *The Iliad of Homer, Translated by Alexander Pope: A New Edition,* 4 vols. (London 1806), vol. I, pp. vi–vii.
34. As pointed out by Wakefield in ibid., pp. xxi–ii.
35. *The Sacred Classics Defended and Illustrated* (1737), cited by Andrew Ashfield and Peter de Bolla, eds., *The Sublime: A Reader in British Eighteenth-Century Aesthetic Theory* (Cambridge 1996), p. 18.
36. Paul Hammond, ed., *Selected Prose of Alexander Pope* (Cambridge 1987), p. 8.
37. H. R. Woudhuysen, ed., *Samuel Johnson on Shakespeare* (Harmondsworth 1989), p. 145.

I am indebted to Stuart Gillespie, Paul Hammond, Charles Martindale, and Tom Mason for their helpful comments on earlier drafts of this chapter.

CHAPTER 16

'There is no end but addition': the later reception of Shakespeare's classicism

Sarah Annes Brown

Today's readers of *The Two Noble Kinsmen* will already have most of Shakespeare's more celebrated *oeuvre* under their belt, and thus may experience a sense of *déjà vu* when they turn to this late work, written in collaboration with Fletcher. We are introduced to the Athenian Duke Theseus, who has just won Hippolyta as his bride, and watch him try to arbitrate in the quarrels of two young noblemen who are both in love with the same girl. Of course these features are already present in Chaucer and Boccaccio; but the unnamed 'second countryman' cannot be traced back to any such obvious source. He and his companions, who are planning a May Day dance to entertain the court, have few classical credentials:

> All the boys in Athens
> Blow wind i'th breech on's. And here I'll be,
> And there I'll be for our town and here again,
> And there again. Ha, boys, heigh for the weavers!
> (2.3.46–9)[1]

This over-enthusiastic weaver irresistibly recalls Bottom; it is as though, following *A Midsummer Night's Dream*, he and his comrades are now immutably part of the Athenian landscape, always rehearsing to please the Duke. Within the complex historical and geographical matrix of educated reading practice there is a corner of a classical Athenian wood which will be forever Elizabethan England.[2] The mechanicals' memorable performance also haunts this play. When the jailor's daughter enters a wood near Athens at night, and first thinks her beloved has mistaken the place before worrying that he has been killed by a beast, we are reminded of the woes of Thisbe, specifically Flute's Thisbe if she is portrayed as a rustic rather than a classical heroine. The link is further confirmed when we later hear that the love-maddened girl has been heard muttering 'Palamon is gone, / Is gone to th' wood to gather mulberries' (4.1.67–8), for the mulberry tree's berries were first dyed purple by the blood of Pyramus (*Metamorphoses* 4.126). Thus it would seem that even for Shakespeare himself certain classical topics had become inseparable from the Shakespearean texts they influenced.

Such reinflections of classicism are part of Shakespeare's legacy, and so powerfully so that it is difficult to determine whether these apparently significant links between *A Midsummer Night's Dream* and *Two Noble Kinsmen* are indeed a function of Shakespeare/Fletcher's literary memory or whether their resonance should rather be ascribed to our own instinct to highlight those few details which map onto our conception of Shakespeare, and Shakespeare's classicism, at the expense of other allusions to say *Othello* or *Hamlet*, or indeed to other works by the comparatively little read Fletcher. But even if the latter scenario is more accurate, our privileging or constructing of certain literary narratives, those which generate most (inter)textual energy, can scarcely be avoided. However we may try to historicise our readings of Shakespeare or any other playwright we can never gain unmediated access to the complex of impulses lying behind his works.

This chapter attempts to offer some thoughts about the ways Shakespeare and the classics have converged in the last four centuries, both through reconceptualisations of links already present or implicit in Shakespeare's own works, and through the development of fresh interaction between Shakespeare and classical literature. It is not intended to be representative of Shakespeare's classicism – a bias toward Ovid may be noted – or even of the reception of Shakespeare's classicism (in which it might be argued that Joyce plays a more important role than C. S. Lewis), but it does attempt to identify and analyse a range of processes and procedures at work in later texts where Shakespeare and the classics are both present. My main contention in this chapter is that the relationship between Shakespeare and the classics is still evolving, that it has been created rather than simply discovered by later writers who, even when simply recontextualising established points of contact between Shakespeare and his sources, almost inevitably transform the nature of the interface.

For example, although the twin presences of Perdita and Proserpine (twinned because the latter is mediated through the former's famous flower speech in *The Winter's Tale*) retain much of their original resonance in *Paradise Lost*, the Christianised Miltonic context brings new pressures to bear on the relationship. Eve's alignment with Proserpine is well known, and is described in a memorable passage:

> Not that fair field
> Of Enna, where Proserpine gathering flowers
> Her self a fairer flower by gloomy Dis
> Was gathered . . .   (4.268–71)[3]

The more ghostly presence of Perdita, a harvest queen in act 4 of *The Winter's Tale*, may be signalled by the following detail:

> Adam the while
> Waiting desirous her return, had wove
> Of choicest flowers a garland to adorn
> Her tresses, and her rural labours crown,
> As reapers oft are wont their harvest queen.
> (9.838–42)

The garland will later be dropped by Adam in horror when he hears that Eve has been tempted to eat the forbidden fruit – 'From his slack hand the garland wreathed for Eve / Down dropped, and all the faded roses shed' (9.892–3) – the connection between girls and faded flowers (implicit in Ovid's account of Proserpine and explicit in *The Winter's Tale* and *Paradise Lost* 4.269–71) is thus reprised; Eve and her garland have both fallen. It is easier to see why Proserpine should become a foreboding figure in *Paradise Lost* – her taste of the pomegranate and subsequent status as queen of the underworld align her too closely with the fallen Eve for comfort – than why Perdita should be implicated in Milton's narrative of the Fall. A partial explanation may be found in the parallels between the uxorious Adam and Prince Florizel; each man testifies to his mistress's perfections:

> What you do
> Still betters what is done. When you speak, sweet,
> I'd have you do it ever . . . Each your doing
> (So singular in each particular)
> Crowns what you are doing in the present deeds,
> That all your acts are queens.
> (*Winter's Tale* 4.4.135–46)

> Yet when I approach
> Her loveliness, so absolute she seems
> And in herself complete, so well to know
> Her own, that what she wills to do or say,
> Seems wisest, virtuousest, discreetest, best . . .
> (*Paradise Lost* 8.46–50)

In each text the lover's devotion involves implicit neglect of a higher authority and precedes disaster. But whereas the comic context of *The Winter's Tale* ensures that disobedience to a mere earthly father can be forgiven, and all barriers to the lovers' marriage circumvented, Adam's rebellion against his heavenly father, his failure to subordinate human to divine obligations, must be punished. Just as Proserpine, a charming if pathetic figure in *The Winter's Tale*, is almost inevitably transformed into a potentially sinister analogue for Eve in *Paradise Lost*, so even Perdita, through her unwitting implication in filial disobedience, even in her innocent desire to be a 'queen', becomes a problematic figure in Paradise, though irreproachable in Bohemia.

But this change of resonance in the Proserpine/Perdita pairing is perhaps rather a contingent effect of recontextualisation than a challenge to Shakespeare, or Shakespeare's classicism, as such. A corrective or dialectical intention may be inferred or read into the poem, but is not clearly signalled – we have only to think of Milton's account of Mulciber's fall (1.740–7) or his description of the Hesperian apples (4.250–1) to be reminded that when Milton wants to be combative he often lets us know about it. Although we can never know precisely what Milton's 'intentions' were the *effect* of intentionality inevitably exerts pressure on our response to the poem. And here Shakespeare's classicism seems rather an incidental, intertextual reflex than a purposefully allusive presence. Indeed what seems to be Shakespeare's classicism is perhaps already Milton's classicism, for by the time he wrote *Paradise Lost* Milton had already conflated Proserpine with Perdita in 'On the Death of a Fair Infant Dying of a Cough'.[4]

The effect of allusion is far more pronounced in some later responses to Shakespeare's classicism which emphasise their own status as imitations, creating a recessive effect through a kind of meta-allusion. Here the fact or act of allusion is as important as its substance. For instance in *The Waste Land*, a poem composed of fragments and quotations, it is significant that one of the most striking Shakespearean borrowings, Enobarbus' speech from *Antony and Cleopatra*, is itself a near quotation from North's Plutarch. It is thus placed within double quotation marks, as it were, by Eliot, and this curious status is reflected in its immediate context in 'The Game of Chess'. Repetition seems to have attenuated its force; the central female image is occluded by paraphernalia; 'the Chair she sat in' is located 'on the marble, where the glass . . . doubled the flames of sevenbranched candelabra' (77–82)[5] – perhaps she is no more than a reflection, a possibility which is strengthened by the transformation of the pretty Cupid-like pages who flank Shakespeare's Cleopatra into two golden Cupidons who frame and support not the woman, but the glass. Even in North and Shakespeare Cleopatra is evoked primarily through her impact upon her surroundings. In *The Waste Land* she is still more elusive: her apparent artificiality is echoed in the poetry, while her borrowed scents and colours are matched by the borrowed fragments which construct her poetically.

This awareness of himself quoting Shakespeare quoting the classics emerges still more forcefully in Eliot's reference to Ovid's tale of Philomela, bracketed between allusions to two Shakespearean moments which reference the same myth. The first is the scene in *Cymbeline* where Iachimo spies on Imogen as she sleeps; the jewels, perfume, and moving candleflames which catch the voyeur's attention all echo faintly in 'A Game of Chess'.[6] Iachimo also notes that Imogen has been reading the *Metamorphoses*:

> Hath been reading late
> The tale of Tereus; here the leaf's turn'd down
> Where Philomele gave up.   (2.2.44–6)

This very obtrusive allusion – the text invoked actually appears on stage as a prop – is matched in *Titus Andronicus* when the heroine Lavinia uses a volume of Ovid's *Metamorphoses* to denounce her attackers. Her fate, more extreme than Philomela's since she loses her hands as well as her tongue, is recalled by Eliot's lines:

> Yet there the nightingale
> Filled all the desert with inviolable voice
> And still she cried, and still the world pursues,
> 'Jug Jug' to dirty ears.
> And other *withered stumps* of time
> Were told upon the walls . . .
>
> (*italics mine*, 99–104)

The present tense of 'and still the world pursues' evokes the stasis of pictorial representation but also the repetition of literary tropes in this mirrored gallery of female victims. By selecting two of Shakespeare's most potently allusive moments, recombining Philomela with her two Shakespearean descendants, Eliot suggests a Modernist Shakespeare, a collagist of flagged fragments, who helped prepare the way for *The Waste Land*'s own textual borrowings and juxtapositions. Shakespeare's classicism is reinvented as an Eliotic classicism.

But this use of Shakespeare's classicism to suggest the persistence of literary archetypes did not originate in the twentieth century. In Keats' *Endymion* too a similar trope of recession can be identified. Keats uses moments of interaction between Shakespeare and the classics, such as the relationship between Ovid and *The Tempest*, to figure the processes of imitation. The sea becomes a locus of literary memory:

> Wide sea, that one continuous murmur breeds
> Along the pebbled shore of memory!
> Many old rotten-timbered boats there be
> Upon thy vaporous bosom, magnified
> To goodly vessels . . .   (2.16–20)[7]

The 'pebbled shore' can be traced back to Shakespeare's Sonnet 60, itself a clear echo of *Metamorphoses* 15. Because the phrase encourages such literary excavations it is now an emblem of memory as well as time. The image is simultaneously an account of literary transmission and a practical demonstration of its processes.[8] Magnification, like reflection in *The Waste Land*, suggests the workings of literary tradition.

We are thus encouraged to interpret Endymion's later journey among such wrecks as a search for traces of a literary as well as a material culture (such an association between literal and metaphorical excavation is very apparent in the works of Renaissance writers such as Du Bellay):[9]

> Old rusted anchors, helmets, breast-plates large
> Of gone sea-warriors; brazen beaks and targe;
> Rudders that for a hundred years had lost
> The sway of human hand; gold vase embossed
> With long-forgotten story . . . mouldering scrolls
> Writ in the tongue of heaven by those souls
> Who first were on the earth; and sculptures rude
> In ponderous stone, developing the mood
> Of ancient Nox . . .   (3.123–33)

Like the 'pebbled shore' passage this is likely to weave together for the reader memories of both classical and English predecessors. Most specifically it recalls Clarence's striking dream from *Richard III* (1.4.9–33), itself an Ovidian reworking. It thus both describes and exemplifies the ways poets salvage the works of their predecessors – an effect which is underlined when Shakespearean classicism mutates into Miltonic classicism towards the end of the extract. As book 3 continues this link between Ovid and Shakespeare will be forged still more strongly; Keats welds together moments from the works of each poet, reifying combinations hitherto only implicit.

Endymion encounters an old man, dressed in a blue cloak which is 'o'erwrought with symbols by the deepest groans / Of ambitious magic' (3.198–9). He bears a 'pearly wand' and a book lies in his lap (3.213–14). This magician with his staff and book might most obviously recall Prospero, but turns out to be the Ovidian Glaucus. (Although there is no strong affinity between Prospero and Glaucus, the phase of the *Metamorphoses* in which the latter appears lent much to *The Tempest*'s atmosphere.)[10] Having conceptualised Glaucus and Prospero together, Keats draws attention to their kinship within a literary line of descent when he describes how Glaucus, Prospero-like, beholds a vessel in trouble:

> On a day
> Sitting upon a rock above the spray,
> I saw grow up from the horizon's brink
> A gallant vessel . . .
>
>   . . . therefore all the billows green
> Tossed up the silver spume against the clouds.
> The tempest came. I saw that vessel's shrouds
> In perilous bustle, while upon the deck
> Stood trembling creatures. I beheld the wreck;
> The final gulfing; the poor struggling souls.
>
>   (3.645–59)

From the wreck emerges one survivor, another old man, who clutches the same scroll and wand now in Glaucus' care, but is lost in the sea before he can be rescued. Glaucus' reading of the scroll is suggestive in its repetition, and in its implied identity with the poem we are reading:

> I read *these words*, and read again, and tried
> My eyes against the heavens, and read again.
>
>   (*italics mine*, 3.682–3)

In fact 'these words' turn out to refer to an inset quotation from the scroll rather than to *Endymion* itself – yet as the subject of these lines is Glaucus, the effect of circularity is compounded:

> *In the wide sea there lives a forlorn wretch,*
> *Doomed with enfeebled carcase to outstretch . . .*
>
>   (3.689–90)

But the 'forlorn wretch' cannot perhaps simply be identified as Glaucus; he is rather as a kind of eternal sea mage figure, in whom Prospero and Glaucus are merged, together with nameless others.[11] It is significant that Glaucus' encounter with his literary double is a moment of pressure and anxiety. He, like Keats himself, seems to be 'wrestling with the dead':[12]

> I knelt with pain – reached out my hand – had grasped
> These treasures – touched the knuckles – they unclasped –
> I caught a finger. But the downward weight
> O'erpowered me – it sank.   (3.671–4)

Earlier in the poem Keats suggested his own anxiety of influence when he blamed the times for the difficulty he experienced in rendering the love of Endymion for Phoebe in poetry:

> Our dazèd eyes
> Have seen a new tinge in the western skies.
> The world has done its duty. Yet, oh yet,
> Although the sun of poesy is set,
> These lovers did embrace . . .   (2.726–30)

Apparently barred from fresh inspiration, Keats tropes his own reliance on his predecessors, signalling his own poem's absorption in old tales through the fable of Glaucus.

The note of desperation in Keats' description of the attempted rescue suggests that the speaker was himself in peril of drowning and was 'o'erpowered' before sinking. And in a sense the drowning man was only another version of Glaucus himself. The scroll imposes a burden on him:

> *He must pursue this task of joy and grief*
> *Most piously: all lovers tempest-tossed,*
> *And in the savage overwhelming lost,*
> *He shall deposit side by side . . .*
>
>   (3.702–5)

Thus numberless lovers are now in his care, held in suspended animation:

> Turn to some level plain where haughty Mars
> Has legioned all his battle . . .
>
>   Imagine further, line by line,
> These warrior thousands on the field supine –
> So in that crystal place, in silent rows,
> Poor lovers lay at rest from joys and woes.   (3.728–36)

Keats' vision of endless self-replicating crystalline suspension is the stuff of science fiction – a genre in which *The Tempest* has of course played its part – and the lovers can be woken only by the tearing of the scroll, the breaking of the continuous loop in which 'Prospero/Glaucus' is trapped. The presence of a literary line of lovers, culminating in Endymion himself, mirrors the poem's accumulation of textual traces, a hall of mirrors stretching back into tropic antiquity. The particular links Keats here effects between Shakespeare and the classics reflect his own perception of poetry's developments and his place within these. He describes this awareness of his own poetic lineage in an early sonnet:

> How many bards gild the lapses of time!
> A few of them have ever been the food
> Of my delighted fancy – I could brood

> Over their beauties, earthly, or sublime;
> And often, when I sit me down to rhyme,
> These will in throngs before my mind obtrude . . .[13]

Endymion's vision of lovers multiplied in a literary hall of mirrors suggests the power of certain romantic archetypes. Star-crossed lovers are packed as tightly as Glaucus' tempest-tossed collection in the intertextual continuum. The highly self-conscious Thisbe of David Slavitt's 1994 translation certainly seems aware of pressures which postdate Ovid, most notably *Romeo and Juliet*:

> And she is at once transformed
> Into the noble heroine of the story she is composing,
> Seeing how it has to go for symmetrical reasons . . .
> . . .   Their parents, life, and the world itself
> she would dismiss in a single painful action and triumph –
> at least in the beautiful story she reads in her mind's text.[14]

Here we see how Shakespeare has influenced our reception of the classics. It is as though he is so central to our culture that we find it difficult to conceive of a world whose (moderately well-educated) inhabitants would not spot any obvious similarities between their own lives and Shakespeare's plays. Similarly, though more briefly, does Ted Hughes' Thisbe inscribe her fate within a larger, post-classical, literary landscape. She and Pyramus arrange to meet:

> Their rendezvous the mulberry tree
> Over the tomb of Ninus, a famous landmark.[15]

The last phrase is an addition; we may infer that the 'landmark' is a literary as well as a geographical *topos*, made famous originally by Ovid, and then still more memorably by Shakespeare in *A Midsummer Night's Dream*. These later Thisbes contradict Barthes' account of the lover: 'But he who utters this discourse and shapes its episodes does not know that a book is to be made of them; he does not yet know that as a good cultural subject he should neither repeat nor contradict himself.'[16]

However the relationship between Shakespeare and the classics in later literature goes beyond Shakespeare's own proven borrowings and influences. The modern reception of classical texts is often mediated through Shakespeare, creating relationships between his plays and works which he might not even have read. When, in his free version of the *Tristia*, David Slavitt makes the exiled Ovid speak of his metamorphosis:

> I change
> Into something poor and strange
> (1.7)[17]

the reader is encouraged to embark on an investigation of the suggestive
connections between Ovid, exiled in a surreally hostile environment where
the Getae cannot speak his language, and the equally forlorn Prospero.
Both Ovid's exile poetry and Shakespeare's *The Tempest* are 'last' works; the
gulf between the status of *The Tempest* as one of Shakespeare's greatest plays
and the common characterisation of the exile poetry as the work of a poet
in decline is figured in the metamorphosis from 'rich' to 'poor' in Slavitt.

A more complex Shakespearean moment is discovered in Slavitt's translation of Seneca's *The Phoenician Women*. Here we see how Shakespeare's
works, like the most celebrated classical texts, have the capacity to generate characters who are *loci classici* of their types. Sometimes he himself
drew attention to his characters' archetypicality – by linking Lavinia with
Philomela, for example. Sometimes the connections between classical and
Shakespearean archetypes must be revealed if not created by later writers,
including Slavitt. In *The Phoenician Women* the blinded, unthroned king,
supported by his daughter, is perched on the rugged cliffs of Cithaeron:

> O great of soul, I beg you, father, consider!
> Listen to me, your wretched loving daughter.
> Those thunderstorms of the passions are all behind you,
> As distant as the grandeur of your throne.
> We look down as a pair of soaring birds
> On tiny creatures we know to be men and women,
> Animated by joys and sorrows we scarcely
> Credit now . . .   (181–7)[18]

The interpolated lines (184–6) confirm the play's Shakespearean resonances.
In Antigone's words to Oedipus we can trace both the reunion of Lear and
Cordelia and the vertiginous encounter between the blinded Gloucester
and his son Edgar in disguise.

> We too alone will sing like birds i'th' cage . . .
> (5.3.9)

> Half way down
> Hangs one that gathers samphire, dreadful trade!
> Methinks he seems no bigger than his head.
> (4.6.14–16)

The figure of Seneca, introduced into the play by Slavitt, comments on the
drama's inevitability:

These characters . . . just stand there and endure, acting out the same tawdry and stupid plot with no possible evasion or escape. Nothing they do can lessen the disasters that await them with each new performance of each new version.[19]

Of course as a character himself, Seneca is implicated in this criticism. Authors re-enact the same stories just as actors play out the same scenes time after time. The character goes on to confirm this identification:

We are all in this together, audience, playwright . . . even the actors. The story is old, is there, like a mountain, and each new ascent is a new one with its own risks and its own rewards.[20]

From the perspective of this fictional Seneca the audience can only plot his Oedipus against other versions of the story, but the translation's modern readers are likely to encounter the play after *King Lear* and, in collaboration with Slavitt, reinvent *The Phoenician Women* as one of Lear's precursors. David Hopkins describes how, for the eighteenth-century reader, Shakespeare's status as a 'classic' was commensurate with Homer's standing as a similarly sublime if defective genius. By the twentieth century, Shakespeare had superseded Homer as a classic, becoming, for the Western world, originary.

Thus even classical translations which do not share Slavitt's fondness for quirky interpolations can have a Shakespearean resonance. Take the following passage:

And do thou, O Sleep, vanquisher of woes, rest of the soul, the better part of human life, thou winged son of thy mother Astrea, sluggish brother of cruel Death, thou who dost mingle false with true, sure yet gloomy guide to what shall be . . .[21]

Most readers, tolerably versed in Shakespeare, would be reminded by this Senecan passage of Macbeth's famous speech. This is in fact a fairly neutral translation – the choice of 'sluggish' to translate *languide* even detracts from its potential to invoke *Macbeth*. (In the discussion of the passage in Charles and Michelle Martindale's *Shakespeare and the Uses of Antiquity* the more 'Shakespearean' 'soothing' is provided).[22] But almost any translation of the passage would, simply through the act of translation, by the creation of a portrait of Sleep as a refuge from cares through the build up of possessive clauses, inevitably suggest *Macbeth*. Thus even without the translator's or editor's intervention certain passages from classical texts will have been virtually highlighted, as it were, and we read almost with the sense that the text in front of us is one of Shakespeare's progeny, not one of his precursors. In *Allusion and Intertext* Stephen Hinds considers what the effect would have been had Ovid not simply included a 'Little *Aeneid*' in the

Metamorphoses, but had in fact quoted Virgil's entire poem. He notes several ways – the problematisation of Augustan teleology for example – in which Ovid would have transformed even a repetition of Virgil.[23] Because *Macbeth* is so familiar, no such direct textual juxtaposition is necessary for Seneca to be similarly transformed by association with Shakespeare. As for Pierre Menard's *Don Quixote*, repetition inevitably involves recontextualisation and thus reconstruction.[24] Truly, as T. S. Eliot asserted, the past has been altered by the present.[25]

The process whereby new connections are established between Shakespearean and classical archetypes can be seen particularly clearly in C. S. Lewis' *Till We Have Faces*, a novel based on the myth of Cupid and Psyche, retold by Apuleius in *The Golden Ass*. Here the main focus is not on the beautiful Psyche but on her ugly elder sister Orual. Much of the detail which Lewis adds to the story can be traced back to *King Lear*. The melancholy but humorous slave, Fox, fulfils a function similar to that of Lear's fool. The character of Psyche's father, irascible and finally mad, echoes Lear himself. Orual's pessimistic, melancholy view of the world seems inspired by the words of Gloucester:

> As flies to wanton boys are we to th' gods,
> They kill us for their sport.   (4.1.36–7)

The gods never send us this invitation to delight so readily or so strongly as when they are preparing some new agony. We are their bubbles; they blow us big before they prick us.[26]

Orual continues with another simile, reminding us that however powerful the impulse binding Shakespeare together with certain classical texts, Shakespeare is conflated with no author so readily as himself:

But I held my own without that knowledge. I ruled myself. Did they think I was nothing but a pipe to be played on as their moment's fancy chose?[27]

You would play upon me, you would seem to know my stops . . . 'Sblood, do you think I am easier to be play'd on than a pipe? (*Hamlet* 3.2.364–370)

Further curious little echoes of *King Lear* are thrown up by the text. Orual as Queen challenges the less worthy of two rival brothers to a duel and is threatened with hanging if he conquer her. In *Lear* this is the fate the worse of two brothers succeeds in imposing upon Cordelia. Orual's punishment for pressurising Psyche to look on her husband was that she should 'become' Psyche, and this echo/anticipation of Cordelia is part of that process.

Apuleius is not generally perceived as an important influence on *King Lear*,[28] although *The Golden Ass* would seem to lie behind Bottom's metamorphosis in *A Midsummer Night's Dream*. But Lewis may not have felt that the connection wrought between Lear and Apuleius in *Till We Have Faces* was of his own forging:

And will the gods one day grow thus beautiful, Grandfather?

They say . . . but even I, who am dead, do not understand more than a few broken words of their language. Only this I know. This age of ours will one day be the distant past. And the Divine Nature can change the past. Nothing is yet in its true form.[29]

We may be reminded of Eliot's claim that the introduction of an important and new work of art exerts a retrospective influence, ensuring that 'the relations, proportions, values of each work of art towards the whole are readjusted'.[30]

If we compare Lewis' text with a modern response to *Lear*, Jane Smiley's *1000 Acres*, another characteristic of the Shakespeare/classicism interface is revealed. Although there is no reason to think that Smiley was influenced by Lewis, there are strong similarities between the two retellings, the most obvious being that both are narrated by an 'ugly sister', Orual in Lewis, Ginny/Goneril in Smiley, who is presented in a positive light. This example suggests how Shakespearean texts and cognate classical works tend to grow closer together quite independently, for both are likely to be appropriated and reinvented in similar ways in accordance with the spirit of each age. In other words, the inherent affinities between *Lear* and Apuleius have been enhanced both by the impact of the later, stronger text on the earlier text's reception and through the parallel developments which characterise each work's twentieth-century afterlife.[31]

There are clear affinities between *Lear* and *Cupid and Psyche*, making their cross-contamination in *Till We Have Faces* probable, but relationships can be forged between Shakespeare and more incongruous classical texts. Eliot chose an epigraph from Seneca's *Hercules Furens* for 'Marina', creating a poignant contrast between the situations of a father reunited with a lost daughter and a very different father who was goaded by madness to slaughter his entire family:

> *Quis hic locus, quae*
> *Regio, quae mundi plaga?*[32]

In a letter he wrote in 1930 Eliot explained: 'I intend a crisscross between Pericles, finding alive, and Hercules finding dead – the two extremes of the recognition scene – but I thought that if I labelled the quotation it might lead readers astray rather than direct them.'[33] This unexpected 'crisscross' between the two texts invites the reader to search for relationships between them, perhaps by recalling the shade of incest in *Pericles* which has as destructive and impious an effect on families as murder. The recognition scene in *Pericles* itself is in fact already doubled in this way. For the terms on which the father recognises his daughter take the audience back to another moment of recognition: Pericles' decoding of the riddle set by Antiochus in the play's first act and his discovery of the incestuous father/daughter liaison it conceals. The effect is thus described by Terence Cave: 'The paradoxical metonym with which Pericles addresses Marina at the climax ('O come hither, / Thou that begett'st him that did thee beget') recalls the reversals of the order of generation in the opening incest riddle.'[34] Similarly the shock of recognition felt by Eliot's narrator is matched by the poem's readers, for the grid of sameness and difference which we trace between parents and children is matched by the operations of *différance* in literary relations:

> What is this face, less clear and clearer
> The pulse in the arm, less strong and stronger –
> Given or lent?[35]

The uncertainty of the narrator's vision, the apparent move in and out of focus as though between competing possibilities, matches the reader's uncertainties, forced to negotiate the competing messages of the poem's opposing intertexts. We might say that the Shakespearean Marina, whose parents appear to have been separated by death, resembles Eliot's 'Marina', the child of two influences (Seneca and Shakespeare) apparently quite separate yet ultimately capable of a strange reconciliation – 'more distant than stars and nearer than the eye'.[36] And yet another shock of recognition may come into play for the reader – the recognition of a link between Eliot's use of the classics and Shakespeare's. As a near-translation of a well-known passage from the *Metamorphoses*, Prospero's 'Ye Elves' is almost as paratextual, as it were, as Eliot's Senecan epigraph, and similarly seems – for today's readers if not necessarily for Shakespeare and his audience – to require explanation if not apology. Although Eliot's choice of epigraph is striking, it is no more dissonant than the apparently benevolent Prospero's echo of a far more culpable childkiller, Medea. Here, as in 'Marina', a murderous parent is aligned with a loving parent, but one whose love has been perceived as potentially incestuous.

Recalling the literary wrecks littering *Endymion* it is tempting to interpret the ship described in 'Marina' as similarly intertextual:

> Bowsprit cracked with ice and paint cracked with heat.
> I made this, I have forgotten
> And remember.
> The rigging weak and the canvas rotten
> Between one June and another September.
> Made this unknowing, half conscious, unknown, my own
> The garboard strake leaks, the seams need caulking.[37]

Its subjection to extremes of heat and cold parallels the contrast provided by the poem's principal intertexts, and its leaky, uncaulked sides might figure literary *débordement*, the textual vessel's antipathy for enclosure and containment. But the qualities which would betoken unseaworthiness in a real ship ensure long life in the world of texts; the vessel of Shakespeare's classicism remains buoyant because of its unceasing capacity to absorb fresh material from that 'Wide sea, that one continuous murmur breeds / Along the pebbled shore of memory.' And its voyage is not over yet.

NOTES

1. *The Riverside Shakespeare* (Boston and New York 1997). All subsequent references are to this edition.
2. The connection is discussed by Julia Briggs in 'Tears at the Wedding', in *Shakespeare's Late Plays: New Readings,* ed. Jennifer Richards and James Knowles (Edinburgh 1999), pp. 210–27; James R. Andreas, 'Remythologising The Knight's Tale: *A Midsummer Night's Dream* and *The Two Noble Kinsmen*', *Shakespeare Yearbook* 2 (1991), 49–66; Glynne Wickham, '*The Two Noble Kinsmen* or *A Midsummer Night's Dream Part II?*', *Elizabethan Theatre* 19.7 (1980), 167–96.
3. *Paradise Lost*, ed. Alistair Fowler (London 1971). All subsequent references are to this edition.
4. Ll. 1–10, in John Milton, *Complete Shorter Poems* (London 1971).
5. T. S. Eliot, *Collected Poems 1909–1962* (London 1963). All subsequent references are to this edition.
6. Compare *The Waste Land* 82–91 with *Cymbeline* 2.2.11–24. The connection is mentioned briefly by Stephen Medcalf, 'Ovid and *The Waste Land*', in *Ovid Renewed*, ed. Charles Martindale (Cambridge 1988), pp. 233–46, p. 241.
7. Keats, *The Complete Works*, ed. Miriam Allott (London 1970). All subsequent references are to this edition.
8. This borrowing from Ovid is discussed by Gordon Braden in 'Ovid, Petrarch, and Shakespeare's *Sonnets*', in A. B. Taylor, ed., *Shakespeare's Ovid: The Metamorphoses in the Plays and Poems* (Cambridge 2000), pp. 96–112.
9. See for example Thomas Greene, *The Light in Troy: Imitation and Discovery in Renaissance Poetry* (New Haven and London 1982).

10. Ovid's influence on *The Tempest* is discussed by Jonathan Bate in *Shakespeare and Ovid* (Oxford 1993), pp. 247–9. The importance of *The Tempest* for Keats is discussed by R. S. White in *Keats as a Reader of Shakespeare* (London 1987), pp. 88–103.

11. Karen Swann suggests that he encompasses 'Wordsworth's Leech-Gatherer, Coleridge's Ancient Mariner, Milton's Lycidas, and Spenser's Archimago' ('*Endymion*'s Beautiful Dreamers', in *The Cambridge Companion to Keats* (Cambridge 2001), pp. 20–36, p. 26).

12. Harold Bloom, *The Anxiety of Influence: A Theory of Poetry* (2nd edn, Oxford 1997), p. 80.

13. Keats, *The Complete Works*, p. 59.

14. David R. Slavitt, *The Metamorphoses of Ovid* (Baltimore and London 1994), p. 68.

15. Ted Hughes, *Tales from Ovid* (London 1997), p. 248.

16. Roland Barthes, *A Lover's Discourse: Fragments*, trans. Richard Howard (London 1990), p. 4.

17. David R. Slavitt, *Ovid's Poetry of Exile* (Baltimore and London 1990).

18. Seneca, *The Tragedies*, ed. David R. Slavitt, vol. II (Baltimore and London 1995).

19. Ibid., p. 249.

20. Ibid., p. 249.

21. Seneca, *Hercules Furens*, in *Tragedies*, vol. I, trans. Frank Justus Miller (London 1968), p. 95.

22. Charles and Michelle Martindale, *Shakespeare and the Uses of Antiquity* (London 1990), p. 16.

23. Stephen Hinds, *Allusion and Intertext: Dynamics of Appropriation in Roman Poetry* (Cambridge 1998), pp. 120–2.

24. 'Pierre Menard, Translator of the "Quixote"', in Jorge Luis Borges, *Labyrinths* (Harmondsworth 1970).

25. 'Tradition and the Individual Talent', in T. S. Eliot, *Selected Essays* (London 1932), pp. 13–22, p. 15.

26. C. S. Lewis, *Till We Have Faces* (London 1978), p. 105.

27. Ibid., p. 105.

28. The connections are discussed by J. J. M. Tobin in *Shakespeare's Favourite Novel: A Study of The Golden Asse as Prime Source* (Lanham 1984), pp. 117–21.

29. Lewis, *Till We Have Faces*, p. 316.

30. Eliot, *Selected Essays*, p. 15.

31. Admittedly some of the 'similarities' between Lewis and Smiley may be more apparent than real; although both writers explore the perspective of a marginalised literary character, their motives for doing so are far from identical. In his science-fictional retelling of *Paradise Lost* C. S. Lewis pours scorn on the feminist tendency to champion witches. The evil Weston tempts the second Eve with stories of female empowerment: 'Each had been misunderstood, reviled, and persecuted: but each also magnificently vindicated by the event . . . Ransom had more than a suspicion that many of these noble pioneers

had been what in ordinary terrestrial speech we call witches or perverts' (*The Cosmic Trilogy* (London 1990), p. 257).

32. The epigraph is discussed briefly by E. M. Knottenbelt in '"And to make an end is to make a beginning": A Reading of "Marina"' in *Centennial Hauntings: Pope, Byron, and Eliot*, ed. C. C. Barfoot and Theo D'Haen (Amsterdam 1988), pp. 311–21.

33. Quoted in B. C. Southam, *A Student's Guide to the Selected Poems of T. S. Eliot* (London 1968), p. 146.

34. Terence Cave, *Recognitions: A Study in Poetics* (Oxford 1990), p. 289.

35. Eliot, *Collected Poems*, p. 115. Allusion troped by recognition is discussed by Hinds, *Allusion and Intertext*, pp. 5–16.

36. Eliot, *Collected Poems*, p. 115.

37. Ibid., p. 116.

Select bibliography

compiled by Joanna Paul

There is a vast amount of scholarship on Shakespeare and the classics. This bibliography is necessarily extremely selective, and aims to provide a survey of some of the most important and useful English-language works, particularly those published more recently (for fuller reports see the items in Section 1). The opening sections consist of a range of works on Shakespeare's general approach to antiquity, and, in particular, his use of ancient Rome. The following sections then narrow their focus to individual ancient authors and their importance for Shakespeare, and, finally, to individual Shakespearean works. The overlap between these areas means that some items are duplicated, for ease of reference. On occasion, cross-references are also signalled at the end of the section (for example, for more items on *The Winter's Tale*, see under Ovid).

1. REFERENCE

Bullough, Geoffrey, *Narrative and Dramatic Sources of Shakespeare*, 8 vols. (London 1957–75)

Gillespie, Stuart, *Shakespeare's Books: A Dictionary of Shakespeare Sources* (London 2001)

Velz, John W., *Shakespeare and the Classical Tradition: A Critical Guide to Commentary, 1660–1960* (Minneapolis 1968)

Walker, Lewis, *Shakespeare and the Classical Tradition: An Annotated Bibliography, 1961–1991* (New York and London 2002)

World Shakespeare Bibliography online – www.worldshakesbib.org

2. GENERAL

Altman, Joel B., *The Tudor Play of Mind: Rhetorical Inquiry and the Development of Elizabethan Drama* (Berkeley and London 1978)

Baldwin, T. W., *William Shakspere's Small Latine and Lesse Greeke*, 2 vols. (Urbana 1944)

Boyce, Benjamin, 'The Stoic *Consolatio* and Shakespeare', *PMLA* 64 (1949), 771–80

Brower, Reuben A., *Hero and Saint: Shakespeare and the Graeco-Roman Tradition* (New York 1971)

Bush, Douglas, *Mythology and the Renaissance Tradition in English Poetry* (New York 1963, rev. edn)

Faas, Ekbert, *Shakespeare's Poetics* (Cambridge 1986)

Girard, René, 'Shakespeare's Theory of Mythology', in *Classical Mythology in Twentieth-Century Thought and Literature* (Comparative Literature Proceedings 11), ed. Wendell M. Aycock and Theodore M. Klein (Lubbock, Texas 1980), 107–24

Grafton, Anthony and Jardine, Lisa, *From Humanism to the Humanities* (London 1986)

Jones, Emrys, *The Origins of Shakespeare* (Oxford 1977)

Leech, Clifford, 'Shakespeare's Greeks', in *Stratford Papers on Shakespeare 1963*, ed. B. W. Jackson (Toronto 1964), 1–20

Martindale, Charles and Martindale, Michelle, *Shakespeare and the Uses of Antiquity: An Introductory Essay* (London and New York 1990)

Miola, Robert, *Shakespeare's Reading* (Oxford and New York 2000)

"'An alien people clutching their gods?" Shakespeare's Ancient Religions', *ShS* 54 (2001), 31–45

Muir, Kenneth, *The Sources of Shakespeare's Plays* (London 1977)

Nosworthy, J. M., 'Shakespeare's Pastoral Metamorphoses', in *The Elizabethan Theatre VIII*, ed. George R. Hibberd (Port Credit 1982)

Peyré, Yves, 'Iris's "rich scarf" and "Ariachne's broken woof" – Shakespeare's Mythology in the Twentieth Century', in *Shakespeare and the Twentieth Century (The Selected Proceedings of the International Shakespeare Association World Congress, Los Angeles 1996)*, ed. Jonathan Bate (Newark and London 1998), 280–93

Root, Robert Kilburn, *Classical Mythology in Shakespeare (Yale Studies in English 19)* (New York 1965, first published 1903)

Sowerby, Robin, *The Classical Legacy in Renaissance Poetry* (London 1994)

Thomson, J. A. K., *Shakespeare and the Classics* (New York 1952)

Tiffany, Grace, 'Shakespeare's Dionysian Prince: Drama, Politics, and the 'Athenian' History Play', *RQ* 52 (1999), 366–81

Velz, John W., 'Some Modern Views of Shakespeare's Classicism: A Bibliographical Sketch', *Anglia* 81 (1963), 412–28

'The Ancient World in Shakespeare: Authenticity or Anachronism? A Retrospect', *ShS* 31 (1978), 1–12

White, Howard B., *Copp'd Hills Towards Heaven: Shakespeare and the Classical Polity (International Archives of the History of Ideas 32)* (The Hague 1970)

3. SHAKESPEARE AND ROME

Cantor, Paul A., *Shakespeare's Rome: Republic and Empire* (Ithaca 1976)

Crowl, Samuel, 'A World Elsewhere: The Roman Plays on Film and Television', in *Shakespeare and the Moving Image: The Plays on Film and Television*, ed. Anthony Davies and Stanley Wells (Cambridge 1994)

Holderness, Graham, Loughrey, Bryan, and Murphy, Andrew, eds., *Shakespeare: The Roman Plays* (London and New York 1996)

Hughes, Geoffrey, '"A World Elsewhere": Romanitas and its Limitations in Shakespeare', *English Studies in Africa* 28 (1985), 1–19

Hunter, G. K., 'A Roman Thought: Attitudes to History Exemplified in Shakespeare and Jonson', in *An English Miscellany Presented to W. S. Mackie*, ed. Brian S. Lee (Cape Town 1977), 93–115

Kahn, Coppélia, *Roman Shakespeare: Warriors, Wounds and Women* (London 1997)

Kayser, John R. and Lettieri, Ronald J., '"The Last of All the Romans": Shakespeare's Commentary on Classical Republicanism', *Clio* 9 (1979–80), 197–227

MacCallum, M. W., *Shakespeare's Roman Plays and their Background* (London 1910, 1967)

Marshall, Cynthia, 'Shakespeare, Crossing the Rubicon', *ShS* 53 (2000), 73–88

Miles, Gary B., 'How Roman are Shakespeare's Romans?', *ShQ* 40 (1989), 257–83

Miles, Geoffrey, *Shakespeare and the Constant Romans* (Oxford 1996)

Miola, Robert S., *Shakespeare's Rome* (Cambridge 1983)

Nuttall, A. D., *A New Mimesis: Shakespeare and the Representation of Reality* (London and New York 1983) (Chapter 3 on *Julius Caesar* and *Coriolanus*)

Ronan, Clifford, *'Antike Roman': Power Symbology and the Roman Play in Early Modern England, 1585–1635* (Athens, Georgia 1995)

Simmons, J. L., *Shakespeare's Pagan World: The Roman Tragedies* (Charlottesville, VA 1973)

Spencer, T. J. B., *Shakespeare: The Roman Plays* (London 1963)

Wells, Charles, *The Wide Arch: Roman Values in Shakespeare* (New York 1993)

4. INDIVIDUAL ANCIENT POETS

APULEIUS

Holloway, Julia Bolton, 'Apuleius and *A Midsummer Night's Dream*: Bottom's Metamorphoses', in *Tales Within Tales: Apuleius Through Time*, ed. Constance S. Wright and Julia Bolton Holloway (New York 2000), 123–37

McPeek, James A. S., 'The Psyche Myth and *A Midsummer Night's Dream*', *ShQ* 23 (1972), 69–79

Starnes, D. T., 'Shakespeare and Apuleius', *PMLA* 60 (1945), 1,021–50

Tobin, J. J. M., *Shakespeare's Favorite Novel: A Study of The Golden Ass as Prime Source* (Lanham, MD 1984)

ARISTOTLE AND PLATO

Elton, William R., 'Aristotle's *Nicomachean Ethics* and Shakespeare's *Troilus and Cressida*', *Journal of the History of Ideas* 58 (1997), 331–7

Everett, Barbara, 'Good and Bad Loves: Shakespeare, Plato, and the Plotting of the Sonnets', *TLS* (5 July 2002), 13–15

Medcalf, Stephen, 'Shakespeare on Beauty, Truth and Transcendence', in *Platonism and the English Imagination*, ed. Anna Baldwin and Sarah Hutton (Cambridge 1994), 117–25

Shorey, Paul, *Platonism and English Literature* (Berkeley 1938)
Soellner, Rolf, 'Shakespeare, Aristotle, Plato and the Soul', *Shakespeare-Jahrbuch (Bochum)* (1968), 56–71
Wheater, Isabella, 'Aristotelian Wealth and the Sea of Love: Shakespeare's Synthesis of Greek Philosophy and Roman Poetry in *The Merchant of Venice* (I-II)', *RES* 43 (1992), 467–87 and 44 (1993), 16–36

CICERO

Vawter, Marvin L., '"Division 'tween our souls": Shakespeare's Stoic Brutus', *ShSt* 7 (1974), 173–95
'"After their fashion": Cicero and Brutus in *Julius Caesar*', *ShSt* 9 (1976), 205–19

GREEK ROMANCE

Adams, Martha Latimer, 'The Greek Romance and William Shakespeare', *University of Mississippi Studies in English* 8 (1967), 43–52
Archibald, Elizabeth, *Apollonius of Tyre: Medieval and Renaissance Themes and Variations* (Woodbridge 1991)
Comito, Terry, 'Exile and Return in the Greek Romances', *Arion* 2 (1975), 59–80
Gesner, Carol, *Shakespeare and the Greek Romance: A Study of Origins* (Lexington 1970)

GREEK TRAGEDY

Arnold, Margaret J., '"Monsters in Love's Train": Euripides and Shakespeare's *Troilus and Cressida*', *Comparative Drama* 18 (1984), 38–53
Bryant, A. J. Jr., '*Julius Caesar* from a Euripidean Perspective', *Comparative Drama* 16 (1982), 97–111
Bushnell, R. W., 'Oracular Silence in *Oedipus the King* and *Macbeth*', *Classical and Modern Literature* 2 (1981/2), 195–204
Paolucci, Anne, '*Macbeth* and *Oedipus Rex*: A Study in Paradox', in *Shakespeare Encomium*, ed. Anne Paolucci (New York 1964), 44–70
Poole, Adrian, *Tragedy: Shakespeare and the Greek Example* (Oxford 1987)
Schleiner, Louise, 'Latinized Greek Drama in Shakespeare's Writing of *Hamlet*', *ShQ* 41 (1990), 29–48
Silk, Michael, ed., *Tragedy and the Tragic: Greek Theatre and Beyond* (Oxford 1998)
Stump, Donald V., 'Greek and Shakespearean Tragedy: Four Indirect Routes from Athens to London', in *Hamartia: The Concept of Error in the Western Tradition: Essays in Honor of John M. Crossett*, ed. Donald V. Stump *et al.* (New York 1983), 211–46
Wilson, Douglas B., 'Euripides' *Alcestis* and the Ending of Shakespeare's *The Winter's Tale*', *Iowa State Journal of Research* 58 (1984), 345–55

HORACE

Edden, Valerie, 'The Best of Lyrick Poets', in *Horace*, ed. C. D. N. Costa (London 1973), 135–60

Martindale, Charles, 'Horace, Ovid and Others', in *The Legacy of Rome: A New Appraisal*, ed. Richard Jenkyns (Oxford 1992), 177–213

Martindale, Charles and Hopkins, David, eds., *Horace Made New: Horatian Influences on British Writing from the Renaissance to the Twentieth Century* (Cambridge 1993)

Westbrook, Perry D., 'Horace's Influence on Shakespeare's *Antony and Cleopatra*', *PMLA* 62 (1947), 392–8

LIVY

Barton, Anne, 'Livy, Machiavelli, and Shakespeare's *Coriolanus*', *ShS* 38 (1985), 115–29

Donaldson, Ian, *The Rapes of Lucretia: A Myth and its Transformations* (Oxford 1982)

LUCAN

Blissett, William, 'Lucan's Caesar and the Elizabethan Villain', *SP* 53 (1956), 553–75

Logan, George M., 'Lucan-Daniel-Shakespeare: New Light on the Relation between *The Civil Wars* and *Richard II*', *ShSt* 9 (1976), 121–40

Ronan, Clifford J., 'Lucan and the Self-Incised Voids of *Julius Caesar*', *Comparative Drama* 22 (1988), 215–26

'Lucanic Omens in *Julius Caesar*', *Comparative Drama* 22 (1988), 138–44

LUCIAN

Kott, Jan, 'Lucian in *Cymbeline*', *MLR* 67 (1972), 742–4

Robinson, Christopher, *Lucian and his Influence in Europe* (London 1979)

OVID

Armitage, David, 'The Dismemberment of Orpheus: Mythic Elements in Shakespeare's Romances', *ShS* 30 (1987), 123–33

Barkan, Leonard, '"Living Sculptures": Ovid, Michelangelo, and *The Winter's Tale*', *Journal of English Literary History* 48 (1981), 639–67

The Gods Made Flesh: Metamorphosis and the Pursuit of Paganism (New Haven and London 1986) (Chapter 6 – 'Shakespeare and the Metamorphoses of Art and Life', 243–88)

Barnett, Louise, 'Ovid and *The Taming of the Shrew*', *Ball State University Forum* 20.3 (1979), 16–22

Bate, Jonathan, 'Ovid and the Sonnets; or, Did Shakespeare Feel the Anxiety of Influence?', *ShS* 42 (1990), 65–76

Shakespeare and Ovid (Oxford 1993)

Brown, Sarah Annes, 'Ovid, Golding and *The Tempest*', *Translation and Literature* 3 (1994), 3–29.

The Metamorphosis of Ovid: From Chaucer to Ted Hughes (London 1999)

Carroll, William, *The Metamorphoses of Shakespearean Comedy* (Princeton 1985)

Dean, Paul, '*Antony and Cleopatra*: An Ovidian Tragedy?', *Cahiers Elisabéthains* 40 (1991), 73–7

Dundas, Judith, 'Ovidian Shakespeare: Wit and the Iconography of the Passions', *Illinois Classical Studies* 12 (1987), 121–33

Enterline, Lynn, *The Rhetoric of the Body from Shakespeare to Ovid* (Cambridge 2000)

Forey, Madelaine, '"Bless thee, Bottom, bless thee! Thou art translated!": Ovid, Golding and *A Midsummer Night's Dream*', *MLR* 93 (1998), 321–9

Keach, William, *Elizabethan Erotic Narrative: Irony and Pathos in the Ovidian Poetry of Shakespeare, Marlowe, and their Contemporaries* (London 1977)

Lamb, M. E., 'Ovid's *Metamorphoses* and Shakespeare's *Twelfth Night*', in *Shakespearean Comedy*, ed. Maurice Charney (New York 1980), 63–77

'Ovid and *The Winter's Tale*: Conflicting Views Toward Art', in *Shakespeare and the Dramatic Tradition: Essays in Honor of S. F. Johnson*, ed. W. R. Elton and W. B. Long (Newark 1989), 69–87

Martindale, Charles, ed., *Ovid Renewed: Ovidian Influences on Literature and Art from the Middle Ages to the Twentieth Century* (Cambridge 1988)

Mueller, Martin, 'Hermione's Wrinkles, or, Ovid Transformed: An Essay on *The Winter's Tale*', *Comparative Drama* 5 (1971), 226–39

Nosworthy, J. M., 'Shakespeare's Pastoral *Metamorphoses*', in *The Elizabethan Theatre VIII*, ed. G. R. Hibbard (Port Credit, Ontario 1982), 90–113

Phillippy, Patricia B., '"Loytering in Love": Ovid's *Heroides*, Hospitality, and Humanist Education in *The Taming of the Shrew*', *Criticism* 40 (1998), 27–53

Rudd, Niall, 'Pyramus and Thisbe in Shakespeare and Ovid', in *Creative Imitation and Latin Literature*, ed. D. West and T. Woodman (Cambridge 1976), 173–93

Stapleton, M. L., *Harmful Eloquence: Ovid's Amores from Antiquity to Shakespeare* (Ann Arbor 1996)

'Venus as Praeceptor: The *Ars Amatoria* in *Venus and Adonis*', in Philip Kolin, ed., *Venus and Adonis: Critical Essays* (New York and London 1997), 309–21

Staton, W. F. Jr., 'Ovidian Elements in *A Midsummer Night's Dream*', *HLQ* 26 (1962–3), 165–78

Taylor, A. B., ed., *Shakespeare's Ovid: The Metamorphoses in the Plays and Poems* (Cambridge 2000)

Truax, Elizabeth, *Metamorphosis in Shakespeare's Plays: A Pageant of Heroes, Gods, Maids, and Monsters* (Lewiston 1992)

Velz, John W., 'The Ovidian Soliloquy in Shakespeare', *ShSt* 18 (1986), 1–24

Wilkinson, L. P., *Ovid Recalled* (Cambridge 1955)

Willmott, Richard, 'Helen's Crime or Golden Love? A Study of the Influence of Ovid's *Amores* on the Plays of Marlowe and Shakespeare', *Shakespeare Yearbook* 9 (1999), 282–305

PLAUTUS AND TERENCE

Arthos, John, 'Shakespeare's Transformation of Plautus', *Comparative Drama* 1 (1967–8), 239–53

Beck, Ervin, 'Terence Improved: The Paradigm of the Prodigal Son in English Renaissance Comedy', *Renaissance Drama* 6 (1973), 107–22

Bruster, Douglas, 'Comedy and Control: Shakespeare and the Plautine Poeta', *Comparative Drama* 24 (1990), 217–31

Coulter, Cornelia C., 'The Plautine Tradition in Shakespeare', *JEGP* 19 (1920), 66–83

Gill, E. M., 'A Comparison of the Characters in *The Comedy of Errors* with Those in the *Menaechmi*', *University of Texas Studies in English* 5 (1925), 79–95
   'The Plot Structure of *The Comedy of Errors* in Relation to its Sources', *University of Texas Studies in English* 10 (1930), 13–65

Harrold, William E., 'Shakespeare's Use of *Mostellaria* in *The Taming of the Shrew*', *Deutsche Shakespeare-Gesellschaft West* (1970), 188–94

Hosley, R., 'The Formal Influence of Plautus and Terence', in *Elizabethan Theatre (Stratford-upon-Avon Studies 9)*, ed. John Russell Brown and Bernard Harris (London 1966), 131–45

Knox, Bernard, '*The Tempest* and the Ancient Comic Tradition', in *English Stage Comedy (English Institute Essays)*, ed. W. K. Wimsatt (New York 1955)

Louden, Bruce, '*The Tempest*, Plautus, and the *Rudens*', *Comparative Drama* 33 (1999–2000), 199–23

Miola, Robert S., *Shakespeare and Classical Comedy: The Influence of Plautus and Terence* (Oxford 1994).
   'New Comedy in *King Lear*', *PQ* 73 (1994), 329–46
   'The Influence of New Comedy on *The Comedy of Errors* and *The Taming of the Shrew*', in *Shakespeare's Sweet Thunder: Essays on the Early Comedies*, ed. Michael J. Collins (Newark 1997), 21–34

Riehle, W., *Shakespeare, Plautus, and the Humanist Tradition* (Cambridge 1990)

Rudd, Niall, *The Classical Tradition in Operation* (Toronto 1994)

Salingar, Leo, *Shakespeare and the Traditions of Comedy* (Cambridge 1974)

Svendsen, James, 'The Fusion of Comedy and Romance: Plautus' *Rudens* and Shakespeare's *The Tempest*', in *From Pen to Performance: Drama as Conceived and Performed III*, ed. Karelisa V. Hartigan (New York 1983), 121–35

PLINY THE ELDER

Baldwin, T. W., 'A Note Upon William Shakspeare's Use of Pliny', in *Essays in Dramatic Literature: The Parrott Presentation Volume*, ed. Hardin Craig (New York 1967), 157–82

Simmons, J. L., 'Holland's Pliny and *Troilus and Cressida*', *ShQ* 27 (1976), 329–32
Truchet, Sybil, 'The Art of Antiquity in Works by Lyly and Shakespeare', *Cahiers Elisabéthains* 24 (1983), 17–26

PLUTARCH

Cook, Albert, 'The Transmutation of Heroic Complexity: Plutarch and Shakespeare', *Classical and Modern Literature* 17 (1996–7), 31–43
Dillon, Janette, '"Solitariness": Shakespeare and Plutarch', *JEGP* 78 (1979), 325–44
Doyle, Brian, 'The Soul of Plutarchos', *American Scholar* 69.3 (2000), 111–22
Evans, Robert C., 'Flattery in Shakespeare's *Othello*: The Relevance of Plutarch and Sir Thomas Elyot', *Comparative Drama* 35.1 (2001), 1–41
Graves, Wallace, 'Plutarch's *Life of Cato Utican* as a Major Source for *Othello*', *ShQ* 24 (1973), 181–7
Green, David C., *Plutarch Revisited: A Study of Shakespeare's Last Roman Tragedies and Their Source* (Salzburg 1979)
Homan, Sidney, 'Dion, Alexander, and Demetrius – Plutarch's Forgotten *Parallel Lives* – as Mirrors for Shakespeare's *Julius Caesar*', *ShSt* 8 (1975), 195–210
Honigman, E. A. J., 'Shakespeare's Plutarch', *ShQ* 10 (1959), 25–33
Marshall, Cynthia, 'Shakespeare, Crossing the Rubicon', *ShS* 53 (2000), 73–88
McGrail, Mary Ann, ed., 'Shakespeare's Plutarch', *Special Issue of Poetica* (Tokyo 1997)
McJannet, Linda, 'Antony and Alexander: Imperial Politics in Plutarch, Shakespeare, and Some Modern Historical Texts', *College Literature* 20.3 (1993), 1–18
Mueller, Martin, 'Plutarch's *Life of Brutus* and the Play of its Repetitions in Shakespearean Drama', *Renaissance Drama* 22 (1991), 47–93
Pelling, C. B. R., ed., *Plutarch: Life of Antony* (Cambridge 1988)
Rothschild, Herbert B. Jr., 'The Oblique Encounter: Shakespeare's Confrontation of Plutarch with Special Reference to *Antony and Cleopatra*', *ELR* 6 (1976), 404–29
Russell, D. A., *Plutarch* (New York 1973)
Shackford, Martha Hale, *Plutarch in Renaissance England, With Special Reference to Shakespeare* (Wellesley 1929)
Spencer, T. J. B., *Shakespeare's Plutarch* (Baltimore 1964)
Wofford, Susanne L., 'Antony's Egyptian Bachanals: Heroic and Divine Impersonation in Shakespeare's Plutarch and *Antony and Cleopatra*', *Poetica* 48 (1997), 33–67

SENECA

Arkins, Brian, 'Heavy Seneca: His Influence on Shakespeare's Tragedies', *Classics Ireland* 2 (1995), 1–16
Boyle, A. J., *Tragic Seneca: An Essay in the Theatrical Tradition* (London 1997)

Braden, Gordon, *Renaissance Tragedy and the Senecan Tradition: Anger's Privilege* (New Haven 1985)

Brooks, Harold F., '*Richard III*, Unhistorical Amplifications: The Women's Scenes and Seneca', *MLR* 75 (1980), 721–37

Cunliffe, John W., *The Influence of Seneca in Elizabethan Tragedy* (London 1893)

Ewbank, Inga-Stina, 'The Fiend-Like Queen: A Note on *Macbeth* and Seneca's *Medea*', *ShS* 19 (1966), 82–94

Frank, M., 'Did Shakespeare Owe Anything to Seneca? The Debate Outlined', *Akroterion* 42 (1997), 36–42

Helms, Lorraine, *Seneca By Candlelight and Other Stories of Renaissance Drama* (Philadelphia 1997)

Hunter, G. K., 'Seneca and English Tragedy', in *Seneca*, ed. C. D. N. Costa (London 1974), 166–204

Kaufman, R. J., 'The Seneca Perspective and the Shakespearean Poetic', *Comparative Drama* 1 (1967), 182–98

Kiefer, Frederick, 'Seneca's Influence on Elizabethan Tragedy: An Annotated Bibliography', *Research Opportunities in Renaissance Drama* 21 (1978), 17–34
'Senecan Influence: A Bibliographical Supplement', *Research Opportunities in Renaissance Drama* 28 (1985), 129–42

Langford, Larry, 'The Story Shall Be Changed: The Senecan Sources of *A Midsummer Night's Dream*', *Cahiers Elisabéthains* 25 (1984), 37–51

Miola, Robert S., *Shakespeare and Classical Tragedy: The Influence of Seneca* (Oxford 1992)
'Othello Furens', *ShQ* 41 (1990), 49–64

Muir, Kenneth, 'Shakespeare and the Tragic Pattern', *Proceedings of the British Academy* 44 (1958), 145–62

Ornstein, Robert, 'Seneca and the Political Drama of *Julius Caesar*', *JEGP* 57 (1958), 51–6

Stapleton, M. L., *Fated Sky: The Femina Furens in Shakespeare* (Newark and London 2000)

Truax, Elizabeth, '*Macbeth* and *Hercules*: The Hero Bewitched', *Comparative Drama* 23 (1989–90), 359–76

Wallace, John M., 'The Senecan Context of *Coriolanus*', *Modern Philology* 90 (1992–3), 465–78
'*Timon of Athens* and The Three Graces: Shakespeare's Senecan Study', *Modern Philology* 83 (1980), 349–63

SUETONIUS AND TACITUS

Berry, E. G., 'Shakespeare and Suetonius', *The Phoenix* 2 (1947–8), 73–81

Montgomerie, William, 'More an Antique Roman Than a Dane', *Hibbert Journal* 59 (1960–1), 67–77

Price, George R., 'Henry V and Germanicus', *ShQ* 12 (1961), 57–60

Womersley, D. J., '*3 Henry VI*: Shakespeare, Tacitus, and Parricide', *N&Q* 230 (1985), 468–73

VIRGIL

Bates, Paul A., 'Shakespeare's Sonnets and Pastoral Poetry', *Shakespeare Journal* 103 (1967), 81–96

Black, James, 'Hamlet hears Marlowe, Shakespeare reads Virgil', *Renaissance and Reformation* 18 (1994), 17–28

Bono, Barbara J., *Literary Transvaluation: From Vergilian Epic to Shakespearean Tragicomedy* (Berkeley 1984)

Bulman, James C., 'Shakespeare's Georgic Histories', *ShS* 38 (1985), 37–47

Hamilton, Donna B., *Virgil and 'The Tempest': The Politics of Imitation* (Columbus, OH 1990)

    'Re-Engineering Virgil: *The Tempest* and the Printed English *Aeneid*', in *The Tempest and Its Travels*, ed. Peter Hulme, William H. Sherman, and Robin Kirkpatrick (Philadelphia 2002), 114–20

James, Heather, 'Cultural Disintegration in *Titus Andronicus*: Mutilating Titus, Vergil, and Rome', in *Violence in Drama*, ed. James Redmond (Cambridge 1991), 123–40

    Shakespeare's Troy: Drama, Politics, and the Translation of Empire (Cambridge 1997)

    'Dido's Ear: Tragedy and the Politics of Response', *ShQ* 52 (2001), 360–82

Knight, G. Wilson, *Vergil and Shakespeare* (Exeter 1977)

Kott, Jan, '*The Aeneid* and *The Tempest*', *Arion* 3 (1978), 425–52

Miola, Robert S., 'Vergil in Shakespeare: From Allusion to Imitation', in *Vergil at 2000: Commemorative Essays on the Poet and his Influence*, ed. John D. Bernard (New York 1986), 241–59

Nuttall, A. D., 'Virgil and Shakespeare', in *Virgil and his Influence*, ed. Charles Martindale (Bristol 1984), 71–93

Pitcher, John, '"A Theatre of the Future": *The Aeneid* and *The Tempest*', *Essays in Criticism* 34 (1984), 194–215

Savage, Roger, 'Dido Dies Again', in *A Woman Scorn'd: Responses to the Dido Myth*, ed. Michael Burden (London 1998), 3–38

Tudeau-Clayton, Margaret, *Jonson, Shakespeare, and Early Modern Virgil* (Cambridge 1998)

Wiltenburg, Robert, '*The Aeneid* in *The Tempest*', *ShS* 39 (1986), 159–68

Wright, Laurence, 'Epic into Romance: *The Tempest*, 4.1, and Virgil's *Aeneid*', *Shakespeare in Southern Africa* 9 (1996), 49–65

5. INDIVIDUAL PLAYS

ANTONY AND CLEOPATRA

Dean, Paul, '*Antony and Cleopatra*: An Ovidian Tragedy?', *Cahiers Elisabéthains* 40 (1991), 73–7

Westbrook, Perry D., 'Horace's Influence on Shakespeare's *Antony and Cleopatra*', *PMLA* 62 (1947), 392–8

See also Shakespeare and Rome, Plutarch

AS YOU LIKE IT

Hunt, Maurice, '*Kairos* and the Ripeness of Time in *As You Like It*', *MLQ* 52 (1991), 113–35

Knowles, Richard, 'Myth and Type in *As You Like It*', *Journal of English Literary History* 33 (1966), 1–22

THE COMEDY OF ERRORS

Baldwin, T. W., *On the Compositional Genetics of 'The Comedy of Errors'* (Urbana, IL 1965)

Gill, E. M., 'A Comparison of the Characters in *The Comedy of Errors* with those in the *Menaechmi*', *University of Texas Studies in English* 5 (1925), 79–95

'The Plot Structure of *The Comedy of Errors* in Relation to its Sources', *University of Texas Studies in English* 10 (1930), 13–65

CORIOLANUS

Barton, Anne, 'Livy, Machiavelli, and Shakespeare's *Coriolanus*', *ShS* 38 (1985), 115–29

Heuer, Hermann, 'From Plutarch to Shakespeare: A Study of *Coriolanus*', *ShQ* 10 (1957), 50–9

Pelling, Christopher, 'The Shaping of *Coriolanus*: Dionysius, Plutarch, and Shakespeare', *Poetica: An International Journal of Linguistic–Literary Studies* 48 (1997), 3–32

Velz, John W., 'Cracking Strong Curbs Asunder: Roman Destiny and the Roman Hero in *Coriolanus*', *ELR* 13 (1983), 58–69

Wallace, John M., 'The Senecan Context of *Coriolanus*', *Modern Philology* 90 (1992–3), 465–78

CYMBELINE

Bergeron, David M., '*Cymbeline*: Shakespeare's Last Roman Play', *ShQ* 31 (1980), 31–41

Gesner, Carol, '*Cymbeline* and the Greek Romance: A Study in Genre', in *Studies in English Renaissance Literature*, ed. Waldo F. McNeir (Baton Rouge 1962), 105–31, 226–31

Kott, Jan, 'Lucian in *Cymbeline*', *MLR* 67 (1972), 742–4

HAMLET

DiMatteo, Anthony, '*Hamlet* as Fable: Reconstructing a Lost Code of Meaning', *Connotations* 6 (1996–7), 158–79

Eckert, Charles W., 'The Festival Structure of the Orestes–Hamlet Tradition', *Comparative Literature* 15 (1963), 321–37

Findlay, L. M., 'Enriching Echoes: *Hamlet* and Orpheus', *MLN* 93 (1978), 982–9
Kilpatrick, Ross, 'Hamlet the Scholar', in *Mélanges Offerts en Hommage au Révérend Père Étienne Gareau*, ed. Pierre Brind'Amour (Ottawa 1982), 247–61
Kott, Jan, 'Hamlet and Orestes', *PMLA* 82 (1967), 303–13
Miola, Robert S., 'Aeneas and Hamlet', *Classical and Modern Literature* 8 (1987–8), 275–90
Schleiner, Louise, 'Latinized Greek Drama in Shakespeare's Writing of *Hamlet*', *ShQ* 41 (1990), 29–48

HENRY IV

Stewart, Douglas J., 'Falstaff the Centaur', *ShQ* 28 (1977), 5–21

HENRY V

Betts, John H., 'Classical Allusions in Shakespeare's *Henry V* with Special Reference to Virgil', *Greece and Rome* 15 (1968), 147–63
Merrix, Robert P., 'The Alexandrian Allusion in Shakespeare's *Henry V*', *ELR* 2 (1972), 321–33

HENRY VI

Womersley, D. J., '*3 Henry VI*: Shakespeare, Tacitus, and Parricide', *N&Q* 230 (1985), 468–73

JULIUS CAESAR

Blits, Jan H., *The End of the Ancient Republic: Essays on 'Julius Caesar'* (Durham, NC 1982)
Bryant, A. J. Jr., '*Julius Caesar* from a Euripidean Perspective', *Comparative Drama* 16 (1982), 97–111
Gentili, Vanna, 'Shakespeare's *Julius Caesar* and the Elizabethans' Roads to Rome', in *Shakespeare Today: Directions and Methods of Research*, ed. Keir Elam (Florence 1984), 186–214
Green, David C., *'Julius Caesar' and Its Sources* (*Jacobean Drama Series* 86) (Salzburg 1979)
Homan, Sidney, 'Dion, Alexander, and Demetrius – Plutarch's Forgotten *Parallel Lives* – as Mirrors for Shakespeare's *Julius Caesar*', *ShSt* 8 (1975), 195–210
Miller, Anthony, 'The Roman State in *Julius Caesar* and *Sejanus*', in *Jonson and Shakespeare*, ed. Ian Donaldson (New Jersey 1983), 179–201
Miola, Robert S., '*Julius Caesar* and the Tyrannicide Debate', *RQ* 38 (1985), 271–89
'Shakespeare and his Sources: Observations on the Critical History of *Julius Caesar*', *ShSt* 40 (1987), 69–76
Ornstein, Robert, 'Seneca and the Political Drama of *Julius Caesar*', *JEGP* 57 (1958), 51–6

Roe, John, *Shakespeare and Machiavelli* (Woodbridge, Suffolk 2002) (Chapter 5 on *Julius Caesar*)
See also Shakespeare and Rome, Cicero *and* Lucan

KING LEAR

Miola, Robert S., 'New Comedy in *King Lear*', *PQ* 73 (1994), 329–46

LOVE'S LABOUR'S LOST

Evans, Malcolm, 'Mercury Versus Apollo: A Reading of *Love's Labour's Lost*', *ShQ* 26 (1975), 113–27

MACBETH

Bushnell, R. W., 'Oracular Silence in *Oedipus the King* and *Macbeth*', *Classical and Modern Literature* 2 (1981–2), 195–204
Ewbank, Inga-Stina, 'The Fiend-Like Queen: A Note on *Macbeth* and Seneca's *Medea*', *ShS* 19 (1966), 82–94
Paolucci, Anne, '*Macbeth* and *Oedipus Rex*: A Study in Paradox', in *Shakespeare Encomium*, ed. Anne Paolucci (New York 1964), 44–70
Truax, Elizabeth, '*Macbeth* and *Hercules*: The Hero Bewitched', *Comparative Drama* 23 (1989–90), 359–76

MEASURE FOR MEASURE

Rosenheim, Judith, 'The Stoic Meanings of the Friar in *Measure for Measure*', *ShSt* 15 (1982), 171–215
Rowe, M. W., 'The Dissolution of Goodness: *Measure for Measure* and Classical Ethics', *International Journal of the Classical Tradition* 5 (1998–9), 20–46

THE MERCHANT OF VENICE

Wheater, Isabella, 'Aristotelian Wealth and the Sea of Love: Shakespeare's Synthesis of Greek Philosophy and Roman Poetry in *The Merchant of Venice* (I–II)', *RES* 43 (1992), 467–87 and 44 (1993), 16–36

THE MERRY WIVES OF WINDSOR

Hinely, Jan Lawson, 'Comic Scapegoats and the Falstaff of *The Merry Wives of Windsor*', *ShSt* 15 (1982), 37–54
Steadman, John M., 'Falstaff as Actaeon: A Dramatic Emblem', *ShQ* 14 (1963), 231–44

A MIDSUMMER NIGHT'S DREAM

Carroll, W. C., *The Metamorphoses of Shakespearean Comedy* (Princeton 1985)

Doran, M., *A Midsummer Night's Dream: A Metamorphosis* (*Rice Institute Pamphlets* 46) (1960), 113–35

Fender, S., *Shakespeare – A Midsummer Night's Dream* (*Studies in English Literature* 35) (London 1968)

Garber, Marjorie B., *Dream in Shakespeare: From Metaphor to Metamorphosis* (New Haven 1974)

Holloway, Julia Bolton, 'Apuleius and *A Midsummer Night's Dream*: Bottom's Metamorphoses', in *Tales Within Tales: Apuleius Through Time*, ed. Constance S. Wright and Julia Bolton Holloway (New York 2000), 123–37

Kott, Jan, 'The Bottom Translation', *Assays: Critical Approaches to Medieval and Renaissance Texts* 1 (1981), 117–49

Langford, Larry, 'The Story Shall Be Changed: The Senecan Sources of *A Midsummer Night's Dream*', *Cahiers Elisabéthains* 25 (1984), 37–51

McPeek, James A. S., 'The Psyche Myth and *A Midsummer Night's Dream*', *ShQ* 23 (1972), 69–79

Muir, Kenneth, 'Pyramus and Thisbe: A Study in Shakespeare's Method', *ShQ* 5 (1954), 141–53

Taylor, A. B., '"When Everything Seems Double": Peter Quince the Other Playwright in *A Midsummer Night's Dream*', *ShS* (forthcoming)

See also Ovid

OTHELLO

Evans, Robert C., 'Flattery in Shakespeare's *Othello*: The Relevance of Plutarch and Sir Thomas Elyot', *Comparative Drama* 35.1 (2001), 1–41

Graves, Wallace, 'Plutarch's *Life of Cato Utican* as a Major Source for *Othello*', *ShQ* 24 (1973), 181–7

Miola, Robert S., 'Othello Furens', *ShQ* 41 (1990), 49–64

PERICLES, PRINCE OF TYRE

Greenfield, Thelma N., 'A Re-Examination of the "Patient" Pericles', *ShSt* 3 (1967), 51–61

THE RAPE OF LUCRECE

Allen, Don Cameron, 'Some Observations on *The Rape of Lucrece*', *ShS* 15 (1962), 89–98

Donaldson, Ian, *The Rapes of Lucretia: A Myth and its Transformations* (Oxford 1982)

Hulse, S. Clark III, '"A Piece of Skilful Painting" in Shakespeare's *Lucrece*', *ShSt* 31 (1978), 13–22

Muir, Kenneth, '*The Rape of Lucrece*', in *Shakespeare the Professional and Related Studies* (London 1973), 187–203

RICHARD II

Leon, Harry J., 'Classical Sources for the Garden Scene in *Richard II*', *PQ* 29 (1950), 65–70
Logan, George M., 'Lucan–Daniel–Shakespeare: New Light on the Relation between *The Civil Wars* and *Richard II*', *ShSt* 9 (1976), 121–40

RICHARD III

Brooks, Harold F., '*Richard III*, Unhistorical Amplifications: The Women's Scenes and Seneca', *MLR* 75 (1980), 721–37

ROMEO AND JULIET

Porter, Joseph A., *Shakespeare's Mercutio: His History and Drama* (Chapel Hill, NC 1988)

THE SONNETS

Bate, Jonathan, 'Ovid and the Sonnets; or, Did Shakespeare Feel the Anxiety of Influence?', *ShS* 42 (1990), 65–76
Everett, Barbara, 'Good and Bad Loves: Shakespeare, Plato, and the Plotting of the Sonnets', *TLS* (5 July 2002), 13–15
Leishman, J. B., *Themes and Variations in Shakespeare's Sonnets* (London 1961)

THE TAMING OF THE SHREW

Barnett, Louise, 'Ovid and *The Taming of the Shrew*', *Ball State University Forum* 20.3 (1979), 16–22
Harrold, William E., 'Shakespeare's Use of *Mostellaria* in *The Taming of the Shrew*', *Deutsche Shakespeare-Gesellschaft West* (1970), 188–94
Phillippy, Patricia B., '"Loytering in Love": Ovid's *Heroides*, Hospitality, and Humanist Education in *The Taming of the Shrew*', *Criticism* 40 (1998), 27–53

THE TEMPEST

Brown, Sarah Annes, 'Ovid, Golding and *The Tempest*', *Translation and Literature* 3 (1994), 3–29
Nosworthy, J. M., 'The Narrative Sources for *The Tempest*', *RES* 24 (1948), 281–94
Wills, Robin Headlam, 'Blessing Europe: Virgil, Ovid, and Seneca in *The Tempest*', in M. Marrapodi, ed., *Shakespeare and Intertextuality: The Transition of Cultures Between Italy and England in the Early Modern Period* (Rome 2000), 69–84
See also Virgil, Plautus, *and* Terence

TIMON OF ATHENS

Wallace, John M., '*Timon of Athens* and The Three Graces: Shakespeare's Senecan Study', *Modern Philology* 83 (1980), 349–63

TITUS ANDRONICUS

Broude, Ronald, 'Roman and Goth in *Titus Andronicus*', *ShS* 6 (1970), 27–34

Ettin, Andrew V., 'Shakespeare's First Roman Tragedy', *ELH* 37 (1970), 325–41

Hunter, G. K., 'Sources and Meanings in *Titus Andronicus*', in *Mirror up to Shakespeare: Essays in Honour of G. R. Hibbard*, ed. J. C. Gray (Toronto 1984), 171–88

James, Heather, 'Cultural Disintegration in *Titus Andronicus*: Mutilating Titus, Vergil, and Rome', in *Violence in Drama*, ed. James Redmond (Cambridge 1991), 123–40

Law, Robert Adger, 'The Roman Background of *Titus Andronicus*', *SP* 40 (1943), 145–53

Miola, Robert S., '*Titus Andronicus* and the Mythos of Shakespeare's Rome', *ShSt* 14 (1981), 85–98

Pincombe, Michael, 'Classical and Contemporary Sources of the "Gloomy Woods" of *Titus Andronicus*: Ovid, Seneca, Spenser', in *Shakespearean Continuities: Essays in Honour of E. A. J. Honigmann*, ed. John Batchelor, Tom Cain, and Claire Lamont (Basingstoke 1997), 40–55

Waith, E. M., 'The Metamorphosis of Violence in *Titus Andronicus*', *ShS* 10 (1957), 39–49

West, Grace Starry, 'Going By The Book: Classical Allusions in Shakespeare's *Titus Andronicus*', *SP* 79 (1982), 62–77

TROILUS AND CRESSIDA

Arnold, Margaret J., '"Monsters in Love's Train": Euripides and Shakespeare's *Troilus and Cressida*', *Comparative Drama* 18 (1984), 38–53

Bradshaw, Graham, *Shakespeare's Scepticism* (Brighton 1987)

Elton, William R., 'Aristotle's *Nicomachean Ethics* and Shakespeare's *Troilus and Cressida*', *Journal of the History of Ideas* 58 (1997), 331–7

Henderson, W. B., 'Shakespeare's *Troilus and Cressida*: Yet Deeper in its Tradition', in *Essays in Dramatic Literature: The Parrott Presentation Volume*, ed. Hardin Craig (New York 1967), 127–56

Hunter, G. K., '*Troilus and Cressida*: A Tragic Satire', *ShSt (Tokyo)* 13 (1974–5), 1–23

Muir, Kenneth, 'Shakespeare and the Tale of Troy', *Aligarh Critical Miscellany* 5 (1992), 113–31

Presson, Robert K., *Shakespeare's 'Troilus and Cressida' and the Legends of Troy* (Madison, WI 1953)

Simmons, J. L., 'Holland's Pliny and *Troilus and Cressida*', *ShQ* 27 (1976), 329–32

Smith, Valerie, 'The History of Cressida', in *Self and Society in Shakespeare's 'Troilus and Cressida' and 'Measure for Measure'*, ed. J. A. Jowitt and R. K. S. Taylor (Bradford 1982), 61–79

Suzuki, Mihoko, '"Truth tired with iteration": Myth and Fiction in Shakespeare's *Troilus and Cressida*', *PQ* 66 (1987), 153–74

TWELFTH NIGHT

Lamb, M. E., 'Ovid's *Metamorphoses* and Shakespeare's *Twelfth Night*', in *Shakespearean Comedy*, ed. Maurice Charney (New York 1980), 63–77
Taylor, A. B., 'Shakespeare Rewriting Ovid: Olivia's Interview with Viola and the Narcissus Myth', *ShS* 50 (1997), 81–9

VENUS AND ADONIS

Froes, João, 'Shakespeare's Venus and the Venus of Classical Mythology', in *Venus and Adonis – Critical Essays*, ed. Philip C. Kolin (New York and London 1997), 301–7
Hamilton, A. C., '*Venus and Adonis*', *SEL* 1 (1961), 1–15
Maguin, Jean-Marie, 'The Mythical Background of *Venus and Adonis* – Intertexts and Invention', in *William Shakespeare, Venus and Adonis: Nouvelles Perspectives Critiques*, ed. Jean-Marie Maguin and Charles Whitworth (Montpellier 1999), 19–42
Streitburger, W. R., 'Ideal Conduct in *Venus and Adonis*', *ShQ* 26 (1975), 285–91

THE WINTER'S TALE

Hanna, Sara, 'Voices Against Tyranny: Greek Sources of *The Winter's Tale*', *Classical and Modern Literature* 14 (1993–94), 335–44
Wilson, Douglas B., 'Euripides' *Alcestis* and the Ending of Shakespeare's *The Winter's Tale*', *Iowa State Journal of Research* 58 (1984), 345–55
See also Ovid

Index

References in bold type refer to main treatment of the topic